Classic
AMERICAN TRACTORS

OLIVER HART PARR

C.H. WENDEL

©2005 KP Books
Published by

kp books
An imprint of F+W Publications, Inc.

700 East State Street • Iola, WI 54990-0001
715-445-2214 • 888-457-2873

Our toll-free number to place an order or obtain
a free catalog is (800) 258-0929.

Library of Congress Catalog Number: 2004115349

ISBN: 0-87349-929-8

Printed in the United States of America

Table of Contents

Introduction

With roots going back well over a century, the study of Oliver Corporation is, in a sense, a microcosm of mechanized agriculture. American Seeding Machine Company is one such example. Beginning as several individual companies, it was the result of a merger at the turn of the century. Each of these smaller firms contributed to the development of the grain drill; combining these developments resulted in an impressive machine. With the grain drill, farmers were able to place seeds correctly in the soil. The grain drill not only saved seed, it also was a mechanized method which was more time-efficient than anything the world had ever known in the art of planting seeds in the soil.

Nichols & Shepard Company began in 1848 with a small and rather crude threshing machine, but it evolved through the years, finally ending in the famous Red River Special Line. N & S also got into the steam engine business. However, N & S made no move to broaden the line to any further extent; they were quite satisfied to do one thing and do it well. Thus, American Seeding Machine sold the grain drills to plant the seed, while Nichols & Shepard sold the threshing machines to remove them from the mature plants.

Oliver Chilled Plow Works began in the 1850s, and of course, their specialty was tillage equipment, especially plows. Preparing the seedbed was the first requirement for planting, and so, this trio of Oliver, Nichols & Shepard, and American Seeding Machine were each able to provide different product lines for the Oliver Farm Equipment merger of 1929.

Hart-Parr Company, the fourth company of the 1929 merger, offered farm tractors, yet another distinctly different and non-competing line. Hart-Parr had gained great fame in their field, as did the other partners withing their specialties. Unlike several mergers of the time, there was almost no duplication of the manufacturing effort. Many other mergers were not so fortunate, and were of necessity forced to dump overlapping product lines.

Extensive information was located on most of the tractor lines, although it was in short supply or non-existent for some of the implements. This is to be expected, and in some cases, may not appear in this book. Likewise, there is the possibility that a few tractor models may have been omitted, not necessarily because they were overlooked, but simply because no information could be located.

Beyond all this, simple typographical errors likely do exist, despite repeated proofreading. Should errors be located, kindly contact the Author, in care of Motorbooks International. Please note also, that no specific method has been used to inventory the photographs used in this book, making it difficult to impossible to provide additional prints for a specific purpose.

The serial number listings are, we believe, fairly complete, and are as accurate as we could make them. A simple typographical error can make a big difference within these lists, and therefore, the reader is cautioned that these lists are presented purely for informational purposes. If precise serial number data is required, consulting with the manufacturer or successor is the only reliable method of obtaining this information.

It has indeed been a pleasure to prepare this book, although it has entailed literally thousands of hours in research, photography, and writing. Many more hours were spent in proofreading, and in the many final details which go into the production of a book.

C. H. Wendel

Flow Chart

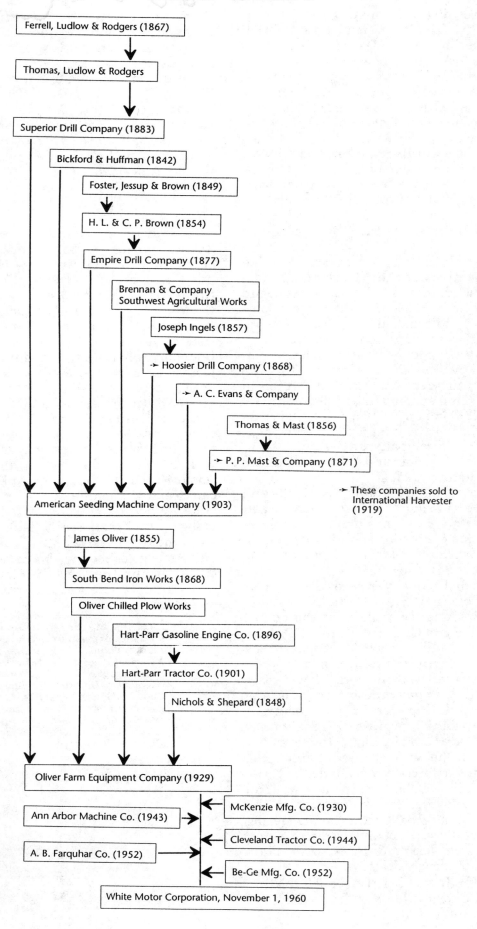

Ferrell, Ludlow & Rodgers (1867)

Thomas, Ludlow & Rodgers

Superior Drill Company (1883)

Bickford & Huffman (1842)

Foster, Jessup & Brown (1849)

H. L. & C. P. Brown (1854)

Empire Drill Company (1877)

Brennan & Company
Southwest Agricultural Works

Joseph Ingels (1857)

Hoosier Drill Company (1868)

A. C. Evans & Company

Thomas & Mast (1856)

P. P. Mast & Company (1871)

These companies sold to
International Harvester
(1919)

American Seeding Machine Company (1903)

James Oliver (1855)

South Bend Iron Works (1868)

Oliver Chilled Plow Works

Hart-Parr Gasoline Engine Co. (1896)

Hart-Parr Tractor Co. (1901)

Nichols & Shepard (1848)

Oliver Farm Equipment Company (1929)

Ann Arbor Machine Co. (1943)

McKenzie Mfg. Co. (1930)

Cleveland Tractor Co. (1944)

A. B. Farquhar Co. (1952)

Be-Ge Mfg. Co. (1952)

White Motor Corporation, November 1, 1960

American Seeding Machine Company

American Seeding Machine Company was organized in 1903. This merger brought together several competing companies. Ostensibly, the plan was to achieve the benefits of mass production by eliminating a great deal of competition among several small companies. The plan was partially successful in that it staved off the inevitable for another three decades. Ultimately, there were too many companies manufacturing grain drills for a saturated market, and many of them slowly withered out of existence. Others, like American Seeding Machine Company, were fortunate enough to maintain a future through yet another merger. Thus it was that American was one of the partners in the Oliver merger of 1929.

The partners in the 1903 American Seeding Machine merger included the Hoosier Drill Company at Richmond, Indiana. This firm was begun by Joseph Ingels in 1857. Initially, Ingels operated at Milton, Indiana. During 1868 it was reorganized as Hoosier Drill Company.

Corn drills were added to the Hoosier line in 1870, followed by broadcast seeders in 1877. The following year Hoosier removed from Milton to Richmond, Indiana and built a new factory there.

P. P. Mast & Company, Springfield, Ohio was another member of the American Seeding Machine merger. This company was established in 1856 by John H. Thomas and P. P. Mast under the name of Thomas & Mast.

Initially, Thomas & Mast built grain drills and cider mills, but during the 1860s they began making cultivators and other implements. During 1871 Thomas & Mast dissolved partnership, being then known as P. P. Mast & Company. This company built the Buckeye drill.

Superior Drill Company was established at Springfield, Ohio in 1867 as Ferrell, Ludlow & Rodgers. Their Superior drills used the double distributer patents of C. E. Patric. In 1872, John H. Thomas (also of Thomas & Mast) purchased Ferrell's interest, with the new company being named Thomas, Ludlow & Rodgers. Eleven years later, in 1883, the company was incorporated and established as the Superior Drill Company. A significant contribution to grain drill design was patented by C. E. Patric in 1882. On November 21 of that year he was granted Patent No. 267,985 covering a 'force-feed grain drill.'

The Empire drill was built by the Empire Drill Company of Shortsville, New York. This firm had its beginnings in the 1840s with the pioneering work of Gilbert Jessup. At a subsequent point, the firm of Foster, Jessup & Brown was established to build this early design.

During 1854 H. L. and C. P. Brown left the firm and moved to Shortsville, New York. Through them the Empire Drill Company eventually emerged. In 1866 they developed a single run distributor which was long known as the Empire feed. By 1878 the Empire drill had assumed the general form it would follow until the American Seeding Machine merger. During 1877 other partners came into the firm, along with the Brown's and at that time the company was given the name of Empire Drill Company.

Bickford & Huffman was yet another partner in the American Seeding Machine Company merger of 1903. This company was first organized in 1842, and was incorporated as Bickford & Huffman in 1893.

Little historical data has been located on yet another partner to the American Seeding Machine merger. This firm was Brennan & Company, also known as the Southwestern Agricultural Works. Situated at Louisville, Kentucky this company built the Kentucky drill.

After the 1903 merger, manufacturing operations of Brennan & Company and of Empire Drill Company were moved to the Richmond, Indiana factory formerly operated by Hoosier Drill Company. International Harvester Company contracted with American in 1912 to sell the entire output of this factory, and in 1920 International bought out the Richmond factory. In effect, this puts the historical chronology of Hoosier, Evans, and P.P. Mast under the vast domain of International Harvester Company. At this point American Seeding Machine Company chose to concentrate its efforts on drills and other implements being built at their Springfield, Ohio plant. This too came to an end on April 1, 1929, for on that day American Seeding Machine Company and three other partners lost their individual identity under the new umbrella of Oliver Farm Equipment Company.

Although Superior Drill Company was preeminently a builder of grain drills, the company also built corn planters and other equipment prior to the 1903 American Seeding Machine Co. merger. Shown here is the Simplex Corn Planter of 1896, with this advertisement noting that the Simplex was 'made in both Plain and Fertilizer styles.' At this time, Superior was also offering the Evans potato planter, apparently a product of A. C. Evans Company. In 1903 the latter firm would also become a part of American Seeding Machine Company.

Many New and Important

Send for Particulars

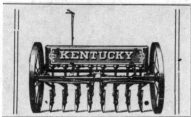

The Kentucky Drill was a product of Brennan & Company, Southwest Agricultural Works. Located at Louisville, Kentucky this firm was strategically located, and was able to serve a very large farming area. Although little history of Brennan & Company has been located, it is apparent that this firm enjoyed a substantial business. However, like the other firms of the American Seeding Machine merger, it too, suffered from the effects of overproduction and a saturated market by the dawn of the twentieth century.

P. P. Mast & Company offered the Thomas grain drill for many years. This design resulted from the partnership of John H. Thomas and P. P. Mast at Springfield, Ohio. Established already in 1856, this company diversified by the 1860s into cultivators and other farm implements. John H. Thomas was also financially interested in the firm of Thomas, Ludlow & Rodgers, a firm that became Superior Drill Company in 1883.

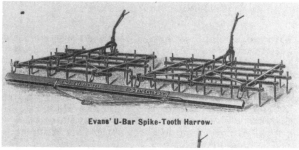

Evans' U-Bar Spike-Tooth Harrow.

A. C. Evans Company at Springfield, Ohio built the Buckeye grain drills. Their implement line also included a wide variety of tillage implements, including harrows and cultivators. Precise information is unavailable, but it appears that Evans began their operations during the 1870s, continuing into the American Seeding Machine Company merger of 1903. The virtual plethora of implement makers during the latter part of the nineteenth century served the valuable purpose of pushing technology forward to new heights. Unfortunately, many aspiring inventors and manufacturers would find little tangible reward for their efforts.

Although this advertisement dates from 1908, the New Empire drill shown here was little different than had been built by Empire Drill Company prior to the merger into American Seeding Machine Company. For several years, the individual entitities functioned as divisions of American Seeding Machine Company. It is entirely possible that this maneuver was designed to preclude government interference under the Sherman Anti-Trust Law. History shows that at this point in time, International Harvester Company was involved in litigation in this regard. For International, the case was in the courts for nearly twenty years. Meanwhile, IHC operated several separate business entities under their corporate umbrella.

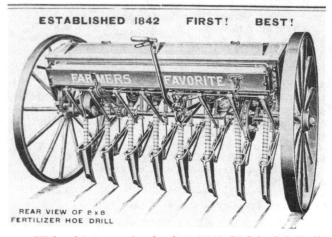

REAR VIEW OF 8 x 8
FERTILIZER HOE DRILL

With a history going back to 1842, Bickford & Huffman laid rightful claim to be the first American manufacturer of grain drills. Although a few grain drills had been built earlier in local shops, it was the Farmers Favorite which first underwent any sort of mass production. By the time of the American Seeding Machine Company merger, Bickford & Huffman had developed an extensive line of grain drills. Included were single and double disc drills, spring hoe drills, and various other styles.

American Seeding

Bickford & Huffman used a very interesting trademark. The patriotic background included a pair of flags. The large horseshoe symbolized good luck, and the centerpiece was a finely shaped sheaf of grain. The scroll reads, "As ye sow, so shall ye reap," a Biblical paraphrase of Galatians 6:7. During its career, Bickford & Huffman introduced several significant developments in grain drills, as well as building numerous other farm implements.

Hoosier Drill Company offered one of the most extensive grain drill lines in the industry. Taking all available sizes and styles, there were over five hundred combinations available for virtually any seed crop or any farming practice. Due to varying soil types, numerous furrow openers were required. Certain seed crops and individual preference created a need for several different distributor mechanisms. Small farms needed a small drill, and large wheat farms needed the largest possible sizes.

In a 1908 advertisement, Hoosier Drill Division of American Seeding Machine Company was offering over 800 styles and sizes of corn drills, corn planters, wheat drills, cotton drills, and various other seeding machines. By the time of the 1903 merger, grain drills had been fully developed, and subsequent crop years saw little or no change in the designs. Only in recent decades have grain drills changed substantially from the designs of a century ago, and many of these changes are more cosmetic than real. A study of grain drill development inevitably leads to the conclusion that our ancestors were indeed inventive geniuses.

After the merger of 1903, American Seeding Machine Company heavily promoted the Superior line of grain drills. Shown here is a Superior Hoe Drill of the 1920s. This one is of the spring hoe type, and technically speaking is a 9 x 7 style, with nine hoes having a seven inch spacing. However, this particular model is a fertilizer drill rather than a grain drill. It is equipped with flexible steel ribbon tubes. The latter design was a great advance in drill design, for it permitted constant flexing of the hoes without retarding the flow of grain or fertilizer to the boot.

With the development of tractor power, Superior was quick to offer a new grain drill design that included a power-lift mechanism. It was controlled by a rope, and could be operated from the tractor seat. Although it was possible to remodel a horsedrawn drill for tractor use, this drill was designed especially for the purpose, and undoubtedly was far better than a modified version. However, a great many horsedrawn grain drills were modified by enterprising farmers and skilled blacksmiths. It is to be imagined that some of these rebuilt jobs were better than others.

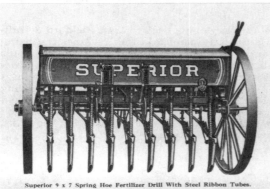

Superior 9 x 7 Spring Hoe Fertilizer Drill With Steel Ribbon Tubes.

Superior Tractor Drills

Front View Tractor Drill With Steel Wheels.

Ann Arbor Machine Company

The history of Ann Arbor Machine Company goes back to 1882. The company began in a small way building hay presses and other machines. Their heavy duty Columbia hay press was sold nationally and internationally. Of significance, the Columbia was the original horizontal continuous type baling press from which all others have more or less been copied.

The Columbia was the one and only model built for over thirty years. Then in 1905, Ann Arbor introduced their Model 20 to fill the need for a lightweight machine. By comparison, the Model 20 weighed 3,400 pounds, while the large Columbia press scaled at well over three tons! Two main ideas were built into the Model 20. First of all, it was particularly adapted to baling alfalfa, a relatively new forage crop. Secondly, it was developed with an eye toward using the relatively new power source of the gasoline engine. A major design change was the use of a plunger stroke and a feed opening some six inches longer than in the Columbia. The primary object of the extra long feed opeing was to aid in saving the leaves of the alfalfa by minimizing the breakage of the stems through crowding into a smaller opening.

Model 20 hay presses were built into the early 1920s. In 1924 the company introduced their Model 40 as its successor. This machine was essentially the same in general design, but was more rugged and provided even greater capacity. In addition, wherever possible, fabricated steel sections replaced castings to provide the ultimate in strength, yet retaining the lightweight design.

The original Columbia hay press used a double-geared design. The Model 40 was offered in both the single-geared style and as a double-geared machine. Also of significance, Ann Arbor produced a gasoline traction hay press about 1910. It is illustrated on page 25 of the Author's *Encyclopedia of American Farm Tractors* (1979: Crestline Publishing Company). Designed to carry the engine and baler on a single chassis, it was also capable of propelling itself from job to job. This particular design was marketed for only a short time.

During the 1920s, Ann Arbor began experimenting with a traveling field baling press to automatically pick up the crop and bale it while traveling over the windrow. This significant development was the subject of a paper presented at the November 1932 Annual Meeting of the American Society of Agricultural Engineers. This machine embodied a pick-up mechanism, along with a power transmission system which was able to utilize the relatively new tractor power take off shaft, offered on many tractors of the early 1930s.

Although Ann Arbor's engineers attempted to adapt various combine pick-up units to their new Hay & Straw Combine, these experiments were unsatisfactory, and as a result, they developed a pick-up unit designed especially for the purpose. Developing the force-feed system was a matter of no small consequence. One engineer noted that 'some lost sleep and headaches resulted along with a lot of waste paper from the drawing board.' Initially, a ground-drive system was thought to be desirable for the pick-up mechanism. After considerable experimenting this was abandoned in favor of a power-driven pick-up system. The latter arrangement also had the advantage of allowing normal operation, even when working as a stationary hay press. Another unique feature of the Hay & Straw Combine was the use of 1 1/8 inch shafting throughout the unit, except for the baling press unit. Thus, all fifteen of the cast iron self-aligning bearings were interchangeable. Proof of the success of this new machine was substantially verified in 1932. A unit which had been sold in May of the previous year had already baled over 2,500 tons!

Ann Arbor Hay Press Company began operations in 1882 at Ann Arbor, Michigan. In the 1920s the firm removed to Shelbyville, Illinois as the Ann Arbor Machine Company. In 1943 Oliver Farm Equipment Company made a long-term lease agreement for the Shelbyville factory, and it was eventually absorbed into Oliver Corporation. The Shelbyville plant was closed in 1970 and was absorbed by facilities at South Bend, Indiana, Charles City, Iowa, and Brantford, Ontario.

In 1882 the Ann Arbor Hay Press Company began operations at Ann Arbor, Michigan. Their original product was the Columbia Hay Press. This machine would remain the keystone of the Ann Arbor line for several decades. An early style of the Columbia is shown here. It was built largely of wood and cast iron, and weighed over three tons. A fist points toward the continuous feed mechanism that was pioneered in the Columbia. With its system, each tuft of hay was securely pushed into the chamber. Despite the huge size of the machine, ten horsepower was usually ample to operate the Columbia.

Ann Arbor Machine Company

In addition to the Columbia, Ann Arbor also built this early cantilever machine. Shown here in the transport position, its front wheels were removed when in actual operation. A long sweep arm is directly over the extended tongue and the toggle linkages. In operation, a team of horses walked around the center pivot, pulling the sweep arm behind them. By multiplying the power through a series of linkages, two horses were able to deliver the powerful forces required to compress hay into compact bales. While this machine had but a fraction of the capacity of the Columbia, it was ideally suited for the small farm.

For the largest baling jobs, Ann Arbor offered the Model 60 Twin-Gear hay press. Until the late 1920s, this big machine was built only on special order, but eventually it became a part of the regular line. Although a belt-driven model is shown here, the Model 60 was also available with an auxiliary power unit. This big hay press was available with three different bale chambers, namely, 14 x 18; 16 x 18; and 17 x 22 inches. This huge machine had a capacity approaching 70 tons of baled hay over a ten hour period.

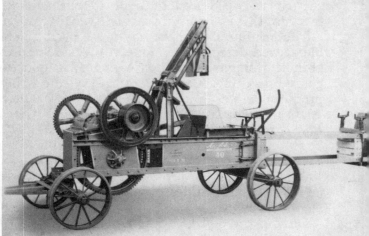

Ann Arbor advertised heavily in the *American Thresherman* and other farm-oriented magazines. This advertisement of the early 'teens illustrates an Ann Arbor press with a mounted engine. Mounting the engine directly on the machine precluded the need to align a drive belt for each set, and in fact, eliminated the need for a steam engine or tractor to operate the press. All that was necessary was a team of horses to move the press from one location to another.

This Model 40 hay press is shown with the single-gear design, although it could also be purchased as a double-gear machine. Obviously, the baling mechanism was where the greatest strains were encountered. Depending on the service to which the machine would be subjected, the single-gear was satisfactory for light work, and the double-gear was essential for large production. In the mid-1930s the Model 40 was available in 14 x 18 and 17 x 22 inch sizes; the earlier 16 x 18 model had been discontinued by that time. Both sizes were priced between $500 and $600. Adding a Wisconsin VF-4 engine added $350, and using a Continental PF-140 motor added $445 to the base price.

Ann Arbor Machine Company

The Model 18 was a small press intended for the average farm, or for a group of farmers. This model was offered in 14 x 18 and 16 x 18 inch sizes, with the price coming to about $370. Adding the self-feeding block dropper raised the price by $55, and adding a Wisconsin one-cylinder Model AHH engine raised the price by another $205. Of course none of these models tied automatically. Baling wire was used, and it was placed around the bales and tied by hand. The job was not extremely difficult, but this was more than offset by the dust and dirt emanating from the chamber with each stroke of the plunger.

The notation with this photograph reads, "Baling 1,535 bales hay in one day. Ann Arbor baler." Since these bales averaged about 80 pounds, this totals well over 60 tons of hay in a single day, or about 6 tons an hour. The man standing above assisted in feeding the hay into the chamber, and either he, or another person, was needed to drop the bale blocks in place at the proper time. Bale blocks were used to divide one bale from another. Usually they were made with channels that permitted the tyers to run the wires through from bottom to top.

Shown here is a top view of the double-gear baling mechanism as was used on the Ann Arbor hay press. The belt pulley is on the extreme right of the countershaft. Its two pinions engage larger gears on the pinion shaft; they are situated outside the frame. Within the frame the two small pinion gears can be observed; they mesh with the huge gears that carry the connecting rod to the bale plunger. Note that the countershaft carries two sizable flywheels to assist during the plunger stroke.

Here is an Ann Arbor Model 40 hay press, with a closeup view of the feeder mechanism. The feeder bill is about midway in its travel, with the dotted line view illustrating its position when actually forcing the hay into the chamber. Of course this part of the mechanism was timed through gearing so that there could be no interference with the plunger. Also visible in this illustration are the two large final drive gears which actually operate the bale plunger.

In large ranching areas, huge hay stacks emerged every summer. The photograph probably does not do justice to this scene, especially since at least four large stacks are visible to the right, along with several smaller ones to the left of this illustration. Baling the hay required far less space than was needed with loose hay, and required far less labor for the daily feeding of livestock. Unfortunately, no details accompany this interesting look at our agricultural past.

Here's a Caterpillar Twenty powering a Model 40 Ann Arbor hay press. The location is unknown. Also of curious interest, another Caterpillar Twenty is in the background, apparently pushing the loose hay into piles. This photograph was obviously taken prior to the 1932 introduction of the Ann Arbor Hay & Straw Combine. Rather than load the hay onto wagons, it likely was easier to bale directly from each haycock, although it was still necessary to load the big 80 pound bales for transportation to a barn or a haystack.

This Model 40 hay press of the 1930s is equipped with rubber tires. During World War Two however, this was not considered essential, and only steel wheels were available for the duration. A Continental PF-140 engine is powering this model; its $445 cost was nearly as much as the $590 price of the bare bones baler. Although not shown in this photograph, many baler engines were furnished with a tall air intake stack to minimize the chaff and dust entering the air cleaner. As could be expected, this accessory required frequent cleaning.

Apparently the Ann Arbor line was sold by Oliver Farm Equipment Company for a time before the 1944 buyout of this Shelbyville, Illinois firm. In the 1929 merger that formed Oliver Farm Equipment, none of the partners had a hay baler, yet this machine was becoming an important part of the 1930s farm scene. This Model 18 hay press has the Oliver logo directly beneath the feed table. It is powered by an early style of Wisconsin air cooled engine.

During the 1930s Ann Arbor Machine Company pioneered the use of pneumatic tires on its hay presses, and was also instrumental in adapting this machine for use with the tractor power take off shaft. In so doing, all need for auxiliary engines was eliminated, as was the perpetual problem of aligning a drivebelt for the stationary models. The 14 x 18 Model 18 baler weighed 2,800 pounds, and the 16 x 18 size was a hundred pounds heavier. The large screws at the back of the bale chamber are used to adjust the weight of the bale. Heavy springs under the hand cranks maintain the pressure at the same level.

Ann Arbor Machine Company

This photograph of July 1931 illustrates a Caterpillar Twenty tractor pulling an Ann Arbor Combine Baler. The location is Paschendale Farms at Antioch, Illinois. A caption with the original photograph indicates that Paschendale Farms used Caterpillar tractors exclusively, having 13 different units in operation at that time. This Caterpillar Twenty is equipped with a rear pto shaft to operate the baler. In the early 1930s, Ann Arbor made farm equipment history by being the first company to offer a baler with a pickup attachment for direct baling from the windrow.

This early model of the Hay & Straw Combine would see very few changes for a decade. The hay was carried up the first elevator to a cross-conveyor. The latter was equipped with a reverse mechanism. With a signal bell, the operator was cautioned to drop a divider block into the bale chamber. In order to facilitate this, the cross conveyer was reversed to clear the throat of any hay; this would keep the block from dropping into place. Slip clutches were widely used on this machine, and of course this was a definite advantage. Ann Arbor noted in the 1930s that their baling equipment was in use on every continent in the world.

An interesting study is presented with this photograph of a small Caterpillar Ten and an Ann Arbor Hay & Straw Combine. This machine is not be confused with a 'combine' in the usual sense of the word...the harvesting abilities of this machine consisted of picking up hay or straw from a windrow, conveying it to the bale chamber, and delivering 80 pound bales at the rear exit. At this time the bales were still tied by hand, using pre-cut baling wires. The automatic wire tie or twine tie baler was yet in the future.

Shown here is an Ann Arbor Hay & Straw Combine in heavy hay. Despite its baling capacity, this machine required ten horsepower or less for successful operation. It is being towed by a Silver King tractor (Fate-Root-Heath Company) of about 1936 vintage. A close inspection of this photograph reveals however, that this hay baler was equipped with an auxiliary engine. While Ann Arbor was of course, proud to illustrate its revolutionary new baler, tractor companies weren't at all adverse to the idea of displaying their latest models either.

Shown here is the tying crew behind an Ann Arbor Hay & Straw Combine. More often than not, two men did the tying. Each of the two wires was started through the cavities in the drop blocks, sometimes called separator blocks, and the person on the opposite side took the wires across the side of the bale and passed the ends through the opposite drop block. Some preformed bale ties utilized a twisted loop on one end and a small preformed button on the other. Since the bale remained quite compressed this far ahead in the chamber, it was a relatively easy matter to join hook and eye together. As the bale left the chamber, the compressed bale took up the slack in the ties.

Ann Arbor Machine Company

An IHC Farmall leads this parade of an Ann Arbor baler and behind it is a wagon to receive the finished bales. Probably due to the intense summer heat, a canvas sunshade has been improvised over the tying benches. As those who have endured this task can relate, this job was one that few people wanted. With each stroke of the bale plunger came a cloud of dust and chaff. This, mixed with the sweat of the day, made the job uncomfortable at best, and depending on the crop, virtually unbearable at the worst. Perhaps the homemade sunshade on this outfit helped placate those unfortunate souls assigned to the tying platform.

This 1930s photograph illustrates an Ann Arbor Hay & Straw Combine mounted on a motor truck. A. B. Caple Company of Toledo, Ohio mounted their Ann Arbor Combines on motor trucks, for a very mobile unit, and one that was capable of moving from farm to farm with the greatest of ease. This unit has been equipped with a rear hitch to accommodate a wagon for direct loading of the bales. Ann Arbor Machine Company made a tremendous investment while experimenting with and developing this machine. The gamble paid off, for many thousands of units were built, even during the difficult financial times of the Great Depression.

Tulare, California and the farm of Joe Lang was the scene of this interesting photograph. The Ann Arbor is baling wheat straw at the rate of 2 1/2 tons per hour. A note on the back of the original indicates that it was taken on July 26, 1940. Of further interest is the tractor pulling this Ann Arbor hay press. It is a Minneapolis-Moline Model GT. In itself the tractor is not colossally unusual. The unique feature is that this tractor is equipped to burn propane fuel. Minneapolis-Moline was a pioneer of adapting tractors to this type of fuel, and excelled in the art.

With the onset of World War Two, many field hands who had perhaps been tying bales the year before, would gladly have opted for their old job instead of one that required marching through mud, dodging incoming artillery, or escaping enemy torpedoes. Due to the wartime scarcity of farm labor, these WACS, made a part of the regular armed forces by Congressional action, celebrated their new status by volunteering to help with the hay crop. This photograph was taken near the Army Air Force Training Command School at Scott Field, Illinois.

By 1944, Oliver had concluded a long-term lease agreement with Ann Arbor Machine Company. In effect, the Ann Arbor name soon disappeared from view. From its legacy came the Oliver hay baler line. Within a short time, automatic wire-tie and twine-tie balers would be a reality. This Oliver-Ann Arbor machine was equipped with a fully automatic hydraulic threader that eliminated the drop blocks or dividers, and made the tying process far easier than before. By eliminating the drop blocks, continuous feeding was possible, and this permitted a daily output as much as 30% higher than before.

Cleveland Tractor Company

The story of the Cletrac crawler begins already in 1911. That year, Rollin H. White and his brother, Clarence G. White began developing a farm tractor. Their design was revolutionary in that it incorporated the implement as an integral part of the tractor. White was a pioneer designer and inventor, having previously developed the White steam car, and many other inventions. That particular branch of endeavor would eventually become internationally known as White Motors Corporation.

The initial success of the White tractor did not satisfy White, and so the early wheel-type design was redesigned in 1912, and again in the following two or three years. White finally concluded that the crawler design would be ideal for farm work, especially since this design compacted the soil far less than conventional wheel-type tractors. Thus came the patented Controlled Differential Steering mechanism which typified the Cletrac design for all time.

The Cleveland Motor Plow Company was incorporated on January 20, 1916. A new manufacturing plant was built, and production of the Model R Cletrac tractor began. This little tractor weighed only 2,500 pounds, and was capable of 10 drawbar horsepower. The fundamental design of the Model R was carried through subsequent years. A year after being organized the company name was changed to Cleveland Tractor Company, and in 1918 the "Cletrac" trademark was adopted.

During 1918 the Model R was redesigned---- the new Model H incorporated a water-type air cleaner, used anti-friction bearings in the lower track wheels, and several other changes. This model also was capable of 12 drawbar horsepower.

Additional changes came in 1919 with the Model W, a 15 1/2 horsepower model that used manganese tracks instead of cast iron. An oil filter was added, but overall, the Model W was essentially of the same design as its immediate predecessor, the Model H. An interesting sidebar is the model designation for the first three tractor models. In order they were R, H, and W; the initials for Rollin H. White. Coincidence? Hardly!

Rollin H. White introduced the Cletrac Model F tractor in late 1918. This was the first crawler tractor designed for cultivating and other row-crop duties. Evidence of its unique design is shown in the adjustable height and width of this tractor. When reduced to its narrowest width the Model F could operate between corn rows. Provision was made to raise and widen the tractor if needed to straddle other crops. This was the first

such tractor to incorporate such a revolutionary design.

Concurrently with the development of the Model F, Mr. White developed a series of push-type implements to be fitted to the tractor. Initially, a cultivator was adapted to this service, but levelers, seeders, and other implements were eventually added.

With the development of the Model R tractor, Mr. White patented a number of new designs. In 1917 he received Patent No. 1,170,692 covering an Agricultural Machine. In January of the following year, Patent No. 1,253,319 was issued for a Tractor. This one essentially covered the differential mechanism which eventually came to be known as Tru-Traction. This essential design would forever remain with the Cletrac design, despite numerous modifications and improvements.

The next patent, No. 1,258,286 of March 1918 covered an agricultural machine. This patent had been filed in 1913 and did not cover a crawler design. When this patent was filed, Rollin and Clarence G. White were developing a wheel-type tractor with integral implements. By the time the patent was issued, White had abandoned attempts along this line and was concentrating on crawler tractors. (Only those crawler tractors built by Caterpillar Tractor Company can be called "Caterpillar" since this is a company trademark. Therefore, all other crawler tractors must be called crawlers or tracklayers, but they cannot be called "Caterpillars.")

Patent No. 1,260,738 of March 1918 covers "Power-Propelled Agricultural Machinery." This patent illustrates a wide drive drum, together with integral implements. This patent was applied for in 1912 when the brothers White were still developing a wheel-type tractor.

A significant Cletrac crawler patent is No. 1,261,082 issued in April 1918. This patent covers the track design of the Cletrac. It was applied for in 1917. In August 1918, two significant Cletrac patents were issued. The first one, No. 1,275,343 covered the main frame and traction frame design. Application for this patent had been filed in October 1917. The next patent, No. 1,275,344 covered additional aspects of the main frame and traction frame design. It was filed in January of 1918. Then in November of 1918, White received Patent No. 1,285,861 covering a multiple cylinder engine as used in the Cletrac at that time. All of these patents were assigned to the Cleveland Tractor Company.

When the Nebraska Tractor Tests began in 1920, Cletrac was there with their Model W,

Cleveland Tractor Company

Rollin H. White organized the Cleveland Tractor Company and incorporated it on January 20, 1916. Mr. White and his brother Clarence were prolific inventors who had actually begun experimenting with tractors as early as 1911. R. H. White had invented the White steam car, and from this small beginning the White Motors Corporation finally evolved. During his lifetime, Rollin H. White saw White Motors grow from a relatively small company building a few steam cars to a major truck builder. The Cleveland Tractor Company was a separate entity from White Motors.

12-20 model. It was tested in August 1920 with the results appearing in Test No. 45. This was the first crawler tractor tested at Lincoln. The test model was equipped with a Weidely engine. Curiously, the Model F, 9-16 model was not tested at Nebraska until 1922; the results are shown in Test No. 85. Subsequently, the vast majority of Cletrac models made their appearance at the Test Laboratory.

In 1925 Cletrac expanded the line to include the Model K-20 tractor, and subsequently the Model A and the Model 40 tractors were added. Both of these models saw development of a rear pulley and a power-take-off shaft. Cletrac placed the Model 15 on the market in 1931---it was the first crawler tractor built with a one-piece forged track shoe.

Model E Cletrac crawlers appeared in 1936 to supersede the venerable Model F. Model E crawlers were offered in several widths to accommodate various row crops.

All Cletrac models were redesigned in 1937 to include a streamlined hood and to provide better eye appeal. The small Model HG crawler saw first light in 1938. Eventually, Cletrac built crawlers in excess of 100 horsepower. In 1944 Cleveland Tractor Company became a part of the Oliver Corporation. The latter continued building crawler tractors. When White Motor Corporation purchased Oliver in 1962 the crawler tractor plant was relocated at Charles City, Iowa and remained there until crawler production was discontinued in 1965. Between 1916 and 1944, Cletrac produced on the order of 75 distinct tractor models.

Cleveland Tractor Company also produced numerous tracked vehicles for the U. S. Military. These are well illustrated in Fred Crismon's *U. S. Military Tracked Vehicles* published in 1992 by Motorbooks International, Osceola, Wisconsin.

The early tractor designs of Rollin H. and Clarence G. White were aimed at a wheel-type tractor. It went through several design changes but never saw more than very limited production, if in fact, it ever went beyond a few prototypes. Shown here is a rare photograph of one of the early Cleveland Motor Plow Company designs. There is no doubt that this tractor is the same design as shown in Patent No. 1,260,738 of March 1918. However, the latter date is not nearly so significant as the filing date of 1912, since it was during this period that the brothers White were concentrating on wheel tractor designs. By the time the patent was issued, the Model R crawler had already come and gone, and the Model H was fully into production.

To what extent the Cletrac crawlers were used in World War One is now unknown. However, at least a few of them made it to Europe during the conflict. This old photograph is now in the archives of the Floyd County Historical Society at Charles City, Iowa. It shows a Cletrac in France during 1918, pulling General Pershing's car out of the mud. However, the notes with the photograph say nothing at all about whether General Pershing was present for this heroic rescue.

Cleveland Motor Plow introduced their Model R crawler in 1916. "Geared to the Ground" was a slogan that accompanied this new crawler. Built only during 1916 and 1917, it used a Buda engine according to most accounts. However, there are also indications that some of the Model R tractors may have been equipped with an engine designed by Rollin H. White and built in the Cleveland Tractor Company shops. To confuse the issue still further, a manufacturer's listing appears in the July 12, 1917 issue of *Farm Implement News* which indicates that Waukesha and Buda engines were both used in the Model R tractor.

The second Cletrac style was the Model H, built in the 1917-19 period. This one apparently was equipped with a Weidely engine. At this point the design was fairly well established, and for some years to come, at least some of the Cletrac models would carry a front-mounted belt pulley. The Model H was replaced in 1919 with the Model W. It was essentially the same tractor, but with some improvements in design. Note that this model carries a top track idler, but this was not used on the subsequent Model W design.

Eventually the Cletrac crawlers would find their way into the construction industries. Initially though, it appears that White was aiming his Cletrac crawler at the farmer, rightfully claiming that the crawler caused very little soil compaction compared to ordinary wheel tractor designs. Power farming demonstrations were popular at the time, and the Cletrac was there, along with many competitors. Plow companies were there too, as evidenced by this Cletrac Model H pulling a Vulcan plow at an unnamed demonstration.

An early Cletrac catalog illustrates the comparison between the crawler and the wheel tractor. Regarding the 30-60 Case tractor to the right it is stated that 'The constant downward pressure of the wheels packs the soil hard.' To the left is the Cletrac, of this design it is stated, 'The Cletrac travels on top of the soil---doesn't sink or pack.' Yet it would be many years before soil compaction was fully recognized as a detrimental practice.

Cleveland Tractor

In their sales pitch to farmers, Cletrac went all out in emphasizing the benefits of minimal soil compaction. To the left is a workman pushing a heavy wheelbarrow through soft ground. Yet, on the right, the same wheelbarrow is pushed along easily when running on a plank road. To clinch the case, the lower illustration notes that 'The Cletrac runs on a pair of tracks like a locomotive.' Apparently the Cletrac advertising campaign was reasonably successful---thousands of Cletracs were sold!

So far as is known, no yearly serial number lists exist for the early Cletrac crawlers. The cumulative lists show that the Model H began in 1917 with No. 1001, and ended in 1919 with No. 13755. The Model W followed with No. 13756. By the time production ended in 1932, it closed with No. 30971. Assuming that the tractors were built consecutively, this totals over 17,000 Model W tractors built in a thirteen year period, or an average of 1,300 per year. A Weidely engine was used into at least 1920, although by 1923 it appears that Cletrac was using their own engine.

Cletrac first offered front-mounted cultivators to fit their tractors, eventually offering a number of other machines adapted with an 'easy-on, easy-off' system. Cletrac was also early to adopt an air cleaner system, recognizing its benefits in extended engine life. Because of its high clearance the Model W was able to work in growing crops. The unique differential system patented by R. H. White also minimized damage when turning.

Also known as the 12-20 model, the Cletrac Model W was the first crawler tractor ever tested at the world-famous Nebraska Tractor Test Laboratory. The test model went through its paces in August 1920. Although it weighed but 3,300 pounds, the Model W pulled 1,734 pounds, or about 52% of its own weight. The test tractor was equipped with a Weidely engine---a four-cylinder design having a 4 x 5 1/2 inch bore and stroke. Full details of the Cletrac Model W may be found in Nebraska Test No. 45.

About 3,000 Model F Cletracs were built between 1920 and 1924. This interesting model was unique in that it used a top drive sprocket somewhat resembling modern design. Rated at 9 drawbar and 16 belt horsepower, the Model F continued to use the front-mounted belt pulley. One forward and one reverse speed were built into this model, and Cleveland used their own four-cylinder engine. Rated at 1,600 rpm, this engine carried a 3 1/4 x 4 1/2 inch bore and stroke. For its day, the rated engine speed was quite high, especially when many of the heavyweight tractors were operating at one-fourth that speed.

Cleveland Tractor Company

Apparently the Model F Cletrac was designed especially for use with cultivators and other front-mounted implements. While it was equally useful for other duties within its capacity, it appears that Cleveland went to great lengths in adapting various front-mounted implements to this particular model. In 1923 this tractor carried a list price of $595. It was only 43 inches wide, stood 50 inches high, and weighed 1,865 pounds. A 1923 advertisement indicates that in addition to front-mounted implements, two different manufacturers were offering rear-mounted implements designed especially for the Model F tractor.

Production of the Model 20K, also known as the 20-27 tractor, ran from 1925 to 1932. If the serial numbers ran consecutively, and if in fact, all the numbers were used, then this would indicate that about 10,000 of these units were produced. This model was equipped with Cletrac's own four-cylinder engine. It used a 4 x 5 1/2 inch bore and stroke, and was the same engine as used in the concurrently built 12-20 model. Shipping weight was 4,390 pounds.

The "20" model designator shines forth on the radiator of this tractor. Apparently, this one was late in the 1925-32 production period, since the new style front track idler is visible, and the carriage rollers have been modified from the original design. While some manufacturers of crawler tractors were aiming primarily at the construction and industrial market, it appears that Cleveland Tractor Company set their sights on the farm market, with the industrial side taking second place.

Model 30A (30-45) tractors were built between 1926 and 1928. This model was followed in 1929 and 1930 with the 30B tractor. Production of both was rather limited, especially when compared to the ever-popular Model W. A Wisconsin six-cylinder engine was used---it carried a 4 x 5 inch bore and stroke. Shown here is a Cletrac toward the end of the assembly line. Specially built carriers moved the tractor along the track. This one is nearing completion except that the track pads and some of the accessories yet await. For some years Cleveland furnished some of their tractor models with engines built within the Cletrac shops.

Cleveland Tractor

Cletrac Model 55 tractors were produced in the 1932-36 period. This tractor was a successor to the earlier 55-40 tractor, built during 1931 and 1932. In fact, the serial numbers are consecutive. Going back a step further, the latter model was a successor to the Model 40 tractor which originated in 1928. The serial number listings begin with No. 101 for the Model 40, and close with No. 1833. Then comes the 55-40 with No. 1835, and continuing to No. 1889. With the introduction of the Model 55 in 1932, the serial numbers continue with No. 1890, ending in 1936 with No. 3852.

Production of the Cletrac "40" (40-55) tractor ran from 1928 to 1931. About 1,700 units were built. This big tractor used a six-cylinder Beaver engine having a 4 1/2 x 5 inch bore and stroke. It was rated at 1,575 rpm. An innovative feature was electric starting. Weighing slightly over 12,000 pounds, the Model 40 could pull nearly 10,000 pounds on the drawbar. This converted to about 55 drawbar horsepower, hence its rating. A copy of the Model 40 was sent to the Nebraska Tractor Test Laboratory, and the results are posted in Test No. 149. During 1931 and 1932 Cleveland offered the 55-40, essentially the same tractor as before. However, production of the latter style was quite limited, since only about 50 copies were built during this two year period.

Although some of the big Model 55 crawlers probably ended up doing farm work, it appears that this large tractor was intended primarily for heavy construction. In fact, this one is equipped with a large air compressor. A big six-cylinder Wisconsin engine was used in the Model 55.

To describe the Cletrac Model 100 as huge would be to minimize the term. This gigantic crawler weighed almost 28,000 pounds. The Wisconsin six cylinder engine burned gasoline, probably in large quantities with its 6 x 7 inch bore and stroke. It was given an SAE horsepower rating of 86, but was probably capable of much more on peak loads. Using the serial number list as a guide, approximately fifty copies of the Model 100 were built between 1927 and 1930.

A popular Cletrac style was the Model 15, introduced in 1931. Thousands of Model 15 crawlers were built between 1931 and 1933. Its successor was the Model 20-C, built in the 1933-36 period. From the latter came the Model AG, built in the 1936-37 era. When Cleveland began streamlining their tractors in 1936 and 1937, the AG reappeared with a new serial number series in 1937, along with a streamlined grille. Production of the Model AG finally ended in 1942. Throughout production, from the Model 15 to the Model AG, a Hercules four-cylinder engine was used. It carried a 4 x 4 1/2 inch bore and stroke.

Cleveland Tractor Company

A front view of the Model 15 tractor illustrates its clean lines, its simplicity, and the ample ground clearance. Cleveland Tractor sent a Model 15 to the Nebraska Tractor Test Laboratory in July 1931 for testing. The company rated this tractor at 15 drawbar and 22 belt horsepower. During Test No. 196 it yielded almost 17 drawbar horsepower, and exerted nearly 26 belt horsepower. A modified version of the Model 15 appears in Test No. 202; it yielded approximately the same test results.

Among the many modifications and attachments for the Cletrac crawlers were wide track pads, as shown here. Under certain conditions, extra flotation was needed, and this was one way to solve the problem. Front and rear power-take-off shafts were available for the Model 15, and for all other models of this period. A rear power pulley was also available for all models. Other options included a full cab, radiator guard, electric lighting, and a canopy top. In addition to the standard configuration, Cletrac offered their tractors as in logging, industrial, hillside, orchard, and factory versions, plus of course, the Swamp Special shown here.

The Model 20-C Cletrac was built between 1933 and 1936. This $1,445 machine weighed about 6,000 pounds. Like the Model 15, it used a Hercules four-cylinder engine having a 4 x 4 1/2 inch bore and stroke. Obviously, this 1933 model was equipped with a hydraulic system to operate the dozer blade. The Cletrac design used a very simple track roller system which was rebuildable by the average machine shop. In contrast, some of the competing models utilized designs which precluded easy repairs in the field.

Delco-Remy battery ignition and electric starting were regular features of the Cletrac 25 tractor. Introduced in 1932, it was tested at Nebraska in April of that year; results of the test are given as No. 201. Weighing slightly over 7,000 pounds, the Model 25 carried a 1933 list price of $1,850. Each track was driven through a cast steel sprocket which meshed with rollers in the track system. Although sidecurtains were standard equipment, the majority of them disappeared in the field, especially when working at high ambient temperatures.

Cleveland Tractor Company

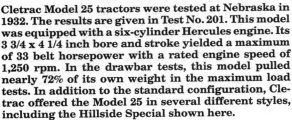

Cletrac Model 25 tractors were tested at Nebraska in 1932. The results are given in Test No. 201. This model was equipped with a six-cylinder Hercules engine. Its 3 3/4 x 4 1/4 inch bore and stroke yielded a maximum of 33 belt horsepower with a rated engine speed of 1,250 rpm. In the drawbar tests, this model pulled nearly 72% of its own weight in the maximum load tests. In addition to the standard configuration, Cletrac offered the Model 25 in several different styles, including the Hillside Special shown here.

Another method of utilizing the Cletrac 25 was the addition of this electrical generating plant. It was operated through the rear-mounted power take off shaft. As with air compressors and other construction equipment, this portable electric plant served a valuable role in construction work. During the 1930s many areas had little or no electrical power, especially those areas which were some distance from a central power plant. Thus, an electric generating plant was a virtual necessity. With this unit, electrical power could be taken to the job, instead of requiring line construction and its related expenses.

Cletrac 25 tractors were popular for farm purposes, but also found an important niche on the construction scene. This Model 25 is equipped with an air compressor unit, obviously powered from the rear pto shaft. Since the Model 25 could negotiate rough terrain, this unit made it possible to move an air supply to rough ground and other remote locations. A few companies specialized in equipment designed specifically for the Cletrac tractors.

Relatively few details are available for the Model 30 Cletrac tractor. Built only during 1935 and 1936, its production appears to have extended to only a couple hundred copies. Model 30 tractors were equipped with a Hercules JXC engine. This six-cylinder style was capable of about 33 flywheel horsepower, and used a 3 3/4 x 4 1/4 inch bore and stroke. A noticeable change is the modified carriage roller system which is partially enclosed behind steel shielding.

Cletrac "35" tractors were powered by a six-cylinder Hercules Model WXT engine. Rated at 1,450 rpm, it was capable of 46 belt horsepower. A major advantage of the Hercules engine design was the force-feed lubrication of the main bearings, connecting rods, and cam bearings. By comparison, many tractors of 1932 were still using dip pans under each connecting rod. This, together with a slinger attached to the rod cap constituted the oiling system. Force-feed lubrication put the lubricant inside the bearing instead of splashing the oil about the crankcase.

Weighing some five tons, the Cletrac Model 35 tractor listed at about $2,500. During its 1932-36 production run the 35G (as compared to the 35D, a diesel model) it appears that slightly over 2,000 units were built. It also appears that the 40-30 was an immediate predecessor of the Model 35, with the Model CG, built from 1936 to 1942, being a direct descendant. All three models used the same parts book. This Model 35 is shown with a leaning wheel grader, building up a roadbed.

Like other Cletrac models, the "35" could be equipped with a wide variety of options. This particular copy is set up as a Swamp Special with its extra-wide track pads. Given this equipment, the Model 35 was able to negotiate soft, mucky ground where most other tractors feared to tread. Although the Model 35 was available with magneto ignition and a hand crank, the preferred equipment was battery ignition and an electric starter. The 40-30 tractor was the immediate predecessor of the Model 35.

Rated by Cleveland Tractor Company at 30 drawbar and 44 belt horsepower, the 40-30 saw first light in 1930. When production ended the following year, only a few hundred copies had been built. Features included a Hercules six-cylinder engine. Rated at 1,450 rpm, it carried a 4 1/4 x 4 1/2 inch bore and stroke. This model was tested at Nebraska under No. 195 of 1931. In the maximum load test, the 40-30 pulled 7,580 pounds, or slightly 78% more than its test weight of 9,700 pounds.

Cleveland Tractor Company

The Cletrac Model DD tractor began life in 1935 as the Model 40 Diesel, and even before that as the Model 35 Diesel. The scenario begins in 1934 with the Model 35D, powered by a Hercules DRXH diesel engine. The following year the Model 40D emerged, and it remained in production until 1936. When the Cletrac tractor line was revamped and streamlined in 1936 the Model 40D was designated as the Model DD tractor. Weighing just short of six tons, the Model 40D was sent to Nebraska's Tractor Test Laboratory in June 1935, with the results appearing in Test No. 235. It developed over 63 belt horsepower.

Another interesting development was that of the Model 80 Cletrac. An early variation apparently was the 50-60 tractor, equipped with a Wisconsin DT-3 gasoline engine. This style was built from 1930 to 1932. The latter year, the DT-3 engine was replaced with a larger DT-4 Wisconsin engine, but production of this model ended the same year it began. After this came the 80G tractor, built in the 1932-36 period. This model was equipped with a Hercules HXE engine. The huge six-cylinder power plant used cylinders having a 5 3/4 x 6 inch bore and stroke, and could develop well over 100 belt horsepower. This model was capable of a drawbar pull exceeding 19,000 pounds.

Built in the 1933-36 period, the Model 80 Diesel tractor carried the same essential specifications as the comparable gasoline model, except of course, for the type of engine. In this instance a Hercules six-cylinder DHXD engine was used. It was designed with a 5 x 6 inch bore and stroke. Standard features included Leece-Neville starting and lighting equipment. This tractor weighed over 24,000 pounds. Only about 300 units were built during its 1933-36 production run.

The 1936 *Tractor Field Book*, published early that year, shows all the Cletrac models in an unstyled version. However, the following year, some of the crawlers have an entirely new streamlined look, even though the tractor beneath the sheet metal was still essentially unchanged. One popular model was the Model E. It was built in several configurations, including the EN style. Hercules supplied the four-cylinder gasoline engine; it used a 4 x 4 1/2 inch bore and stroke. Rated speed was 1,250 rpm. Three forward speeds were provided.

Cleveland Tractor

While the Cletrac DG tractor was powered by a gasoline engine, the Cletrac DD was equipped with a Hercules DRXB six-cylinder diesel design. Rated at 1,200 rpm, it used a 4 3/8 x 5 1/4 inch bore and stroke. The engine featured a Bosch fuel injection system. Electric starting was of course, standard equipment. The Cletrac DD was tested at Nebraska under No. 235 of June 1935. In this test it yielded almost 68 belt horsepower, along with a deliver of 61-plus horsepower at the drawbar.

By 1937 Cleveland Tractor Company was offering their Cletrac in four different models with diesel engines, and in eleven different models with gasoline motors. In all, the Cletrac line of 1937 ranged from 22 to 94 horsepower. The extensive nature of the line is better appreciated when it is noted that the Model E Cletrac alone was available in five different widths. This was done to accommodate virtually any row crop requirements, and at this point in time, Cletrac was firmly committed to finding new agricultural uses for its crawler tractors. This Cletrac is pulling a couple of spring-tooth harrows; apparently the two men on board the harrow are attempting to provide some extra ballast.

No reference can be found regarding this specially equipped Cletrac diesel model. It obviously uses a gasoline-powered starting engine. The general appearance of the tractor leads to the conclusion that this was probably an option for cold climates where electric starting would work if there were enough batteries. The extended crank for the starting engine is obvious, and the company was proud enough of this attachment to attach their customary Cletrac decal to the engine side panel.

Throughout their years in the crawler tractor business, Cleveland Tractor Company emphasized their unique, and patented, Controlled Differential Steering. Under this system, first developed by Rollin H. White, the whole differential assembly turned together when going straight ahead. However, when turning, both tracks were under power, and this permitted the Cletrac to turn on a true course, and under complete control of the operator. In contrast, simple clutch steering was unable to secure this kind of control over the tractor.

Cleveland Tractor Company became a part of Oliver in 1944. When White Motors bought out Oliver in 1960 the Cletrac operations were moved to Charles City, Iowa. However, all crawler tractor production ceased in 1965. Thus, Rollin White's dream of the ultimate in crawler tractors lasted for a half century, not very long by some standards, but a long time indeed, compared to some of the many companies who entered the tractor business.

Production of the Cletrac CG began in 1936. This model was a derivative of first the 40-30 tractor, then the Model 35. The 40-30 began life in 1930, followed in 1932 with the Model 35. All used the Hercules WXT engine, and in fact, all three models used the same parts book. To be sure, there were differences among the three tractors, but essentially they were of the same design and in the same horsepower class. Cleveland sent a CG tractor to Nebraska in September 1937, and the results appear in Test No. 289. In this test the CG managed a maximum output of nearly 46 drawbar horsepower. Operating weight was 11,700 pounds.

Cleveland announced the Model D tractor in 1936. Interchangeably it was called the DG (gasoline) as compared to the DD (diesel) model. This big tractor used a six-cylinder engine having a 4 5/8 x 5 1/4 inch bore and stroke; as with most others of the series, the engine was built by Hercules. Capable of approximately 61 brake horsepower, this tractor was also capable of a drawbar pull exceeding 11,000 pounds. This tractor was never tested at Nebraska.

Weighing nearly 13,000 pounds, the Cletrac DD was virtually identical to its gasoline-powered brother, the Model DG. In this instance, Cletrac used a Hercules DRXB six-cylinder diesel engine. Its 4 3/8 x 5 1/4 inch bore and stroke yielded a displacement of 474 cubic inches. It was rated in excess of 60 drawbar horsepower. Three forward gears were provided with speeds ranging from 1.8 to 4.3 mph. Initially, the Model DD was built with the unstyled design. During 1937 it was restyled and streamlined, although the basic tractor specifications remained unchanged.

The D-Series Cletracs were available in standard and Hillside Special models. Essentially, this meant that the two tractors used different track widths. The standard model had an overall width of 68 1/2 inches, while the Hillside Special was spread out to 81 1/2 inches. The extra width provided the additional stability needed when working on sidehills and slopes. In addition to the need for this design in hilly farm ground, it was also widely used for construction work. This Model DDH Cletrac is equipped with a Drott Hi-Lift loader.

Cleveland Tractor Company introduced their Model E crawler in 1934. It was built in E-31, E-38, E-62, and E-68 models, with these numerals indicating the width between tracks. Until 1938 it was not streamlined, having the same general appearance as other Cletrac models of the early 1930s. The gasoline model used a Hercules OOC four-cylinder engine. Its L-head design used a 4 x 4 1/2 inch bore and stroke, with a rated speed of 1,300 rpm. Operating weight was 6,100 pounds.

By offering various track widths, the Model E Cletrac could be adapted to many different crops and farming practices. Cletrac continued to point to the lightfootedness of their crawler tractor, noting that it had only about a third of the ground pressure of a man walking across the ground. A 1939 Cletrac catalog again emphasizes that the Cletrac was 'The Only Crawler Tractor with Power on Both Tracks.' Cletrac's Controlled Differential Steering had been pioneered by Rollin H. White in 1916. Shown here is an EHG High Clearance model.

Model E Cletrac tractors were also built in a diesel version. Shown here is an ED-42 model with a 42-inch track gauge. This tractor was equipped with a Hercules DOOC four-cylinder diesel engine having a 4 x 4 1/2 inch bore and stroke for a displacement of 226 cubic inches. In all other respects, this model was no different than the gasoline model. Various styles of front-mounted cultivators were available for the Model E tractor. Cletrac heavily stressed a design that permitted easy servicing. Adjusting the steering bands required only the removal of a handhole and adjusting a single self-locking nut. The ED2 diesel model was equipped with a Buda diesel engine.

Initially, the Model F Cletrac assumed this non-streamlined appearance. This huge tractor weighed over 13 tons and was equipped with a gasoline engine capable of over 113 brake horsepower. By today's standards this is relatively small, but for 1936, this was indeed a huge tractor. A Hercules HXE engine was used. Its six cylinders were designed with a 5 3/4 x 6 inch bore and stroke. Rated speed was 1,120 rpm. In Nebraska Test No. 262 the Model F (also called the FG) made a maximum pull of over 19,000 pounds.

In Nebraska Test NO. 262 the Cletrac FG consumed gasoline at the rate of 12 gallons per hour in the maximum load tests. Using a ten-hour day and gasoline at $1.15 a gallon would leave a gasoline bill of $138 per day at present prices. All this calculates to about 25 ounces of gasoline every minute! The FG was equipped with three forward speeds from 1.75 to 4.3 mph. It was eight feet wide, 14 1/2 feet long, and 7 feet tall. This model replaced the earlier Model 80 Cletrac. Using the serial number lists as a guide, only about eight of these huge tractors were built.

The Cletrac Model F tractors were intended for the largest and heaviest construction work. This early, unstyled Model FD was essentially the same as the gasoline model, except of course, that a diesel engine was used. The engine was by Hercules, of six-cylinder design, and used a 5 x 6 inch bore and stroke. It was rated at 1,300 rpm. This model was a successor to the Model 80 Diesel of the 1933-36 period. Initially, the FD used a four-speed transmission, but from 1938 upward, a six-speed gear box was featured. It appears that production of the FD tractor with its variations totaled about 400 units.

Cleveland Tractor Company

From its 1936 inception, the Model F series included the Model FDL Logger Special. It was equipped with a special radiator grille and a massive steel bumper. It also had a high clearance of 19 1/2 inches, lower track and wheel bearing guards, plus a steel transmission case and steel bell housing and crankcase guard. Like all other Cletrac diesels, the FDL featured full electric starting. The FD tractors weighed well over 27,000 pounds, with the special equipment on the Logger Special probably pushing the operating weight to nearly 15 tons!

Crawler tractors have been used extensively for snow removal. Rural roads of the 1930s and 1940s often had little or no grade, and ditches to catch drifting snow were often non-existent. This unidentified photograph shows a Cletrac equipped with a huge snow plow, and bucking drifts higher than the tractor itself. In many instances, snow drifted so high that even the fence posts were covered. For those areas not fortunate enough to have a large plow like this, there were two alternatives. One was for neighbors and townspeople to gather with shovels and make a path of their own. The other alternative was to wait until the spring thaw.

Model F Cletracs were used primarily for heavy construction. However, the FD diesel model was tested at Nebraska in 1936, with the results appearing in No. 263. It was again tested in 1939 under Test No. 326. The latter test manifested a maximum output of 107 belt horsepower and fuel consumption of 14 horsepower hours per gallon of fuel. The earlier FD tractor delivered 91 belt horsepower, but with nearly identical fuel economy. Thus it appears that Cletrac was hoping that some of their FD tractors would find their way into agriculture. But, at this time there were virtually no implements built for use with such a large tractor.

Operating a huge tractor like the Cletrac FD was undoubtedly a thrill, especially since it was one of the largest tractors on the 1936 market. The same Controlled Differential system which Rollin H. White patented in 1916 was still being used in the big FD crawler. Cleveland Tractor stressed the benefits of this system, with a 1939 catalog noting that their 'True-Course' steering system was possible only because of the unique differential design. The company also laid great stress on their main frame design with its inherent stability.

Cleveland Tractor Company

From 1939 to 1942, Cleveland Tractor Company departed from usual practice and built a wheel-type tractor. The little General Model GG tractor used a Hercules IXA four-cylinder engine with a 3 x 4 inch bore and stroke. Rated at 1,400 rpm, it was capable of 10 drawbar and 19 belt horsepower. Operating weight was 3,115 pounds. No specific information has surfaced, but it seems entirely logical that production of the Model GG was suspended in 1942 due to the onset of World War Two. In 1939 this little tractor listed at $595.

An unidentified photograph of about 1940 illustrates the Model GG wheel tractor to the right. It is almost completely dwarfed by a huge Model FD crawler in the center. The GG tractor had a blood relative in the Model HG tractor, also introduced in 1939. This small crawler model also carried the same Hercules engine as used in the Model GG wheel tractor. However, the crawler tractor was rated at 1,700 rpm, compared to 1,300 rpm for the Model GG tractor. In 1943 Cleveland Tractor Company was offering ten different models, ranging from the small HG crawler up to the huge Model FD.

Three forward speeds, ranging from 2 to 5 1/4 mph were provided in the Model HG tractor. As previously indicated, it used the same Hercules IXA engine as was used in the Model GG tractor. Cleveland Tractor sent a copy of the Model HG to Lincoln, Nebraska in August 1939 for testing. The results appear in No. 324. In this test the 3,500 pound Model HG pulled 2,800 pounds, or nearly 80% of its own weight. After Oliver Corporation bought out Cleveland Tractor Company in 1944, some of the Cletrac models remained in production for a time, and eventually were replaced with crawlers of Oliver's own design. Further information on Oliver crawler tractors may be found in the *Tractors* section of this volume.

In the early 1940s Cleveland Tractor attempted to market a crawler model using rubber tracks. It was an excellent idea, and in fact, the idea has been reintroduced in recent years. Unfortunately, the rubber tracks kept stretching, and technology of the 1940s was unable to come up with a relatively stable rubber track. Recognizing the problems with this design, Cletrac voluntarily recalled the rubber-track machines already in the field and retrofitted them with standard steel tracks. A very few of these machines still exist in their original condition.

Cockshutt Farm Equipment Company

James G. Cockshutt founded the Cockshutt Plow Company in 1877. It was under his direction until the company was incorporated in 1882. This company operated at Brantford, Ontario until it was purchased by White Motor Company in February 1962.

The Cockshutt factories originally specialized in plows and other tillage implements. About the turn of the century, Cockshutt contracted for the production of Frost & Wood Company at Smiths Falls, Ontario. This company dated back to the small shop of Ebenezer Frost, begun in 1839. Frost & Wood had a wide reputation for reapers, and in later years, grain binders. Although Ebenezer Frost began with a one-man shop, he took in a partner, Alexander Wood, in 1846. Thus came the title of Frost & Wood.

While the Cockshutt implements contributed mightily to agricultural development in Canada, their tractors are of special interest. The two digit models were built between 1946 and 1957, with the first Cockshutt 30 coming off the assembly

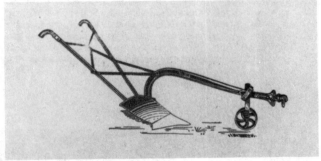

Cockshutt gained first fame with a line of plows designed especially for the Canadian market. Although it is rather difficult to elucidate to any extent regarding plows, untold hours of work went into their design. When it came to drawing out and sharpening the plow lays, a blacksmith who did not understand plow work could turn a good plow into virtually a non-performer. This No. 53 1/2 Walking Plow from Cockshutt was built in 7, 8, 9, 10, 12, and 14-inch sizes.

Cockshutt plows often were named after various aspects of the Dominion of Canada. An example is the "Maple Leaf" gang plow. It was originally built from 1904 to 1936. The following year it was redesigned, but continued to be known as the Maple Leaf gang plow. Other interesting titles were the Canadian Wonder gang plow, the Die Boer plow, and the Beaver gang plow. Cockshutt built a full line of plows for every need, including subsoil and road plows.

line on October 10, 1946. During the 1946-57 period, Cockshutt built the 20, 30, 35, 40, 50, Golden Eagle, and Golden Arrow models. The numbered models were sold as the Co-op tractors in the United States, and were designated as the E2, E3, E4, and E5 tractors. Cockshutt tractors were also sold in the United States under the Blackhawk name. The Gamble's Farmcrest Model 30 was identical to the Cockshutt Model 30. The Cockshutt tractors of this period were painted red and cream, while the Co-op models were painted orange and got a set of Co-op decals. It is also significant that the Cockshutt 30 was the first Canadian tractor to be tested at Nebraska. This test, No. 382, was run in the summer of 1947.

Between 1957 and 1961 Cockshutt produced the three digit series, namely the 540, 550, 560, 570 and 570 Super tractors. In addition, the 411R and 411G tractors were sold between 1961 and 1965. The two latter models were purchased from Fiat of Italy. Of further note, all Cockshutt tractor production at Brantford ended on February 1, 1962. At that time, Cockshutt tractor operations were moved to Charles City, Iowa. Beginning about 1950, and continuing a few years, Cockshutt maintained facilities at Bellevue, Ohio. With the merger of Oliver, Cockshutt, and other companies into White Motor Company, the individual entities blended into a faceless continuum of an earlier, and perhaps more enjoyable time.

By 1954, Cockshutt had developed a series of implements for use with the three-point hitch system. Included was a series of mounted plows. The No. 1230 plow featured full floating action with the 3-point hitch. Positive depth control was achieved with a crank-adjusted gauge wheel. In addition, a wide variety of conventional pull-type plows came from the Cockshutt factory. In 1954, Cockshutt offered four distinct plow models. With their variations, a total of 32 different plows were available. In addition, each of these models could be equipped with any of eight different moldboard styles.

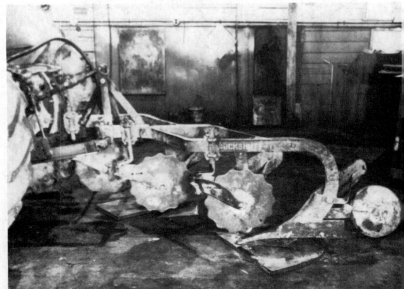

Cockshutt Farm Equipment Company

No. 16 TRACTOR DISC HARROWS

The Cockshutt tillage line included many different implements, including a variety of disc harrows. This No. 16 model could be furnished with rope or hydraulic control. While the latter was distinctly preferable, many farmers of the early 1950s did not yet have tractors equipped with a hydraulic system. As a peripheral note, the lack of tractor hydraulics propagated a flourishing business for a few years of building a hydraulic system which could be attached to any farm tractor. It was operated either from the belt pulley or from the pto shaft. The No. 16 tractor disc harrow shown here was available in 7, 8, and 10-foot models.

No. 10 STIFF TOOTH CULTIVATOR

The No. 10 Stiff Tooth Cultivator was but one of many different tillage implements from Cockshutt. It was built extra heavy to withstand the pulling strains of large tractors, as well as the unexpected shock of hidden rocks and roots. Small units, designed for use with live horsepower were available into the early 1950s. In addition, the tractor drawn models could be furnished with a mechanical or hydraulic lift, as desired. In addition to primary tillage implements, Cockshutt also built an extensive line of secondary tillage tools, including many different styles of cultivators.

Many different styles of disc plows were available from Cockshutt. These included numerous horse-drawn and tractor-powered designs. For example, the Cockshutt Canadian rotary disc plow was a horse-drawn style available in two- or three-furrow sizes. The Cockshutt reversible disc plow was a unique single-furrow machine that permitted a farmer to begin plowing at one side of the field without having to lay out the headlands. Included too were numerous sizes and styles of tractor-drawn disc harrows.

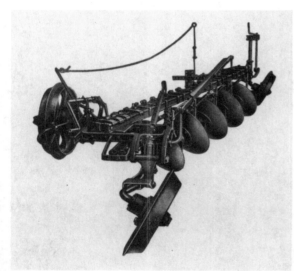

The No. 33 Tiller Combine was designed for deep cultivation. Without the seeding attachment it was ideal for summer fallow, or for discing after the harvest. With the seeding attachment, the No. 33 was ideal for once-over spring seeding and tillage. A major reason for this method was that it conserved soil moisture. Other disc harrows were designed for shallow cultivation, and permitted cultivating, seeding, and packing in one operation. Numerous sizes and styles were available to meet individual needs.

For commercial gardeners and nurserymen the Cockshutt No. 1 transplanter manifested a great labor savings. This machine was equipped with seven different sprocket wheels so that plants could be spaced anywhere from 12 1/2 to 55 inches. Cockshutt pointed out the obvious advantages of this machine, especially to growers of tobacco, cabbage, cauliflower, eggplant, tomatoes, sweet potatoes and strawberries.

This No. 625 Cockshutt spreader was built in the 1950s. It had a 125 bushel capacity. For some years before, Cockshutt offered various spreader models. Included was the No. 5 spreader, a lightweight machine suited to the needs of the small farmer. The No. 6, first offered in the 1940s was designed for use with a tractor, and the No. 4 was of the four-wheel design, but could be used with horses or a tractor, as desired.

Not only did Cockshutt offer a full line of tillage implements; this company also built farm wagons for a number of years. Shown here is their No. 95 wagon of the 1950s. This model had a capacity of 6,000 pounds. An unusual feature shown on this model is the front and rear spring bolster, available at extra cost. Although the front and rear axles were free to oscillate about the reach, adding the spring bolsters cushioned the load.

This No. 5 Frost & Wood binder was built from 1928 to 1933. Its immediate predecessor was the No. 4, built in the 1917-27 period. Many other models came before and after this time, but of significance is the No. 1 tractor binder, first built in 1928, with production ending in 1936. Cockshutt began marketing the Frost & Wood line in the early 1900s, and eventually the two firms blended into one. Curiously, Cockshutt did not make any overt moves into building their own threshing machines, preferring instead to concentrate on grain binders and other machinery.

During its career, Cockshutt built many different mowers. By the 1950s the company was offering this No. 315, tractor mower. It was an outgrowth of the earlier No. 15AS power mower, first offered in the 1940s. In addition, Cockshutt continued to offer a variety of horsedrawn mowers, including the Giant 8A model. It was a successor to the earlier Giant No. 8, a model which Cockshutt had sold throughout the world. In fact, various models of Giant mowers were marketed by Cockshutt for half a century.

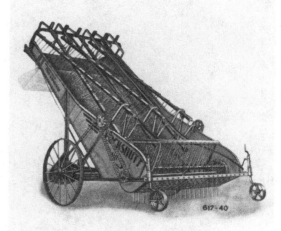

No. 3 HAYLOADER

The Cockshutt hay line included rakes, hayloaders, and other necessary equipment. This No. 3 hayloader was an all-steel design that used a combination cylinder and push bar design. The revolving cylinder picked up the hay from the windrow, and the reciprocating push bars moved it forward and upward to the hay wagon. Another style was the No. 2, designed with a cylinder and carrier apron rather than the push bars. Both styles worked satisfactorily, with the choice being primarily one of farmer preference.

COCKSHUTT "112" PLANTER

About 1950 Cockshutt set up facilities at Bellevue, Ohio. Apparently this facility was connected with the National Farm Machinery Co-op in the same city. The latter built the Blackhawk corn planters and other implements. In this same connection came a catalog of the Cockshutt-Blackhawk planters. Eight different planter models were available in 1954. Included were horsedrawn and tractor drawn models. This Cockshutt No. 112 planter is of 1950s vintage.

This very unusual machine is a flax scutcher. It was designed by Frost & Wood, and sold by Cockshutt. The flax scutcher was designed to break, scutch, and clean flax straw in a single operation. The end result was the fiber used in making linen. Prior to scutching the flax was retted, which essentially means that the straw was permitted to cure, or partially decay until the connective tissue was destroyed. The success of the scutcher depended in large part on the degree of retting and the moisture in the material. Obviously, this machine was sold to a very small, but nevertheless, a very important market.

prevent grain loss — reap a fuller harvest at low cost!

With the coming of combines came a need for the windrower or swather. (The latter two terms are used interchangeably). Swathing permitted cutting of the grain earlier, thus hastening maturity. It was also done to avoid insect damage. Ordinarily the No. 2 swather was furnished with a 12-foot cutting width, but a 3-foot extension was available for an effective width of 15 feet. This model was powered from the tractor pto. To accommodate the windrowed crop, Cockshutt furnished a special pick-up attachment for their combines.

Cockshutt Farm Equipment Company

No. 7 HARVESTER COMBINE

Prior to Cockshutt's 1962 acquisition by White Motor Company, this No. 423 swather was marketed in a 16-foot size. Actually, the No. 423 was not built by Cockshutt, even though it carried the Cockshutt color scheme and their logo. Instead, this machine was built by Hesston Mfg. Company at Hesston, Kansas. The self-propelled design had many inherent advantages. Among them was unexcelled maneuverability. The operator's platform was directly above the cutter bar for completely unobstructed vision.

Current research has not been able to ascertain the exact beginning of Cockshutt combine production. Presumably the company was involved in combine research during the 1930s, One early example was the No. 6 combine, built in 1939 and 1940. It was followed by the No. 7, introduced in 1941. This pull-type model is shown here with a pto drive, but it was also available with a Hercules engine. This No. 7 used a 62-inch cut and had a 35 bushel grain tank. The No. 7 was also built with an 8-foot cut.

"422"

Introduced in 1954, the No. 422 Cockshutt combine featured a 75-inch cutter bar, along with a straight-through body design. A huge 66-inch width was provided through the entire machine from the cylinder through the straw racks. An exclusive feature was the variable speed cylinder drive. It provided cylinder speeds of 600 to 1600 rpm by simply turning a crank. An auxiliary engine or a pto drive could be used, and numerous options were available. Production of this model ended in 1962.

Cockshutt initiated production of self-propelled combines with their SP-110 and SP-112 models in 1946. A variation of the SP-112 was the SP-115 model. The latter used a 15-foot cutting width, compared to 12 feet for the SP-112. The SP-110 was a smaller machine with a 10-foot cutting width. Forward features of the SP-110 included a 45 horsepower engine, and a 35 bushel grain tank. The complete unit weighed 5,500 pounds. Production of the SP-110 ended in 1951.

Along with the Drive-O-Matic traction drive, Cockshutt SP-132 and SP-137 combines featured a single-lever adjustment for the concaves and four full-length, all-steel straw walkers. The SP-132 carried a 67 horsepower Chrysler engine; its six cylinders used a 3 3/8 x 4 1/8 inch bore and stroke. The SP-137 featured a Chrysler 72 horsepower engine with a 3 7/8 x 4 1/4 inch bore and stroke. Low pressure 16.00 x 16 Flotraction tires were another feature, along with a live axle drive. Power steering was yet another feature of the innovative models.

A Chrysler six-cylinder industrial engine was featured in the SP-110, 112, and 115 combines. The latter two sizes carried a 60 horsepower style; six cylinders with a 3 3/8 x 4 1/16 inch bore and stroke. Eight forward speeds were provided, and an undershot feeder house was used to carry cut grain to the cylinder. Heavy duty v-belts were used wherever possible, along with ball or roller bearings. All-steel straw walkers were another feature, and the reel was power-driven. The SP-112 listed at $4,260. For a time during the 1950s, Cockshutt combines were sold in the United States by the National Farm Machinery Cooperative at Bellevue, Ohio.

COCKSHUTT "SP427"
DRIVE-O-MATIC
Deluxe

The Cockshutt SP-132 and SP-137 combines were built in the 1952-58 period. Both sizes were available in cutting widths of 10, 12, or 15 feet. Both featured a one-piece platform with center delivery, using an undershot auger. Hydraulic platform control was also a standard feature. The Cockshutt Drive-O-Matic traction drive was a new feature. It consisted of four-speed transmission coupled with an infinitely variable sheave drive. The variable pitch sheaves were hydraulically controlled with a foot pedal. Using this system, ground speeds could be varied from 5/8 to 9 mph.

Production of the Cockshutt SP-427 combine ran from 1956 to 1958. By the end of production this model was retailing at $6,039. The SP-427 was designed with a 12-foot cutting width, but was furnished with a larger engine than its predecessor the SP-132. In this instance, a Chrysler 72 horsepower engine was used. In addition, greater use was made of hydraulics, and power steering was a standard feature. The power-driven reel used on the Cockshutt combines was an innovative feature.

Cockshutt Farm Equipment Company

Cockshutt SP-428 combines were built from 1956 to 1962. Although the standard machine used a 12-foot header, the SP-428 could also be furnished with 10 and 15-foot headers at the buyer's option. When equipped with a 15-foot header, the SP-428 weighed over 7,700 pounds. To carry this machine, the drive wheels were equipped with high flotation 16.00 x 16 tires. Extras include a straw spreader, lights, and a spike tooth cylinder in lieu of the standard rasp bar design. In 1962 the SP-428 sold for $7,400.

Weighing 8,800 pounds, the SP-429 combine was furnished with big 13-26 drive wheels. This machine sold for $7,231 in 1962. Production began already in 1954. Like other Cockshutt self-propelled combines, the SP-429 was equipped with the Cockshutt Drive-O-Matic variable speed drive. One feature of the SP-429 was its high underframe clearance to permit harvesting in soft fields with little danger of damaging the underside of the combine. The SP-429 could be furnished with special equipment for virtually any seed crop.

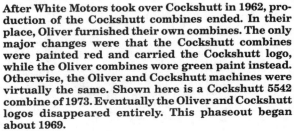

After White Motors took over Cockshutt in 1962, production of the Cockshutt combines ended. In their place, Oliver furnished their own combines. The only major changes were that the Cockshutt combines were painted red and carried the Cockshutt logo, while the Oliver combines wore green paint instead. Otherwise, the Oliver and Cockshutt machines were virtually the same. Shown here is a Cockshutt 5542 combine of 1973. Eventually the Oliver and Cockshutt logos disappeared entirely. This phaseout began about 1969.

On May 21, 1947 Cockshutt Plow Company presented their new Model 30 tractor to the Nebraska Tractor Test Laboratory. This is significant, since the Model 30 was the first Canadian tractor tested at the University of Nebraska. It is shown here during the actual test, No. 382, run between May 21 and June 3, 1947. The "30" was also built for, and was identical to, the Model E3 Co-op tractor sold in the United States by the National Farm Machinery Cooperative, Bellevue, Ohio.

Cockshutt 30 tractors could be furnished for use with gasoline, distillate, and propane fuels. Production of this model ran from 1946 to 1956. By the end of production it carried a list price of $2,478. Between 1949 and 1956 Cockshutt also built a Model 30 Diesel. The latter style listed at $3,255. The 30D featured a four-cylinder Buda engine with a displacement of 153 ci. Also of significance, the Cockshutt 30 was marketed as the Farmcrest 30. The gasoline model featured a Buda four-cylinder engine. Rated at 1,650 rpm, it carried a 3 7/16 x 4 1/8 inch bore and stroke. It was capable of about 30 belt horsepower.

Nebraska Test No. 474 of 1952 was run on the Cockshutt 20 tractor. This model was equipped with a Continental four-cylinder, L-head engine. Rated at 1,800 rpm, it was capable of about 26 belt horsepower. This model was sold in the United States as the Co-op E-2 tractor. Some were also sold in the U.S. as Blackhawk tractors. The only difference was that while Cockshutt tractors were painted red and cream, the Co-op tractors were painted orange and carried Co-op decals.

Here they are   THE NEW FARMCREST "30"s

Production of the Cockshutt 20 ran from 1952 to 1958. This model was available only for use with gasoline fuel. The list price of $2,101 was for the tricycle model; adding the wide-front axle shown here increased the list price by $104. The hydraulic system and three-point hitch came as standard equipment; if not wanted, there was a price deduct of $221 from list. Other standard features included the pto and pulley drive, and power-adjusted rear wheels. The Model 20 weighed 2,813 pounds.

As previously indicated, the Cockshutt 30 was sold for a time as the Farmcrest 30 from Gamble's Stores. An advertisement of the early 1950s illustrates the Farmcrest 30 in narrow front and standard-tread styles. In addition, the narrow front could be replaced with an adjustable-width front axle. Since there was no difference in the Cockshutt and Farmcrest models, both titles were included in Nebraska Test No. 382. Apparently, the Cockshutt 30 Diesel was not sold to any major extent in the United States. It was not tested at Nebraska.

The National Farm Machinery Cooperative sold the Cockshutt 40 as their Model E-4. The spark-fired model was available for use with gasoline, distillate, and LP-gas fuels. Production of this model ran from 1949 to 1957. The Cockshutt 40 was tested at Nebraska under No. 442. This photograph illustrates the Model 40 while under actual brake horsepower testing during June 1950. A Buda six-cylinder engine was featured; its 3 7/16 x 4 1/8 inch bore and stroke gave a displacement of 230 ci.

Live power take off was a standard feature of the Cockshutt 40 tractor. The six-cylinder design featured a Buda engine with a 3 7/16 x 4 1/8 inch bore and stroke. Six forward speeds were provided, ranging from 1 5/8 to 10 1/2 mph. Primarily for the Canadian market, the Cockshutt D40 was a diesel model which was essentially the same as the spark-fired design. However, the D40 used a Buda diesel engine of the same bore and stroke. This engine used a Bosch fuel system. In 1958 the 40 gasoline model listed at $3,586 and the diesel model sold at $4,512. Cockshutt 40 Diesel tractors were built from 1950-1957.

Cockshutt Golden Eagle tractors were built only in a diesel version. The Golden Eagle was sold in the United States, and was identical to the Cockshutt 40D4 tractor sold in Canada. Production of this tractor ran from 1955-57 and was marketed in the 1956-58 period. The Buda diesel formerly used was replaced with a Perkins four-cylinder engine. Other equipment was essentially the same as used on the Model 35 or Golden Arrow models.

A Buda engine with a 273 ci displacement was featured in the Cockshutt 50 tractor. This gasoline model was capable of 58 belt and 52 drawbar horsepower. It could be furnished in various configurations, such as the standard-tread design shown here. It could also be furnished with a tricycle front. A live pto was standard equipment, along with a six-speed transmission and live hydraulics. The Cockshutt 50 was tested at Nebraska under No. 488 of 1952. Production of this model ran from 1952 to 1957.

Cockshutt 50 tractors were built in gasoline and diesel models. Production of the 50 Diesel ran from 1952 to 1957. This model was equipped with a Buda 6DA273 engine capable of about 50 brake horsepower. Rated as a four-plow tractor, the D50 delivered a maximum pull of 6,319 pounds in Nebraska Test No. 487 of 1952. Bare weight of the D50 was 5,988 pounds, but for purposes of the above test considerable ballast was added. The Cockshutt 50 was also sold in the United States as the Co-op E-5 tractor.

Golden Arrow and Cockshutt 35 tractors were actually Cockshutt 30 tractors using a 550 Hercules engine. The Golden Arrow and Golden Eagle tractors were transitional models as Cockshutt changed over from two-digit models to the three-digit models. The Model 35 was built between 1955 and 1957, while the Golden Arrow was built only in 1957. Both styles were made only for use with gasoline fuel. The Cockshutt 35 was not marketed by National Farm Machinery Cooperative.

In 1958 Cockshutt announced an entirely new line of tractors. The small end of the line included this 540 model. Rated as a two-plow tractor, it used a 162 ci engine built by Continental. The dual-range, six-speed transmission provided the optimum speed for virtually any kind of field work, and draft control hydraulics were standard equipment, as was the three-point hitch system. This model was available only with a gasoline engine. It listed at $2,750.

Cockshutt 550 tractors were built in gasoline and diesel versions. Only the diesel model was tested at Nebraska, with the results appearing in Test No. 681 of 1958. The gasoline version was equipped with a Hercules four-cylinder engine; this model listed at $3,310. The 550 diesel model used a Hercules engine with a 198 ci displacement. Power steering was a $169 option, as were the special crown fenders for an additional cost of $68. The 550 diesel was rated at about 35 brake horsepower.

A Perkins four-cylinder diesel engine was featured in the 560 Cockshutt tractor. Built in the 1958-61 period, this model was offered only as a diesel for the U. S. market, but was also available with a four-cylinder, 198 ci gasoline engine. Weighing 7,295 pounds, the 560 was capable of 43 rated belt horsepower. A new depth and draft control system on the 500-Series tractors kept implements at a pre-set depth. A transfer system automatically placed more weight on the rear wheels as the draft increased.

Cockshutt 570 tractors were built primarily as a diesel model, and this tractor was tested at Nebraska under No. 683. This model featured a Hercules six-cylinder engine; it was capable of 54 rated belt horsepower. The 570 was also available with a gasoline engine, at least for the Canadian market. The 298 ci engine made the 570 a full 5-plow tractor. Weighing 7,175 pounds, it was ordinarily furnished with 13.6 - 38 tires, but various other sizes were available to suit individual requirements. Production of the 570 ran from 1958 to 1960. During 1961 and 1962 the Cockshutt 570 Super Diesel was built. This model was the end of the Cockshutt tractor line.

A live pto system was standard equipment on the Cockshutt 560 tractor. Other features included double disc brakes, and live hydraulic power. The Perkins diesel engine featured a three-bearing crankshaft, replaceable precision type main and connecting rod bearing inserts, high performance aluminum pistons, full floating piston pins, and full pressure lubrication. Production of the 560 diesel ended in 1961.

After White Motors acquired Cockshutt in 1962, production of the Cockshutt tractor ended. After this time came Oliver tractors painted red, and carrying the Cockshutt logo. This Cockshutt 1250 is actually an Oliver 1250; the latter having been built in the 1965-69 period. In addition, two Fiat tractor models were sold in the 1961-65 period. These were the 411R diesel and 411RG gasoline models. The latter tractors were purchased from Fiat and sold with the Cockshutt logo.

Arthur B. Farquhar was born in 1838 at Sandy Springs, Maryland. In 1856 he moved to York, Pennsylvania and apprenticed with W. W. Dingee & Company. The latter was building grain threshers. In 1858 Farquhar bought an interest in the company, and shortly thereafter the firm was renamed as Pennsylvania Agricultural Works. Shortly after, the plant burned to the ground. Dingee and Farquhar dissolved their partnership, with the latter resuming business as the sole proprietor. Dingee eventually went to work for the J. I. Case Threshing Machine Company at Racine, Wisconsin. The company shops were destroyed by fire again in 1876, but were quickly rebuilt. In 1889 the company name was changed to A. B. Farquhar Company Ltd.

Farquhar began with threshers and other farm machines, expanding gradually into cultivators and other implements. Steam engines of stationary and portable types appeared about 1880, and traction engines followed a few years later.

In 1915 the company made a brief excursion into the gasoline engine and tractor business, but both were discontinued within a few seasons.

A. B. Farquhar died in 1925, and the business was taken over by his son, Francis.

With the decline of steam power, the company bought out the Iron Age implement line in 1930, and the Portable Machinery Company in 1931.

In 1952 the A. B. Farquhar Company was sold to Oliver Corporation. The latter gradually phased out all operations at York, and when White Motor Corporation acquired Oliver in 1960, the Farquhar plant was not included in the transaction.

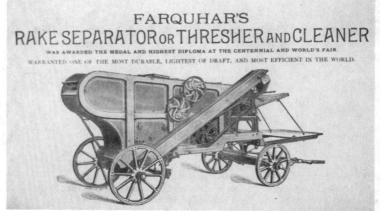

Arthur B. Farquhar apprenticed with W. W. Dingee & Company at York, Pennsylvania during 1856. The latter was building grain threshers at the time, and eventually, Dingee became the chief thresher designer at J. I. Case Threshing Machine Company. Initially, it is to be assumed that the products consisted of plain threshers and perhaps a rake separator, not unlike the model shown here. Farquhar became a partner with Dingee in 1858. Shortly afterward, the plant burned to the ground. Dingee left York at that time, and Farquhar rebuilt from the ashes he left behind.

Into the early 1900s, Farquhar continued to offer an overshot separator, with or without the Railway Power shown here. The latter was essentially a treadmill, but the unusual name was derived in part from the design of this machine. The Railway Power was available alone, or in combination with the overshot machine shown in this illustration. It was built only with a 26-inch cylinder size. With two horses, and average grain, this machine could thresh 150 to 200 bushels of wheat per day.

Farquhar continued to offer rake separators as late as 1910, and perhaps even longer. This, despite the fact that the vibrator separator had been available for decades. Perhaps this type of machine was better adapted to certain crops than the vibrator, but the more likely answer is that some farmers preferred this style to the 'new-fangled' vibrator machine. At the turn of the century, many active farmers had witnessed the transition from flail to the groundhog thresher. Then came the rake-type machine, followed by the vibrator design. Perhaps they were not about to tolerate any further changes in grain harvesting methods!

A. B. Farquhar Company

Farquhar plain threshers undoubtedly dated back to the 1850s, yet they were available into the early 1900s. As its name implies, this machine was essentially a spiked cylinder and concave teeth. It was of course, fed by hand...the feed table is visible at the far right of this illustration. Plain threshers could be furnished with a shaker attachment, as shown here to the back of the cylinder, but could also be shipped without this attachment. In thresherman's lingo, plain threshers were also called groundhog threshers or chaff pilers.

Since most small farms could not afford a steam engine, and since gasoline engines weren't well developed in the 1890s, the horse power or sweep power attained great popularity. It was a simple means of converting animal power into a rotating mechanical force. Shown here is a one-horse sweep power. It made 11 revolutions of the output shaft to one turn of the horse around the circle. This machine carried an 1897 list price of $58.

Farquhar rake separators could be furnished with the mounted Climax sweep power shown here in the foreground. Its four sweep arms could accommodate up to eight horses. Power was transmitted through tumbling rods and 'knuckles' or universal joints to gears on the thresher. Suitable stakes and braces prevented any movement of the sweep power. W. W. Dingee perfected many features of the sweep power, and undoubtedly, his earlier connections with A. B. Farquhar proved beneficial in later improvements to these important sources of power.

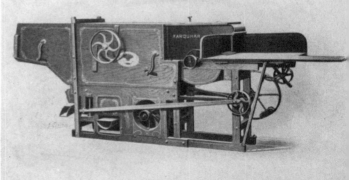

Farquhar Baby Vibrator.

While it has not been precisely determined when Farquhar introduced their vibrator machine, presumably it came onto the scene by the 1880s. While the rake machine used an open raddle to carry the straw to the rear of the machine, the vibrator used straw shakers or straw racks to move the straw rearward, meanwhile dropping the grain to the grain pan below. The low-down design was unique, especially since this machine was only about six feet from the ground. The low height was advantageous when threshing from stacks or when barn threshing. It was also a distinct advantage in traveling over hilly ground.

Farquhar offered their Baby Vibrator at least until World War One. This small stationary style was primarily intended for threshing from barns. In some areas, the grain was harvested and set into shocks. After a suitable curing time in the field, the bundles of grain were brought to barns and stored there for further drying and curing. During those seasons when other work was slack, farmers would then thresh the grain which had been harvested several months before. The grain was put into bins, and the straw remained in the barn for animal bedding.

All Farquhar vibrator cylinders were 22 inches in diameter over the spikes. This size remained constant, regardless of cylinder width. Double bars were used to add weight and strength to the cylinder. The additional weight gave a flywheel effect to help the cylinder go through heavy grain or wet straw. This design also strengthened the cylinder bars considerably. Each cylinder tooth was designed with a long tapered shank which was pulled tightly into a socket on the cylinder bar. Also evident in this illustration are the heavy iron bands shrunk over the cylinder bars to hold them tightly in place.

With its bright red finish, yellow striping, and yellow wheels, the Farquhar Vibrator was an impressive sight. This view illustrates a Vibrator equipped with a self-feeder and a pneumatic stacker. Due in part to the overall design of the machine, this model was equipped with a countershaft at the top. Power from the cylinder shaft was transmitted by belt to the countershaft, and then via another pulley, downward to the stacker pulley. Each thresher builder had their own special method of arranging the many belts and pulleys.

About 1896 Farquhar introduced the use of chain belts, as they were called at that time. This was far preferable to using leather or rubber belting with slats bolted on at frequent intervals. For those wishing to adapt the chain belt to an existing machine the malleable iron links were available for 16 cents per foot, and each elevator bucket was priced at eight cents. Within a short time after the development of the chain belt, virtually ever thresher manufacturer was using this design.

Farquhar, like most other thresher companies, persisted in building their machines of wood until competition finally forced them to begin building all-steel machines. Curiously, it was W. W. Dingee, the original founder of what would become Farquhar, who was instrumental in developing the all-steel thresher over at J. I. Case Threshing Machine Company. The latter machine was first marketed in 1904. The 1910 model of the Farquhar vibrator is equipped with a hand feed board and a slat stacker. Using the slatted stacker was preferable for some farmers over the pneumatic stacker.

As thresher sales declined in the 1920s the number of models steadily decreased. This all-steel machine of the late 1920s typifies the Farquhar line at that time. Recognizing the new dominance of the small farm tractor, Farquhar offered this small 22 x 36 machine. The Fordson and other small farm tractors could handle this machine with relative ease. The first figure of 22 indicates the cylinder width in inches. The latter figure of 36 indicates the width of the separating unit behind the cylinder.

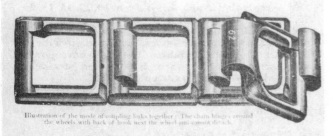

Illustration of the mode of coupling links together. The chain hinges around the wheels with back of hook next the wheel and cannot detach.

Showing application of chain to driving pulleys. The motion is positive, avoiding friction and strain on journals.

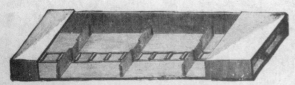

Tailings Elevator and Scraper Attachment.

A. B. Farquhar Company

New Farquhar Number 26 Separator

In 1900, Farquhar introduced their Number 26 separator. This model was made with a 22 inch cylinder and a 31 inch separator. It could be equipped with a side gear for use with a sweep power, or could be furnished as a belted machine. Steel wheels were standard, as shown here, but the Number 26 could also be furnished with wooden wheels, at the purchaser's option. Although this illustration shows a machine without a rear stacker, this could also be furnished as an option.

Designed to be the hallmark of simplicity, this Farquhar 22 x 36 machine opens up completely on the back. This permitted easy changing of sieves, as when changing from one type of grain to another. Of course, it also permitted easy access for repairs and servicing of the machine. Nothing more was needed than to drop the stacker belt, remove a few bolts, and open the entire back of the machine. Arthur B. Farquhar operated the company until his death in 1925, after which control of the company was assumed by his son, Francis Farquhar.

By 1900, and perhaps earlier, Farquhar offered the trade a pea vine thresher and shredder. This machine was designed especially for separating peas and beans from the vines, and delivering them from the spout, just like grain from a threshing machine. The vines were shredded for use as forage. In addition, this machine was capable of shelling and cleaning corn, while also shredding the corn fodder. Due to its special design, this machine was totally unsuited to threshing ordinary small grain crops.

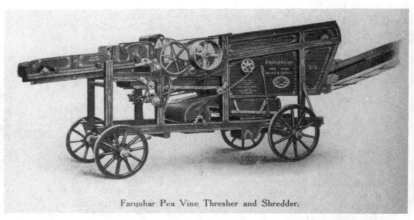

Farquhar Pea Vine Thresher and Shredder.

DOES NOT CRACK THE GRAIN, THRESHES CLEAN FROM THE STRAW, AND DELIVERS WITHOUT WASTE, CLEAN OF ALL FILTH, READY FOR THE MILL.

Ajax Center Crank Engines likely had their beginnings in the late 1880s. While no specific information has been located, it seems entirely likely that Farquhar was building steam engines prior to that time. The Ajax Center Crank was built in 10, 12, 15, 18, 20, 25, 30, and 35 horsepower sizes. The smallest model used a 7 x 10 inch bore and stroke; it had an 1897 list price of $450 without the stack, but complete with all other fixtures and appliances. The big 35 horsepower size carried an 11 x 15 inch bore and stroke; it weighed 14,000 pounds and sold for $935.

Recognizing the special needs of the rice grower, Farquhar offered this special rice separator as early as 1897. It was built following the design of the ordinary thresher, but was specially modified for the rice crop. Few specifics have been located regarding this machine. A special catalog was issued for those interested parties. Certain types of rice were notoriously difficult to thresh, and so this required special design work at the cylinder end. The cylinder speed was modified, and the separating mechanism was also redesigned to permit the efficient harvest of an important crop.

A. B. Farquhar Company

The mounted vertical engines represented an unusual design. To simplify moving from place to place, the engine and boiler were simply tilted forward over the rear axle for easy transportation. Thus equipped, the 6 horsepower size sold for $325, while the slightly larger 8 horsepower model listed at $365. Adding the four-wheel trucks only added about $30 to the price of the plain unit designed for stationary mounting. These engines were illustrated as late as 1910, and may have been offered for several years beyond that time.

Farquhar billed their vertical engines as a 'specialty.' This small outfit was compact, having the engine mounted directly to the vertical boiler. The small 5 hp model used a 4 1/2 x 7 inch bore and stroke; as shown here, it listed at $195 in 1897. The large 10 horsepower model was designed with a 6 1/2 x 9 inch bore and stroke. When equipped as shown in this illustration, it carried an 1897 retail price of $420. The largest size weighed 4,100 pounds.

A 1910 catalog illustrates this Ajax Center Crank Engine, with this one specifically being the Style D model. It obviously is equipped with a return flue boiler, although it could also be purchased with a standard locomotive boiler. In addition to their other enterprises, the Farquhar people made a specialty of boiler work, and could supply boilers of almost any size or for any application. Portable engines like this one were used to a limited extent, but were never as popular as a traction engine of comparable size.

In addition to the mounted center crank Ajax engines, Farquhar also offered this style mounted on skids for semi-portable or stationary use. When this engine was illustrated in 1910, many factories and small shops were still operated with an engine like this one. In addition, a substantial number found their way to sawmills. With this application, operating costs were reduced to almost nothing, since the fireman burned green slab wood for fuel. Firing with green slabs was, and is, entirely possible. However, it requires firing skills somewhat in advance of the neophyte.

By 1910 the Farquhar portables had gained essentially the form they would retain until the 1940s. Even though steam traction engine production was halted in the late 1920s, it appears that Farquhar continued to offer stationary and portable engines for some years to follow. Whether these were carried in stock or built to order is unknown. Either way, it is likely that Farquhar maintained the foundry patterns and machining jigs, so building an engine was relatively simple, even though full production had long since come to an end.

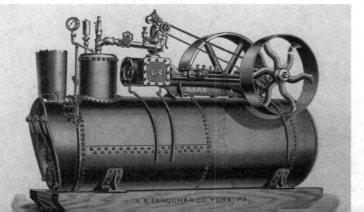

A. B. Farquhar Company

Ajax center crank engines were available for stationary mounting, as shown in this 1910 catalog illustration. The engine was virtually identical to those mounted on a boiler, except that the main frame was designed with mounting feet especially for a masonry foundation. Engines like this one were designed with particular care. All parts were heavily proportioned. A great many of them operated six or seven days a week for years on end, but required virtually no repair work.

Farquhar built their sidecrank engine with a Corliss-style girder frame for several decades. Specific production periods have not been located, however. While some engineers and users preferred the center crank design, others preferred the side crank style shown here. Each design had its advantages, and for various reasons, the side crank style seemed to be the most popular. The Corliss-style girder frame seems to have had its beginnings with Edwin Reynolds at E. P. Allis Company. This style mounts the main bearings and the cylinder separately to the floor, in effect, using the foundation as the main frame. The casting bolted between the cylinder and the main bearings serves to tie the two sections together, as well as carrying the crosshead.

Another variation was this square bed frame style. It could be furnished in a center crank or a side crank design. The heavy base section also functioned as the crosshead guide, and the bottom half of the main bearings were an integral part of the main casting. Although this square bed frame engine is shown on a masonry foundation, it could also be furnished as a mounted style, using either the return flue or the locomotive style boiler.

This large stationary engine is of the Corliss-style girder frame design. Using a sidecrank concept, these big engines were built in sizes ranging from 100 to 300 horsepower. The 300 horsepower engine used a 24 x 36 inch bore and stroke; this engine weighed 47,000 pounds. A 1907 Farquhar catalog notes that several of these engines were then being used in the building of the Panama Canal, and three more had recently been shipped to Cuba. To accommodate virtually any situation, these engines could be furnished either right-hand or left-hand, as desired. The left-hand style is shown here.

J. I. Case Threshing Machine Company made a lot of advertising hay with their Case Eagle trademark. Not to be outdone, the 1906 catalog of A. B. Farquhar Company illustrates their version of an eagle trademark, noting it to be 'The Original Eagle.' Research into the Patent Office records has not come up with conclusive answers as to whether Farquhar was actually using this mark prior to J. I. Case. In truth, it may have been in use for several years, or even several decades before it was finally registered as a trademark. In fact, trademarks were not registered by the U. S. Patent Office until 1870. Most of the early trademarks were for everything from snake oil to whisky; few farm equipment trademarks were issued prior to 1900.

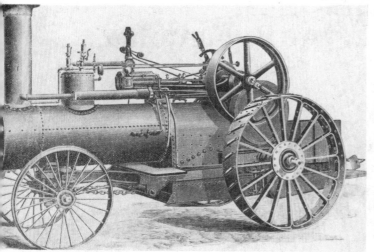

The Pennsylvania Traction Engine of 1897 was offered in five sizes, ranging from 10 to 20 horsepower. At the small end of the line was the 10 horsepower size with a 6 1/4 x 8 inch bore and stroke. It sold for $1,000. The largest model used a 9 x 11 inch bore and stroke; this model listed at $1,600 in 1897. Farquhar laid great emphasis on their boilers. The company specialized in boilermaking, and was prepared to offer boilers as large as 300 horsepower for virtually any purpose.

A 1906 Farquhar catalog notes that their Pennsylvania traction engine featured the standard Ajax center crank engine, but equipped with a link reverse. A canopy is shown on this engine, but Farquhar catalogs indicate that a canopy was never furnished, except on special order. These traction engines placed the flywheel on the left side, while almost all other manufacturers put the flywheel on the righthand side. Farquhar catalogs indicated that this was done to better adapt the Pennsylvania traction engine to sawmill work. The 1906 Farquhar catalog also indicates that Arthur B. Farquhar commenced manufacturing at York on April 7, 1856.

About 1907 Farquhar introduced their Style K traction engines. Four sizes were built: K-10, 7 3/4 x 10 inch; K-12, 8 1/4 x 10 inch; K-15, 9 x 11 inch; and K-20, 10 x 11 inch cylinder. As is obvious in this illustration, the Style K was of the sidecrank design, rather than the center crank style. While the Pennsylvania traction used a link reverse, the Style K featured a single eccentric reverse of the sliding block variety. Another important feature was the heavy duty boiler, intended for a 130 psi working pressure.

Already in 1906 Farquhar was advertising their new Style L traction engine. This double cylinder style was rated at 30 horsepower. This big engine used two cylinders with an 8 x 10 inch bore and stroke. The crankshaft was 3 1/2 inches in diameter, and was fabricated from a solid steel forging. The boiler was designed for a working pressure of 150 psi, and was of the standard open bottom style. By 1910 the Style L would be billed as a Road Engine, in reference to its use for heavy contractor work, hauling, and similar tasks. Initially though, the Style L was ostensibly intended to be a prime mover which would put thousands of acres under the plow.

Farquhar constantly stressed what they thought was the salient feature of their traction engines; the independent mounting system. Using heavy steel side plates and channels securely riveted together, and attached to the front and rear axles, the engine and gearing were carried entirely independent of the boiler. A unique design feature was that there were no stud bolts whatever in the boiler. All attachments were made with rivets. All gearing was of steel and malleable iron, except the wheel hub, which was cast, built up, and riveted together. The cannon box supporting the rear axle and countershaft was cast in one piece for added strength.

A. B. Farquhar

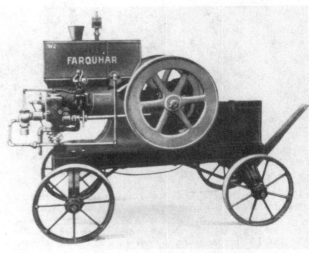

In addition to being built as a regular traction engine, the Style K was also available in a Contractors version, as shown here. It was first marketed about 1905. Special equipment on this engine consisted of open-hearth cast steel gearing, a one-piece solid steel cannon box, and a special rear hitch. A 1910 catalog indicates that the big 20 horsepower engine weighed 22,400 pounds, compared to 15,500 pounds for the 10 horsepower model. The engine dimensions were the same as for the Style K engine as previously indicated.

Between approximately 1910 and 1915, Farquhar built gasoline engines. This was probably in response to the tremendous market for engines at the time. This two horsepower model followed the ultimate in design features. A lay shaft parallel with the cylinder operated the valve and ignitor mechanisms. Engine speed was controlled through a flyball governor geared to the lay shaft. Unfortunately, no records exist to indicate the extent of Farquhar gas engine production.

In the words of Farquhar's 1910 catalog, the Style L Road Engine was 'built like a road roller---only better---for hauling and plowing. This double-cylinder model used an 8 x 10 inch bore and stroke. Operating at 250 rpm, and a boiler pressure of 150 psi, it was probably capable far in excess of its nominal rating of 30 horsepower. The engine design was similar to that used in the single-cylinder Style K engine. Standard features included the independent mounting, straight-line drive, steel gearing, brass-bushed bearings, and a coal capacity of 800 pounds.

A locomotive style cab was available on special order for the Style L Road Engine. Curiously, a power steering attachment was not offered, despite the size of this huge engine. Large water bunkers were provided, and to save fuel, the boiler waist and the steam dome were jacketed. With regular drivers, this engine was 8'-2" wide and 18 feet long. Farquhar indicated that this engine weighed about 10 tons, but chances are that its operating weight with fully loaded coal bunkers and water tanks approached 15 tons. Production of this style was probably very limited.

Farquhar got into the tractor business about 1915 and continued to produce a few tractors for the next decade. The 18-35 shown here was built with a four-cylinder engine. Its 6 x 8 design was built by Farquhar. This model weighed about 16,000 pounds. The large metal box at the front is the radiator, and mounted high above the radiator are the fuel tanks. A canopy was standard equipment, probably intended more for protection of the tractor engine than for the comfort of the operator. Farquhar also built a big 25-50 tractor. It featured the company's own four-cylinder engine, using a 7 x 8 inch bore and stroke. The 25-50 weighed 19,000 pounds.

FARQUHAR, 18-35

A. B. Farquhar Company

As late as 1923 the Farquhar 15-25 tractor was listed in the tractor directories. Weighing 5,700 pounds, this model was equipped with a Buda four cylinder engine having a 4 1/2 x 6 inch bore and stroke. Two forward speeds were provided of 2 1/2 and 4 mph. The transmission was of the worm gear type, with enclosed external spur gears in the final drive. Sales of this model were probably very small, particularly since Farquhar advertised their tractor very little.

Farquhar began building grain threshers in the 1850s. However, the company also branched out into other endeavors over the following years, with sawmills becoming a specialty. This mill is equipped with the Ajax belt feed works. The belt feed and a friction reverse were combined for a simple, efficient feed system. The cone pulleys on the feed permitted three different speeds, depending on the available power and other factors. The large structure behind the drive pulley is a tensioning device for the drive belt.

The Farquhar sawmills were also available with a friction feed system. The small wooden lever shifted a friction wheel in relation to the face of the large driving disk. By this means, both the feed and gig-back motions were under infinitely variable control of the sawyer. The large vertical lever controlled the feed and gig-back motions. While the husk, mandrel, and other appliances shown here look fairly simple, a considerable amount of engineering was involved for a dependable, and ultimately successful sawmill.

Yet another feed system available on Farquhar sawmills was the Reamy feed. This patented design was used on several makes of sawmills, although each builder made slight alterations. The feed was operated and controlled completely by a single lever. Through a forward or reverse motion the feed and return motions were achieved. In addition, side-to-side movement of the lever controlled the speed of the feed and gig-back motions. The primary objection to the Reamy system was the regular attention that was needed for the paper friction wheels.

Farquhar Company

For large sawing operations, Farquhar mills could be equipped with a top saw rig. This device greatly increased the capacity of the mill where very large logs were frequently encountered. Frequently though, sawyers were forced to ingenuity when encountering a very large log. Usually, the procedure was to cut around the log, taking as much cut as possible, then turning the log for another cut. Eventually the cant was squared up sufficiently to permit a regular cut.

Farquhar sawmills could be furnished with a friction power receder for the knees. This was regularly furnished as standard equipment on the larger mills, but as an extra on the smaller sizes. To operate the receder, the flat pulley in the lower part of the illustration was forced into contact with a wood rail beneath. Also shown here is the Farquhar patent chain set works. It was simple and efficient, yet was free from a complicated mechanism. Depending on requirements, Farquhar sawmills could be furnished with many different knees, setworks, and other accessories.

This No. 7 Farquhar mill used the double-belt feed which eventually gained wide popularity. This model of the 1940s was typical of the Farquhar line at the time. Future changes would include the use of ball bearings in the mandrel, along with other modern features. When Oliver purchased the Farquhar factories in 1952, sawmills were continued for a short time, but eventually, almost all of the Farquhar operations were phased out. When White Motor bought out Oliver in 1960, the Farquhar plant was not included in the acquisition.

The Farquhar Peerless Baling Press was available for several years beginning about 1900. As with much of the Farquhar line, little is known of the Peerless press, except from the company's own literature. Like many other farm equipment builders of the time, Farquhar advertised but little in the trade papers. Apparently, the company had developed a sufficient trade to keep the shops busy, and perhaps there was no need to advertise further.

Farquhar Chilled Plow.

As previously indicated, Farquhar diversified into various farm implements during the 1860s. One early product was their chilled iron plow. It was built in virtually the same style for several decades. As its name implies, the moldboard was made of chilled iron, similar to that used in railroad car wheels. It was mixed in the proper proportions with charcoal iron to gain the proper amount of strength and toughness, while maintaining an extremely hard surface.

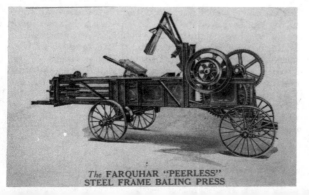

The FARQUHAR "PEERLESS" STEEL FRAME BALING PRESS

This all-steel spring tooth harrow was but one of several different harrows offered by Farquhar. This one was made with 14, 16, 18, 20, and 22 teeth, depending on farmer preference. Spike-tooth harrows were also available, along with numerous other tillage implements. From all appearances, Farquhar marketed these implements on a fairly localized basis, and probably enjoyed a substantial market.

Included in the Farquhar implement line was the Pennsylvania Low-Down force feed grain drill. This one is shown with a spring hoe drag bar. The Low-Down feature was an important one, since it permitted much easier loading of the hopper than was afforded by some of the competing models. Arthur B. Farquhar singlehandedly improved and patented many of the machines offered by his company. For nearly half a century he was at the helm of the company he organized in 1856.

Intended for truck farmers and small fields, the Farquhar Keystone planter was a single row outfit that could be pulled by a single horse or mule. The double-wheel design shown here was ordinarily furnished, but in lieu of this, the Keystone could be shipped with a concave single wheel. The seed mechanism was operated through a chain driven, by the ground wheel. A small hand lever on the handle permitted the farmer to disengage the planting device at will.

Concerning the Pennsylvania cultivator an 1897 catalog notes that it "was made specially for the Pennsylvania, New Jersey, and New York trade." Farming methods differ from one area to another, and apparently the Pennsylvania was built to suit the needs of farmers in these states. The double tongue provided great strength, and each cultivator sweep could be equipped with a spring trip or the common pin trip. The latter consisted of a wooden pin driven into the mating holes between shank and shovel. If an obstruction was hit, the wooden pin sheared off, minimizing any damage to the cultivator.

Pennsylvania walking cultivators were available for those preferring this style over the chance to ride. Some farmers would have nothing but a walking cultivator; they were convinced that a riding cultivator was a device built for lazy people. In addition, the extra burden of carrying the operator was deemed to be too hard on the horses. This walking model is shown with six shovels and a middle, or seventh shovel. Various styles of shovels were available for virtually any cropping requirement.

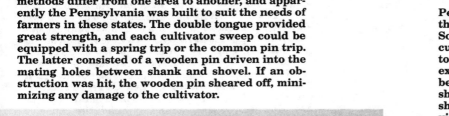

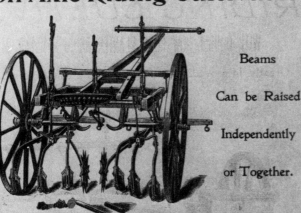

"IMPROVED" PENNSYLVANIA

xtension Axle Riding Cultivator

uble Tongue,

hree Levers,

Pin or

Spring Hoe.

Beams

Can be Raised

Independently

or Together.

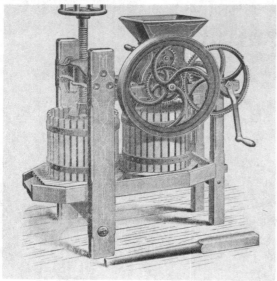

Early in its manufacturing career, Farquhar began building cider mills. This one of the 1890s typifies the size and style ordinarily found on farms and country homes. This one was built with a double crank, permitting two people to reduce the apples to pomace. The latter dropped into the slatted vats for pressing out the juice. It ran across the bottom board into a waiting tub or bucket. While two people were filling one vat with pomace, another person was pressing out the juice in the other. A hardwood lever was placed between the lugs on the screw wheel. Eventually, Farquhar would build large commercial mills and pressing equipment.

Another interesting Farquhar implement was this Archimedean stump puller and rock lifter. The complete machine weighed about 600 pounds, but the unique system of levers permitted two men to multiply their lifting force to about 25,000 pounds. Various methods for stump removal have been employed over the years, with this being one approach. Others employed capstans, tackle blocks, and other mechanical means. Still others preferred a couple sticks of dynamite.

A wagon jack was an essential tool on every farm. Many were homemade or came from the ideas of the local blacksmith. Others were available at the local hardware store. One such example is this Little Giant wagon jack. An 1890s advertisement from Farquhar notes that "This machine is sold in Pennsylvania exclusively by us, and is beyond comparison, the best lifting jack in use." Where sufficient manpower was available, more often than not, a couple of men would simply pick up one side of a wagon while others placed suitable blocks beneath the axle.

THE LITTLE GIANT.

The Champion water drawer was built for drawing water from shallow wells or cisterns. It consisted of a small bucket elevator turned by a hand crank. The buckets delivered water to the spout. As an advantage, it was pointed out that the water drawer was much preferable to the pump, being less apt to get out of order. An early Farquhar advertisement notes that "The Champion with Covered Top is the handsomest and most complete machine for drawing water in the market."

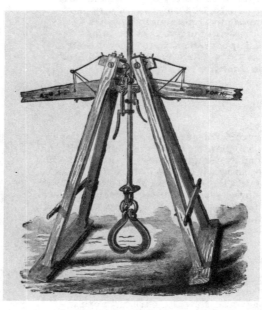

Another important implement on the farm of the 1890s was the corn sheller. Shelling corn by hand was slow and tiresome work. This so-called double spout machine could also be called a two-hole sheller, meaning that two ears of corn could be fed at a time. A unique feature was that a special shaker device was used to clean the shelled corn, and then delivered it from a spout to a waiting basket. Using belt power, this sheller had a capacity of about 300 bushels per day. However, when cranked by hand, the capacity dropped to half that figure.

A. B. Farquhar Company

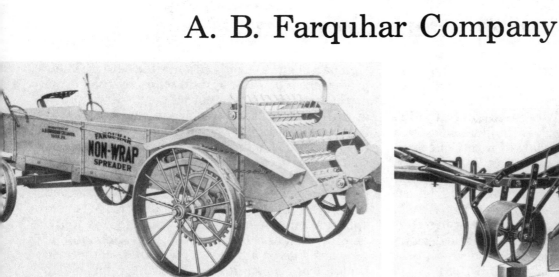

During the 1930s Farquhar developed their Non-Wrap spreader. It more or less followed conventional design, but apparently the No-Wrap concept involved the wide-spread attachment at the rear of the spreader. With certain makes, and under certain conditions, this device became wrapped with straw, necessitating the rather unpleasant job of removal. While the spreader was and is, one of the most unglamorous implements on the farm, the alternative was far less enchanting. The alternative was to load a wagon by hand and spread the manure over the field with a fork.

Already in early 1900s, Bateman Mfg. Company was offering a potato digger. This machine dug the potato crop, with the raddle chain serving to separate most of the dirt, while leaving the crop lying on the ground behind the machine. Again, the savings of labor over hand methods was beyond accurate description. Bateman had developed a most complete line of potato machinery prior to 1910. Farquhar was also offering a potato digger under their name by 1915, but quite possibly, this machine was being built by Iron Age.

With the decline of the steam engine and thresher business, Farquhar diversified into other implement lines. Included during the 1930s was the Farquhar Star planter. This unique design is shown with disk closers rather than the common press wheel found on most planters. As has been pointed out previously, certain crops and specific farming practices necessitated the development of unique farm implements, and the Farquhar Star was no exception.

In 1930 Farquhar bought out the Iron Age implement line pioneered by Bateman Manufacturing Company, Greenloch, New Jersey. The latter had developed many specialized implements including potato planters and diggers, sprayers and dusters, transplanters, and other equipment. Shown here is an Iron Age transplanter. Even though working on a transplanter was a strenuous job, it saved a tremendous amount of labor over conventional methods of setting each plant by hand labor.

Iron Age implements included an extensive variety of sprayers and dusters. These were available in power and traction models; the latter style was powered from the implement wheels. It required no auxiliary engine of any kind. While the average grain farmer had little use for a machine of this type, it found wide use on truck farms. Dusters were likewise available with either power or traction drive. The machine shown here had a tank capacity of 100 gallons. The pump was capable of pressures up to 300 psi, and could handle four rows at a time with its twelve nozzles.

Hart-Parr Company

In 1872, Charles Walter Hart was born at Charles City, Iowa. The Hart family had arrived on the Massachusetts shore in 1632...this particular scion of the family came to Iowa in 1871.

After childhood, C. W. Hart taught school for a time, finally enrolling at Iowa State College in Ames for the 1892-93 school year. A year later, Hart transferred to the University of Wisconsin. In September of that year he met Charles H. Parr, and the two young men became fast friends. Eventually, Hart and Parr would work together on their Special Honors thesis...from the designs thus created, the two men created their first engine. The thesis was presented in 1896.

The first section of the Hart and Parr thesis deals extensively with the historical development of internal combustion engines. A second section delves into the atomization and successful burning of various fuels, and using various modifications to the fuel mixing devices. At one point they related, "Our experience has shown that in many cases where electric ignition is used and thought to be faulty, the real fault lies in improper or irregular mixtures." The thesis later notes, "At first thought it may seem an easy task to construct a mixing device, but when we consider [various problems]...we begin to see the difficulty imposed." From this section of the thesis it becomes readily apparent that Hart and Parr were wrestling with the problems of atomizing the fuel; a problem that plagued gasoline engine development for many years.

Section 3 of the Hart and Parr thesis deals with ignition systems, and problems with ignition. Considering that ignition systems of 1896 were indeed poorly developed and thoroughly unreliable, Hart and Parr made some interesting observations. Regarding the low-tension, make-and-break ignitor the writers noted, "Our experience has shown that platinum points for the contact pieces within the cylinder are unnecessary. Wrought iron points are just as reliable and require no more current, and with proper combustion of the gases do not become coated." Hart and Parr go on to point out the continuing cost and the poor reliability of batteries. Then comes the statement, "There is another method of producing the current for ignition which we believe is destined to supersede the battery and which adds complications of a simpler nature only. This is the magneto generator." Considering the timeframe in which this statement was written, the observation was indeed, profound.

When Hart and Parr wrote their thesis in 1896 they preferred the hit-and-miss method of governing, noting that the throttling governor design had been used only to a limited extent. Their preference was for a system whereby the governor controlled the exhaust valve, holding it open at the top end of the rated speed, and permitting it to operate normally when permitted to do so by the governor. A significant statement appears in this section of the thesis: "We believe that for the best results in governing in this way the valve mechanism should be such that the admission valve be held shut while the exhaust valve is held open." Numerous companies would later adopt a modification of this concept. In fact, Section 3 of the thesis gives a better idea of their conviction that hit-and-miss governing was preferable to volume governing: "The best and most economical governing is obtained by holding the exhaust valve open and the inlet valve shut. Where very uniform motion is desirable even at the expense of economy, we believe it can be obtained by using a small clearance space or explosion chamber and varying the quantity of the mixture."

Part 5 of the Hart and Parr thesis involved the valve operating system. For their thesis, the two men developed a 30 horsepower, two-cylinder vertical engine. Their design included mechanically operated intake and exhaust valves; both valves being closed by flat steel springs. The thesis contends that this was an advantage over the usual conical spring, since the entire spring was kept away from the excessive heat of the cylinder head under their plan. For the purposes of this book, it is important to note that using many of the ideas developed at the University of Wisconsin, Hart and Parr appear to have built five engines during 1896.

The Hart-Parr Company was organized at Madison, Wisconsin on April 29, 1897. From then until 1901 they operated their engine factory at Madison. During this period they also perfected their valve-in-head engine design, as well as a cooling system employing oil as the cooling medium.

It is unclear whether Hart and Parr had illusions of building gas tractors initially, or whether this idea was developed in the latter part of the Madison years. However, the demand for their engines continued to grow, and larger facilities were needed. Unable to secure expansion capital in the Madison area, Hart and Parr turned to Hart's father in Charles City. The latter, along with C. D. and A. E. Ellis, persuaded Hart-Parr Company to move to Charles City. Eventually though, the era of good feeling between Ellis and Hart would wane, and Hart would leave the company.

Hart-Parr Company was organized on June 12,

Hart-Parr Company

1901 at Charles City, Iowa. Ground was broken for the new factory on July 5 of that year. By the following December the transfer of all machinery and equipment from Madison to Charles City had been completed. Hart-Parr Company was now ready to do business and had an authorized capitalization of $100,000.

Although 1901 is generally credited as the year when Hart-Parr built their first 'gasoline traction engine,' there are strong indications that it was not actually completed until 1902. In fact, a family photograph of this tractor reads, "First Traction Engine, July 1902." Another family photo reads, "Second Traction Engine, October 1902." Then there is the historical information from C. H. Parr, who also indicated that 1902 was correct.

During 1903 the Hart-Parr factory came into full production. Gas engines were still being built, with tractors actually being a secondary product at this time. The following year of 1904, Hart-Parr decided to build "gasoline traction engines" exclusively, and over the next few years the Hart-Parr gasoline engines were gradually phased out.

Also of significance during this period, Hart-Parr placed their first magazine advertisement in the December 1902 issue of *American Thresherman*. This journal was read by many farmers and virtually every thresherman in the country. It emerged from Madison, Wisconsin every month, under the careful eye of Bascom B. Clarke. When the old-line steam engine builders saw an advertisement for a gasoline traction engine in their favorite magazine, many, if not most of them, nearly had apoplexy. In fact, some threatened to pull all their advertising from Clarke. The latter was well gifted with turning a phrase, and invited them to do just that if they so desired. None did. However, this was the beginning of the end for the steam traction engine. In another two decades the steamer was well on its way to obsolescence, and within three decades, farmers would get their first taste of row-crop farming with no need of either horses or steam engines.

By 1907 the Hart-Parr Company was well established. Demand for their tractors had grown to the point that by the end of 1908 there were six major branch houses, in addition to the ever-growing factories at Charles City. Part of the factory facilities included a unique engine testing system. At the power house, numerous generators were set in place. As each tractor came off the assembly line it was belted to one of the generators. This provided a load for running in

the engine and providing a full-scale test prior to leaving the factory. The power thus generated was not wasted, but was sent back into the factory as electrical power. Also in 1907, Hart-Parr started the use of the term, 'tractor' instead of the clumsy term of 'gasoline traction engine.' Actually, the term 'tractor' goes back to the time of Shakespeare, but this was apparently its first use in connection with gasoline-powered traction engines.

Hart-Parr Company grew by leaps and bounds, employing some 1,100 people by 1911. To accommodate them, Mr. Hart directed the company to buy farmland on the east side of Charles City. This was then platted for houses to be rented or sold to Hart-Parr employees. C. W. Hart was also very active in civic and community affairs.

With tractor production growing each year, it soon became obvious to Hart that transportation facilities in and out of Charles City were dreadfully inadequate. So, C. W. Hart masterminded the Charles City Western Railroad. It was a 13-mile line running from Charles City to Marble Rock, Iowa. At this point it connected into the Rock Island Railroad. There are indications that Hart built an automobile sometime during the 1906-08 period, as well as an experimental crawler tractor. During World War One, it appears that Hart-Parr Company built, or at least intended to build, motor trucks for the U. S. Military.

By 1915 the Hart-Parr Company was capitalized at $2.5 million. Hart was riding a wave of success, but this was soon to change. The company began retooling for the manufacture of munitions in 1915. Tractor sales were not maintaining the brisk pace of the past, and a disastrous fire struck the factory in 1916. In addition, it is said that Hart-Parr had sold tractors in Europe, and many of these were not paid for. After spending considerable money on tooling up for the British munitions contract, a military change in plans saw an abrupt cancellation of the project. This left Hart-Parr sitting high and dry with a lot of partially completed shell casings. In addition, C. W. Hart had designed special lathes for machining the shell casings; these lathes were designed, cast, and built within the Hart-Parr factories.

Rumors have circulated for decades that another contributing factor was the allegation that the Ellis family, which was heavily invested, quietly picked up all available stock, and eventually took over the managerial control of the company.

It appears that numerous factors were in-

Hart-Parr Company

volved, with some probably being more factual than others. Regardless, C. W. Hart left Charles City in 1917. He did not reside there again. From Charles City, Hart and his family headed for Montana, apparently in the spring of 1918. They landed at a town called Hedgesville. In the fall of 1918 the family moved back to Milwaukee, Wisconsin. Meanwhile, C. W. Hart remained in Montana, attempting to commute when possible, and dividing his time between his family and the wheat ranch.

Apparently, Hart found time to experiment with a new tractor design during this period. It resulted in a three-cylinder model which eventually bore Patent No. 1,509,293. Two or three of these tractors were built and shipped to Montana, along with a large supply of spare parts. Hart also worked with C. E. Frudden in tractor development. The latter had been Hart's chief engineer at Charles City, but apparently Frudden left at the same time as Hart, or shortly thereafter. He relocated to the Milwaukee area and was a tractor engineer at Allis-Chalmers for many years. Hart's involvement with Frudden regarding the development of the early Allis-Chalmers tractors remains unclear. There have been various statements from family members in this connection, but it is our belief that the full details of this arrangement will probably never be known. The important point is that once Hart built the three-cylinder tractors, his career as a tractor builder ended. Hart now concentrated on wheat farming and oil refining in Montana.

In 1919 C. W. Hart applied for Letters Patent on a header barge, although the patent application simply stated, "Method of Harvesting Grain." On June 19, 1923 Patent No. 1,458.936 was issued to Mr. Hart. Some wheat growing areas used headers...a machine which left as much standing straw as possible, while cutting the stalks just below the grain. The header barge was designed receive the headed grain from the sickle. While traveling through the field, the headed grain tends to settle in the barge, and by the time it is filled, it has become a compact mass. On arriving at a suitable dump site, the header barge simply deposits its load and returns for another.

After the 1920 harvest, C. W. Hart set up a small refinery as a commercial experiment. This would soon become the Hart Refinery. Oil came from Cat Creek Field, Montana's first commercial oilfield. Ostensibly, Hart set up the refinery to obtain kerosene for use in his tractors. In fact, it appears that the gasoline was sold off to local garages and filling stations. Eventually, Hart had ten filling stations to which he supplied gasoline and other petroleum products.

On the basis of the successful refinery at Hedgesville, Hart and a partner set up a larger refinery at Missoula, Montana in 1924. As with the tractor company, financial troubles again loomed, but Hart remained indomitable. Various family members have described his character, using adjectives ranging from grumpy to reclusive. Perhaps his dislike for bureaucrats illustrates C. W. Hart's clever mind:

In 1931 the Montana Legislature passed a law stating that gasoline sold in Montana could not contain more than two-tenths of one percent sulphur. Gasoline from the Hart Refinery was above this level, and he had no plans to change his refining methods. After a long war of words, and when it appeared the bureaucrats were about to close in, Hart made a clever move. Virtually overnight, Hart changed all the signs and all the advertising to read, "Hart Auto Fuel." This of course, was no longer gasoline, but auto fuel, and there was nothing in the law to cover it. So the bureaucrats took their lumps and Hart went on with business as usual.

As with the tractor company, the first few years of the Hart Refinery were profitable. As with the tractor company, a major fire in the Hart Refinery was a precursor to financial difficulties. After the disastrous refinery fire in 1929, plus the Great Depression which struck at the same time, Hart Refinery went into debt. Yet, C. W. Hart remained indomitable. During 1935 and 1936 he signed a contract for construction of a refinery near Cody, Wyoming. This particular field had been discovered in 1931, but the major refiners were not interested in the crude because of its low grade. However, Hart designed a cracking still, refinery, and auxiliaries to successfully refine the low-grade crude. This was the last major project for C. W. Hart.

On Sunday, March 14, 1937 C. W. Hart died from a heart attack at the age of 65. His remains were returned to Charles City, Iowa with his old partner, Charles Henry Parr delivering a burial dedication for his longtime friend.

Thus ended the career of a most interesting and innovative personality. Various writers have pointed to the man's qualities and to his faults. There is no question that Charles W. Hart was one of those farsighted men who made 'tractor power' a reality. There is no question of his inventive genius, and there is no question of his business acumen. Yet, it is equally obvious that C. W. Hart was plagued with a heaping measure of life's adversities. In fact, his entire career is checkered with numerous high points, and other times which epitomized hardship and trouble. It has been said that Hart was essentially good-hearted, but that some of the various reverses in his life caused him to be bitter and harsh in his later years. Yet, for the purposes of this study, it is perhaps best that those purely personal aspects of Mr. Hart's life be left at rest. Perhaps it is better that this study should concentrate instead on Mr. Hart's technological developments, especially regarding the development of the farm tractor.

Charles Henry Parr

While considerable research has been conducted regarding Charles W. Hart, relatively little history had come to light in connection with Charles H. Parr. As indicated in the previous section on Mr. Hart, the two young men met at the University of Wisconsin. From all appearances, Hart was the quintessential extrovert, bold in actions, and possessing a keen mind. Parr on the other hand, appears to have been a comparatively reserved personality. Various writers have concluded that it was Hart who came up with the ideas, and it was Parr who was able to make the drawings and reduce ideas into practical terms.

During the time that Hart and Parr worked together (into 1917) there are indications that Hart worked in the daytime, while Parr was the night superintendent. Yet, when Hart left the company, Parr remained, apparently content to maintain status quo, rather than strike out on his own. Despite their different personalities, Hart and Parr remained friends, even though their paths took distinctly different directions.

In 1918, and apparently after Hart had left the tractor company, C. H. Parr wrote up a history of Hart-Parr Company. Parr noted that they began business as Hart & Parr, Madison, Wisconsin. By that time they had several engine designs and several sets of foundry patterns. Yet, investment capital was very difficult to obtain, and the two partners were forced to operated under the most meager circumstances.

Although the business was organized in 1896 as Hart & Parr, it was reorganized as Hart-Parr Company on April 29, 1897. This company had an authorized capitalization of $24,000. The first annual stockholders meeting of January 4, 1898 showed an operating loss of $354. The following year of 1899 indicated an operating loss of $491, but in 1900 there was a profit of $454. In January 1901 the company had a profit of $1,564.

By now it was obvious that the company needed growth capital. Yet, no serious investors could be found. In the early part of 1901, C. W. Hart was visiting his family at Charles City, and related his problems to his father. The elder Hart discussed the matter with some of the bankers and businessmen in Charles City. Thus, on May 14, 1901 the Hart-Parr Company at Madison, Wisconsin voted to accept a proposition to move to Charles City. On June 12, 1901 the Hart-Parr Company was organized at this place with an authorized capital of $100,000. Among the original investors were C. D. Ellis and A. E. Ellis, two brothers who were bankers in Charles City.

Parr's history of the company also relates that the Hart-Parr gasoline engines were especially intended for the large grain elevators. From Parr's history, and from other sources, it appears that the company did indeed ship many of its gasoline engines to the western prairie states for use in grain elevators. Parr also relates that the first tractor was sold to a farmer near Mason City, Iowa. The first owner used the tractor for several years, and then it was sold to a neighbor who continued to use it for threshing. As late as 1917, the engine was still operating, but by now the chassis had been scrapped, with the engine operating a factory and repair shop.

Other typewritten notes indicate that when Hart left the company in 1917, [Parr] was "not in a position to leave at once, [and] accepted a position in the Engineering Department under the new management, which he held till November 1923." Other file notes indicate that during this time Parr designed special tools and foundry equipment for use in the production of war materials. From November 1923 to July 1924 Parr was Chief Engineer for the Elgin Street Sweeper Company of Elgin, Illinois. Apparently, Parr then returned to the Engineering Department of Hart-Parr Company. When the later merged with other companies in 1929 to form Oliver Farm Equipment Company, Mr. Parr remained with the new firm. Charles Henry Parr died in 1941, and is buried in Charles City, a short distance from his associate, Charles Walter Hart.

Hart-Parr Company

While the previous paragraphs have provided a cameo view of Hart and Parr, this section deals with the Hart-Parr Company from its meager beginnings, and continuing up to its merger into Oliver Farm Equipment Company in 1929. Since the principals, Hart and Parr, are inextricably entwined, a certain amount of redundance is present. However, it has been virtually impossible to separate these two men, even from a biographical viewpoint, from the company which they founded.

As previously indicated, the firm of Hart & Parr officially began building gasoline engines at Madison, Wisconsin in 1896. At what point these two men first planned on a gasoline traction engine is unknown. However, given Hart's creative mind and his indomitable disposition, this may have been in the plans from the very beginning. Yet, the partners remained in the gasoline engine business at Madison until 1901. Conjecture has it that they had plans for building a traction engine prior to leaving Madison, and some rumors exist to the effect that they actually did build some type of tractor there.

It has been often related in the tractor industry that being unable to secure growth capital for their enterprise, Hart and Parr moved to Hart's boyhood home of Charles City, Iowa where liberal capital was available. During the years at Madison, Hart and Parr had perfected their original valve-in-head engine design, and indeed, by 1900 they were building engines that used an oil coolant rather than water. The higher coolant and cylinder temperatures were conducive to the use of low-grade fuel. Another major advantage was that freezing weather had no effect on the coolant. At the time, the only available anti-freeze solutions were calcium chloride and a mixture of water and alcohol. The latter began evaporating at something like 160 degrees F., and so constant replacement was necessary. Calcium chloride is very destructive of iron, so it too, was not very desirable.

Although the industry usually indicates 1901 as the beginning of the Hart-Parr gasoline traction engine, ample evidence indicates that the first tractor was not completed until the summer of 1902. Yet, the company's official production records show that No. 1205, Tractor No. 1, was built in 1901. If so, could it have been partially built at Madison? It is unlikely that precise answers will be found. More importantly, this tractor was the first of many which ultimately would revolutionize farming methods, and which eventually helped to relegate the steam traction engine to an abandoned corner of the barnyard. This first tractor carried a two-cylinder horizontal engine with a 9 x 13 inch bore and stroke. The huge flywheel weighed 1,000 pounds.

Tractor No. 2 emerged late in 1902, and embodied numerous changes over the first model. With No. 2 (Serial No. 1206) came the first use of the induced draft cooling system which characterized the Hart-Parr tractors for some years to come. Like No. 1, it also used an oil coolant. Hart and Parr were as yet convinced that hit-and-miss governing was more desirable than volume governing. This system was mechanically complicated, but very simple electrically. Educated engineers of 1900 knew relatively little about electrical systems, whereas the mechanical parts were much easier to master.

The No. 3 tractor evidenced numerous refinements. Introduced in 1903, it set the pattern for Hart-Parr tractor design...a pattern which remained fertile for several years. This model carried a two-cylinder horizontal engine having a 10 x 13 inch bore and stroke. Make-and-break ignition was used. Tractor No. 3 was rated at 18 drawbar and 30 belt horsepower. During 1903 Hart-Parr sold fifteen of these 18-30 tractors...operating weight for this monster was nearly 15,000 pounds.

During 1903 Hart-Parr introduced the 22-45 model. It was an improved version of the No. 2 tractor of 1902. The 22-45 was the first standardized model in the Hart-Parr line. Earlier models were essentially hand-built from beginning to end, and it would not be totally unfair to state that those models prior to the 22-45 were in essence, prototype models. In 1904 Hart-Parr introduced a new kerosene carburetor. C. W. Hart also received Patent No. 774,752 covering a "Cylinder Cooling System." Curiously, the patent drawings illustrate the inverted vertical stationary engine combined with the induced draft radiator as used on the tractors. In 1904 Hart-Parr also introduced magneto ignition for their tractors, apparently using a low-tension ignition dynamo. The following year of 1905 saw the introduction of the force-feed lubricator for precise and reliable oiling of essential engine components. Hart-Parr would continue this lubrication system until the advent of unit frame designs in the late 1920s.

During these formative years at Charles City, Hart-Parr continued building gasoline engines. From all appearances, production of the stationary engines came to about 1,300 units by 1904. Other indications show that engine production was gradually phased out after this time, finally ending altogether in 1908.

Through the years, vintage tractor enthusiasts and historians have commented regarding the design similarities of the Hart-Parr with the somewhat later Rumely OilPull. Indeed, there are similarities. One was that both used an oil coolant. The most obvious is the similarity of the cooling system. Both used an open radiator design. Above the radiator tubes or section plates, the engine exhaust was directed into vertical nozzles. The high velocity of the exhaust gases passing upward through the open stack created an induced draft beneath, and this pulled cool air over the radiator. Since the volume and velocity of the exhaust gases moving up the stack varied proportionally to the engine speed and the load, the cooling system was virtually automatic. It is significant that several other companies also made use of an induced draft cooling system, including the early Avery tractors. A major difference between the Hart-Parr and the OilPull was that the latter used volume governing by interposing a slide (and later a butterfly) in the air intake stream. Hart-Parr on the other hand, continued to use hit-and-miss governing for several years. Some years ago the Author was told that Hart-Parr actually cast and machined the major engine components for the OilPull prototypes. While this is entirely possible, our research has found nothing to either confirm or deny the story.

Between 1907 and 1918 Hart-Parr produced what was to be one of their most popular tractors for the period...the invincible "Old Reliable" 30-60 model. Top speed was 300 rpm. However, at this speed there were two pistons of 10-inch diameter traveling within cylinders having a 15-inch stroke. In fact, Hart-Parr built 205 copies of the 30-60 in 1907. By comparison, less than 400 tractors had been built in the period from 1901 through 1906. Over 200 of the 30-60 tractors emerged in 1908...there was now no doubt whatever that Old Reliable was on its way to the history books!

As has been indicated earlier in this section, Hart-Parr experienced growing pains almost immediately after setting up shop in Charles City. Plant expansion was the rule rather than the exception, and by 1908 the company had established six major branch houses in addition to the Charles City factory. Also in 1908 the company began its first major exports to foreign countries.

In 1907 Hart-Parr first began applying the use of 'tractor' to what had formerly been 'gasoline traction engines.' Initially, it was probably an advertising gimmick, but the new designation was much more simple than the old one, and it stuck. Before long, 'tractor' was a household term. Also of significance is the fact that when Hart and Parr set up their Charles City factory, it was the first one in history to be designed for the exclusive production of tractors. Thus, Hart and Parr deserve recognition as truly being the founders of the farm tractor industry.

The great success of the 30-60 model prompted Hart-Parr to develop an even larger trac-

tor...their 40-80. Built in the 1908-1914 period, this huge four-cylinder tractor weighed some eighteen tons! Oil cooling was used, along with high tension ignition and a magneto. As was typical of Hart-Parr tractors, this one also used a force-feed lubricator, with oil making one trip through the engine. Although wasteful of oil, compared to present standards, it must also be remembered that this system helped keep the engine clean, thus prolonging its life. Efficient oil filter systems simply were not the reality in tractors of this period.

Recognizing the need for a smaller tractor as well, Hart-Parr then introduced the 15-30 model in 1909. Built until 1912, its original design used an engine with two opposed cylinders of 8-inch bore and 9-inch stroke. This was later replaced with a vertical engine design. This was also the first Hart-Parr tractor to be furnished with two forward speeds.

Huge steam traction engines and huge tractors were sensations of the early 1900s. Like some of the other companies, Hart-Parr also built a colossal giant, the huge 60-100. Relatively little is known of this tractor, even by those who have studied the company extensively. The serial number lists tend to indicate that a dozen or so were built. However, the 60-100 was the largest tractor of its time...it weighed something over 52,000 pounds. Where they were shipped or whether they were at all successful is unknown. Rumors have abounded that the remains of a 60-100 rested, or perhaps still rest, in a Montana scrap yard, but the rumor has never been substantiated. Only during 1911 and 1912 were any of these gigantic tractors built. After that time the company followed the demands of farmers for a small, lightweight tractor suitable for their average quarter-section spread.

Tractor production continued apace with the introduction of the Hart-Parr 20-40 in 1912...it remained in the lineup until 1914. Again, a two-cylinder vertical engine was used, along with force-feed lubrication and a K-W magneto. An overlapping design was the Hart-Parr 12-27 model which emerged in the 1914-15 period. This smaller, one-cylinder tractor was oil cooled, used jump spark ignition, but had no magneto. The engine carried a 10-inch bore and stroke.

In 1913 and 1914 the Bull tractor came on the scene. Despite its faults, and despite the simple fact that the Bull was essentially a poor design, it was nevertheless a small, lightweight tractor that farmers would buy. Between its obvious usefulness, its low price, and an eminently successful advertising campaign, Bull tractors hit the industry like a firestorm. Eventually, many of the competitors either capitulated to light-weight designs or left the market altogether. Hart-Parr chose to respond with their 'Little Red Devil.' It was altogether unlike anything that Hart-Parr had ever built. In fact, given C. W. Hart's business acumen, it seems entirely possible that he acceded to the Little Red Devil purely from a business standpoint, rather than looking at it as the epitome of tractor design.

Rated at 15 drawbar and 22 belt horsepower, the Little Red Devil was powered by a two-cylinder, two-cycle engine. The single rear wheel obviated the need for a differential. Since the two-cycle engine was reversible, there was no need for a transmission, and of course this engine style had no valve mechanism. Production of this tractor began in 1914 and ended in 1916.

The Hart-Parr Oil King 18-35 model first ap-

peared in 1915, with production ending in 1918. Its one-cylinder vertical engine retained the oil cooling system and the induced draft radiator. Apparently, a substantial number of these tractors were exported. In 1919 the Hart-Parr "35" Road King tractor appeared as an improved version of the 18-35 Oil King. Production began and ended that same year, and this marked the end of the Hart-Parr heavyweight tractor designs.

As noted in the biographical sketch of C. W. Hart, the company became involved in military ordnance production for Great Britain during World War One. This required a considerable investment in new equipment, and due to the scarcity of specialized machinery, Hart-Parr designed and built much of it at the Charles City factories. During this time however, C. W. Hart was busy at an entirely new tractor design...in fact, when he abruptly left the company in 1917, the new tractor hadn't even been built yet. In fact, after 1917 the Hart-Parr Company and C. W. Hart had but one thing in common, and that was the use of his name on the billhead! His final legacy to the company was the New Hart-Parr 12-25 which emerged in 1918.

With the coming of the New Hart-Parr 12-25 the company once again changed the face of the tractor industry. In this same connection though, tractor collectors often comment about the similarities between the New Hart-Parr and the concurrently built Waterloo Boy tractors. To be sure, there are similarities, but whether by accident or whether by design, no information has ever surfaced to precisely indicate how Hart-Parr developed their concept of the ideal small tractor. Similarities aside, the New Hart Parr and its siblings immediately became very popular with

A 1909 letterhead of the Hart-Parr Company indicates that the company was still offering 'oil-cooled gasoline engines' in traction, portable, and stationary designs. About this time, M. Rumely Company at LaPorte, Indiana began marketing their OilPull tractor, using similar designs. Yet, a few years later, Hart-Parr would modernize with some entirely new tractor designs, while Rumely would continue with their OilPull far beyond its useful time. By the time this letter was written in 1909, Hart-Parr had already discontinued production of the portable and stationary engines.

Charles Walter Hart was born near Charles City, Iowa in 1872. His parents were Lovira Maria and Oliver Wales Hart. The latter family had come to Massachusetts in 1632, with this family scion coming to Charles City, Iowa in 1871. As is detailed in various sections of this book, Hart was the consummate inventor. His earliest developments with gasoline engines led directly to the development of the world's first company devoted exclusively to tractor production. The Hart-Parr Company remained in Hart's control until 1917. After this time Hart followed several enterprises, primarily that of the Hart Refineries in Montana. Mr. Hart died suddenly in 1937 and was returned to his native home of Charles City, Iowa for burial.

HART-PARR CO.

MANUFACTURERS OF

OIL COOLED GASOLINE ENGINES

Traction, Portable, Stationary,

Cable Address,-
HARTPARR.
Lieber's Code.

CHARLES CITY IOWA.

Sep 15, 1909

farmers.

Right on the heels of the New Hart Parr 12-25 came the Hart-Parr 15-30 "A" tractor. This model was built in the 1918-22 period. When the Nebraska Tractor Tests began in 1920, the Hart-Parr "30" as it was known, made its debut in June of that year. It yielded an impressive fuel economy of 8.04 horsepower hours per gallon of kerosene. Subsequently, Hart-Parr introduced their "20" tractor in 1921, continuing it until 1924. Also in 1921, Hart-Parr introduced stationary engines, using the comparable tractor engines, but mounting them on a substantial cast iron base. This continued until at least 1929. Numerous improvements and new models appeared during the 1920s. Yet, the days of the Hart-Parr were numbered...farmers wanted row-crop tractors.

An interesting diversion of the 1924-27 period was the Hart-Parr washing machine. Apparently the company decided to cash in on what was then a booming market, and in fact, it appears that this machine was innovative and fairly popular. Despite all the positives, sales were apparently not so great...if they had been, the Hart-Parr washing machine probably would have been on the market for more than three years.

With the Hart-Parr 28-50 of 1927-30 the era of

C. W. Hart's tractor designs was ending. The company was in serious financial problems, so serious in fact, that a merger seemed the only sensible thing to do. Thus, on April 1, 1929 Hart-Parr Tractor Company merged with Oliver Chilled Plow Works, Nichols & Shepard, and American Seeding Machine Company to form the Oliver Farm Equipment Company. The following year came the Oliver-Hart-Parr 18-28 tractor, an entirely new model with a unit frame design and a vertical engine. In the 1935-37 period the Hart-Parr name was dropped, and from that time onward the tractors came out under the Oliver banner. It is indeed ironic that the Hart-Parr name was dropped about the same time as C.W. Hart departed this earth in 1937. Four years later, in 1941, Charles Henry Parr would be buried in the same Charles City cemetery where he had earlier delivered a graveside eulogy for his lifelong friend, Charles Walter Hart.

Charles Henry Parr was born in Wyoming Township, Wisconsin during 1868. In September 1893 Parr met another engineering student, Charles Hart while registering for classes at the University of Wisconsin. The two young men soon became fast friends, and developed several gasoline engines of their own design during their university days. Their work was detailed in a Special Honors Thesis published in 1896. Of the two partners, Hart and Parr, the latter seems to have been the quiet one, and ultimately, the one to reduce Hart's ideas into practical designs. C. H. Parr died in 1941 and is buried in the same Charles City, Iowa cemetery with C. W. Hart.

By 1906 the Hart-Parr stationary engines were at their brief zenith. Shown here is a refined version of their inverted vertical design...it was built in sizes of 4, 7, and 12 horsepower. However, this later style was water cooled, rather than the oil-cooling method offered as well. Ignition was of the hot tube and electric styles, giving the user the choice of either. For engines of 1906 vintage, this was no bad idea, since low-tension electric ignition was not always reliable, and the hot tube was a logical backup system.

Hart-Parr Company

Opinions differ as to whether the Hart-Parr No. 1 was built in 1901 or 1902. Given the specific dates of the move from Madison, Wisconsin to Charles City, the latter date is probably more accurate. In the background is shown the small brick building that housed the first factory at Charles City. In the foreground is Tractor No. 1. The large bulbs above the engine were expansion bulbs for the oil coolant. This tractor used a two-cylinder engine having a 9 x 13 inch bore and stroke.

The most commonly seen photograph of the Hart-Parr stationary engines is shown here. Its legend indicates that it was of 1898 vintage and used oil cooling. Hart and Parr were initially convinced that the inverted vertical engine design was superior, although their ideas later moved toward standard vertical and horizontal designs. The radiator is simply a cast iron heating radiator as was commonly used in heating a house or other building.

Style No. 11.—Stationary, Oil Cooled, Vertical—Electric Ignition.
SIZES, 4, 7 AND 12 HORSE POWER.

Hart-Parr stationary engines of about 1906 were offered as shown here, with oil cooling, inverted vertical design, and fully electric ignition. The company recommended the water-cooled style where there was no danger of freezing the cooling water. A catalog notes that "The lack of vibration, strength of construction, simplicity of design, durability, convenience, and general efficiency make it unapproachable."

The Hart-Parr Style No. 11 engine was essentially like the engine shown here, except that this particular style used a one-piece cast iron base. The regular style was built over a substantial wood base of planks and sills. The cast iron base also served as a gasoline reservoir, and in addition, it could be mounted on portable trucks, if so desired. All pipe connections were made at the factory, thus requiring only the addition of fuel and water, connecting the batteries, and some minor adjustments.

By 1906, and perhaps earlier, Hart-Parr was offering stationary engines in a horizontal style. The 12, 15, and 20 horsepower stationary engines were but single cylinder versions of the ordinary double-cylinder engines as used in the tractors. Only the mounting method was changed...in this case, a large cast iron base and mounting standards replaced the normal components of the tractor frame. Also note the flat steel springs used for actuating the intake and exhaust valves. Early Hart-Parr designs favored this style over the standard conical springs.

2 H. P. SIZE.

An interesting and unusual Hart-Parr engine style is this 2 horsepower vertical stationary model. It appears in the 1906 Hart-Parr catalog. Note that this engine, like earlier Hart-Parr models is in a completely enclosed crankcase. In general, the 2 horsepower model was a hallmark of simplicity. Three sections of ordinary domestic heating radiator were used for the cooling system, and a large expansion bulb at the top took care of varying volumes with changes in temperature.

In their 1906 catalog, Hart-Parr illustrate their portable engines in sizes of 12, 15, and 20 horsepower. An interesting feature of these engines was the hemispherical head, cast in place, with no packed joints to worry about. According to catalog information, the 15 horsepower portable engine is shown in this engraving. In addition to the fully enclosed crankcase, these engines used a very simple and positive governor, a high-tension ignition system, and the same gasoline feeder [carburetor] that had been used successfully for the previous ten years.

Rated at 17 drawbar and 30 belt horsepower, Hart-Parr No. 1 is generally recognized as the first successful production tractor ever built. With its announcement in late 1901 or early 1902, Hart-Parr Company justly deserves recognition as 'founders of the farm tractor industry.' The access covers to the huge engine crankcase are visible in this illustration...Hart-Parr No. 1 used a two-cylinder engine having a 9 x 13 inch bore and stroke. The huge flywheel weighed half a ton. With No. 1, Hart and Parr established and refined special design features, including the unique oil-cooled engine and their own version of the valve-in-head design.

For large stationary power needs, Hart-Parr offered their 30 and 40 horsepower engines, being identical to those used in concurrently built tractors. These engines could be furnished with oil cooling or water cooling as desired. This catalog illustration shows the double cylinder engine mounted on a substantial cast iron base. A huge clutch pulley is attached to the crankshaft, and it is actuated from a large lever in the foreground. Oftentimes the engine would be located in a basement, and the clutch lever would extend upward through the floor above.

Hart-Parr Company

The December 1902 issue of *American Thresherman* carried this advertisement of the Hart-Parr 22-45 model, frequently referred to as Tractor No. 2. This model was substantially different in appearance, due mainly to an entirely different cooling system. The big two cylinder engine operated at 280 rpm. When the Hart-Parr advertisement appeared, several of the old-line steam engine builders snorted that if B. B. Clarke at *American Thresherman* accepted any more Hart-Parr advertising, they would pull their advertising contracts. Clarke snorted back that they should go ahead...that the Hart-Parr money was just as good as theirs. He didn't, they didn't, and before long there were numerous gas tractor builders advertising in Clarke's famous journal.

Hart-Parr No. 3 was built in 1903. This tractor now rests in the Smithsonian Institution Museum, Washington, D. C. It is said to be the oldest gasoline tractor still in existence. No. 3 was sold August 5, 1903 to George Mitchell, near Charles City. The price was $1,580. On July 8, 1924 Hart-Parr issued a check to George Mitchell in the amount of $72.75 for this old tractor. The payment was made on the basis of 50 cents per hundred pounds of tractor weight.

Old Number 3 was used on Iowa farms for about 24 years. A telegram to the Hart-Parr factory from the sales department noted, "MITCHELLS OLD SIXTY WORTH THOUSANDS TO US FOR FAIRS AND PUBLICITY PURPOSES AND IT IS LAST OF EARLY TRACTORS AVAILABLE STOP BUY IT IMMEDIATELY PULL INTO FACTORY AND PUT IN RUNNING ORDER." This telegram was dated February 13, 1924 and the following day, a letter went out from the Hart-Parr factory to Mr. George Mitchell, confirming the purchase of "your old Hart-Parr tractor."

The Hart-Parr No. 3 used a two-cylinder engine having a 10 x 13 inch bore and stroke. Oil was used as the cooling medium, and like several early Hart-Parr models, this one used low-tension ignition with a make-and-break ignitor on each cylinder. The forward and backward motion of the tractor was controlled by a single lever. At this point in time, even Hart-Parr was still using the term, 'gasoline traction' as applied to these big prime movers. Not until 1907 did the company began using the word 'tractor.' Actually, the word itself is very old, dating back at least to the time of Shakespeare.

Hart-Parr Company

Growth of the Hart-Parr factories at Charles City was phenomenal. Actually, Hart-Parr had grown so rapidly that by 1908 the firm had made its first foreign sales, and the factory seemed to be in a constant state of expansion. By the end of 1908 there were six major factory branches across the United States, and these in addition to the huge factory complex shown in this 1909 photograph. With their own foundry and a complete manufacturing shop, virtually all tractor components were built on-site, rather than being farmed out to other companies.

Obviously the first years of Hart-Parr tractor production were in part, experimental. This 17-30 was a continuation of the No. 3 tractor, and it in turn evolved from the No. 1 model. The unique enclosed outer shell of the radiator seems to have depended on all cooling air rising from the bottom side of the radiator. Later designs would use a square radiator with open fins on the sides and on the bottom. Produced in the 1903-06 period, this 17-30 model weighed nearly 15,000 pounds.

A 1906 Hart-Parr catalog illustrates the 'right side, 17 and 22 nominal horsepower, standard gear engines.' Actually, this referred to the 17-30 and 22-40 models. Both were of double cylinder design, with the 17-30 having a bore and stroke of 9 x 13 inches; the larger model carried dimensions of 10 x 15 inches. These models used piston pins having a diameter of three inches; the crankshaft was four inches in diameter, as was the rear axle. Shipping weight of the 17-30 was 7 1/2 tons, and the 22-40 weighed in at 8 1/2 tons.

In addition to the 'standard gear' engines, the 1906 Hart-Parr catalog also indicates that the 22-40 model was available with as a special plowing engine. This model carried the same basic engine dimensions as the standard gear 22-40, but the engine speed was increased for the plowing engine by 20 rpm to a rated speed of 300 rpm. This model had a shipping weight of 9 tons, due primarily to the heavier gearing. By 1905 Hart-Parr had adopted the force-feed lubricator system, and by 1906 the engine design was modified to use removable valve cages.

Hart-Parr Company

A platform view of the early Hart-Parr tractor line shows standing room only on the platform. Despite the hard and sometimes hazardous duty of operating a gasoline traction engine in unknown terrain, and often under unsafe conditions, relatively little thought was given to the comfort of the operator. The lack of rear wheel fenders must surely have created a horrible dust bath for the engineer, together with a bountiful supply of grasshoppers and various other unwelcome little critters on the platform. Only the slightest protection was offered by the footboard, and these models did not so much as include a plain, pressed steel seat.

The Hart-Parr 22-45 model was built in the 1903-06 period. Initially, the Hart-Parr tractors used a fuel pump to deliver fuel to the carburetor or atomizer. By 1906 however, this was changed to a float-feed carburetor and a gravity fuel system. It is shown here, with the larger kerosene tank to the bottom, and the smaller gasoline tank atop. By 1905 Hart-Parr had developed an entirely new spur-gear differential. Continually raising the tractor horsepower required heavier gears and other components. To their credit, Hart-Parr was very innovative in the use of cast steel, steel forgings, and other high strength components.

From a 1906 Hart-Parr catalog comes this threshing scene from South Dakota. In the foreground is a Hart-Parr 22-45 tractor operating a threshing machine of unknown make. Obviously, the crew has taken time to pose for the camera, with a couple of them standing on the machine, and several in the foreground, near the tractor. Many midwestern farmers of 1906 were immigrants who could barely communicate in the English language. Thus, they often tended to congregate in their own communities where they could retain their native tongue and at least some semblance of their native ways.

A 1906 catalog engraving illustrates a front view of the Hart-Parr 22 horsepower model. The front axle was strongly trussed, and was designed with a ball and socket coupling. Also evident is the air venting at the bottom of the radiator box. This permitted cool air to rise into and up the radiator cooling fins. An induced draft was created by the engine exhaust, and this assisted greatly in maintaining the proper coolant temperature.

Hart-Parr Company

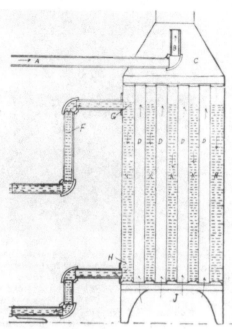

This diagram from a 1906 Hart-Parr catalog illustrates the simple radiator system. The vertical radiator tubes were filled with oil coolant. Hot oil from the cylinders circulated to the top of the radiator, while cooled oil returned to the engine cylinders through the lower pipe. The engine exhaust is piped to a vertical nozzle that terminates in the air stack. Hart-Parr noted that, "as there is no waste of the oil, the original supply furnished with the engine should last as long as the engine itself."

Shown here is a 22-40 Hart-Parr tractor of 1905 vintage. It is breaking timothy sod somewhere on the prairie loam soil of northern Iowa, and is cutting to a depth of 6 inches. Pulling eight bottoms, this tractor plowed twenty acres in a ten hour day. Given the available horsepower of this engine, and given the tremendously increased efficiency over animated horse power, this was indeed a remarkable accomplishment.

Another plowing scene of 1906 illustrates the Hart-Parr 22 horsepower engine working in North Dakota. In this instance it is pulling four gangs, or a total of 12 discs. It is cutting an 11-foot furrow about 8 inches deep, and is turning over about 23 acres per day, with the operating expenses coming to about 50 cents per acre. Hart-Parr noted that in a full day of stiff work their 17 horsepower engine would not burn over 30 gallons of gasoline per day, and usually, considerably less. At this time, most gasoline and kerosene was delivered in barrels...there were very few bulk plants in 1906.

Although this 17 horsepower Hart-Parr was obviously bigger than necessary, it still was easier than trying to shell corn with a portable engine. With the tractor, all that was necessary was to align the drive belt and block the rear wheel. With a portable engine, aligning the drive belt was in itself a challenge, and keeping it sufficiently tight was yet another. For obvious jobs like sawing wood and shelling corn, farmers were innovative in adapting tractor power to other daily tasks.

Beginning in 1905, Hart-Parr redesigned the differential gear for their Special Plowing Engine. The company noted that the ordinary bevel-gear differential was quite suitable for ordinary traction work as encountered in threshing and other light traction duties. However, for continuous traction work like plowing, the spur gear differential was designed for extra strength and more working surfaces.

Hart-Parr Company

On the back of this ancient photograph is written, "The Hart-Parr 60 in 1904. Still in successful operation." Apparently the reference was to the earlier Hart-Parr 22-45, built in the 1903-1906 period. Obviously this one either was not furnished with a canopy, or it was lost somewhere along the way. It is also obvious that it is keeping the belt tight on some heavy threshing work. The Old Reliable 30-60 used two cylinders having a 10-inch bore and a 15-inch stroke.

This unidentified sales branch of the Hart-Parr Company illustrates the sales and repair force, along with a couple of tractors. Below the billhead is written, "The Modern Farm Horse. Does Plowing for 40 to 60 cents an Acre." Selling a Hart-Parr was one thing...training the buyers was yet another. Many farmers of the early 1900s were immigrants who barely spoke the language, and whose notion of horsepower had recently conceived of nothing more than something with four big feet and a long tail. So the company put a great many 'experts' in the field; men who could teach farmers how to operate the engine, and who could also make the inevitably necessary repairs.

Hart-Parr placed heavy emphasis on the engine design. For instance, a 1908 catalog notes that for several years the company had used a cast-steel connecting rod, but due to the possibility of hidden flaws, they had experienced problems. This was remedied by using drop-forged connecting rods. The crankshaft was either of a steel drop forging or a hammered forging from a single billet of open-hearth steel. Shown here is the double cylinder engine used in the 45 horsepower tractor. Bevel gears and a lay shaft terminate in a cross shaft to which the valve cams are mounted. Also visible is the belt-driven governor.

This sectional view illustrates the unique engine used in the early Hart-Parr tractors. One secret of its success was that the crankshaft centerline was set below the centerline of the cylinders. This altered the geometrics significantly, and tended to diminish some of the vibration. Note also the cylinder arrangement whereby both valves were operated from a single rocker arm.

While the earliest Hart-Parr designs used a fuel pump and an overflow carburetor, the company experienced problems with maintaining the fuel pump, among other things. A major difficulty was that the gasoline quickly destroyed the pump packing, and of course the gasoline then had an unimpeded exit. The gravity system with a float-operated carburetor was the adapted by Hart-Parr, and this was then the method of choice. According to a 1908 catalog, "Our feeder has no needle valves or small passages to choke (the smallest passage being one-fourth inch in diameter), and provision is made for separating paraffin, sediment, or water from the fuel."

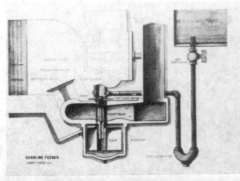

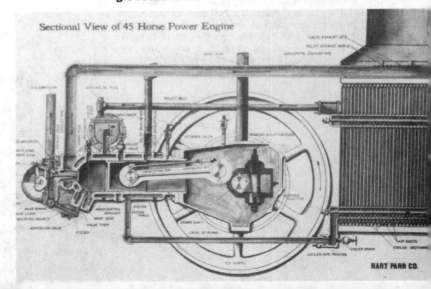

Sectional View of 45 Horse Power Engine

Fortunately, a very few Hart-Parr 30-60 tractors still remain. Built in the 1907-1918 period, this tractor was a descendant of the Hart-Parr 22-45 (1903-06), and its antecedent, the Hart-Parr No. 2 tractor of 1902. Hit-and-miss governing was used, and this gave the 30-60 an unusual exhaust sound, especially when under a load. The 30-60 had one forward speed of 2.4 mph...it operated at 300 rpm, but this was probably its safe limit, given the bore and stroke dimensions of 10 x 15 inches.

All details regarding this interesting photo have been lost. Obviously, six plows are behind this Hart-Parr, probably in land that has never before felt the plow. Despite its present-day glamour, breaking the prairies was an unpleasant task in many ways, and often the results were less than satisfactory. Breaking the prairie was only part of the task...then came the ethereal task of planting the seed in the hopes of a crop. A timely rain and a respite from grasshoppers or chinch bugs often meant the difference between success and failure. In 1916 the 30-60 tractor had a cash price of $2,600.

This file photo of 1908 or 1909 illustrates a Hart-Parr 30-60 tractor pulling an elevating road grader. The latter machine pulled dirt from the side ditches, and actually elevated it up to the road bed as shown here. With pass after pass, the grade was lifted. Many rural roads were thus built, and remain as a tribute to machines like these. No details regarding this photograph have been located, but fortunately it remains in the Oliver-Hart-Parr Archives held by the Floyd County Historical Society at Charles City, Iowa.

A four-cylinder engine was used in the big 40-80 tractor. Built in the 1908-1914 period, it featured heavy use of drop forgings and steel castings. Virtually the only cast iron parts were the engine cylinders, the flywheel, and the belt pulley. The engine used an oil coolant, and featured jump-spark ignition with dry cells and a high tension magneto. A force-feed lubricator was also part of the standard equipment.

Practically all the working parts of the 40-80 tractor were made of steel. This included the gears. Some of the mammoth dimensions included a crankshaft with a diameter of six inches. The differential shaft used bearing of six inch diameter and a width of thirteen inches. The huge rear axles were 5 1/2 inches in diameter. Great care was taken to make all the working parts as accessible as possible, and this was very important with component parts being so heavy and large.

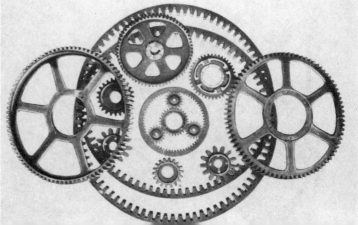

Hart-Parr Company

A 1908 Hart-Parr catalog notes that the first 40-80 tractor was demonstrated at the Minnesota State Fair in September 1908. Its' plowing demonstrations there were witnessed by thousands of farmers. After then, it worked near Rudd, Iowa for several years, but its eventual whereabouts remain unknown. It is shown here with a 24-disc plow, making a 20-foot furrow. Although Hart-Parr still insisted on hit-and-miss governing for the 30-60 Old Reliable tractor, this four-cylinder tractor used throttle governing.

Hart-Parr 40-80 tractors carried a 9 x 13 inch bore and stroke. The engine operated at 400 rpm. As previously indicated, the crankshaft was six inches in diameter, and used a five inch crankpin. Each drive wheel was 28 inches wide and 98 inches high. The crankshaft made 48.2 revolutions for every turn of the rear wheels in low gear, and 33.8 revolutions for every turn of the rear wheels in high gear. This resulted in theoretical road speeds of 2.4 and 3.4 mph. According to Hart-Parr catalog information, this tractor weighed 34,000 pounds.

It appears that the Hart-Parr 15-30 appeared in late 1909 or early 1910. Initially, it was built with a double-cylinder opposed engine, as shown here. The massive radiator and exhaust stack were directly forward of the operator's platform. This, together with the fuel and water tanks, served to limit the operator's visibility. Apparently, this engine used a bore and stroke of 8 x 9 inches. Production of the 15-30 with the horizontal engine continued for perhaps a few months. Within a year, this style was replaced with a two-cylinder vertical model.

The Hart-Parr 15-30 saw total production of about 100 copies in the 1910-1912 period. Some historians have it that the 15-30 emerged in 1909, but the company's production records do not show this model until No. 2332 of 1910. Later models used a two-cylinder vertical engine, apparently of the same, or approximately the same dimensions as had been used with the horizontal style. Hart-Parr offered the 15-30 as a regular threshing engine, and also provided it as a special plowing engine...the latter being equipped with heavy-duty gearing.

Despite a concerted effort over many years, very little information has surfaced on the Hart-Parr 60-100 tractor. This was the largest model built by Hart-Parr, and remains as one of the largest tractors ever built. A limited number were built in 1911 and 1912, but no records have been located to indicate where they were shipped, or even if they operated with any degree of success. Apparently, this huge tractor weighed over 50,000 pounds and used drive wheels 9 feet high! The 60-100 used a four-cylinder vertical engine.

The Hart-Parr 20-40 was built from 1912 to 1914; it was apparently a successor to the 15-30 model of 1910-1912. Rated at 400 rpm, it featured two forward speeds of 2.2 and 4.0 mph. Every gear in this tractor was of steel, and the high-speed gears were machine cut for quiet operation. Hart-Parr noted that they owned and operated their own open-hearth steel foundry. No other tractor builder of the time was thus equipped. Even the crankshaft was forged, heat-treated and ground to size in the Hart-Parr shops.

This early photograph illustrates a pair of Hart-Parr 12-27 tractors pulling road graders in about 1914. The first of the Hart-Parr "27" tractors appeared in late 1914, with about 200 being built before production ended the following year. A single-cylinder vertical engine was used...it had a 10-inch bore and stroke. The heavy steel canopy was standard equipment. High-strength steel components were used throughout...even the rear wheels were cast of steel.

Following the 12-27 tractor came the 18-35 Oil King model. Like its immediate predecessor, it too used a single cylinder vertical engine. The Hart-Parr designs were notable for their great strength, but by this time Hart-Parr Company was looking at ways of giving great strength with less weight. Thus, it is evident the tractor frame has been lightened, as seen by the 'weight holes' in the frame, just forward of the flywheel. The huge cast steel wheels were virtually indestructible. Also note the attachment lugs provided on the rear wheels for extension rims.

A 1915 Hart-Parr catalog illustrates the rear wheel design used on these tractors. These wheels were a one-piece steel casting, and in some tests, one of these wheels withstood a blow of 216,000 pounds without cracking or breaking. In addition, this wheel illustrates the famous Hart-Parr "Hold-Fast" extension lugs. Hart-Parr noted that the "Hold-Fast" lugs were designed to get a deep bite, yet were able to pull away without tearing up the soil.

A 1917 Hart-Parr photograph illustrates a "35" tractor with an Austin grader. This rig was building roads near Red Oak, Iowa. Despite its apparent popularity, only about 250 copies of the 18-35 tractor were built between 1915 and 1918. More often than not, road builders of the time opted for a larger tractor like the Hart-Parr 30-60. Then too, there was tremendous competition among the tractor builders for road building tractors. These factors, and an ever-changing market, all served to hold the total production down, and also forced manufacturers to come forth with new and innovative designs.

Hart-Parr Company

Left Side "35"

This rear view of the 18-35 Oil King tractor illustrates the compact platform. The fuel tanks are hung above the operator. The steering wheel is obvious, and the second hand wheel is the gear shifter; it operated a rack-and-pinion to shift between high, low, and reverse gears. Like the earlier 12-27 model, the Oil King "35" also used a single cylinder engine with a 10-inch bore and stroke. The combustion chamber was designed to handle gasoline, naphtha, kerosene, and other fuels. The huge 10-inch piston carried five rings!

Before leaving the factory, Hart-Parr tractors were thoroughly tested. This included a visual inspection, followed by a field run. If these tests were satisfactory, each tractor was belted to a dynamo for 20 to 40 hours of service. Self-recording meters were used to follow the performance of each tractor under test. Then, during the last hour of the test, each tractor was required to carry far more than its rated load, a test that each one was required to pass before leaving the factory. Each purchaser received a certified copy of the test report with the tractor. After three successful years (1915-18) with the 18-35 Oil King, Hart-Parr offered a final model in this series. Only in 1919 did the company offer the 18-35 Road King model. In fact, confidential company records indicate that only fifty numbers were assigned to the Road King, but there is no indication of how many of this number block was assigned to tractors actually leaving the factory.

Hart-Parr guaranteed the Oil King "35" to be capable of 35 belt horsepower. This model was capable of a maximum 23 drawbar horsepower. Of single-cylinder design, it used a 10-inch bore and stroke. The crankshaft was 3 3/4 inches in the bearings, with a 3 7/8 inch crank pin. The piston pin was 2 1/2 inches in diameter, and rated engine speed was 500 rpm. Each cast steel drive wheel was 74 inches in diameter, with an 18 inch face. This tractor weighed in at 11,400 pounds, was perhaps not as heavy as some tractors of the period. With its heavy use of steel forgings, castings, and other steel components, the early Hart-Parr models certainly epitomize the early trend to high strength with a minimum of weight.

Late in 1914, Hart-Parr assigned about 25 serial numbers for the "Little Red Devil," an entirely new tractor model. Advertising of the time stated, "Make the Mare Go. Make the LITTLE DEVIL Go. Does the Work of Eight Mares." Undoubtedly, this model was in response to other new, lightweight, and sometimes radically different tractor designs of the period. Although most were consigned to failure, even before being built, many of the new designs had salient features which would later be embodied in a more practical way. Since this tractor had only a single rear drive wheel, no differential was required.

Hart-Parr Company

A Hart-Parr advertising folder delivers the story on the "Little Devil." It was equipped with a two-cylinder, two-cycle engine of horizontal design. It used a 5 1/2 x 7 inch bore and stroke, with a rated speed of 600 rpm. The Little Devil had two forward and two reverse speeds, with only seven gears and pinions. To reverse the tractor, one reversed the two-cycle engine...this was best accomplished by bringing the engine to a slow idle, killing the spark, and then closing the spark again as the engine came up on the compression stroke. This caused the engine to kick backwards, and of course, this was the goal.

Few front views have been located for the Little Devil tractor, but as is shown here, it was capable of straddling corn rows for cultivating purposes. In 1915 the Little Devil sold for $850, but the following year the price jumped to $1,000. Hart-Parr called this model "The Only Small Oil Tractor in the World." but the simple truth was that the Little Devil did little to capture the burgeoning small tractor market. Meanwhile, Hart-Parr was busy designing an entirely new series of tractors.

About 1917 Hart-Parr Company built a prototype truck design. Possibly the prototype was intended for possible sale to the war effort of World War One. Perhaps Hart-Parr saw some openings in the relatively new market for motor trucks. At least one truck was built, and is shown here...the legend reads, "Hart-Parr Manufactured Truck, Driven by George Newton." Thus far, nothing further has surfaced in the company records or from any other source concerning this unique design.

In 1914 Hart-Parr offered the "Money-Maker" separator. Actually, it was a thresher built by Robinson & Company, Richmond, Indiana. For 1914 this machine was offered only in a single size, having a 29-inch cylinder width, and a 48-inch separator. Prices varied somewhat, depending on the geographical location, but when picked up at the factory, this machine had a cash price of $705. Hart-Parr apparently enjoyed some success with the Money-Maker line, for a 1916 price book indicates four different Money-Makers available. These ranged up to a huge 37 x 60-inch machine with a list price of $850. All machines were priced, f.o.b., Richmond, Indiana.

In 1918 Hart-Parr Company introduced the New Hart-Parr 12-25 model. Designed primarily by C. W. Hart and C. H. Parr, this tractor would be Hart's legacy to the company. For a variety of reasons, Hart left the company in 1917, even before the new tractor model was introduced to the market. Gone was the oil-filled radiator, and gone was the huge and heavy engine of days gone by. In its place came a relatively light weight, water-cooled engine operating at 750 rpm. The New Hart-Parr would typify the company's tractor designs for more than a decade.

Hart-Parr Company

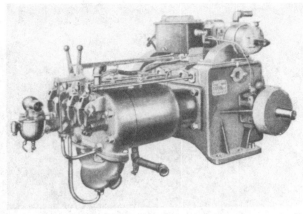

A catalog view illustrates the power plant as used in the Hart-Parr "30" tractor. The exhaust manifold is obvious below the cylinder head, as is the kerosene shunt which assured atomization of the kerosene fuel. A Schebler carburetor is obvious, as is the Madison-Kipp force-feed lubricator. By providing the main bearings, connecting rod bearings, and cylinders with fresh oil at all times, engine life was lengthened considerably.

Shortly after its introduction the New Hart-Parr 12-25 was re-rated upward as the 15-30 "A" tractor. With this style, Hart-Parr also introduced its system of external counterweights on the engine crank, plus a new kerosene atomizer system. A unique feature of this entire series was the method of driving the cooling fan. A friction pulley was mounted on the fan shaft. A small handwheel permitted the operator to pull the friction pulley into contact with the side of the flywheel. The system was simple and straightforward, and this was definitely an advantage.

An early Hart-Parr photograph illustrates a New Hart-Parr 12-25 moving a Mexican pool hall having a weight of about 1,000 pounds. The caption with the original photo does not indicate whether the pool hall was permanently mobile, or whether the proprietors were simply packing up for a better location. Since it is said to have weighed only about half a ton, the building must not have been very large, and given the pool tables of the time, with their two-inch slate floor, it must either have been a very light building or a very small pool table!

The kerosene shunt shown here was developed in the Hart-Parr factories. When working at full load, the carbureted fuel goes directly to the engine, but on an idling load it travels downward through the chamber built into the exhaust manifold. This system provided heated kerosene at light loads for better atomization. Actually, kerosene does not vaporize as does gasoline, and therefore it is essential that it be atomized as completely as possible before entering the cylinders; otherwise crankcase oil dilution is bound to occur.

The Northern Hart-Parr Company (address unknown) demonstrated this 15-30 Hart-Parr and a three-bottom Vulcan plow. Hart-Parr was one of the earliest tractor builders to enclose the engine, and pioneered the use of enclosed transmission gears. Yet, the final drive gears remained in the open. Lubricating oil from the force-feed lubricator traveled through the engine and finally made its way to the final drives, and from there to the ground. Depending on the soil type, this often resulted in a caked mass of dirt and oil inside each rear wheel.

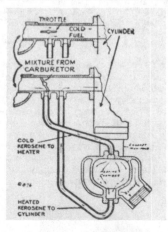

Hart-Parr Company

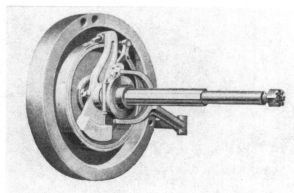

The Hart-Parr "30" used a band clutch as shown here...later models would use a plate clutch. However, this clutch had the advantage of requiring but a single adjusting point, and simplicity was always a hallmark of the Hart-Parr designs. The engine flywheel was of course, bolted to the crankshaft. The output shaft shown here passed through the transmission case, and its outer end carried the belt pulley. When properly adjusted the band clutch was capable of gentle engagement, yet when fully engaged, it could carry all the power of which the engine was capable.

Beginning with the New Hart-Parr and continuing into 1929, all Hart-Parr models were built over a substantial channel-iron frame. It was precisely bent to shape, and securely fastened with hot rivets. On this foundation, Hart-Parr attached the engine, transmission, and drive train. The dependability of the Hart-Parr tractor frame was unquestioned, and compared to earlier tractors, it gave tremendous strength with but a fraction of the weight.

Plenty of Flexible Power for Belt Work." In this case a Hart-Parr "30" is barking at an ensilage cutter. For those who have been so fortunate (?) as to have fed an ensilage cutter, this machine did have the advantage of being able to thoroughly test the average farm tractor. Especially when a farmer thought his tractor to be invincible, the neighbors often proved that it wasn't. With the heavy work pushed onto many of the early tractors, it is amazing that so many of them still survive, albeit as reminders of the past.

Hart-Parr tractors became very popular for road maintenance work. Although customs varied from one area to another, the Author recalls that in Iowa, each township was responsible for its roads. Many times, a local farmer would contract with the township or with the county to maintain several miles of roadway. If the weather cooperated, the task was fairly simple. But after long bouts of wet weather, the roads were often cut up so bad that it required several days of work to make them somewhat passable.

The 15-30 Hart-Parr saw several changes during its production run, as did the 16-30 Hart-Parr which followed. In 1918 the 12-25 New Hart-Parr was introduced, followed shortly thereafter by the 15-30 Type A tractor. This model was produced into 1922, ending with s/n 21000. The Type A had the water pump on the fan shaft, and had exposed valve levers and push rods. Beginning with No. 21001 in 1922, the 15-30 Type C tractor placed the water pump on the governor shaft. In addition, the valve levers were in a housing, and the push rods ran in tubes. Following this was the 16-30 Type E tractor, effective with No. 22501 of 1924. Its most noticeable feature was the enclosed drive gears.

Hart-Parr Company

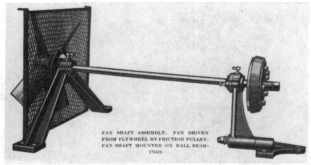

A unique feature of the Hart-Parr was this unusual fan shaft assembly. The fan was driven from the engine flywheel by the friction wheel shown to the right in this photograph. By releasing the spring tension on the friction wheel, the operator could actually disengage the fan, as when warming up during very cold weather. Replacing the friction element was fairly simple, and was seldom required. Ball bearings were used on the fan shaft.

HART-PARR "12-24" ENGINE, A COMPACT, ACCESSIBLE KEROSENE-BURNING POWER PLANT

The Hart-Parr 12-24 engine is shown here, but all Hart-Parr engines were of the same essential design, varying primarily in size and horsepower output. As a part of the very simple, very straightforward design, the engine was bolted directly to the heavy channel iron frame, being shimmed as required to align with the transmission shaft. That was it...there was nothing else to align, or for that matter, to get out of alignment. All of the Hart-Parr engines were designed to burn either gasoline or kerosene fuel.

CRANK-CASE ASSEMBLY, FRONT VIEW. LARGE, EASILY ADJUSTED BEARINGS. SIMPLE CAMSHAFT ASSEMBLY AND TIMING GEARS

CRANK-CASE, REAR VIEW, SHOWING SIMPLE METHOD OF ATTACHING CYLINDER BLOCKS

A breakdown of the Hart-Parr engine illustrates its simplicity. The crankcase itself was a fairly simple casting, yet it embodied considerable size and weight compared to some of the competing models. Building a strictly first-class tractor engine in the face of tremendous competition made the salesman's job more difficult, but farmers of the 1920s had already given the Hart-Parr wide acceptance. A unique feature of these engines was the fact that the crankshaft centerline was placed slightly below the cylinder centerline. This altered the geometrics of the piston movement considerably, and appears to have enhanced the lugging power of the Hart-Parr tractors. It also eliminated much of the vibration inherent with the design.

A major selling point for the Hart-Parr tractors was their straight-line design. Recognizing the imperative need that pulled implements operate from the center of the tractor pull, Hart-Parr emphasized this concept in their advertising. Although this idea is commonly accepted in today's practices, there were numerous tractor designs of the 1920s which did not follow this pattern. The result was almost always unsatisfactory, either because of the side-pull on the tractor, or due to the deleterious effects of sidedraft on the towed implement.

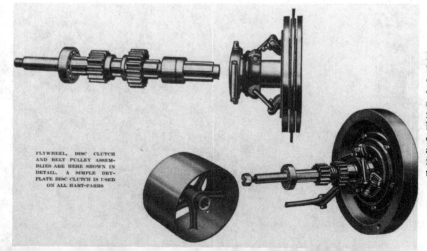

FLYWHEEL, DISC CLUTCH AND BELT PULLEY ASSEMBLIES ARE HERE SHOWN IN DETAIL. A SIMPLE DRY-PLATE DISC CLUTCH IS USED ON ALL HART-PARRS

From the flywheel, power was transmitted through the clutch to the transmission case, as well as to the external belt pulley. The initial design used a band clutch. This was later changed to a plate clutch as shown here. A possible reason for the changeover might have been that if there was slight misalignment between the center of the crankshaft and the center of the transmission shaft, this appears to have created breakage problems with the band clutch. From its beginnings, Hart-Parr made heavy use of heat treated shafts and gears.

Hart-Parr Company

Production of the little 10-20 Type B tractor began in 1921, effective with No. 35001. During that year and the following one, Hart-Parr built this smaller version of the famous 15-30 model. In the 1922-24 period Hart-Parr offered the 10-20 Type C tractor. It was similar except that it used a 5 1/2 inch cylinder bore, compared to 5 1/4 inches for the Type B tractor. With this exception there were few differences between the two tractor models.

Left side view of Hart-Parr "20"

A rear view of the Hart-Parr tractor line illustrates the large platform, with all controls in easy reach of the operator. The advertisement specifically points to 'operator comfort,' thus indicating that the company was looking at this as a selling point for its tractors. A Hart-Parr 20 was sent to the Nebraska Tractor Test Laboratory in June 1921. It yielded 23 maximum brake horsepower. Details are found in Test No. 79.

About 1925 Hart-Parr began demonstrating the 12-24 tractor at fairs all over the country. This special demonstration as shown here, consisted of the tractor actually lifting its own weight with the aid of cables and pulleys. Called, "The tractor that lifts itself by its own bootstraps," the demonstration was an immense success, in that it dramatized the pulling power of the 12-24 in a unique manner. The 12-24 Type E tractor saw first light in 1924, and was tested at Nebraska that year under No. 107.

Hart-Parr 10-20 tractors evolved into the 12-24 model during 1924. As otherwise indicated, the evolutionary process actually began with the 1921 introduction of the 10-20 Type B tractor with its 5 1/4 x 6 inch bore and stroke. During 1922 this was modified to a 5 1/2 inch engine bore. Weighing 3,990 pounds, the Hart-Parr 20 carried a 1923 list price of $920, while the larger Hart-Parr 30 listed at $1,160. Note that this model used conventional steel wheels rather than the expensive cast steel wheels of earlier days.

Hart-Parr Company

LEFT SIDE VIEW OF HART-PARR 16-30

The Hart-Parr 16-30 Type E tractor was introduced in 1924. This model featured enclosed drive gears, compared to the open gears of earlier models. The gears were lubricated with used engine lubricant...Hart-Parr used a once-through, force-feed lubricating system. Once the oil left the engine, it was piped to the enclosed final drives. Overflow pipes in the gear enclosures permitted the excess lubricant to find its way to the ground. While the earlier Hart-Parr 30 and the new 16-30 both used the same double-cylinder, 6 1/2 x 7 inch engine, the latter model was much heavier. In Nebraska Test No. 106 the 16-30 weighed in at 6,000 pounds. By comparison, the earlier 15-30 tractor of Test No. 26 weighed 5,450 pounds.

As with vintage tractors, vintage photographs are also subject to the ravages of time, as is obvious here. This 1920s scene illustrates a 16-30 tractor pulling a corn binder. Hart-Parr offered numerous options, including a special 'air washer.' It was designed to remove dirt and dust from the air before entering the carburetor. The air washer used water as a filtering agent, and in freezing weather the company recommended using 'kerosene instead of water.' Special tractor models included the 15-30 Type B as a "Special Model A Road Tractor." Another was the 15-30 Model C built as a Model D, Special Road Tractor.

Wheel equipment for the Hart-Parr tractors included many different styles of lugs, each intended for specific problems. At the extreme left is the spud lug intended for grassy areas, roads, and other locations where a minimum ground disturbance was required. Second from left is a plain bar lug, again used where minimum ground disturbance was needed. The two-bolt spade lugs were first used in 1927. Four different styles of angle lugs are shown on the right. In addition, the Special Road Tractor models could be furnished with heavy cast steel wheels, having either integrally cast lugs, or with bolted lugs.

Various attachments were offered for the Hart-Parr tractors. Late in production, probably about 1928, the company offered Tractor Lighting Outfits. The Agricultural Type was intended for plowing and other farm work. It consisted of one front head light and one on the rear fender. Complete with generator, it sold at $55. The Agricultural Type is shown here. Also available was the Industrial Type, with two front headlights and a rear tail light. It listed at $57. Both styles used a low-tension generator, belt-driven from the outside counterweight on the crankshaft.

Designed especially for road building and maintenance work, Hart-Parr offered many of its models with special equipment for this duty. A usual feature was the cast steel wheel equipment...this particular model has the lugs cast integral with the wheels. Additional lug equipment could be added if needed. Where flotation was a problem, extension rims could also be provided. Note the large internal-tooth bull gears. These were exposed to dust and dirt, and consequently were subject to heavy and premature wear.

Hart-Parr Company

Tell 'em and Sell 'em

With Hart-Parr Road Signs
The Year Around Silent Salesmen

For the benefit of Hart-Parr dealers the company offered an attractive road sign, calling it "The Year-Around Silent Salesman." The dealer's name was handpainted on every sign, and the company noted that the signs were worth $5 each, with Hart-Parr paying half the cost, or leaving the dealer to pay only $2.50 per sign. Given the high value of vintage tractor signs, it's entirely likely that today's Hart-Parr collectors would become completely ecstatic should a previously undiscovered carton of these signs somehow emerge!

This photograph carries the date of December 4, 1920. Shown is a trainload of 100 Hart-Parr 30 tractors on rail via Cedar Rapids, Iowa with a final destination of Denver, Colorado. A placard on the side of the load states that this shipment has been paid for in cash by Anderson Hart-Parr Company at Denver...the small lettering at the bottom of the placard states, 'Business is picking up.' There is no doubt of the popularity of the Hart-Parr 30 tractors. Sales remained relatively good, even during the early 1920s when many competitors were going broke. Yet, by the time of the 1929 Oliver merger, Hart-Parr was in desperate need of a new row-crop design.

An overhead view of the Hart-Parr 30 illustrates its great simplicity. The large platform gave the operator plenty of room, and the seat and steering wheel were strategically located for maximum visibility. There were relatively few controls to worry about, and these were within easy reach. In fact, virtually everything on the Hart-Parr 30 was accessible either from the platform or from the side of the tractor. The transmission cover is removed in this illustration...the Hart-Parr gearbox was yet another hallmark of simplicity.

Hart-Parr 16-30 tractors used a 6 1/2 x 7 inch bore and stroke, for a displacement of 232 cubic inches. The two cylinders were cast enbloc. In firing order, the right cylinder was first, followed by the left cylinder in the same revolution of the crankshaft. Each of the two main bearings were 2 1/2 inches in diameter, and 5 9/16 inches long. The connecting rod bearings were 3 1/2 inches long and of the same diameter. A Madison-Kipp lubricator was standard equipment, and Hart-Parr was early to adopt the Alemite system for all hard-oil lubrication. the radiator held eleven gallons of water.

Farmers were quick to adapt tractor power to many different tasks. Some farmers chose to invent their own one-man grain binder attachment, while a few companies actually offered such devices to farmers. Through ropes, pulleys, and an extended steering shaft, one man could operate the grain binder as well as the tractor. Of course, this saved one man, probably to set the new bundles into shocks, rather than the relative ease of riding the tractor.

THE HART-PARR 16-30 WORLD'S RECORD NON-STOP
CHAMPION. ALL PARTS ACCESSIBLE FOR INSPECTION
AND ADJUSTMENTS. THE ENGINE IS LUBRICATED BY
THE HART-PARR FORCE-FEED, FRESH-OIL SYSTEM

Hart-Parr Company

ON *the* HILLS *of a* WASHINGTON WHEAT RANCH

Hart-Parr sent a copy of their 16-30 tractor to Lincoln, Nebraska in October 1924. At the Tractor Test Laboratory, it was assigned Test No. 106. The test model was not equipped with a Robert Bosch magneto, as was later used, but instead, it carried a K-W Type T magneto. Also included with the test model was a Stromberg Model MB-3 carburetor. This tractor developed a maximum of 24.79 drawbar horsepower, and also elicited a maximum brake horsepower of 37.03, somewhat higher than its rated performance. Production of the 16-30 Type E tractor began in 1924 and ended in 1926.

A Robert Bosch magneto came as standard equipment on the Hart-Parr 16-30 tractor. This model used a 22 gallon fuel tank, with a small one gallon gasoline tank for starting purposes. Two forward and one reverse speed came standard, and the dry plate clutch featured Raybestos clutch lining. Less water, oil, and lugs, this tractor weighed 5,470 pounds. It was capable of handling a three-bottom plow under most conditions, and under favorable circumstances it could power a 28-inch threshing machine.

The 12-24 Type H tractor was the end of this series. Its production ran from 1928 to 1930. In addition to other features, this model included a three-speed transmission...this change actually took place on the last of the 12-24 Type E tractors, effective with No. 37901. The list price averaged at $1,050.

For road maintenance and industrial purposes the 12-24 Hart-Parr was available with hard rubber tires as shown here. Apparently this option was not available until 1927, since it does not appear in the price lists for 1926 and prior years. For 1927 this rubber-tired version listed at $1,450. By comparison, the standard steel-wheeled farm version sold for $1,050. The power take off attachment was available, with pricing from the factory. Hart-Parr also offered a 'line-drive' attachment for the 12-24 and 18-36 models. It permitted complete control of the tractor from a grain binder or other implement. This attachment listed at $25.

In 1923 Hart-Parr introduced their 22-40 tractor. This four-cylinder model was really nothing more than a pair of 10-20 engines set side by side, and in fact, each pair of cylinders had its own carburetor. A 1923 price list indicates that several variations of the Hart-Parr 40 were available. The standard model included 13-inch cast iron wheels, and listed at $2,250. When equipped with 18-inch rear wheels the price climbed to $2,400. An air cleaner was available at a $10 additional cost. At this time, Hart-Parr also offered the Vulcan plow line to its customers. An inventory was maintained at the Charles City factory, although the plows were actually made at Evansville, Indiana.

RIGHT-SIDE VIEW HART-PARR 22-40 SHOWING STURDY CONSTRUCTION AND CRANK CASE ACCESSIBILITY. ALL ADJUSTMENTS ARE MADE FROM THE SIDE OR THE PLATFORM

Although Hart-Parr promoted their '40' tractor heavily for road building and maintenance duty, it does not appear that the company made any overt efforts to include graders as part of the overall company offering to the trade. Even though Hart-Parr offered plows, and even sold threshing machines for awhile, they do not appear as sales agents for graders. However, there are strong appearances that the 22-40 was indeed a very popular road tractor. It remained on the market until 1927 when it was replaced with the 28-50 tractor.

Hart-Parr put a pair of 10-20 engines together to make the 22-40 power plant. The company called this their 'twin-two' construction. Like the two-cylinder 10-20, the four-cylinder 20-40 used a 5 1/2 x 6 1/2 inch bore and stroke. This tractor used a firing order of 1-2-4-3, with No. 1 cylinder being on the right-hand side of the tractor. Hart-Parr sent a copy of the 22-40 to Nebraska in July 1923. Two Schebler Model D carburetors were used, and the test tractor used a K-W Model TK magneto. Later on, this was changed to a Robert Bosch magneto. An oversized water pump was available for this tractor, and the tractor tested at Nebraska was thus equipped.

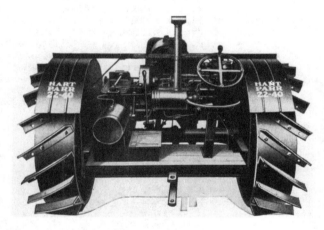

This rear view of the 22-40 Hart-Parr illustrates the large, roomy platform. In Nebraska Test No. 97, the 22-40 delivered 28 maximum drawbar, and 46.4 brake horsepower. During its rated load tests the 22-40 consumed nearly 5 gallons of kerosene per hour of operating time, and also consumed an equal amount of water. During its 1923-27 production run, a total of 496 Hart-Parr 40 tractors were built, the last number being 70500 of early 1927.

In 1926 Hart-Parr ended production of the venerable 16-30 Type E tractor. In its place came the 18-36 Type G tractor. When first introduced, the 18-36 came with a two-speed transmission. The first 18-36 tractor, No. 26001, used a 6 3/4 inch bore. Effective with No. 28851 of 1927 the 18-36 tractor gained a three-speed transmission. As with the 12-24 and the 28-50, this 18-36 model could be purchased with hard rubber tires as special equipment. A Hart-Parr price list of May 1927 shows that the 18-36 with standard equipment sold for $1,350. A special road maintenance model with steel wheels listed at $1,625, and this model with dual rubber wheels sold at $2,075.

It appears that Hart-Parr offered a power take off shaft as special equipment beginning about 1925. The Model G power take off unit was used until 1927, and was replaced with the Model H pto unit at that time. This change seems to coincide generally with the concurrent addition of a three-speed transmission to the tractor line. In 1928 the power take off attachment listed at $50. The Hart-Parr 18-36 appears in Nebraska Test No. 128 of October 1926. The two-cylinder, 6 3/4 x 7 inch engine yielded a maximum of 42.85 belt horsepower at 800 rpm.

Extension Power Shaft Coupling

Power Take Off Clutch Lever Within Reach Of Operator

Dust Proof Oil Tight Enclosure

Bolted Rigidly To Frame

Independent Clutch Band Operating On Crankshaft Counterweight

Hart-Parr Company

The caption with this photo says, "Shipped to Montana, March 5, 1928." Apparently this trainload of 28-50 Hart-Parr tractors were destined to a life of work in the Montana wheat country. This model weighed 8,600 pounds and sold at approximately $2,085. Designed to operate a 36-inch threshing machine, it was also capable of pulling a five or six-bottom plow. A 28-50 Hart-Parr was submitted to Nebraska for testing in April 1927. For reasons unknown this tractor was withdrawn. It was eventually tested in August 1927 under No. 140.

Essentially, the 28-50 Hart-Parr consisted of two 12-24 engines set side-by-side. In Nebraska Test No. 140 this tractor delivered over 64 belt horsepower at its rated engine speed of 800 rpm. Over 43 maximum drawbar horsepower was also indicated. In 1928 the standard 28-50 model listed at $2,085, but if the cab was not wanted, there was a deduction of $75 from the list price. A special road tractor was available for $2,380, and the industrial version with its hard rubber tires sold at $2,850. The 1928 price list indicates that the 28-50 standard model weighed in at 7,980 pounds. Various changes and modifications raised this figure to as high as 10,500 pounds. Production of the 28-50 ended in 1930.

HART-PARR "40" STATIONARY ENGINE.

Beginning in 1923 and continuing into 1930, Hart-Parr offered an air compressor unit built over the standard tractor engines. During this entire period, only about a dozen of the 55 cubic foot models were built, along with about three dozen of the 90 cubic foot size. Apparently, a 180 cubic foot model was offered, but none were sold. The compressor unit was supplied by Buhl Company of Chicago, Illinois. A 1925 price list indicates that the 55 cubic foot model listed at $500; the 90 cubic foot size sold for $650; and the 180 cubic foot compressor retailed at $1,200. Photographs of the Hart-Parr compressors have not been located as this book goes to press, but apparently, one cylinder was used to power the compressor, with the other actually serving as the air compressor cylinder.

In the 1921-29 period, Hart-Parr offered their tractor engines as stationary power units. Each of the tractor engines was offered as a stationary, concurrent with its production as a tractor engine. A 1928 price book indicates that the 24 horsepower engine, complete with fuel tank and cooling system retailed at $775. The 36 horsepower model, the same as used in the 18-36 tractor, was priced at $875, and the four-cylinder, 50 horsepower engine could be purchased at $1,325.

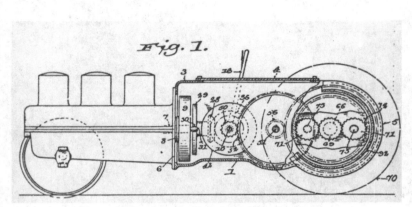

C. W. Hart left Charles City and the tractor business in 1917. With some slight occupational detours he then plunged into the oil refining business. Yet, his love of the tractor business remained. On March 18, 1920 he filed this patent application for a tractor design. Letters Patent for this three-cylinder design were issued to C. W. Hart under No. 1,509,293 on September 23, 1924. Apparently, three tractors were built...along with numerous spare parts. One or two of these were used in Hart's Montana wheat venture. Eventually, the tractors fell out of use and the idea was abandoned.

Beginning in 1924, Hart-Parr entered the washing machine business. A 1925 price list shows that the electric washer when fitted with a gas heater sold at $155; without the heater, the price dropped by $5. The washing machine market was no less competitive than the tractor market, making it difficult for Hart-Parr to capture any major portion of the sales. One possibility is that Hart-Parr chose to enter this market to partially offset the poor tractor sales of the 1920s; this was caused in large part by the post-war depression of the period.

A 1920s tour through the Hart-Parr factories probably began with the huge foundry buildings. From its very beginnings, Hart-Parr operated its own foundry, and in fact, it became well known for its iron and steel castings. At one point the foundry workers became disgruntled over a labor-management problem. Hart was always thinking ahead, anticipated the problem, and dealt with it quickly and firmly. Thus, what might have been a long and costly strike was avoided in one fell swoop.

Looking down one of the many machine tool aisles, nothing is visible except for machine tools and neat stacks of castings. Above, and to the right is one of several huge cooling fans...an essential appliance to maintain a livable working environment. Although a few belt drives are visible, Hart-Parr had apparently adapted most of the factory equipment to electric motor drives. This forward step was a major advancement in factory modernization.

Hart-Parr Company

Hart-Parr Company used a great many innovative machines in its manufacturing operations. Likewise, the company was early to adopt production line methods to tractor building, and the use of precision machining methods. The latter concept was more expensive to set up initially, but proved to be cost effective regarding the assembly of certain components. These benefits also redounded to the farmer-buyer in that repairs were minimized, and when necessary, the cost of needed repairs was substantially reduced.

This battery of drilling machines is obviously being operated by a lineshaft. Earlier, most of the factory was operated by lineshafts and leather belts, but the advent of individual electric motor drives simplified this aspect. Typical of certain factory operations, these workers of the 1920s might well have spent years of their lives working at the same station, operating the same machine, as days turned into weeks, weeks became years, and years eventually rolled into a lifetime of work.

This battery of Hart-Parr stationary engines is set up with electric generators in the Hart-Parr factory complex. A certain number of these units were kept on line to handle normal plant operations, and additional power came from the tractors on the test stands. This unique system provided an excellent means of 'running-in' a new tractor, but the power was put to good use in helping to operate the factory.

This factory photograph illustrates a number of Hart-Parr tractor engines ready for further assembly. Apparently the engine components were assembled separately into a complete engine, and this component was then installed on the tractor frame. The carburetor, force-feed lubricator, and the magneto were purchased outside of the company. With these exceptions, virtually all of the tractor was built within the walls of Hart-Parr Company.

Hart-Parr Company

While many manufacturers of the time preferred to buy crankshafts from those specializing in this art, Hart-Parr made their own. This photograph from the 1920s shows a Hart-Parr worker grinding a crankshaft. A flood of water and soluble oil is flowing over wheel and work as each bearing is brought to its final dimensions and given a mirror finish. Experienced workers could finish off a complete crankshaft in a remarkably short time, and could maintain remarkably accurate dimensions from one part to another.

This Hart-Parr worker is grinding a camshaft for a tractor that will soon rise from the erecting floor. Camshaft grinding was (and is) a complicated task. In fact, the internal combustion engine industry was and is still learning about the influence of cam design on engine performance. However, in the case of the Hart-Parr engines, the design was rather straightforward, since the engines were relatively low speed, compared to later designs.

This photograph illustrates a stack of engine crankcases mounted on a huge planing mill. By this means an essential component could be converted from a rough casting to a finished piece of work, and with great accuracy. In a factory like that of Hart-Parr, many ordinary machine tools were modified to suit a specific application, and probably spent their entire working life on that single operation. Chances are that this planing mill cut many tons of metal chips each year.

Shown here is a test battery for Hart-Parr tractors. Each completed tractor was required to spend several hours on the test stand. After thorough testing within the factory, there was far less probability of trouble when the tractor went into the field. Despite the quality of the Hart-Parr tractor line, farmers of the 1920s were becoming less and less interested in the heavy, fixed-tread models like those shown here. Row-crop tractors were on the horizon, but it would take a combination of Hart-Parr with several other companies to produce a row-crop tractor with Hart-Parr roots.

Hart-Parr Company

The Hart-Parr factories of the 1920s covered many acres. The large foundry was a major portion of the company. Castings usually were placed outdoors to cure or normalize for several months prior to being used. The machine shops covered several acres, and the forging and heat treating shops were sizable. Once the individual parts were machined, assembly began in areas designated especially for the purpose. The paint shop was yet another area, and the testing area was a small, but very essential part of the overall plant. Add to this the office facilities required for everything from design work to filling orders for repair parts, and the plant was indeed a very large operation.

Once the tractors were completed, came the task of loading them onto rail cars for dispatch to various branch houses or to Hart-Parr tractor dealers. A fair number of Hart-Parr tractors were exported, and these required special handling. Each tractor needed special treatment to minimize breakage or damage, and was then securely encased in a huge wooden crate. Ordinary surface shipments like this one required only that the tractors be secured firmly to the flat car.

During World War One, the Hart-Parr Company took on a contract to manufacture shell casings. This proved to be a costly venture, and one that probably brought Hart-Parr near to financial ruin. In 1915 and 1916 Hart-Parr took a British contract to make shell casings. Virtually everything that could go wrong went wrong. In fact, Hart-Parr designed and built equipment within its own factory to do the job. Shown here is one of the special automatic lathes designed and built by Hart-Parr for shell manufacturing.

Hart-Parr built a great many shell casings during World War One. By the time the problems were worked out, there was no longer a need for that particular size or style of casing, and so, Hart-Parr was left with thousands of useless castings and forgings. C. W. Hart left the company in 1917, and so by the time the smoke cleared from this sad episode, Hart was in Montana, and would soon gain a reputation in the oil refining business. C. H. Parr left for a short time, but soon returned, and remained with the company until retirement.

Minneapolis-Moline Company

As with the Cockshutt line, the Minneapolis-Moline line had no connection with Oliver Corporation in the strictest sense. The commonality lies in the acquisition of Minneapolis-Moline, Cockshutt, and Oliver by White Motor Corporation in 1969. These companies were acquired by the parent White Motor Corporation as wholly owned subsidiaries and merged to form the White Farm Equipment Company. Headquarters were at Oak Brook, Illinois. White Farm Equipment functioned as a division of White Motor Corporation. Ironically, Oliver had acquired the Cleveland Tractor Company some years earlier; it had its beginnings with Rollin H. White, also of White Motors.

A pictorial history of Minneapolis-Moline was published by Motorbooks International in 1990 by this Author. Although it is not a comprehensive, in-depth study of Minneapolis-Moline and its ancestors, it does provide a thumbnail sketch of the company, particularly regarding its tractors.

Minneapolis-Moline began in 1929 with the merger of three companies; Moline Plow Company, Minneapolis Threshing Machine Company, and the Minneapolis Steel & Machinery Company. Each had in its own right established a brief niche in the farm equipment industry, and each had made its own contributions.

A significant development of Moline Plow Company was their Moline Universal tractor. It represented a radical departure from usual practice, in that the drivewheels were in the front, with the implement attached to the rear of the tractor. This concept of an integral tractor and its implement was not new, but Moline developed it to an extent that was previously unheard of. Despite its brief popularity, the Moline Universal lasted for only a few years, after which Moline Plow retreated to manufacturing implements, never again entering the tractor business.

Regarding the Moline implement line, it is worthy of notice that Flying Dutchman implements were well received and enjoyed a wide market. Yet, by the 1920s, the implement market was changing. It was saturated with horsedrawn implements. The fact was that few farmers went out to buy a new cultivator every few years; the one they bought twenty years earlier was probably still cultivating the same fields in the same time-honored way. Changing over to tractor power required new implements, tailored especially for the purpose, and this was an intensely competitive market. Thus, Moline Plow found itself in tight financial straits by the late 1920s.

Minneapolis Threshing Machine Company offered an excellent line of threshing machines and had even made pioneering efforts in the combine business. Their tractors were equivalent to most others of the time. Yet, Minneapolis was not a full-line builder. Threshing machines, corn shellers, and tractors comprised the bulk of the Minneapolis line. By the 1920s the farm equipment industry had changed. Instead of a host of specialized concerns or short-line companies, the trend was toward full-line dealers who could offer everything needed on the farm under the same trademark. Thus, Minneapolis Threshing Machine Company was in difficulty by this time.

Minneapolis Steel & Machinery Company, like the other two partners, found itself in fierce competition for the available tractor sales by the late 1920s. Undoubtedly the Twin City line of tractors and threshing machines was among the finest in the industry. Yet, sales of new threshing machines were slow. The market was saturated, and replacement machines sold at a far slower pace than during those wonderful years when almost any threshing machine could be sold at almost any time. Again, the Twin City line was limited to a few items, and again, combining the effort seemed to be the only possible choice.

Ironically, the Minneapolis-Moline merger occurred in 1929, the same year as the Oliver-Hart-Parr merger. For Minneapolis-Moline, the merger provided a new lease on life, and in fact, gave the company another four decades of useful activity. During these forty years, Minneapolis-Moline pioneered numerous innovations in the farm equipment industry, one notable example being the development of propane equipment for tractors and its practical application thereto. For about five years following the 1969 acquisition of Cockshutt, Minneapolis-Moline and Oliver, the White Farm Equipment Company offered tractors under the individual trademarks. However, the tractors were the same. For instance, the Oliver 2055 and the M-M G1050 were the same. Another example is the Oliver 1265. It was also sold as the White 1270 and the M-M G350. Eventually, the silver and gray finish of a new tractor series appeared, and with its inception the Prairie Gold of the M-M line disappeared.

Beginning in 1969 the following tractor models were essentially the same, except for colors and decals:

White-Oliver 1555 and M-M G-50
White-Oliver 1655 and M-M G-750
White-Oliver 1855 and M-M G-940
White-Oliver 1755 and M-M G-850
White-Oliver 1865 and M-M G-950

Minneapolis-Moline Company

White-Oliver 2055 and M-M G-1050
White-Oliver 2155 and M-M G-1350
Oliver 2655, M-M A4T and White Plainsman
Oliver 1265, White 1270, and M-M G-350
Oliver 1365, White 1370, and M-M G-450
White 1870 and M-M G-955
White 2270 and M-M G-1355

The photographs and captions accompanying this section present only a brief highlight of Minneapolis-Moline tractor activities during their 1929-69 operating period. A comprehensive look at this company and its ancestors is beyond the scope of this book.

Minneapolis-Moline did as much or more than any other tractor builder to promote the use of propane fuel in farm tractors. Their experiments began in the early 1940s, and perhaps already during the 1930s. These efforts proved successful, and the Model U Standard was the first tractor to be tested at Nebraska using propane fuel. This test, No. 411, was run in June 1949. Except for some modifications to the hood design, and an altered compression ratio, this model was identical to the gasoline version of the Model U. Production of the Model U began in 1940, with various models being offered as late as 1955.

Introduced in 1951 as the Model BF, this little tractor had first life in 1945 with the B. F. Avery Company, Louisville, Kentucky. Minneapolis-Moline took over Avery in 1951 and continued to build derivations of this small tractor until 1955. The Model BF used a four-cylinder Hercules engine with a displacement of 133 ci. It was capable of about 25 belt horsepower. The Model BF was tested at Nebraska during October 1951 by Minneapolis-Moline Company. Results appear in Test No. 469.

During 1955, Minneapolis-Moline introduced a new style of their Model G propane tractor. Production of this model apparently ended the following year. Data from Nebraska Tractor Test No. 545 indicates that this model delivered nearly 70 belt horsepower. The four-cylinder engine had a displacement of 403 ci, using a 4 5/8 x 6 inch bore and stroke. Rated speed was 1,300 rpm. The tractor tested in No. 545 was equipped for propane fuel; data on the gasoline model may be found in Test No. 547.

Production of the Minneapolis-Moline Model GTA tractor began in 1942. Subsequently came numerous other styles in the G-Series tractors, including the GTB, GTC, and others. Rated at over 50 belt horsepower, this Model G was tested at Nebraska in 1950 under No. 437. The 403 ci, four-cylinder engine was built by Minneapolis-Moline; it used a 4 5/8 x 6 inch bore and stroke. Production of various G-Series tractors ran until 1956. This tractor is shown during the actual belt testing procedures at the Nebraska Tractor Test Laboratory.

As previously indicated, Minneapolis-Moline performed pioneering development in the application of propane fuel to farm tractors. As also noted, production of the Model U began already in 1940. Subsequently the Model U was modified as technology advanced. With the introduction and widespread use of rubber tires in the 1930s, tractors changed dramatically in appearance and usefulness. As engine designs changed, power was increased. As new technologies, such as hydraulics, became better refined, they too, gained wide acceptance. Thus, it was a constant struggle for a tractor builder to remain in a very competitive market, and still retain a selling advantage. The ever-popular Model U was able to hold its own niche in the market, being offered in several versions until about 1955. It was tested at Nebraska under No. 521 of 1954.

Capable of about 30 pto horsepower, the 335 Minneapolis-Moline tractor saw first light in 1956. It was tested at Nebraska in June of the following year, with the data appearing in Test No. 624. Priced at $2,500 the 335 came with an independent pto and power-adjustable rear wheels as standard equipment. Power steering was a $110 extra-cost option, as was the Ampli-Torc drive at an additional $148. A front pto shaft was another option; it was priced at $42.50.

In 1956 Minneapolis-Moline introduced their 445 tractor, a new model with radically new styling. Gone was the streamlined hood that had served since before World War Two. In its place came a new swept-back design that epitomized modern tractor design. Rated at about 38 pto horsepower, the Model 445 was tested at Nebraska in June 1956 where it delivered a creditable performance in Test No. 578. However, production of the 445 tractor ended the same year that it began.

Minneapolis-Moline built their 5-Star tractors in the 1957-61 period. Rated at approximately 50 drawbar horsepower, the 5-Star was built in gasoline, propane, and diesel models. Nebraska Test No. 651 was run on a propane model; the gasoline version was apparently not tested. The following test, No. 652 was run on the 5-Star diesel model. While a 283 ci inch engine was used for the propane model, a 336 ci engine was used for the 5-Star diesel. As a price comparison, the 5-Star gasoline model sold at about $4475, while the comparable diesel model retailed at $5250.

Minneapolis-Moline Company

The 4-Star tractors were built only in gasoline and propane models. Both delivered about 40 drawbar horsepower. Both were essentially the same, except that the propane model used a compression ratio of 8.75 to 1, compared to 7.2 to 1 for the gasoline version. Priced at $3,300 the 4-Star did not include power steering with the package; it added another $144 to the list price. Other extra-cost items were the propane equipment at $270, and power-adjustable rear wheels at $120. Production of this model ran from 1959 to 1962.

Rated at about 70 drawbar horsepower, the big G-vi tractor was produced in the 1959-62 period. It was available with a 425 ci propane or diesel engine. Both were of six-cylinder design and both used a 4 1/4 x 5 inch bore and stroke. Both were rated at 1,500 rpm. While the serial number lists indicate that production ended in 1962, industry data shows this model being available into the 1964 model year. Priced at $6,400 for the diesel, the propane version was built for $300 less. Power steering was standard equipment for this model; a belt pulley was available for an additional price of $128.

Although White Farm Equipment acquired Minneapolis-Moline in 1969, the G-1355 was presented for testing at Nebraska in 1973 as a purely M-M model. Rated at 2,200 rpm, this tractor was capable of over 140 pto horsepower. The M-M 585 ci six-cylinder engine was combined with an Oliver drive train in this model. It was available as M-M with Prairie Gold paint or as an Oliver with green paint. White Farm Equipment marketed this tractor in Canada as their 2270 model from the beginning of production. The power level was later raised to 142 horsepower and the M-M designator was removed, with the White logo being substituted.

A Minneapolis-Moline engine and an Oliver power train were combined to produce the G-955 M-M tractor. It was marketed in Canada as the White 1870 model. This tractor was tested at Nebraska in 1974, where it delivered nearly 100 pto horsepower. The six-cylinder diesel engine had a displacement of 451 ci. When equipped with the six-cylinder, 425 ci propane engine, the G-955 yielded about 92 pto horsepower. Serial number lists indicate that the G-955 was built during 1973 and 1974.

The M-M G-1050 tractor was also built as the Oliver 2055 tractor. The latter was offered only in 1971, with production of the G-1050 running from 1969-71. The six-cylinder, 504 ci diesel engine was naturally aspirated. However, this model was also available in a propane version. Likewise, it could also be secured in row-crop or standard-tread models. Features included the Ampli-torc drive and closed center hydraulics.

Production of the Minneapolis-Moline G-950 tractor ran from 1969 to 1971. In the latter year it was also marketed as the Oliver 1865 tractor. The diesel model listed at $10,375 as a row-crop, or at $8,600 as a standard-tread model. Weighing over 10,000 pounds, this model was equipped with a six-cylinder engine having a 4 1/4 x 5 inch bore and stroke. The independent pto was standard equipment, as was power steering and closed center hydraulics. Extras included a three-speed Ampli-Torc instead of the usual two-speed variety; adding this option raised the list price by $455. A fully-enclosed cab added another $1,175 to the list price.

A customized factory cab was offered as a $1,200 option on the G-1350 M-M tractor. Built in the 1969-71 period, this model was also sold in 1971 as the Oliver 2155 tractor. Propane was the fuel of choice for this model, although it was also built in a diesel version. The propane row-crop model listed at $13,700 and substituting a diesel engine raised that figure by another $600. Although the propane model used an Minneapolis engine, the diesel model appears to have first used the Minneapolis design, followed by a German-built M.A.N. engine. Note that this tractor carries both the Minneapolis-Moline and the White logos.

Between 1969 and 1975, White Farm Equipment offered what were essentially the same tractor models in several different versions. The tractors differed little except for the paint color and the decal work. Some were sold under their generic name, while others were sold as White-Oliver or White-MM. In addition were the Heritage tractors, offered only in certain models during 1969 and 1970. The Heritage tractors carried a special design of red, white, and blue, together with stars. Except for the special colors, these tractors were otherwise identical to those tractors with traditional color schemes. An especially confusing array of models is demonstrated with the M-M G-350 tractor. It was built by Fiat (Italy) and was also sold as the Oliver 1265 and the White 1265. Then in 1970 the White version was redesignated as the 1270. Mercifully, the plethora of virtually identical tractors, their dissimilarity resting in the paint color, ended by 1975.

John Nichols opened a blacksmith shop at Battle Creek, Michigan in 1848. Little is known of Nichols' early life, nor does anything but the most scant history of the early years of his shop still exist. In the early 1850s Nichols took in David Shepard as a partner. During those years the firm built farm machinery, steam engines, and mill machinery. Virtually nothing is known of the early products from Nichols, Shepard & Company. Apparently the products were sold on a more or less localized basis, and word-of-mouth was the primary advertising method.

The Pitts brothers developed their first thresher about 1837. For some years the actual separating of the grain from straw and chaff was achieved by a slatted apron behind the cylinder. These so-called apron machines were the accepted standard for about twenty years. Nichols and Shepard decided that the apron machine was never going to be a complete success. Numerous problems besieged the apron machine. One was that when the apron was overloaded, much of the grain was not separated from the straw. In other words, the cylinder had much more capacity to thresh than the separator had to separate. Numerous improvements were made to the apron machine, with varying degrees of success. One was an octagonal roller which operated beneath the slatted apron. As it turned it was to give the apron a vibrating effect aimed at helping to separate the grain from the straw. About 1850 the beater was developed; it first was equipped with teeth to help in the separation process, but the teeth became tangled with straw. Finally the teeth were removed from the beater paddles. From that time on the beater was essentially developed to its present state.

About 1857 Nichols and Shepard developed their first Vibrator thresher. It utilized an entirely different design. Instead of the endless apron came vibrating straw racks, just as used today. The first year, Nichols and Shepard built ten of these machines. Remarkably, they stayed sold! From this point on, Nichols, Shepard & Company was in the thresher business in a big way.

Limited research material of the period nevertheless indicates that the introduction of the Nichols & Shepard Vibrator created a furor among the competing manufacturers. At the time, no one but Nichols & Shepard was building such a machine; all the others were building their own variation of the endless apron machine. Obviously the intrusion of this newcomer was very upsetting to the established builders.

Within a few years, most thresher manufacturers had adopted some form of vibrating threshing principle, although a few continued building endless apron machines for several decades. In fact, some companies, including Farquhar, previously noted in this volume, continued to offer endless apron machines into the early 1900s.

An 1876 Nichols & Shepard catalog points out numerous design features of the Vibrator machine, especially in comparison to the endless apron design. For example, the Vibrator used only five belts, where others used anywhere from six to ten. Only ten pulleys were used on the Vibrator, compared to thirty or more on many of the apron machines.

At one point in their 1876 catalog, Nichols & Shepard invokes the scriptural injunction that "Cleanliness is next to Godliness," followed by the advice that 'Our Vibrator makes no litterings, and saves the dirty and disagreeable [job] of cleaning up.'

By 1876 Nichols & Shepard was offering their threshers adapted to steam power, as well as the usual geared type. These machines could be furnished for use with virtually any make of steam engine, but the company advised that they could also supply the complete outfit of engine, thresher and accessories. However, virtually nothing is known of the earliest Nichols & Shepard steam engines, except that their first portable appeared in 1877.

During the early 1880s Nichols & Shepard moved from portable steam engines to their own traction engine. With their traction engine development came a legal problem which eventually was decided by the United States Supreme Court.

On May 3, 1880 a patent application was filed with the U. S. Patent Office. This patent was for a steam engine valve gear, and was filed jointly by Elon A. Marsh and Minard Lafever, both of Battle Creek, Michigan. On December 28 of 1880, Patent No. 236,052 was issued to Marsh and Lafever. The result was the Marsh reverse, a style which would become widely known. However, the patent documents contained a technical, albeit a fatal flaw. The patent was inadvertently not signed by the Commissioner of Patents. Thirteen months later the error was detected, and the error was corrected. Meanwhile, Nichols & Shepard began using the design.

Marsh demanded an accounting of Nichols & Shepard for profits derived from use of the patent. However, counsel for the defendants argued that no such accounting could be demanded where the infringement took place previous to the issuance of the validated patent. Further, it was argued that a Special Act of Congress of February 3, 1887 for the relief of Marsh and Lefever could not be construed to have a retroactive effect.

Ultimately, the Supreme Court ruled that since the patent was originally unsigned, it was not valid until the signature of the Commissioner of Patents was placed on the patent. After the smoke cleared, Marsh and Lefever were left with the letter of the law, while Nichols & Shepard were effactually cleared of the charge of infringement. Further details of the Marsh v. Nichols & Co. suit are cited in 15 Fed. Rep. 914 and 24 O.G. 901. This case was decided by the Supreme Court on December 10, 1888.

Shortly after 1900 the company introduced their famous Red River Special line of threshers. Like other threshers of the time, these were of wood construction, with an all-steel machine appearing about 1915. However, the company continued to market selected models of wood machines for a few more years. With the advent of the Red River Special line came the special construction which came to be known as the 4 Threshermen---the Big Cylinder, the Man Behind the Gun, the Steel-Winged Beater, and the Beating Shakers. Until Nichols & Shepard merged into Oliver Farm Equipment Company in 1929 the Red River Special line and the 4 Threshermen were nearly synonymous terms. Subsequently, Oliver continued to build the same threshing machines for some years to follow.

With the development of steam traction engines in the 1880s, Nichols & Shepard continued apace in their development. The company offered numerous sizes in single and double-cylinder styles. However, Nichols & Shepard seems to have been intent on remaining in the engine and thresher business, since early advertising literature makes little or no reference to plows and other farm implements.

The company began developing a gasoline tractor in 1911 and continued with three different models into the early 1920s. At that point the company built began building their own tractors on order, and also sold a Lauson-built tractor under the Nichols & Shepard masthead.

Nichols & Shepard controlled numerous patents. A sampling of these includes: No. 34,071, Grain Separator, January 7, 1862; No. 91,658, Threshing Machine Concave, June 22, 1869; No. 59,440, Thrashing Machine, November 6, 1866; No. 225,560, Traction Engine, March 16, 1880; Re 9951, Valve Gear, November 29, 1881; No. 244,807, Valve Gear, July 26, 1881; No. 265,809, Traction Engine, October 10, 1882; No. 257,435, Grain Separator, May 2, 1882; No. 274,386, Grain Separator, March 20, 1883; No. 303,516, Traction Engine, August 12, 1884; No. 293,876, Thrashing Machine, February 19, 1884; No. 427,372, Thrashing Machine, May 6, 1890; and No. 616,380, Traction Engine, November 8, 1904.

Numerous other improvements to steam traction engines and threshers were also patented by Nichols & Shepard. During the 1920s the company developed a line of combines which would later prove to be the nucleus of further activity on the part of Oliver Corporation. Likewise, Nichols & Shepard also developed a corn picker during the 1920s, and it was the direct ancestor of the Oliver corn picker line which followed.

John Nichols started a blacksmith shop at Battle Creek, Michigan in 1848. Like many other shops of the time, it included a small iron foundry. The full extent of Nichols' activity at this time is unknown, but from company literature it is thought that he built steam engines, farm equipment, and other items. Since mass transportation methods of the time were virtually nonexistent, it is likely that most of this shop's early production was sold to a localized market. John Nichols died in 1891. His son E. C. Nichols took over the reins of the company at that time. However, he was a partner with his father in numerous patents secured for the company prior to that time.

This illustration shows the Nichols & Shepard concern, probably in the early 1860s, especially since some indications have it that the first Vibrator thresher did not appear until 1863. From a historical perspective, it is likely that much normal manufacturing activity was slowed or perhaps ceased altogether during the Civil War. Thus, introducing new machines at this time was probably difficult, if not altogether impossible.

David Shepard became a partner of John Nichols in the early 1850s. Apparently the firm operated for some years under the title of Nichols, Shepard & Company. In 1886 the firm was incorporated as Nichols & Shepard Company, and by this time was one of the leading American thresher builders. Shepard's role in the company has not been well defined, and is now lost to history. However, Shepard remained fairly active in the company until his death in 1904.

A well-worn cover from an 1876 Vibrator catalog tells of Nichols & Shepard products. At the time, the annual catalog was the primary means of getting the Nichols & Shepard message to prospective buyers. The line included traction engines, steam power outfits, separators expressly for steam power, plain engines, clover huller attachments, and horse power establishments (the latter term meaning a fixed or settled machine). The company also pointed toward reliability by noting their 'thirty-three years of continuous and successful business without change of name, location or management.'

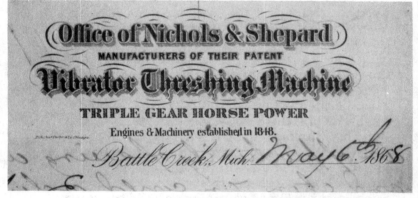

A stained and tattered bill head from Nichols & Shepard dated May 6, 1868 is one of the earliest extant pieces of N & S ephemera to emerge thus far. Typical of the period, there are six lines of type, all of them in a different face, plus numerous type embellishments. Note that the billhead indicates that this firm is the manufacturer of 'their patent Vibrator Threshing Machine.' It was in fact covered by patents, and would be the catalyst which would revolutionize the science of threshing grain.

Into the 1870s, Nichols & Shepard built four sizes of the Vibrator thresher. The 24 and 28-inch machines differed only in cylinder width; both used a 47-inch separating width. However when use with a sweep power, the smaller machine could be operated with six horses, while eight were required for the 28-inch machine. The 32-inch machine was intended for use with a 10 horsepower steam engine; the same held true for the 36-inch machine, the largest of the line.

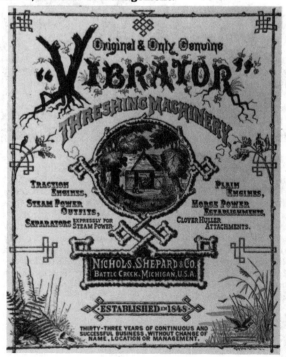

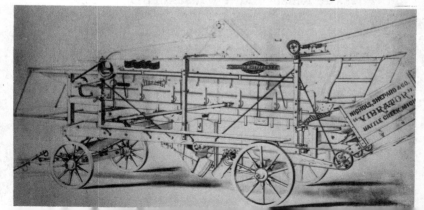

Nichols & Shepard Company

By 1875 the Vibrator thresher had undergone few changes from the original design of 1863. An important feature was the removal of all shafts from inside the machine; this effectually prevented the problems of straw wrapping around shafts and bearings to the point of setting the machine afire or at the least giving the thresherman the awful job of crawling inside with a pocket knife to cut away the unwanted material. By substituting shaking or vibrating straw racks for the endless apron, capacity was increased and the grain was in the sack, not in the stack.

During the 1860s Nichols & Shepard perfected their Triple Gear mounted power. It is shown here staked down and ready for attachment of the sweep arms. This model was designed for operation while on its wheels, as shown in the engraving. Many competing powers required the removal of the wheels for operation in order to sufficiently lower the machine for successful use. Despite the inclusion of N & S sweep powers in catalogs into the 1890s, it is obvious that the company much preferred that threshermen use a separator equipped for steam power.

An 1876 Nichols & Shepard catalog illustrates their belted separator, made expressly for steam power. By this time the Vibrator was well perfected, and would undergo few major changes for another twenty years. By placing the shaker arms outside of the machine, problems with straw wedging or lodging were eliminated. Further, the Vibrator used fewer belts, pulleys, shafts, and bearings than almost any other thresher on the market at that time. This illustration is taken from an early engraving as used in the 1876 catalog.

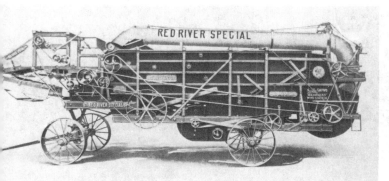

Production data on the Nichols & Shepard line is sketchy prior to 1916. However, production figures exist for separators built 1916 and later. From this data it is known that a limited number of wood machines were built as late as 1922. This was probably in deference to threshermen who preferred wood construction to the all-steel machine. Shown here is a Red River Special of 1914 vintage. Its appearance changed but little for nearly thirty years.

A Nichols & Shepard catalog of about 1906 illustrates the company's attractive logo. About this same time Nichols & Shepard introduced their new Red River Special separator, and the latter term would quickly become synonymous with Nichols & Shepard. In many areas, the Red River Special became that standard by which other threshers were compared. Although the company was successful solely through its engines and threshers, the market eventually became saturated, and eventually began to disappear due to the coming of the combine. Thus, Nichols & Shepard was ripe for merger when the Oliver Farm Equipment Company was formed in 1929.

Nichols & Shepard Company

A cut from the 1914 Nichols & Shepard catalog illustrates the ease of changing sieves whenever required. The large access door permitted installation and removal of the sieves with relative ease. Not shown however is the rather difficult task of positioning the front of the sieve in its proper position or the equally arduous task of locking the rear of the sieve in place. Fortunately, the advent of adjustable sieves minimized the necessity to change sieves to accommodate different kinds of grain or seed crops.

The 1914 N & S catalog indicates that this separator was offered in eight sizes, including the 22 x 36 and 28 x 40 Junior separators. Standard models included the 28 x 40, 30 x 46, 32 x 52, 36 x 56, 40 x 60, and 44 x 64 inch sizes. The latter had a cylinder 44 inches wide with a separating width of 64 inches. This huge machine required a steam engine of at least 80 horsepower to accommodate its tremendous capacity. The latter model was out of production by 1916, since this size does not appear in the extant serial number lists which commence with that year.

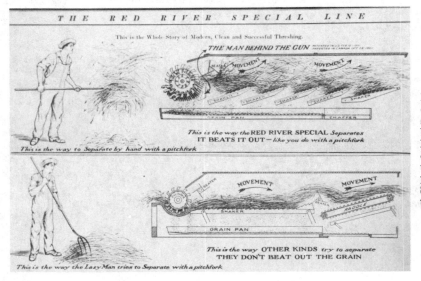

Perhaps this drawing was an oversimplification, or depending on one's perspective, perhaps it overstated the case for the Nichols & Shepard design. The bottom illustration notes that 'This is the way the Lazy Man tries to Separate with a pitchfork.' However, the upper drawing points the right way, noting that 'This is the way to Separate by hand with a pitchfork.' The obvious comparison is that while N & S claimed that other machines tried to *separate*, while the Red River Special *beats it out.*

The Junior Red River Special was a small machine designed for the small farm or a small threshing ring. It was built in two sizes of 22 x 36 and 28 x 40 inches. Standard nomenclature puts the cylinder width as the first figure and the separating width as the second figure. By the early 1920s and perhaps sooner, Nichols & Shepard was equipping their separators with roller bearings on the cylinder and wind stacker shafts. Due to the heavy load at these two points and frequent problems of bearings running hot, the use of roller bearings was well advised. Eventually the Nichols & Shepard line would use ball and roller bearings extensively in its machines.

For many years, Nichols & Shepard promoted its 4 Threshermen as being the successful mark of their separators. The first thresherman was the big cylinder which completely separated the kernels of grain from the stalk. The separating grate and check plate directly behind the cylinder took the name of 'The Man Behind the Gun' or the second thresherman. A steel-winged beater behind the cylinder behind the cylinder was the third thresherman, and the beating shakers were the fourth thresherman. Only the Red River Special used the Man Behind the Gun design.

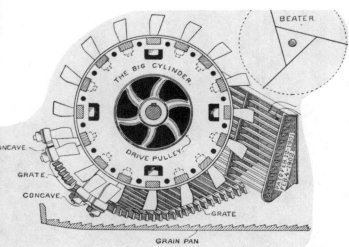

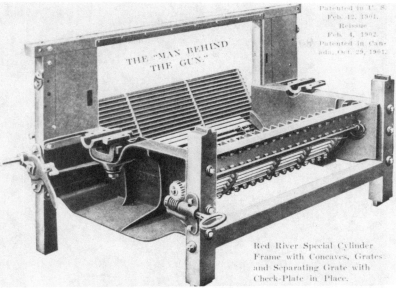

A diagrammatic view illustrates the large diameter cylinder used in the Red River Special threshing machine. Grates were placed beneath the cylinder, and the separating grate and its check plate were the secret of the Red River Special design. By using a large-diameter cylinder it was possible to increase the concave surface. Up to ten rows of concave teeth could be used if necessary. Ordinarily however, only two rows of teeth were used. The steel-winged beater directly behind the cylinder tended to pound any loose grain from the straw.

Red River Special Cylinder Frame with Concaves, Grates and Separating Grate with Check-Plate in Place.

Eli W. Flagg received Patent No. 668,041 on February 12, 1901. It was reissued as No. Re 11,965 a year later. These patents essentially protected the Man Behind the Gun principle used thereafter in the Nichols & Shepard design. Shown here is an early design with plain bearings; roller bearings were substituted in the 1920s. The entire concave unit and separating grate were built as an integral unit of steel and cast iron. The small worm gear and adjusting handle are for the purpose of raising and lowering the concave teeth relative to the cylinder.

In the 1920s Nichols & Shepard issued a special thresher catalog entitled, How Good Threshers are Built. It was a pictorial walking tour through the N & S factory. The Red River Special began life as a mere skeleton of steel and cast iron. All structural components were tied together in such a manner that the resulting framework was analogous to a bridge; great strength with a minimum of weight. All painted parts were finished by dipping to insure that paint would creep into every corner and joint.

After the frame was assembled and placed on wheels, the cleaning mill and grain auger, the cleaning shoe, and the grain pan were installed. Using a progressive assembly line, the Red River Special then moved to the second assembly floor. As shown here, the cylinder and concave unit are being drifted into place. Unit assembly was used wherever possible; that is, units such as this complete cylinder assembly were built in various parts of the plant, and these units were then installed on the machine.

Assembly of the cylinder was a task which required considerable mechanical skill. The cast cylinder heads were first balanced statically, as shown at the right. Lead weights were used to put each head in static balance. At this point the ground cylinder shaft and its two heads were placed on the stand to the left, and the double cylinder bars were put into place. Once these had been placed in suitable notches in the heads, steel bands were shrunk around them. This permanently and effectually made the shaft, the heads, and the cylinder bars an integral unit.

Nichols & Shepard Company

Shown here is a band being driven into place over the cylinder head and bars. Each cylinder bar actually consisted of two high-grade steel bars, one over the other. The bars were punched to receive the cylinder teeth farther down the line. By heating the band to a cherry red and driving it over the head and bars, it squeezed the entire unit together almost as a solid mass. Once the bands were in place the cylinder went down a small trolley line to receive further machining and for the installation of the cylinder teeth.

Once the cylinder teeth were installed, another workman assumed the task of tightening the nuts which held each tooth in place. This job was made much easier by the use of a mechanical device built for the purpose. It is partially visible in the background, as is obvious by the shielded line shaft belt. Chances are that a telescoping shaft with suitable universal joints permitted the tightening of each nut, and presumably the tightening was governed by some sort of torque limiting device.

This threshing cylinder has had the bands shrunk in place and now rests in a special cradle built over a small rail trolley. A workman is installing the cylinder teeth, and is using power equipment to insure that the teeth rest solidly in the square socket already punched into the bars. Great care was exercised throughout the building of the cylinder, since accurate spacing of the cylinder teeth was essential for correct threshing. By adopting numerous assembly line techniques, N & S maintained excellent quality control throughout the process.

After having the teeth driven into place, each completed cylinder was again subjected to a static balance. After this came the dynamic balancing. This running balance was taken with the cylinder at its normal operating speed. Lead weights of various sizes were used to obtain perfect balance, and these could easily be inserted in holes provided for them in the cylinder heads. Highly skilled mechanics were required for this purpose, since much of the machine's reputation rested on whether it would run without shake and vibration in the field.

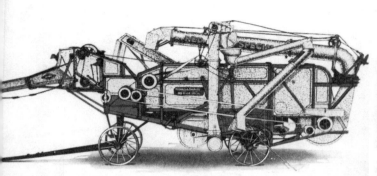

Production of the 22 x 36 all-steel threshers began in 1917 and ended in 1948. This popular machine was a virtual clone of its larger cousins, and embodied all the features found in the bigger machines. Hyatt roller bearings were used extensively; this feature provided an easy running machine with a minimum of maintenance problems. The cylinder was 22 inches wide and also had a diameter of 22 inches over the teeth. At its normal operating speed of 1,065 rpm this gave a tip speed of over 6,000 feet per minute. When fully equipped, this machine weighed 5,650 pounds.

Nichols & Shepard offered their 28 x 40 all-steel thresher in the 1917-21 period. It followed the same design as the other Red River Special threshers, differing primarily in its size. In 1928 Nichols & Shepard adopted the use of Rockwood pulleys. The use of fiber pulleys was a distinct advantage. The Rockwood provided a better grip on the belt for much improved power transmission. Thus began a gradual phaseout of the time-honored cast iron pulleys.

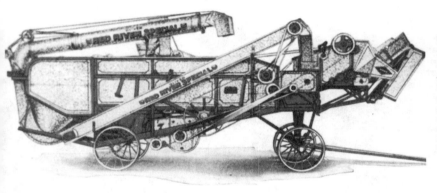

Undoubtedly one of the most popular sizes was the 28 x 46 Red River Special. Built from 1916 to 1948, this ever-popular machine was marketed throughout the Americas. Standard equipment included a Hart feeder and a Hart grain weigher. Special sieves and screens were available for virtually any seed crop. In addition, a pea and bean attachment permitted the threshing and cleaning of these important crops. Fully equipped, the 28 x 46 weighed 6,880 pounds. Fully equipped, it carried a 1927 list price of $1,495.

Red River Special threshers used an overshot cleaning fan driven directly from the cylinder shaft. Wind blinds at each end of the fan controlled the volume of the cleaning blast. Distribution of the blast was controlled by two adjustable wind boards. The cleaning shoe was designed so that chaff and dirt was blown away from the grain and toward the stacker chute. Tailings, or material which was either unthreshed or unseparated was returned via a tailings elevator to the cylinder. In 1917 and 1918 Nichols & Shepard offered a 30 x 46 Red River Special.

The 30 x 52 Red River Special was built in the 1918-28 period. This machine provided slightly more threshing capacity than the popular 28 x 46 model. While the 28 x 46 and smaller models used a 12-bar cylinder, the 30 x 52 marked a change to the 16-bar cylinder. It was 28 inches in diameter over the teeth. Its operating speed of 850 rpm gave a tip speed of about 6,200 feet per minute. The larger cylinder diameter also permitted the use of additional concaves if needed. Up to ten rows of concave teeth could be used, or a total of 125 teeth. Ordinarily, only one or two concaves were used. This machine was priced at $1,930.

Nichols & Shepard Company

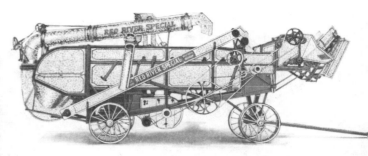

The 32 x 52 Red River Special was offered in an all-steel design between 1917 and 1921. It had previously been offered with wood construction. Grain threshers were almost exclusively shipped by rail. A complete set of belts, sieves, tools, and other items was shipped with each machine. Occasional losses of these items occurred enroute. If the belts and other items were stored inside the machine during shipment, it was relatively easy for those so inclined to crawl inside and avail themselves of these items. Consequently, some manufacturers packed the loose items securely in heavy wooden boxes. Some even went so far as to ship these items separately to prevent their untimely removal.

The big 36 x 60 Red River Special all-steel design was built between 1916 and 1927. By the latter time, combines were already making inroads in the wheat country, and these regions were the home of the largest threshers. A big 2 3/16 inch cylinder shaft was used. It carried 16 double steel bars with a total of 136 teeth. Beneath were the concaves, each holding 31 teeth. Up to five bars could be used, each holding two rows of teeth. For special needs, corrugated teeth could be furnished in lieu of the standard. Weighing nearly 10,000 pounds, the 36 x 60 was over 27 feet long including the feeder and the wind stacker. In 1927 the 36 x 60 Red River Special listed at $2,135.

Red River Special threshers were normally furnished with a specially designed Hart feeder. By loosening the braces the entire feeder could be tilted forward by one man. This provided complete access to the cylinder. In pointing out the advantages of the design, Nichols & Shepard commented: 'When you're running right along, you won't need this tilting feature, but when something happens---when a fork gets into the cylinder, as pitchforks sometimes will...you will surely appreciate the ease with the N & S Hart Special tilts up.' Nichols & Shepard offered their 36 x 56 machine between 1916 and 1921.

With the exclusive 'Beating Shaker' design of the Red River Special machines, the straw racks oscillated at 160 strokes per minute. This rate was far less than was used in most competing machines. The double-drive system simply meant that each end of the shaker crankshaft was driven from the cylinder shaft. In this illustration the tailings return elevator is obvious; it carried tailings from the back of the shoe back up to the cylinder for another pass. A close look shows the adjustable fan blinds, although they are in the closed position. This machine sold for about $2,050. Nichols & Shepard built the 32 x 56 machine between 1916 and 1935.

Production of the big 40 x 60 Red River Special extended only from 1916 to 1919. Its first cousin, the 40 x 64 model was built in 1917 and 1918. The all-steel 44 x 64 machine was built only in 1917; a few 44 x 64 wood machines were built prior to that time. These huge machines were seldom seen in the average midwestern threshing ring. Their huge capacity made them better candidates for the large wheat growing regions where a single job might have several thousand acres to thresh and clean. It was in these same areas that the combine made its first real inroads into the threshing business. By the 1930s the combine was coming on strong, and by the early 1950s the majority of grain was being harvested with combines.

Five different sizes of Nichols & Shepard rice threshers were built, from the 22 x 36 up to the 36 x 60 size. Rice straw when threshed was often in damp or bad condition, making it difficult to separate the kernels of rice from the rice straw without cracking them. From the exterior, this machine appears to be little different than the ordinary thresher. However, the special conditions required special treatment, and this machine was modified especially for the rice harvest. Various attachments were available for ordinary threshers to handle small seed crops such as clover, timothy, and alfalfa.

Unfortunately, little material has been located to fully or even partially indicate the extent of Nichols & Shepard steam engine manufacturing activity. However, it is known that the company was offering single-cylinder engines as late as 1927, only a short time before the Oliver merger. For some years the company built the single-cylinder style in three sizes; 16-50, 20-70, and 25-85 horsepower sizes. For those unfamiliar with steam engine ratings, the first figure is the nominal horsepower, while the second indicates the belt horsepower. However, the latter figure was usually underrated to some extent. As late as 1917 the company also built single-cylinder engines in 13-40 and 30-98 horsepower sizes.

In 1927 the 16-50 single cylinder traction engine sold for $2,550 with a 10% discount for cash on delivery. These engines used a dry bottom in the firebox. The closed or wet bottom style carried water entirely beneath and around the bottom of the boiler. While this may have improved water circulation slightly, the advantage was offset with the problems entailed with sediment collecting in this area. A double-hung link reverse was used on the single-cylinder engines. From the boiler to the smallest detail, Nichols & Shepard insisted on the highest quality materials and workmanship.

The double-hung link reverse was a standard feature of the single-cylinder Nichols & Shepard engines. Two eccentrics were mounted on the crankshaft. Their movement oscillated the curved link over an adjustable pivot point. The large bell crank seen in this illustration was connected to the engineer's reverse lever. Moving it forward or back raised or lowered the curved link, and this moved the engine in forward or reverse motion. This design was very simple, although it had the disadvantage of premature wear in its many pivot points.

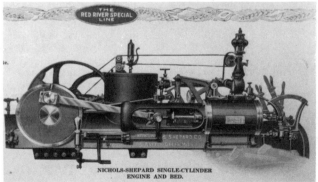

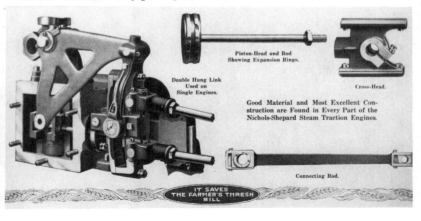

In 1927 the 20-70 single-cylinder engine listed at $3,190 and the big 25-85 style sold for $3,590. An 8 x 12 inch cylinder was used on the 16-50 model, and this was raised to 8 1/2 x 12 inches for the 20-70 sizes. A 9 1/4 x 12 inch bore and stroke was featured on the 25-85 traction engine. The single-cylinder engines also were side-mounted, that is, the stub shafts for the drive wheels were riveted to the side of the firebox. While ordinarily furnished for burning coal and wood, the two largest sizes could also be furnished as straw burners.

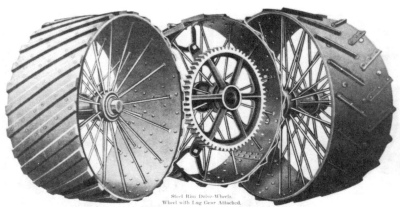

Nichols & Shepard claimed their drive wheels to be the strongest made. Of course the same claim was made by most of the engine builders. However, N & S used an all-steel wheel with cast steel bull gears. To the left is shown a traction wheel with so-called municipal lugs attached. These were also known as road lugs, and were intended to minimize damage to road surfaces. On the right is a special drive wheel designed especially for plowing and other heavy traction work. It was built with three rows of spokes, and could only be used on the 25-85 single-cylinder and the 25-90 double-cylinder styles. For a time the company also built the double-cylinder engine in a 30-98 size.

By about 1920 all Nichols & Shepard double-cylinder engines were built in the rear-mounted design. This meant that the rear axle was placed behind the boiler, thus relieving it from any stresses imposed by the tractive load. Solid steel pinion gears were used, and this made breakage practically unknown. The company strongly recommended the double-cylinder style as a plowing engine. Yet, the use of steam power for plowing had nearly ended by the 1920s, since gasoline tractors were taking over that line of work. This double-cylinder engine is shown without the canopy; it was an extra-cost option.

Nichols & Shepard double-cylinder rear-mounted engines were built in 16-60, 20-75, and 25-90 horsepower sizes. The smallest used two cylinders of 6 1/4 x 10 inch bore and stroke. The bore was increased to 6 5/8 inches for the 20-75, while the 25-90 carried a 7-inch bore. All used a common stroke of ten inches, and all sizes of single and double-cylinder engines operated at 225 rpm. The big 25-90 boiler used 51 flues of 2 1/2 inch diameter, and having a length of 94 inches, or nearly 8 feet.

A rear view of the Nichols & Shepard engines illustrates the ordinary coal and wood burner on the left, with the straw burner on the right. For straw burning, part of the platform was removed to provide better access for the fireman. In certain areas where other fuels were scarce, straw was used as fuel for threshing. It was an excellent fuel but required constant feeding. Old-timers relate that the secret was in keeping a slow but steady stream of straw headed into the firebox, rather than trying to fire with large amounts of straw at irregular intervals.

During 1911 Nichols & Shepard began testing a gasoline tractor. However, like many of the other old-line steam engine builders, steam had been and always would be the king. Yet, when Nichols & Shepard decided to build a tractor, their design epitomized the concept of heavy duty tractors of the time. Weight was a minor factor at the time. Note the heavy structural steel foundation of the 35-70 Nichols & Shepard tractor. Two sizes were offered initially; the 25-50 and the huge 35-70.

A Nichols & Shepard catalog notes that Pickering governors were used on their tractors. The governor was identical to that used on the Nichols & Shepard traction engines. The Ball Ranger unit on the Pickering governor provided variable engine speeds ranging from 125 to 375 rpm. However, it was recommended that the engine be run at its normal speed of 375 rpm for plowing and threshing. Shown here is the Pickering governor, together with an attached carburetor.

Nichols & Shepard tractors used a two-cylinder engine. The cylinders were placed side-by-side so that the cylinder heads, valve gear, and all of the working parts were within easy reach of the operator. The double water-jacket was cast en bloc. This tied the cylinders together as an integral unit. This held the moving parts in rigid alignment. Note the heavy lugs used to secure the cylinders to the crankcase; also the heavy mounting feet at the head-end of the cylinders for attachment to the tractor frame.

In the Nichols & Shepard tractor design the valves were placed on an angle relative to each other. This construction permitted the use of large valves, a requirement for efficient use of large cylinder bores. The cylinder head was cast integral with the cylinder barrel, eliminating problems with leaky cylinder heads. The hemispherical design of the cylinder head was another feature. Each valve operated within its own removable cage, making repair work much easier.

As is obvious from this illustration, Nichols & Shepard tractors used a turned rod. This means that the connecting rod was either forged roughly to size and then turned to final dimensions, or it was machined from a solid block of steel. The bearing caps were secured to the connecting rod with two large bolts. This method permitted easy replacement of a connecting rod liner, and this was a distinct advantage when working many miles from the nearest repair shop. Nichols & Shepard catalogs also note that '...we have never heard of a case in which it was necessary to remove a crankshaft from a Nichols & Shepard tractor for any reason whatever.'

Shown here are the valve components of the Nichols & Shepard tractor. The valve cage was built with a taper which permitted it to seat tightly in its mating hole within the cylinder head. Four bolts secured the valve cage in this position. To the left of the valve cage is shown the well proportioned rocker arm used to operate the valves. At the extreme left is the huge valve, which includes its threaded end, keeper, and locking nut. Terror of all terrors for an engine was, and is, the loss of the valve keeper and dropping the valve into the cylinder.

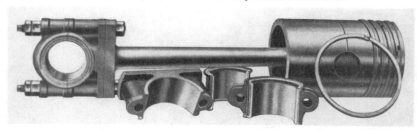

Nichols & Shepard

The heavy duty clutch of the Nichols & Shepard tractor followed the design of its contemporaries. Integral with the clutch spider was a shaft extension which carried the main pinion gear. It could be shifted into or out of mesh with the first reduction gear to the traction gear train. N & S tractors used gears of a coarse pitch and a wide face. This gave each gear tooth greater strength. All-steel pinions were used, and the large gears were made of cast semi-steel. No bevel gears were used in the compensating gear or differential. Instead, spur gears were used.

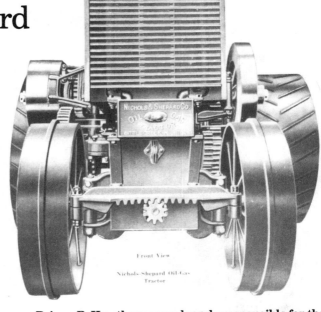

Front View
Nichols-Shepard Oil-Gas Tractor

Primm R. Hawthorne was largely responsible for the design of the Nichols & Shepard tractor. Hawthorne had formerly been associated with Fairbanks, Morse & Company, and before that had been associated with International Harvester Company. One significant patent issued to Hawthorne was No. 1,090,476. It covered the essential radiator design shown here. Issued on March 17, 1914 this patent had been filed about a year before. Curiously, no other patents have been located regarding this tractor, despite some of its unique design features.

Front View
Nichols-Shepard Oil-Gas
Tractor
25-50 H. P. and 35-70 H. P. Sizes

Apparently the radiator design of the Nichols & Shepard tractors changed sometime during production. However, no production figures have been located, nor has any specific data emerged regarding changes to the tractor line. Nichols & Shepard issued a small catalog relating to their so-called Oil-Gas Tractors, but the company never appears to have promoted their tractor line to the extent that they championed their steam traction engines. The two large tanks atop the tractor are for fuel, while the smaller one holds gasoline for starting the engine.

Nichols & Shepard 25-50 tractors were of two-cylinder design and used a 9 inch bore with a 12 inch stroke. The crankshaft was four inches in diameter and used a center bearing for added stability. A force-feed lubricator kept all major bearing surfaces amply supplied with oil. Seven feeds were used. Two of them terminated at slingers mounted to each of the two crank throws. Three were used on the main bearings, and the remaining two were directed to lubricating the engine cylinders. A heavy lay shaft alongside the engine terminated with bevel gears at the cylinder head. A cross-shaft across the front of the cylinder carried the valve cams.

The huge 35-70 Nichols & Shepard tractor was of two-cylinder design. Its 10 1/2 x 14-inch bore and stroke yielded well over 90 belt horsepower, yet its rated speed was only 375 rpm. Unfortunately, no production figures for the 35-70 and 25-50 tractors have been located, although the 25-50 is still listed in the 1927 price list. At that time it carried a retail tag of $2,990. Within a few years after its introduction the 35-70 was relegated to obscurity by the onslaught of small tractors. The fast pace of technological change, coupled with intense competition, and an unfavorable market climate were some major factors which made the 35-70 a virtual exercise in futility.

GIVES AS STRONG, STEADY, RELIABLE POWER TO A THRESHER AS A STEAM ENGINE

About 1920, and perhaps slightly before, Nichols & Shepard offered a third tractor model, their 20-42. This smaller version remained on the market for only a short time. In fact, it was submitted to the Nebraska Tractor Test Laboratory at Lincoln in 1923. However, before testing began the tractor was withdrawn. From all appearances and a perusal of extant literature, the 20-42 left the tractor scene about this same time, so testing procedures quickly became a moot point. Although smaller in size than the 25-50 and the 35-70 it followed the same general design features.

Late in the 1920s Nichols & Shepard offered their 20-40 farm tractor. It was actually a Lauson tractor built by John Lauson Company at New Holstein, Wisconsin. It was sold as the Nichols & Shepard "Lauson-Built" tractor. At least four models were offered; the 16-32 and 20-35, the 20-40, and the 20-40 Thresherman's Special. Prices ranged from $1,650 for the 16-32 up to $2,475 for the Thresherman's Special. The latter included 20-inch rear drive wheels, a canopy top, radiator guard, special thresherman hitch, exhaust whistle, and flat bar lugs. Electric light equipment was available at an extra cost of $85 in 1927.

During the late 1920s Nichols & Shepard began marketing their own combine. A salient feature was the maintenance of the great developments which characterized the Red River Special thresher line. Shown here is a photograph taken in the early 1930s showing a 'solid train load of Oliver Nichols & Shepard combines for Nebraska farmers.' Thus, it can be stated categorically that the Oliver combines had their inception with the machines that had been developed by Nichols & Shepard. In 1927, Nichols & Shepard added another advantage to their machines by using Armco Ingot Iron for all the sheet metal parts.

Nichols & Shepard combines were offered in five main widths of 10, 12, 15, 16 1/2, and 20 feet. Combinations of separating units and power plants were available for virtually any situation. The small ten-foot size was equipped with a Waukesha engine, while all other models were furnished with a Hercules motor. Special protective devices were used on the carburetor, magneto and governor of these engines to minimize problems with dirt and chaff. A special air cleaner was provided, and the radiator was equipped with a protective screen and a special non-clogging core.

This procession of combines is at work on 4,600 acres of wheat near Texhoma, Oklahoma in 1929. A chart in a 1929 Nichols & Shepard catalog notes that the 10-foot Model A had a capacity of 100 to 400 acres per season, while the big Model E with its 20-foot cutter bar could handle up to 1,200 acres in a season. The Model E could handle a 20-foot head in average grain and straw. However, with heavy grain and straw it was advised to windrow the standing grain with a 16-foot cut in order to maintain the cleaning capacity of the machine. A prairie-type Model E combine with a 20-foot cut had a 1927 list price of $2,690. This included a Hercules 38 horsepower engine. The grain tank added another $200 to this price.

Nichols & Shepard Company

This photograph from the Oliver Corporation files illustrates four Nichols & Shepard 20-foot combines at work near Burlington, Colorado in 1929. The land was owned by Burlington Development Company of that city. Every machine in this operation was Oliver-built, including eight Hart-Parr 18-36 tractors. For the 1929 season Burlington Development Company was harvesting 8,800 acres of wheat which averaged 40 bushels, or something over 350,000 bushels!

Hyatt roller bearings were used extensively on the Nichols & Shepard combines. In addition, these machines were equipped with the Alemite zerk lubrication system, relatively new in the 1920s. This eliminated time-consuming grease cups, and virtually eliminated the need for an oil can. To accommodate the excessive width of the machine the header was detachable and could be towed behind the combine. The machine operator stood on a deck which permitted an unobstructed view of the grain coming into the machine. From this platform the operator could control the engine, header, and other essential operations.

Late in the 1920s Nichols & Shepard began marketing their newly developed corn picker. It was built especially for use with the Fordson tractor. It was of single-row design. While this seems inordinately small by today's standards, picking a row at a time by machine was much faster than picking corn by hand. Although some folks enjoyed corn picking by hand, the majority viewed this job as one of drudgery and monotony. The technical challenges of a successful corn picker were so great that harvesting ear corn was one of the last major crops to be mechanized.

From this Nichols & Shepard corn picker of the late 1920s came the Oliver corn picker line. Using the good features and adding new ones took time, and it was not until the mid-1930s that a truly successful corn picker emerged. Here is shown a Nichols & Shepard corn picker as designed for the Fordson tractor. Despite the great popularity of the Fordson, its production in the United States ended about the same time that this picker made its first appearance. Yet, the supply of Fordson tractors remained abundant for some years to come. After the Oliver merger of 1929 marketing of this design was somewhat subdued, since Oliver had its own tractors to sell. It remains significant that one of the last Nichols & Shepard developments would eventually have a profound effect on mechanized farming, yet this N & S development has been virtually forgotten by history.

Oliver Chilled Plow Company

The steel plow was born of necessity. Going back to the time of Thomas Jefferson, the eastern states used cast iron plows. They worked well in the soil found there, but they would not scour in the sticky midwestern soils. Thus, the steel plow saw its development in the 1830s as a solution to this problem. Meanwhile, the cast iron plow remained popular in the eastern states.

Attempts to harden the cast iron plow began almost with the first use of these plows to make them more durable. In these times the chilling process to harden cast iron was not well understood. Making the chilled plow a practical success was due to the efforts of James Oliver. He began experimenting with the chilling process soon after opening his plow factory at South Bend, Indiana in 1853. It should be noted that chilled iron takes its name from the process involved. Normal sand castings are used, but behind a thin wall of sand an iron 'chill' is placed to absorb the heat of the molten metal more quickly. This sudden chilling of the hot metal gives it a tough skin, although the center part of the casting does not become so hard. When Oliver began his experiments, not much had been done in this regard. Many different factors were involved, including the chemical makeup of the iron, size and placement of the chills, to name a few.

The chilled plow, due to its very hard outer skin, was able to scour in heavy, sticky soils. It was also capable of far greater wearability than common cast iron plows. So, Oliver really solved two problems.

Thomas Jefferson had formulated the design of an ideal moldboard, and Jethro Wood had put Jefferson's ideas into practice. Using plows of this design, Oliver began his experiments. Few of the cast iron plows then made even approached the optimum design concerning lightness of draft and a properly laid furrow. One major defect in cast iron plows was the frequent presence of soft spots in the casting. On the other hand, if the casting was chilled to extremes it became brittle as glass. Obtaining sound, uniform castings was one problem which Oliver eventually solved. Eventually he developed a unique annealing process by which it was possible to toughen the metal without softening it. Once this was achieved the Oliver chilled iron plow became a practical success.

Oliver's first patent was No. 76,939 of April 21, 1868. It covered the essential features of the chilled iron plow. In February of the following year, Patent No. 86,579 was issued, covering the unique chilling process which Oliver had developed. A unique plow standard was then developed by Oliver, and this is shown in Patent No. 111,965 of February 21, 1871. No. 128,061 was issued in 1872 and No. 144,785 was granted in 1873. These were the first of a great many patents granted to James Oliver.

During the formative years up to 1868, Oliver kept his foundry busy making castings for Singer sewing machines, casting wagon skeins for Studebaker and others, and making numerous other castings on order. Oliver continued making wagon skeins and other castings until 1874. By that time the volume of the plow business had grown to such an extent that from then on Oliver devoted full time to making chilled iron plows.

On July 22, 1868 the South Bend Iron Works was incorporated to manufacture the Oliver Chilled Plow. Up to that time the business had been run as a partnership. In 1870 the famous Oliver trademark was designed and adopted, and would from that time forward, appear on every Oliver chilled plow.

The *South Bend Register* published by Schuyler Colfax (later a Vice-President of the United States) commented in 1871 regarding Oliver: "If he keeps on improving his plow it will soon have no rivals in the country. The popularity of the Oliver Chilled Plow is almost unprecedented in the history of plows." That year, some 1,500 plows were sold. Three years later the company made 17,000 and had to build a new factory. From this point the company continued to expand, not only its physical plant, but its product line. Eventually, other tillage implements were added. Under careful management the company continued to flourish. After James Oliver died in 1908, his son, J. D. Oliver took over the reins of the company and steered the firm through good times and bad. Proof of the size of the Oliver Chilled Plow Works may be noted from the fact that in 1910 the company purchased over 40,000 tons of pig iron. Parenthetically, James Oliver was a subject of Elbert Hubbard's *Journeys to the Homes of Great Business Men*.

By 1910 Oliver was building an extensive variety of plows and other tillage implements. The company was also building engine gang plows; an entirely new kind of plow from the walking plow or the two-bottom horse gang. The epitome of the Oliver plow line came in 1911 with a huge 50-bottom plow. It was pulled variously by three Rumely OilPull tractors and by three IHC Mogul 45 tractors. This demonstration was held under the auspices of Purdue University. With this plow, about 60 feet of sod was turned over in a single pass. The Purdue demonstrations provided substantial advertising benefits, but after that time

Oliver Chilled Plow Company

James Oliver was born in Whitehaugh, Roxburyshire, Scotland on August 28, 1823. He was the son of a shepherd. The family came to America in 1835, finally settling at Mishawaka, Indiana in 1840. Fifteen years later James Oliver moved to South Bend and began manufacturing plows. After many losses, a lot of hard work, and not a few discouragements, he finally succeeded in making a successful plow using chilled iron. By the time of his death on March 2, 1908 the Oliver Chilled Plow Works covered fifty eight acres, with twenty five of them being under roof.

James Oliver adopted his famous trademark already in 1870, although it was not registered at that time. Probably in reference to the advertising of Deere & Company which states, "John Deere Gave to the World the Steel Plow," this trademark states, 'Oliver Gave to the World the Chilled Plow.' Initially the company made other castings, including the cast iron wagon skeins which were needed in large quantities by the nearby Studebaker Company and others. With the complete success of the chilled plow by the 1870s, Oliver dropped all outside foundry work to concentrate solely on chilled plows, and eventually, other implements.

Oliver placed more emphasis on building smaller tractor plows, correctly anticipating the coming of the smaller two and three-plow tractors.

By the 1920s it was becoming increasingly obvious that a full line manufacturer had the market advantage, and so in 1929 the Oliver Chilled Plow Works merged with Hart-Parr and the others of the combine to form the Oliver Farm Equipment Corporation.

Joseph D. Oliver was the only son of James and Susan (Doty) Oliver. For some years prior to the death of his father, J. D. was the financial manager of the firm, and took the reins of the company after his father's death. J. D. was often in the plow shops. The story is related that one day a couple of patternmakers were arguing about the design of a seat for a gang plow. Mr. Oliver walked over to the sand heap and worked his bottomside into the foundry sand. He got up, dusted the sand from his britches and announced to the two workmen, "Make the seat to fit that!"

A well-worn original photograph of about 1912 illustrates the Oliver Chilled Plow Works of that time. As previously indicated, the plant covered nearly sixty acres, with almost half of it under a roof! Considering the tremendous technical difficulties entailed in the development of the chilled plow, the Oliver success story is truly a story of 'Yankee ingenuity!' James Oliver was a subject included in *America's Successful Men* published by the *New York Tribune* in 1896.

Oliver Chilled Plow Company

For many years this was the largest electric sign in the United States. Situated atop the Oliver Chilled Plow Works, this huge sign was 250 feet in length. At the center, it was 49 feet high. The plow in this sign was 59 feet long from tip to tip. Oliver Works contained a huge foundry that included heating ovens for making malleable iron. Using about 40,000 tons of pig iron per year, Oliver works used a crane with a huge magnet to transfer pig iron in the yard.

Shortly before his death in 1908 a photographer shot this scene of James Oliver plowing his last furrow. Mr. Oliver spent over half a century in the plow business, even though he was past thirty years of age before moving to South Bend and establishing a foundry there. This walking plow with a wood beam was probably similar to Oliver's earliest designs. However, before his death the Oliver Works was building plows in literally hundreds of styles and sizes.

The curious shape of the moldboard belies the intent of this plow. It was called a breaking plow, intended for turning over virgin prairie. These plows were sold by the thousands, and for homesteaders, a plow was one of the essentials. One person could turn over only a few acres in a day, and this only by walking along behind the plow, one foot in the furrow and one out. Incredibly, plows like this one helped to tame the prairies and turn them into vast fields of grain.

One of the many plow variations was this Hillside plow. The moldboard was specially shaped for this work, and this plow is equipped with the adjustable gauge wheel which was patented by James Oliver. Many of the Oliver walking plows were made in various widths, ranging anywhere from 10 inches to 16 inches. By about 1900, most of the walking plows were available with a wooden beam or a steel beam, and attachments included the gauge wheel and various jointers and rolling coulters.

About 1885 James Oliver introduced what would become the No. 40 chilled iron plow. In addition, the Oliver Works built chilled iron plows in many different configurations, each intended for a specific type of soil or a specific plowing method. For many years Oliver printed the *Oliver Plow Book*. It was a detailed explanation of plowing and plowing methods, going so far as to instruct plowmen about the influence and importance of proper plowing methods.

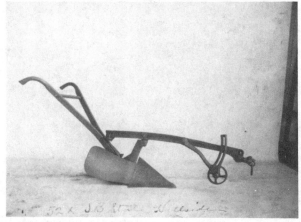

Oliver Chilled Plow Company

A 1920 Oliver catalog notes that 'Government investigation shows that the average life of all walking plows is 11.7 years. [Yet] many Oliver No. 40 plows have been used more than thirty five years and are still in use.' It could be handled by two horses under most conditions, but three could be used in difficult soils. The plow share had a unique shape, in that it extended to the top of the moldboard in front. In effect, this gave the plow a new shin whenever the plowshare was replaced.

A typical plowing scene shows how it really was in the 'good old days.' This farmer is taking his plow down the field, with two sorrels and a bay horse in the lead. After the horses were trained to the plow, they were able to make their way with little assistance from the plowman. Many farmers tied the lines together and put them over their back so that they could steer the team by twisting their shoulders. Once the plow was at its proper depth it took little effort to keep it there. Pushing down on the handles would raise the plow out of the ground, while lifting up on them would cause it to plow more deeply.

This farmer has the lines over his shoulder, permitting him to steer when necessary by simply twisting his shoulders one way or the other. This team even has the comfort of fly nets. Once the successful chilled plow was developed following 1855, its popularity was assured within a few short years. The metamorphosis was not permanent. Recent decades have seen the development of other tillage implements, including the chisel plow. These implements have virtually replaced the plow as a primary tillage tool.

These metal pourers in the malleable iron foundry are waiting for the signal to begin pouring. Each man is equipped with a pouring ladle. Pouring white hot iron was not only a hot and dirty job, it was also exceedingly dangerous. Yet, the job paid well, despite its rigors. Securing high quality castings with daily consistency took no little skill on the part of the foundrymen as well as for those responsible for the metallurgical department.

This workman is pouring molten iron into a sand mold. After being rammed up the pattern is removed and the mold is closed. Suitable pouring sprues are left for the entrance of the molten iron, and the mold is vented to help relieve trapped air and gases. Weights are placed on each mold to keep the top half from rising due to the weight of the molten metal. The original photograph and other factory scenes are contained in an original photograph album which was assembled at the Oliver Works. It is now held by the Floyd County Historical Society at Charles City, Iowa.

Shown here is a workman about to quench a plow share. Proper tempering and heat treating was a prerequisite for plow work. If too soft, the plow share would not wear for long, and if too hard it became brittle and would break easily. Achieving consistent results was undoubtedly one of the biggest challenges to face Oliver's pioneering efforts. James Oliver was ultimately successful, and his success made him an immensely wealthy man. Note the ladder with a re-placement rung nailed in place; truly a safety engi-neer's nightmare!

After being cast, it was necessary for the moldboard to be polished. This huge polishing machine is pow-ered from an overhead lineshaft. The buffing wheels were charged with emery powder. This was secured to the face of the buff with a special cement. After a time, most of the emery was worn off, and workmen then coated it again with cement. After it became tacky it was rolled through the emery powder. Drying overnight, it was ready for use again the next day. This process was repeated day-in, and day-out for years on end.

This workman is fitting moldboards for an Oliver tractor plow. It appears that Oliver began building tractor plows as early as 1910, and perhaps even before that time. The company guessed correctly that the coming of tractor power would require the design of plows especially suited to that purpose. Fitting up a plow was a job which required considerable skill. More than just putting bolts into the proper holes, it also required an innate talent to adjust the plow so that it would work properly in the field. The truth is that far more plows were set incorrectly set than those which had the benefit of proper adjustments.

These workmen are putting the final polish to some plow parts. In order for the plow to scour it was essential that the moldboard have the best possible finish. Otherwise the soil would stick to the mold-board. The only choice for the farmer was to take the plow out of the ground, clean off the moldboard and go again. Farmers were highly protective of a plow that scoured easily and could be equally cantanker-ous if it didn't.

Oliver Chilled Plow Company

The huge production of the Oliver Works required the use of overhead track and trolleys to move component parts from one facility to another. Shown here are plow standards on the left which have just emerged from the paint department, and are now drying. To the right are the frame and axle for Oliver cultivators. While Oliver Works initially built plows exclusively, the line was gradually expanded to include a great many different tillage implements by the onset of the twentieth century.

A 1912 photograph in the engine room shows a huge Corliss steam engine which powered at least a portion of Oliver Works. Of undetermined make, this one is rated at 500 horsepower, and uses a 30 x 60 inch cylinder bore and stroke. Rated speed was probably under 100 rpm. The huge flywheel to the right delivered power via a flat belt to lineshafting. Through a complicated system of shafts, belts, and pulleys the power was transmitted throughout the factory for all belt powered machinery. Each machine had one of several different clutch mechanisms.

Oliver marketed this No. 1 Improved Gang Plow for many years. It used a foot lift mechanism placed in direct line with the seat. Pushing forward raised the bottoms and pushing downward forced them into the ground. The foot lift automatically locked into place when the bottoms were at their correct depth. An auxiliary lever on the landside of the plow gave sufficient leverage for raising the plow under the most difficult conditions. The front end of the furrow wheel connecting rod pivoted over the front furrow wheel axle, allowing the front wheel to turn in or out without affecting the rear furrow wheel. this permitted straight furrows and evenly turned corners.

The sulky plow was nothing more than a wheeled walking plow with a seat. It made plowing a lot easier than when walking behind a plow all day, and it permitted accurate and uniform adjustment of the plow. Yet, a few farmers looked on the sulky plow with disdain; the idea of riding instead of walking seemed nothing more than laziness. Moreover, the additional burden would 'kill the horses.' This plowing scene typifies the equipment and the methods.

Big families with lots of boys meant that more plows could be put to work in season. In this unidentified scene, nine horses are at work with three plows. About 1910 Oliver announced the James Oliver No. 11 sulky plow as the ultimate answer. The company claimed its outstanding feature was the ability to do good work in any and all soils. It was also said that the driver could do better work than with the best walking plow. Obviously this thought was intended to melt those who maintained that the walking plow was the *only* way to till the soil.

Typical of the Oliver plow line into the 1920s was this Oliver No. 9 sulky. Since it was a horsedrawn implement, Oliver also provided an extensive variety of eveners to attach the horses to the plow. If two horses were used then a simple doubletree was all that was necessary. Various styles of three-horse eveners were available. The four-horse evener was a tandem style with two horses abreast. The five-horse model used two horses abreast at the front, in tandem with three abreast at the plow. Six and seven-horse styles were also available.

The Oliver No. 51 sulky was available in 14 and 16-inch models. It used a foot-lift mechanism which provided easy work for the operator. The rear furrow wheel was 24 inches high; this placed the hub far enough above the ground so that it would not gather trash when plowing stubble or heavy weeds. The No. 51 was of the double-bail type, meaning that it would enter the ground point first. This feature provided quick penetration in hard ground with only a short distance of travel.

A great advantage of the No. 11 sulky was its ability to finish a land. This was achieved by an adjustable land wheel that permitted adjustment so that it could be dropped in the furrow and the last strip plowed out full length. Finishing a land had to be done with a walking plow for sulkies not thus equipped. Despite all the polishing done at the factory, the plow would not properly scour until it had taken an earth polish. The easiest way to achieve an earth polish was to take the plow into hard or sandy ground, operating it there until the polish appeared.

An unusual design was the No. 26 sulky plow. Its two-wheel design was intended particularly for very rough and uneven ground. This model was a horse-lift plow. Tripping the lifting latch set the mechanism in motion by locking the shifting lever to the revolving wheel hub. When the plow was raised to its full height the catch automatically released. Oliver went on to note that 'the trip can be operated by hand from the rear of the plow when it is desirable to walk.'

Reversible sulky plows were very popular with truck gardeners for use on level land where farmers desired to plow back and forth from one side of the field to the other. Reversible plows were also popular where irrigation was practiced because they left no dead furrow or back ridges to interfere with the flow of water. A guiding lever changed the angle of the pole or tongue with the plow to the extent that a direct line of draft is secured with either bottom.

Oliver Chilled Plow Company

Oliver No. 134-XX Corn Borer Tractor Sulky Plow

By 1910 Oliver Works was producing their own engine gang plow. It was intended for use with steam or tractor power. Each plow bottom was individually adjustable. A power lift system was provided on some plows but for others it was necessary to raise and lower each bottom individual by means of the hand levers. A plank runway was provided for the plowman to take care of the plows. With a steam outfit and engineer and a fireman were needed at the engine, plus a fuel hauler and a water hauler. So, at least five men were needed for plowing with steam power. Tractor power required only the plowman and the engineer.

Recognizing the threat imposed by the European corn borer, Oliver introduced their No. 134-XX Corn Borer Tractor Sulky Plow in the late 1920s. This big base tractor sulky turned wide, deep furrows to completely bury all stalks, stubble, and trash. This model was also ideally suited for turning marsh and brush land. For many years, farmers had few other methods of taming the voracious appetite of the corn borer. Eventually plant breeders developed resistant varieties to help minimize the problem. Oliver Works even had its own Exposition Room, a showroom of Oliver products. This building was 70 feet wide and nearly 200 feet in length.

By the 1920s Oliver had developed an vast line of tractor plows. Certain features were embodied in every Oliver tractor plow. Included was a positive power lift that permitted full operation from the tractor seat. Plow bottoms were available for virtually any soil type. Oliver plows featured a quick-detachable plow share which permitted changing without a wrench. The Oliver combined rolling coulter and jointer was regular equipment. Shown here is the No. 383 plow of the 1920s. It was available in two, three, and four-bottom sizes. The three-bottom could be converted to a two-bottom if necessary. Likewise, one bottom could be removed from the four-bottom style.

Typical of the 1920s was this Oliver No. 135 tractor plow. Built in a two-bottom size, it was ideal for a small tractor. The power lift was a standard feature, as was the crank-operated leveling device; it is plainly visible here. To get an idea of the size of Oliver's operations at South Bend, there were five miles of railroad track within the plant boundaries. The hydroelectric power plant delivered 3,600 horsepower. This was augmented by an aggregate of 4,500 horsepower available from the steam power house.

Unfortunately, no records have been located to indicate the production period of various Oliver plows. Having outlived their usefulness these records were presumably destroyed. Shown here are the No. 78 and No. 79 tractor plows. This three-bottom design was designed and constructed with the strength and durability to withstand tractor power. To accommodate varying tractor drawbar heights and varying tractor widths, the plow drawbar was designed with many possible settings. This was essential, since the drawbar height materially affected proper operation of the plow.

Oliver No. 135 Tractor Plow

Oliver Nos. 78 and 79 Tractor Plows

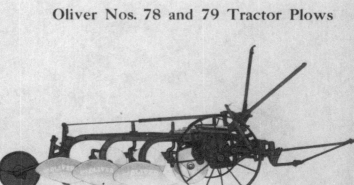

Oliver No. 16 Orchard Plow

Oliver No. 1 Middlebreaker

Oliver produced many different plows for specific applications. Included were a series of orchard plows. A salient feature of this style was its low-profile construction with no levers protruding above the plow frame. The special design permitted close working around trees with a minimal risk of damage. The design of the hitch permitted the tractor to operate in the open space between the trees with the plow running directly under the branches. Oliver even produced an Orange plow, not because it was painted orange, but because it was designed especially for use in orange groves.

Middlebreakers were designed for making furrows or breaking out old cane rows. The middlebreaker could also be used for subsoiling. This implement eliminated much of the hand work formerly associated with cane and cotton production. Oliver also promoted this No. 1 middlebreaker for tearing up old roadbeds and similar heavy duty work. Only a single bottom was used; its double-throw design required considerable power, often much more than was available from a small two-row tractor.

Oliver No. 2 Subsoiler

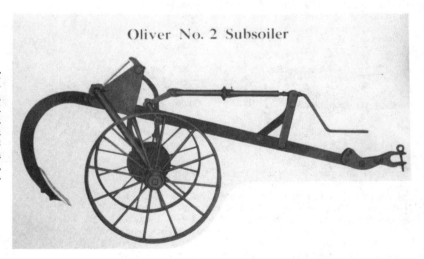

While the middlebreaker could be used for subsoiling operations, Oliver built their No. 2 subsoiler especially for this purpose. Great strength was necessary, since all of the available tractor power was applied to a single plow beam. Subsoiling was often required to break up hardpan, to provide better drainage, and to break up hardpan. Oliver claimed that their No. 2 subsoiler was also very popular as a road plow. Given the power required to operate any kind of scarifier, the single point of the subsoiler was obviously subjected to tremendous strains.

Oliver No. 3 ridge busters were designed to break down two rows or ridges at a time. This left the ground in fairly level condition for planting the next crop. The ridge buster was used after listed crops, in other words crops that had been planted on the ridges left by the lister or middlebreaker. This concept was used in both very wet and very dry ground. On wet ground the ridges gained more light and heat from the sun and the loose soil would dry out more quickly.

The No. 36 Oliver Tractor Cultivator was indeed a heavy duty field cultivator, although its stiff teeth somewhat resemble a contemporary chisel plow. Rather than functioning as a chisel plow however, the tractor cultivator was intended to be an effective weed destroyer. This unit is equipped with a power lift, driven from the ground wheels. Pulling the rope trips the lift mechanism which then lifts the cultivator into transport position. Pulling the rope again trips the lift so that the cultivator once again assumes the cultivating position. A large hand crank was provided to adjust the operating depth.

Oliver No. 3 Ridge Buster

Oliver No. 36 Tractor Cultivator

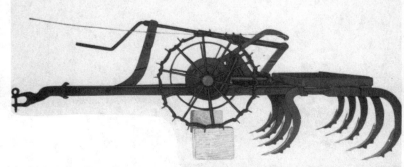

Oliver Chilled Plow Company

Oliver No. 333 Three-Row Tractor Lister

This three-row No. 333 tractor lister was a multi-use implement. It could be equipped with disc attachments for leveling the ridges after they had been formed by the lister. It could be equipped with corn planting attachments for dropping corn as listing progressed. The No. 333 could also be furnished as a lister, as shown here. A power lift mechanism was used on the No. 333; the cleated drivewheel and operating mechanism are plainly obvious in this photograph.

Oliver No. 10 Cane Cultivator

Another unique implement from Oliver Works was this No. 10 Cane Cultivator. It supplemented the work of the middlebreaker and was used for off barring and for cultivating the cane after the rows were formed. Through use of this implement and the middlebreaker, much of the time-honored hand labor associated with cane and cotton crops came to a rapid end. Many other Oliver implements were available for special cropping practices, and for each of them, a multitude of attachments was available.

Due to its low, leverless construction, reversible discs and its wide range of drawbar adjustment the No. D-102 was an ideal orchard disc plow. The ordinary depth and leveling levers were replaced with a simple screw device which does not extend above the wheels of the plow. A power lift system operated on the land wheel and was constructed low to avoid damage to low-hanging branches. As with so many other Oliver implements, this one was tailored especially for a specific crop and certain conditions.

Oliver No. D-102 Orchard Disc Plow

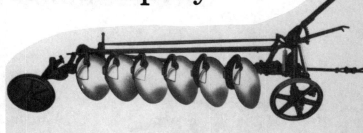

Disc plows are ideally suited for certain crops and certain soil conditions. The disc plow leaves the ground in a looser condition than the moldboard plow. Thus the soil is better able to absorb moisture that may come before fall planting. Disc plows are also commonly used on gumbo, hardpan, and black waxy soils where moldboard plows will not scour. This Oliver No. D-456 tractor disc plow is typical of production from the Oliver Works during the late 1920s.

Oliver Gold Digger Plow

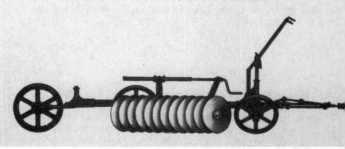

The Oliver Gold Digger Plow was designed especially for the wheat farmer. It was intended to plow every inch of ground, binding the trash between the furrows on top of the ground. This helped hold moisture and retard wind erosion. Ordinarily this machine was run at a depth of four to six inches. However, for summer fallowing it could be run at a shallower depth. Oliver claimed that this machine was also well suited to cutting corn stalks and plowing rice fields.

This photograph of September 1911 illustrates the Oliver No. 8 Chain-Drive Lister. As previously noted, listing offered several advantages. This tillage practice prevented wind erosion of light soils due to the ridges in the field. It saved moisture and promoted the use of more subsoil moisture by putting the roots deeper in the ground. The lister also reduced labor and permitted planting a larger acreage than would otherwise have been possible. With the lister, ridging and planting were achieved in a single operation.

Oliver Chilled Plow Company

Dated June 1911, this photograph shows the Oliver No. 3 Cotton Planter. Presumably this photograph marks the approximate date of introduction for this implement. As with many other implements in the Oliver line, the No. 3 was designed specifically for a special need. Oliver was constantly sensitive to the changing needs of farmers and had no hesitance to develop specialized implements for its clientele. After all, Oliver devoted almost 92,000 square feet of floor space just to fitting up plows and cultivators.

Oliver built this cotton and corn walking planter in several styles. It was intended for accurate planting of cotton, corn and other row crops in conditions that did not warrant the expense of a riding planter. The No. 22 and No. 23 walking planters were equipped with single seed cell cotton drops, while the No. 24 and No. 25 planters were equipped with a force-feed mechanism. Walking planters were available from Oliver at least until the 1929 formation of Oliver Farm Equipment Company, and in fact, appear to have remained on the market until World War Two.

New Britain Machine Company of New Britain, Connecticut introduced a small walking garden tractor during or shortly after World War One. Built in two sizes, it could be equipped with numerous tillage implements. Apparently the New Britain implements were tailored by Oliver Works, as is shown in this original Oliver Works photograph. The New Britain No. 1 sold for $400 in 1920, and the more elaborate, and slightly larger No. 2 sold for $450.

Oliver Works developed a number of different tractor cultivators by the early 1920s. This one was built around the Fordson tractor. At the time, Fordson tractors were in great abundance. The physical size and horsepower of the Fordson made it one of the best tractors of its time for cultivating work. In this instance, the front axle was removed and the cultivator frame was made an integral part of the tractor. While numerous photographs still exist of this particular development, it remains unclear whether it went into any extensive production.

A front view shows the Fordson tractor with the integral Oliver cultivator. Apparently, Oliver began developing this unit sometime prior to 1920. This unit retained the Fordson's front wheels, using them on the extended cultivator frame. A major problem would have been converting the tractor to a cultivator, and then converting it back to a tractor again. For this reason alone, if for no other, this combination unit likely did not gain wide acceptance.

Oliver Chilled Plow Company

Oliver No. 131-B Fallovator
For Tractor Use

For summer fallowing, Oliver offered their No. 131-B Fallovator. It was designed especially for this purpose, and was intended solely for tractor use. Fallowing killed weeds and left the ground with a deep and well pulverized mulch to conserve moisture. The Fallovator broke up the hard surface of the ground so that early rains could penetrate downward. The loose surface mulch left by the Fallovator killed the weeds, and this alone helped to conserve moisture.

By the 1920s the Oliver line included an extensive series of cultivators. In addition to the ordinary styles typically found in the midwest, Oliver also produced literally hundreds of configurations. These were based on about a dozen basic styles, each of which could equipped with special equipment or special shovels to accommodate a specific cultivating task. For many years the Oliver line of tillage implements was sufficient to carry the company through good years and bad. By the 1920s the farm equipment industry was changing to include several full-line manufacturers. This made it all the more difficult for a specialized line, like that of Oliver, to meet an increasingly competitive market.

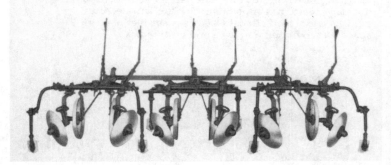

Listed crops required specialized implements from planting to harvest. Recognizing this need, Oliver provided their customers with this No. 39 three-row listed corn cultivator. It was designed especially for tractor power. The change from horse power to tractor power necessitated the design of entirely new implements in most cases. Attempting to convert horsedrawn implements was rarely satisfactory. Even when it was, the horsedrawn implements were not built to withstand the extra strains imposed by tractor power. Oliver claimed that this No. 39 listed corn cultivator could cover about thirty acres in a ten-hour day.

Oliver reversible tractor disc harrows were offered in numerous styles and sizes. The gangs could be set for any inthrow or outhrow desired, and in addition the gangs could be tilted for cultivating ridges or ditches. Oliver claimed their reversible disc harrows to be especially well suited for orchard work, and in fact, Oliver Works even built a special orchard model. These implements were built solely for tractor power, although similar designs were available for use with horses.

Oliver tractor implements were often illustrated with the Fordson tractor. Thousands upon thousands of Fordsons were built during the 1920s, os it was entirely logical to illustrate this popular tractor with implements designed for this purpose. Shown here is a Fordson tractor with a disk plow. The Fordson could handle one or two disks without difficulty; it could also handle a two-bottom moldboard plow under most conditions. Despite the often negative comments about the Fordson, it was instrumental in mechanizing American agriculture.

Oliver ORT Orchard Reversible Disc Harrow

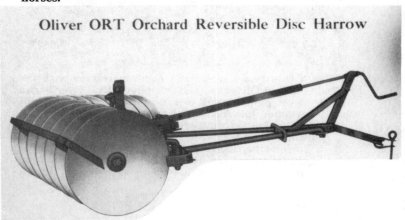

Oliver Chilled Plow Company

Oliver NTDH Tractor Disc Harrow

As with their plows, the Oliver tractor disc harrows quickly etched themselves into American agriculture. The great strength and durability of the design included sufficient flexibility for efficient work. Penetration was obtained by the special design, rather than by the addition of weights. In fact, this model has no weight boxes, nor is there any place for field mounting of additional weights. The adjusting screw at the front of this implement permitted changing of the angle for both the front and the rear gangs.

Oliver TPB Tractor Spring Tooth Harrow

Other Oliver tillage implements included several different styles of spring tooth harrows. Shown here is the Oliver TPB spring tooth model. It was of leverless design, using instead a quick-acting adjustment screw to regulate cultivating depth. A derivation of this style was the Oliver Model MJ quack grass harrow. It was intended to eradicate quack grass, and for this purpose, specially designed teeth were used.

Oliver BTH Brush Tractor Harrow

Many areas of rich cropland were virtually untouchable due to heavy amounts of brush. In fact, until the coming of tractor power, many of these areas remained uncultivated. This special Model BTH brush harrow was designed for breaking virgin brush land, bogs, or cut-over wood land. In many cases the moldboard plow was impractical in these situations. Exceptional strength was essential in the brush harrow, due to the work that was required of it. Large weight boxes permitted adding exceptional amounts of weight for greater penetration.

Oliver OSF Spike Tooth Harrow

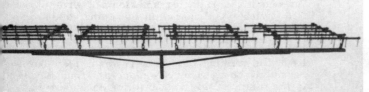

Rounding out the Oliver harrow line was a series of spike tooth harrows. These were built in many different sizes and styles. Again, the extensive range of this simple implement was due partially to specific soil types and certain farming practices. In other instances, the choice of a harrow depended primarily on farmer preference. Of course the harrow dated from antiquity to the time when tree branches were pulled over the soil to level it and prepare a seedbed. By the 1850s the wood-bar harrow with its metal spikes was standard equipment. When the all-steel harrow appeared by the early 1900s, farmers thought this to be the ultimate improvement.

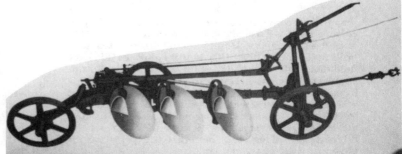

In stubborn soils where the moldboard plow would scour only with great difficulty, the disc plow was an ideal alternative. Beyond this, the disc plow would easily penetrate hard soils, and incorporated enough plant material into the soil to help minimize water and wind erosion. Although Oliver was early to develop disc plows for use with horses, the company was forced to completely redesign its disc plows for use with tractor power. Part of the new design included a much heavier frame to withstand the added strains imposed by a tractor. Added to was a power lift system which permitted easy raising and lowering from the tractor seat.

Oliver Chilled Plow Company

During World War One, many farmers replaced their overalls with a military uniform. In their absence, numerous farm women adapted themselves to jobs usually done by their husbands. This early, and heretofore unpublished photograph shows a farm woman astride an Oliver sulky plow. Historically speaking, this photograph gains further significance when it is remembered that at this point in time, women did not vote, nor did they serve on juries.

Typical of the 1920s is the Farmers Supply Company at a now unknown location. The billboards indicate that the firm sold wagons, buggies, farm implements, and Lion Zinc galvanized fence. A smaller sign in the background indicates that Farmers Supply also sold Oliver Plows and Implements. Farm implement dealers of the 1920s were often a combination of implement dealer, local blacksmith shop, wheelwright shop, and such other enterprises as might have been required by local farmers. Since transportation was much more limited than at present, implement dealers of this period had a much more captive market than in later years.

Oliver Chilled Plow Works took a series of photographs relating to its plowing demonstrations of 1911. These were held under the auspices of Purdue University. An aging photograph album now held by the Floyd County Historical Society at Charles City, Iowa contains many of these images. Due to the effects of aging, and the wrinkled condition of the original photographs, many have been very difficult to reproduce. This one, probably taken in the winter months of 1910-11 shows the famous Oliver fifty bottom plow in the field, waiting only for warm weather to make its trial run.

Few photographs in the annals of mechanized agriculture have been more widely published than this one. It shows three Rumely 30-60 OilPull tractors pulling the huge Oliver fifty bottom plow. In this 1911 field demonstration the race for who could build the biggest tractor was at its zenith. Designing and building a plow that could turn over about three rods of soil in a single pass was indeed a major achievement for Oliver. Likewise, Rumely made advertising hay out of this achievement with their OilPull tractors. Beyond the advertising benefits, the fifty bottom plow had little practical benefit.

The Floyd County Historical Museum at Charles City, Iowa holds a large photograph album of Oliver plows and implements. Included in this aging volume are numerous photographs of the Oliver fifty bottom plow, demonstrated at Purdue University in 1911. This view shows three Rumely OilPull tractors in the lead. The running board ahead of the plow bases permitted the plowman to walk across from one end to the other, raising and lowering each plow base independently.

A heavily worn photograph illustrates how the three tractors remained in alignment with each other during the demonstration of the fifty bottom plow. The tractor closest to the last furrow used that furrow as his gauge. This tractor is fitted with a gauge stick which aligns with the right front wheel of the second tractor, and the second tractor is similarly equipped. However, it would seem that getting the engine speed of each tractor correctly set so that all three tractors pulled evenly would have been a greater challenge.

This Rumely OilPull is pulling an eight bottom Oliver plow at the 1911 Purdue Field Trials. In truth, this was a load more in order for the OilPull, especially in heavy soils, deep plowing, or when climbing hills. Large plowing outfits like this did not appeal to the average midwestern 'quarter-section' farmer. Rather, these large units were better suited to converting huge prairie lands into productive crop ground. For a few years, at least until the majority of the prairie was thus converted, big tractors and big plows were in order.

In this original Oliver photograph the three Rumely OilPull tractors are headed home after the great plowing demonstration. For a time it appears that Rumely sold Oliver plows, but eventually they sold plows under their own trademark, even though it seems that these plows were built by someone besides Rumely. However, Oliver Works and the Rumely factories were close to each other geographically, and the two companies had a good working relationship. Even though the Rumely OilPull has not been built for some sixty years, it remains one of the five most popular vintage tractors.

This side view of the fifty bottom plow shows the plows in the ground, and in fact, it has already made one pass through the field. Oliver advertised this feat to some extent, and Rumely did the same. Even though the fifty bottom plow was not a practical reality, it demonstrated that tractors and tractor plows were a reality. In historical perspective, most farmers of 1911 knew little or nothing about tractors. They plowed their fields one or two furrows at a time, so the concept of a fifty bottom plow did indeed make news.

The Purdue Field Trials of 1911 were not limited to the fifty bottom plow and the Rumely OilPull. This 18-bottom Oliver plow is being pulled by a 30-60 Titan tractor from International Harvester Company. Although the OilPull vastly outsold the IHC Titan, as well as the IHC Mogul tractors, the latter were nevertheless formidable competitions. Extensive research and development work went into IHC equipment, owing largely to the company's size, its good financial position, and consequently, its ability to pour needed monies into developmental work.

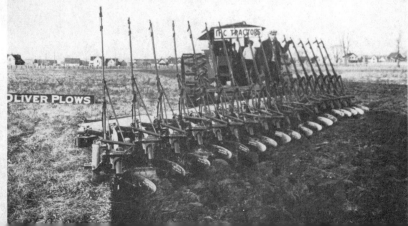

Oliver Chilled Plow Company

Shown here is a Big Four "30" at the 1911 Purdue Field Trials. It is shown with a fourteen bottom Oliver plow. The Big Four was built by Gas Traction Company at Minneapolis, Minnesota. This firm was acquired by Emerson-Brantingham Company in 1912. The large fender on this Big Four also serves as an advertising billboard. Included is a line stating that the Big Four was sold 'Absolutely on Approval.' Another indicates that this tractor was a Gold Medal Winner at the 1910 Winnipeg Agricultural Trials.

Shown here are the plow bases raised into the transport position. Essentially, early engine gangs consisted of a heavy steel frame to which the individual plow beams or bases were attached. Many were equipped with a power lift device, mechanically operated from the land wheel of the plow truck. Others were entirely hand operated, with the plowman raising and lowering each plow by hand. A few companies attempted to use a steam lift arrangement but this was never satisfactory.

This rear view of the Oliver ten bottom engine gang shows a Big Four "30" on the drawbar. The Big Four got its name from the use of a four-cylinder engine as the power plant. In 1910 it was rather unusual for a tractor to have four cylinders, since most others used only one or two cylinders for the job. Two schools of thought prevailed for some years; some people thought that four and six-cylinder engines were nothing more than glorified and oversized automobile engines, and would never stand up to the job. Others decried this notion, pointing to the inherent smoothness of their engines.

Not to be ignored completely, International Harvester sent a copy of their single-cylinder tractor. Capable of about 20 horsepower, the power plant in this tractor was nothing more or less than an IHC Famous stationary engine, suitably adapted to tractor work. The gear train system was a modified version of the Morton traction truck, developed some years before, and adopted on early IHC tractor designs. It was a very simple and straightforward design which used gearing for forward motion and a friction drive for the reverse.

A plowing demonstration of about 1920 shows a three-bottom plow and an All-Work tractor in action. The All-Work was built by the Electric Wheel Company at Quincy, Illinois. This company began offering traction trucks already in 1908; the latter were intended for mounting of any stationary engine of suitable power. Of interest here is the fact that less than ten years after the Purdue Field Trials of 1911, Oliver Works had developed an extensive series of tractor plows, following the general pattern shown here. Having built an exceptional reputation with plows and tillage implements, Oliver Chilled Plow Works contributed mightily to the merger in 1929 which formed Oliver Farm Equipment Company.

Four companies joined forces on April 1, 1929. The Oliver Chilled Plow Company dated from 1855. Hart-Parr Tractor Company began operations in 1897, and the American Seeding Machine Company dated back to 1848. Nichols & Shepard Company likewise began operations in 1848. All four companies emerged from different backgrounds. All were initially directed to satisfying different needs. Historically speaking, these four companies, like others in the budding farm equipment industry, underwent rapid evolvement. In the 1840s the concept of a full-line manufacturer was a moot point, since the total array of farm implements consisted of a plow and a harrow. The remaining implements generally were equipped with handles suitable for hand work.

In the previous pages, numerous points have been made regarding the individual parties to the merger which formed Oliver Farm Equipment Company. By 1929 each of these companies had essentially outgrown its usefulness to the industry. For most of them the market had sometime earlier reached a saturation point. In some instances their machines were badly dated and rapidly approaching obsolescence. For each of these companies to have attempted further activity on a solo basis would almost have certainly been disastrous.

By uniting their various and somewhat diverse product lines into a single company, Oliver Farm Equipment instantly became a virtual full-line manufacturer. In essence, this gave the merged companies a new lease on life, even though their individual identities were masked with the new corporate umbrella. Within a few years after its formation the corporate name was shortened to simply read, Oliver Corporation. For the first couple of years the tractors carried the Oliver-Hart-Parr designation, but the Hart-Parr essence soon disappeared just as an entirely new line of purely Oliver tractors made their appearance.

Subsequent to 1929 Oliver Corporation acquired several successful companies in order to broaden the already extensive Oliver line. One acquisition was that of McKenzie Manufacturing Company. This LaCrosse, Wisconsin firm made potato planting and harvesting machinery. Ann Arbor Machine Company traced its beginnings to the early 1880s. Initially the company was at Ann Arbor, Michigan but in 1920 they moved to Shelbyville, Illinois. Ann Arbor made hay presses their first claim to fame. By the time this plant was closed in 1970 it was building backhoes, balers, siderakes, mowers, loaders, spreaders,

corn harvesters, and seeding equipment. These products were consolidated into the existing lines at the White Farm Equipment plants in South Bend, Indiana and Charles City, Iowa.

Cleveland Tractor Company became a part of the Oliver family in 1944. The Cletrac line was assimilated into the Charles City production effective with the White Farm Equipment merger of 1962. Crawler tractor production ended at Charles City in 1965.

A. B. Farquhar Company of York, Pennsylvania was purchased by Oliver in 1952. For several years this plant continued to produce Oliver sprayers. The Oliver-Farquhar sawmills were also available for a time. Be-Ge Manufacturing Company of Gilroy, California made hydraulic cylinders, scrapers, and land levelers. This company was bought out by Oliver in 1952. When White Motor bought out Oliver, the Farquhar and Be-Ge plants were not included in the merger.

Oliver Chilled Plow Works had built a second plow factory at South Bend in the 1920s. From 1941 to 1943 this plant manufactured guns and shells for the war effort. From 1943 to 1945 it was used as a government depot and warehouse. In 1946 this plant was converted to making gears and other items for various Oliver plants. The South Bend No. 2 plant began producing Oliver's largest tractors beginning in 1947, and the utility tractors were also built at South Bend No. 2, beginning in 1957. The following year this plant was consolidated with facilities at Charles City, Iowa and Shelbyville, Illinois.

White Motor Corporation, Cleveland, Ohio had a long history as a truck manufacturer. On November 1, 1960 White Motor acquired Oliver Corporation as a wholly-owned subsidiary. The Oliver manufacturing operations were then consolidated into existing plants at Charles City, Iowa where tractors were built; the South Bend Works made plows and tillage tools, and the Shelbyville, Illinois factories made pickers, headers, balers, and other machinery. During 1970 the Shelbyville plant was consolidated into the South Bend and Charles City factories, with additional production coming from Brantford, Ontario. The latter facility had formerly been the Cockshutt Farm Equipment Company of Canada, Ltd. This firm was acquired by White Motor in February 1962 as a subsidiary of Oliver Corporation.

Ironically, the Minneapolis-Moline Power Equipment Company was also formed in 1929. It was formed by the merging of Minneapolis Steel & Machinery Company, (Twin City), Moline Plow

With the introduction of new tractor models in 1937, Oliver Corporation provided a graphic parallel between the early Hart-Parr models and their new four- and six-cylinder row-crop tractors. The large sign on the side of the tractor notes that "Oliver Hart-Parr [had provided] 36 years of leadership in the tractor industry; in 1901 Hart-Parr gave the world the word, "TRACTOR." In truth, the term dates back to the time of Shakespeare, although Hart-Parr was first company to use the term on a regular basis. The two syllables of 'tractor' are far easier to pronounce than the cumbersome terminonlogy of gasoline traction engine.

Oliver Corporation made pioneering developments in high-compression engines for tractors. Initially, their designs were not widely used in the industry; most manufacturers of the 1930s were content to stay with heavy, slow-speed engines with a very long stroke as related to the cylinder bore. Although these pioneering efforts were made with gasoline fuel, Oliver was also a pioneer in the devlopment of diesel engines for use in farm tractors. Meanwhile, a few companies were promoting the LP-gas conversion as the ideal tractor fuel. Oliver acquiesced at least partially, and offered LP-gas tractors, either from the factory, or as a field conversion. However, it does not appear that Oliver had their heart in this design; company engineers were much more interested in gasoline and diesel engines.

Company, and the Minneapolis Threshing Machine Company. These three firms experienced difficulties similar to those of the parties which formed Oliver Farm Equipment Company that same year. By merging, the continued growth of the new conglomerate was reasonably assured, but without merging, each one singly would probably have failed. The failure likely would have resulted from the intense economic pressures of the Great Depression, outdated product lines, and numerous other factors.

During the coming years Minneapolis-Moline was content to live within itself, apparently having little interest in acquiring additional firms or broadening their sales base. A notable purchase was that of B. F. Avery & Sons Company at Louisville, Kentucky. Minneapolis-Moline bought this company in 1952, ostensibly to acquire Avery's little BF tractor. Avery dated back to 1825. If there was any family connection with this firm and the Avery Company which operated at Peoria, Illinois there was certainly no corporate connection between the two firms.

Minneapolis-Moline became a wholly-owned subsidiary of White Motor Corporation in 1963, and subsequently the M-M line was blended into that of Oliver until there was virtually no difference between them. Finally in 1969 White Motors formed the White Farm Equipment Company with headquarters at Oak Brook, Illinois. The latter functioned as a division of White Motor Corporation at Cleveland, Ohio. With this corporate change, Minneapolis-Moline, Oliver, and Cockshutt began a change in product color and in name, with the White farm equipment line eventually superseding the earlier product names.

The illustrated product listing on the following pages is intended to show representative examples of the Oliver farm equipment line. No suggestion is made that each and every product ever built by Oliver will be shown herein, although every attempt has been made for completeness. However, in some cases no usable photograph could be located. Instructions and parts manuals for many different products are available from Floyd County Historical Society, Charles City, Iowa at a nominal cost. These manuals generally cover the lines of White, Oliver, Cockshutt, Minneapolis-Moline, Hart-Parr and others. Please contact the Floyd County Historical Society directly, since the Author has only meager samplings of specific product information.

The Oliver baler line had its birth with the acquisition of Ann Arbor Machine Company. The Ann Arbor line was blended into Oliver during 1943. This company had its beginning back in 1882. After moving from Ann Arbor, Michigan to Shelbyville, Illinois in 1920 Ann Arbor continued its development of hay presses and other machinery. After Oliver acquired the Ann Arbor plant the Shelbyville facility was used for production of balers, siderakes, mowers, loaders, spreaders, corn harvesters and seeding machinery. White Farm Equipment closed the Shelbyville plant in 1970, consolidating its products into other WFE plants at South Bend, Indiana and Charles City, Iowa.

Initially, the Oliver hay baler was nothing more than the existing Ann Arbor baler with the Oliver logo attached. Ann Arbor gained precedence with their introduction of the first pick-up device for balers during the 1930s. At this time it was still necessary to tie the bales by hand, since the automatic knotter was not yet successfully developed.

A 1945 Oliver Service Bulletin outlines the method used to indicate the date of manufacture within the baler serial number. The model number was followed by two numerals indicating the year. A letter following the two numerals indicated the month of manufacture, with A being January, B being February, and so forth. The letter I was omitted due to its similarity to the digit '1'. J-14 denoted the Junior 18 baler with a 14 x 18 chamber. J-16 was the Junior 18 was a 16 x 18 inch chamber.

C-17 was the Hay & Straw Combine in the 17 x 22 size. The T-14 was the Automatic Threader in a 14 x 18 size, with T-16 being the same machine with a 16 x 18 chamber. The Improved 18 with a 14 x 18 chamber took the E-14 prefix, and E-16 denote the same machine with a 16 x 18 chamber. No. 40 Twin gear balers took the F-14 designator for the 14 x 18 size and F-17 for the 17 x 22 chamber.

As an example, the serial number of E-14 45 H2 would indicate that this baler was an Improved 18 model in a 14 x 18 size, manufactured in 1945, 'H' denoting August, and the last digit of '2' indicating that this was the second machine built for that month.

Available records do not indicate how long this system was maintained, or whether it extended to other Oliver equipment. However, this information may provide valuable clues regarding the precise age of certain Oliver equipment, particularly since many of the early production records no longer exist.

Oliver Corporation essentially took over Ann Arbor Machine Company in 1943. Ultimately this old-line firm was assimilated into the Oliver corporate structure. This hay press utilized a full-floating, power-driven pick-up system, one that had been originally been developed by Ann Arbor. The Oliver 'sav-a-man' force feeder eliminated the need for a person to feed hay into the chamber with a pitchfork. For some years this was an exclusive feature found only on the Ann Arbor machine. A chain-type cross conveyor carried hay and straw crosswise into the bale chamber.

Oliver produced the Junior 18 baler in the 1949-51 period. This machine was simply an improved version of the earlier Ann Arbor design. The Junior 18 was replaced with this No. 8 Oliver baler in the 1951-53 period. Due to the design of the Junior 18 the hay was tucked into the chamber in such a way that only the tails were cut off, saving as many leaves as possible. The exclusive top shear feeder eliminated the need for a folder, such as was used on many competing machines. The No. 8 was built only as a wire-tie machine.

Balers

An Oliver 66 tractor is on the front end of this Oliver-Ann Arbor hay baler. At this point in time the common practice was to drop the bales on the ground; loading them directly onto a wagon wouldn't come until the 1950s. Laborers followed the baler, loading the bales onto a skid or a specially designed low-profile bale wagon. Water-cooled or air-cooled engines were an option, and a pto drive was available, although far less common than an engine drive.

Production of the Model 100 Oliver baler ran from 1953 to 1958. This wire-tie baler used a 16 x 18 inch chamber with the plunger operating at 38 strokes per minute. Bale length could be varied between 26, 40, and 44 inches. A Wisconsin Model VE-4 air-cooled engine was standard equipment. The automatic wire-tie mechanism used wire from a coil. The wire could be threaded in only a few minutes. The Model 100 was a greatly improved version of earlier styles but retained the cross conveyor system as formerly used. Oliver also built a three-wire Model 101 baler in the 1960-63 period.

The No. 50 automatic twine-tie baler was announced in 1954, and was the first Oliver twine-tie model. The No. 50 was a dramatically improved version over previous models. The cross conveyor was eliminated, and a large screw conveyor carried hay from the pickup directly into the bale chamber. Standard equipment included a two-cylinder engine, but the No. 50 was also available with a pto drive. Production of the No. 50 ran from 1954 to 1957. A further improvement was the No. 60-T (twine) and 60-W (wire) baler of the 1957-61.

Oliver 100 Series balers were built in the 1953-58 period. Shown here is the big No. 103 baler with Oliver's exclusive Roto-Flo feed. It consisted of rotating, rake-type parallel bars which fed material from the pickup mechanism into the bale chamber. One advantage of this system was its ability to fill the top of the bale by creating equal distribution in feeding. Packing fingers assisted the crossfeed in packing hay into the chamber. The No. 103 shown here was equipped with a wide 62-inch pickup unit.

Balers

Oliver No. 102 balers were a three-wire machine for extra large bales. Specific data has not been located, but it appears that production of the No. 102 began about 1959 and ended approximately 1963. Production of Oliver balers was centered at the Shelbyville, Illinois facility. These machines gained an excellent reputation in the industry. This wire-tie machine was especially popular in areas where hay was raised for sale and subsequent shipment to other areas. The wire ties were deemed more secure than those of twine.

Production of the Oliver 520-T baler began in 1966. It was an automatic twine-tie machine with a 14 x 18 inch bale chamber. Weighing 2,500 pounds, the 520-T listed at $2,300. This machine is equipped with an optional No. 14 bale thrower attachment. By using specially designed wagons, bales were thrown directly into the towed wagon, eliminating the need for an extra man and permitting one-man haymaking. The bale thrower necessitate the use of a shorter bale than in ordinary operation.

This Oliver 1850 is towing an Oliver 520 baler. Production of this model extended into 1972, some three years after the merger of Oliver into the White Farm Equipment Company. No. 520 balers could as be purchased as a 520-W wire-tie unit with an automatic-tie device. The basic specifications for this machine differed only in the tying method. Otherwise it was the same machine as the No. 520-T. When equipped with a pto drive the 520-W carried a 1971 list price of $2,500. With an engine drive this same machine retailed at nearly $3,100.

Oliver No. 520 balers were also sold in Canada under the Cockshutt trademark. White Farm Equipment bought out Cockshutt in February 1962. With this buyout certain Cockshutt lines ended and were replaced with machinery built by Oliver. The major difference was that Oliver Green was replaced with Cockshutt Red, along with a different set of decals. In other respects, many of these implements, including the No. 520 baler, were identical to their Oliver counterparts.

Balers

The No. 620 Oliver balers included several exclusive Oliver features, such as a windguard that automatically adjusted to hay flow. A fully-enclosed twine compartment was another feature, along with knotters protected from the dirt and weather. Oliver heavily advertised their 7-way overload protection for greater operator confidence. A simple adjustment permitted any bale length from 12 to 50 inches. A Multi-Luber for the knotter was an optional feature. With a pto drive this machine sold for $2,000.

The No. 15 bale thrower illustrated on this No. 620 baler was one of the many available options. Other optional features included a wire-tie instead of twine-tie; pickup gauge wheel, dual wheels, bale loader, and wagon hitch. With the No. 15 bale thrower it was possible to load bales directly onto a towed wagon. The only limitation was a maximum bale length of 31 inches and a maximum bale weight of 60 pounds. The patented Roto-Flo feeder also remained as an Oliver feature.

Although the No. 710 baler was sold under the Oliver logo, it was essentially built by White Farm Equipment. Most industry listings place it under the heading of the latter company, since Oliver was essentially a dormant entity. Production of the No. 710 medium-duty machine ran from 1972 to 1976. In fact, production of all Oliver and/or White square balers ended about this time. In the 1970-72 period, WFE also built the 1520 and 1720 balers, listing these under the Minneapolis-Moline heading.

As previously indicated, production of Oliver square balers ended about 1976. This No. 720 machine first went into production for the 1967 season, and was available in twine-tie or wire-tie versions. During the latter years of production, the production of many White-Oliver-Cockshutt-Minneapolis machines becomes very convoluted. All were under the control of White Farm Equipment (WFE) but production of some machines was designated for one factory, and some for another. Then, selected models were also designated for Cockshutt, thus creating another apparent model.

Beet Machinery

By the 1920s and perhaps earlier, Oliver Chilled Plow Works had developed various styles of beet lifters. This Oliver-Superior No. 101 riding beet lifter of the 1930s is typical of the period. This particular machine could be operated in one of two ways. It could be set so that the soil was removed on both sides of the beets, leaving them in a standing position. The No. 101 could also be adjusted so that the beets were pulled entirely out of the ground. Note the double rolling coulters on each side of the shovels. They were intended to cut and loosen a slice of soil on each side of the standing beets.

Instead of a drill, some cropping practices demanded the use of a planter. This Oliver No. 19 six-row planter saved seed, fertilizer, and labor over drilling. In addition, this planter was equipped for check-rowing, using planter wire. The buttons on the planter wire were spaced the same distance apart as the individual planting units. This permitted cross cultivation if necessary or desired. The needs of the sugar beet grower were somewhat different than those of the ordinary small grain crops and required specialized equipment for a very important crop.

Following the 1929 formation of Oliver Farm Equipment Company the initial product lines were simply relabeled products from the merged companies. Given some time an entirely new and distinctive Oliver farm equipment line appeared. For some years though Oliver used the 'Superior' tradename formerly promoted by American Seeding Machine Company. This Oliver-Superior No. 9 Beet and Bean Drill of the 1930s is a case-in-point. Although Oliver offered a virtual profusion of grain drill designs, this special machine was intended especially for beet growers.

Beginning in the 1940s Oliver offered various styles of beet lifters. This implement was designed to raise or lift the beet tubers to the surface of the ground. Often acquiring great size, mature sugar beets could not effectively be lifted by hand, so horsedrawn or tractor-powered lifters were essential. Eventually the harvest of this crop was almost completely mechanized, but when this No. 1220 two-row beet lifter appeared, it was indeed revolutionary. Much of the early design work on these implements was done by Oliver Chilled Plow Works at South Bend, Indiana.

Chain Saws

About 1955 Oliver added outboard motors to its overall equipment line. Apparently company management felt that this specialized industry had growth potential, thus the diversification into this line. Little substantive information has surfaced, but from all appearances, Oliver decided subsequently to market chain saws as well. Possibly, this move was intended to expand the overall lawn and garden equipment lines which were growing rapidly at the time.

Regardless of precise manufacturing periods and other details, Oliver did in fact market their WM-19, WM-19D, WM-21, and WM-360 chain saws for a short time. There is no indication that this particular phase of Oliver's sales operations were positively affected through this intrusion into what was already a very competitive industry.

Combines

The history of the Oliver combines undoubtedly represents one of the major odysseys in the annals of mechanized agriculture. Beginning with the efforts of Nichols & Shepard in the 1850s we see a series of small grain threshers. Over the next half century the grain thresher came into its own, emerging as a well developed and very efficient method of separating grain from straw. But, just as the threshing machine entered its golden age about 1900, it was also nearing the end of its usefulness.

When plows turned vast areas of prairie to wheat, the labor-intensive threshing machine was simply no match. After the grain was cut with a binder it took field workers to stand the bound sheaves into shocks to await drying. In a few weeks it was time to load each of the sheaves onto a wagon, unloaded again into the threshing machine, and all of these tasks required large numbers of workers. By combining, that is, cutting the grain and threshing it in one operation, a few people could do the work of many. Thus, already in the 1890s the combine underwent its first serious stages of development.

Meanwhile, the threshing machine industry moved on, with Nichols & Shepard being a leader in this specialized field. This careful, conservative company announced their Red River Special thresher to the world about the turn of the century, and with it their famous "Four Threshermen," with an explanation of this term being found in the *Nichols & Shepard* section of this book.

During the 1920s Nichols & Shepard began developing combines, and marketed some machines prior to the 1929 merger which formed Oliver Farm Equipment Company. Initially known as Oliver-Nichols & Shepard combines, these same machines continued in the Oliver line until the late 1930s; modifications of this original N & S line were built by Oliver into the early 1940s. Oliver advertising continued to reflect on the Man Behind the Gun and other terminology coined by Nichols & Shepard in describing their system of threshing.

With the coming of straight-through designs in the early 1930s, Oliver turned its attention toward similar designs. In 1937 came the first of the Oliver Grainmaster combines, with several models coming in rapid succession. Further development was reduced to a minimum during the 1941-45 period, but in 1946 the Oliver Model 15 combine appeared, and this popular machine was marketed for a decade. Perhaps even more popular was the Oliver Model 18 which followed, and it too, remained on the market for about ten years.

Despite all the developments and refinements of the pull-type combine, the 1950s saw a new impetus in developing self-propelled models. Oliver responded with the Model 33 Grainmaster in 1950, followed by the Model 35 in 1956. A significant development was the 1964 introduction of the Oliver 525; it remained on the market until 1972.

Oliver was acquired by White Motors in 1969. Subsequently the Meadow Green of Oliver implements brightened into the Sumac Red of White Farm Equipment. WFE had also acquired Cockshutt and Minneapolis-Moline, so for a time there were combines with three different names, yet all essentially the same machine. Eventually these lines were integrated into a single series under the White logo. Significant of this period was the 7300 self-propelled combine, built from 1972 to 1981. Various models followed, climaxing with the White 9700 axial combine of 1980. This entirely new design did away with the conventional cylinder and concaves. Ending the series was the White 9720 axial flow machine, built in the 1984-86 period. At that point the White combine line was sold to Massey-Ferguson, with the remainder of the White farm equipment line being sold to Allied Products Corporation.

Combines previously developed by Nichols & Shepard were immediately blended into the Oliver line, subsequent to the 1929 merger. Initially, little more was done than to add the Oliver name and logo to these machines. As otherwise indicated, Nichols & Shepard had a long and illustrious history in the threshing machine business, and successfully transferred this know-how into building combines. The Model A, built by Oliver from 1929 to 1938, was available with a 10 or 12-foot cutting width. Model A Oliver-Nichols & Shepard combines weighed over five tons, complete with a 10-foot header.

Combines

Oliver-Nichols & Shepard Model B combines were nothing more or less than the same machine sold by Nichols & Shepard prior to the 1929 merger. Model B machines were ordinarily furnished with a 12-foot header. The major difference was the header width between the Model A and Model B combines. Both used a 22-inch cylinder with a 30-inch separator. To accommodate the additional grain the Model B was equipped with a 38 horsepower engine, giving it about six more horses than the Model A. Both the Model A and the Model B could be equipped with two or three-foot header extensions for use only in light grain.

Oliver's advertising of the Model A, B, D, and F combines continued to promote the concept of the Four Threshermen, delineated under the *Nichols & Shepard* section of this book. These four threshermen were: The Big Cylinder, The Steel Wing Beater, The Heavy Concaves, and The Man Behind the Gun. Model D combines, were also built in the 1929-38 period. This machine used a 28-inch cylinder with a separating width of 34 inches. It was equipped with a 46 horsepower, four-cylinder engine. During the latter part of the production period the Model D was also built as a Western Special.

Topping the Oliver-Nichols & Shepard combine series was the big Model F. It was available in header widths ranging from 12 to 24 feet, and was powered by a 54 horsepower engine. This big machine used a 32-inch cylinder with a 40-inch separating width. Complete with the header the Model F weighed about six tons. These machines required one man to operate the combine, with another operating the tractor. The grain tank was an option, and these combines could also be equipped with a bagging platform.

Indications are that Oliver first built the Grainmaster combine in 1936. The following year the Model 1 appeared. Its impact on the market is now clouded, but success was finally assured with the 1941 introduction of the Model 2 Grainmaster. It was Oliver's first one-man machine, and was equipped with a five-foot cut. The rasp bar cylinder permitted efficient harvesting of virtually any seed crop, compared to the limited use of the earlier spike-bar cylinder.

First built in 1937, the Model 6 Grainmaster was the first Oliver combine truly representing Oliver's own research efforts. This was also Oliver's first combine to offer an optional pto drive in lieu of the Continental four-cylinder engine which was normally furnished. This machine used a raddle instead of straw walkers, and the rasp bar cylinder permitted the harvesting of almost every seed crop. Model 6 combines were built with a six-foot cutting width. Production ran until 1941.

Model 6 Grainmaster combines required a combine operator in addition to the tractor driver. In lieu of the grain tank shown here the Model 6 could be equipped with a bagging platform and sacker attachment. Additional sieves were available for special crops, along with numerous options for special crops or adverse conditions. Rubber tires were standard equipment. The header could be lowered to within 3 1/2 inches from the ground and could be raised to a maximum height of 28 inches. A Model 5 Grainmaster was apparently built in 1942 but no information has surfaced regarding this machine.

Production of the Model 10 Grainmaster ran from 1937 to 1941. Apparently a Model 8 was also built, but current research has found no information on this model. The Model 10 was offered with 8, 10, and 12-foot headers. It followed the same general design as the earlier Nichols & Shepard machines, in that the cut grain was conveyed sidewise into the cylinder. It also was built only in an engine-powered version; no pto drive was available. The fifty bushel grain tank was standard equipment, but a sacker attachment could be substituted.

Oliver Grainmaster Model 10 combines utilized a rasp-bar cylinder, making them useful in virtually an seed crop. With the development of the rasp-bar cylinder, spike-tooth machines approached the end of their useful life. However, a few companies continued to offer spike-tooth cylinders for some years. In fact, this design was especially suitable for certain crops, more so than the rasp-bar. Oliver continued using the large diameter cylinder pioneered generations earlier by Nichols & Shepard. This design helped to minimize broken straw, thus easing the task of the straw racks to separate grain, chaff, and straw.

Production of the Oliver Model 12 Grain Master ran from 1937 to about 1943. Precise production figures for this model have not been located. This 12-foot machine was equipped with a Continental four-cylinder motor. The grain bin had a capacity of 50 bushels. Operating weight was 5,950 pounds. The list price was $1,413. Model 12 combines used a raddle instead of straw racks. Actually, the raddle was used much earlier than the so-called vibrating design using straw racks. Each had its unique advantages. This Model 12 was equipped with an entirely new rubberized weather-proof draper, replacing the usual canvas conveyor.

Weighing 4,400 pounds, the Model 20 Grainmaster used an eight-foot cut and was normally equipped with a pto drive. This machine used a 26-inch cylinder, but in keeping with the earlier Nichols & Shepard design, it was 20 inches in diameter. Full rotary-type straw walkers were a salient feature, along with a ball bearing pitman. Production of this machine ran from 1939 to 1944. It sold for $965. Parenthetically, Oliver used 'Grainmaster' and 'Grain Master' interchangeably. Technically then, both terms are correct to describe the series.

Oliver built the Model 30 combine in 8, 10, and 12-foot sizes. Production of the 8 and 10-foot models ran from 1939 to 1948; production of the 12-foot size continued into 1953. Both were equipped with a Continental six-cylinder motor, and both weighed slightly over 6,000 pounds. This machine featured a 31-inch cylinder. Oliver built this machine as a combination grain and soybean combine. It was equipped with Oliver's special 'Clip-Cut' cutter bar with a guard spacing of 2 1/2 inches. The header was designed to cut as low as two inches above the ground. A finger-type reel was also available, and this was of special value when harvesting soybeans.

Model 15 Grainmaster combines used a 6-foot cut. They were available initially with a motor drive, but early in production they were also made available with a pto drive. Until the tractor industry standardized pto design, changes to the drive shaft system were often required when changing from one tractor to another. Built in the 1946-56 period, Model 15 Grainmaster combines had a grain tank capacity of 20 bushels. The low profile design was made possible by the use of an unloading auger for the grain tank. In 1956 the Model 15 with a motor listed at $1,800; the same machine with a pto drive sold for $1,360.

Apparently the Model 22 Grainmaster replaced the Model 20 in the Oliver combine line. Production of the Model 22 began in 1944, the same year that the line closed for the Model 20. This ten-foot machine remained available until 1949. A major difference between the Model 20 and the Model 22 was the use of a 10-foot header with the Model 22, compared to only 8 feet for the Model 20. Both were regularly furnished for a pto drive, and both used rotary-type straw walkers. Weighing 4,500 pounds, this Model 22 listed at $1,080.

Oliver's famous Model 18 combine made its debut in 1955. This popular machine was built until 1966; it also marked the end of Oliver pull-type combines. The auger feeder was new, and marked the end of slatted conveyors to carry grain into the cylinder. A new adjustable drawbar made it easier to adapt the Model 18 to a specific tractor. A sturdy tubular frame was the foundation for this machine. It was light in weight but provided tremendous strength while enduring the twisting and jarring common to the grain harvest.

the **MODEL 18**

Within its capacity the Model 18 could well be nominated for excellence among its peers. The Model 18 was simple, well balanced, and did an excellent job of threshing and separating. Ordinarily available with a pto drive, the Model 18 could also be furnished with a motor drive; the Model 18 in this photograph is thus equipped. A hand-lift for the header was standard equipment, but Oliver also offered an optional hydraulic lift. Heavy coil springs permitted the header to float over obstructions. The Oliver semi-revolving reel used cam-controlled bats that always remained vertical, thus saving grain.

In 1956 the Oliver Model 18 combine with a pto drive listed at $1,850. By the time production ended in 1966 this machine was selling for $2,325. The same machine equipped with a motor drive sold for about $2,950. Model 18 combines could also be supplied as a navy bean model at an extra cost of $371. The straw spreader added $66 to the list price. A variable-pitch drive system permitted easy adjustment of cylinder speeds anywhere from 440 to 1,625 rpm. The front of the concave was adjusted by a single hand lever, while the rear of the concave was adjusted by draw bolts. Interestingly, Oliver continued the 'Man Behind the Gun' principle, a combination grate and check plate, that had been developed by Nichols & Shepard many years before. This Model 18 is being pulled by an Oliver 550 tractor.

In 1950 Oliver introduced its first self-propelled combine, the Model 33 Grainmaster. This new machine embodied many features pioneered by Oliver, and even farther back, to Nichols & Shepard. Special emphasis was placed on the threshing and separating mechanism. In this machine the so-called "Man Behind the Gun" prevailed; an explanation of this concept may be found in the *Nichols & Shepard* section of this book. Four rotary straw walkers were featured, and a disc-type straw spreader came as a $43 option.

The center-mounted operators platform gave full vision and was designed for complete control of the machine from one position. A foot clutch controlled ground travel and a hand clutch was used for the combine mechanism. In addition a header and feeder throwout clutch was used. An auger-type platform conveyor with a beater-type feeder was standard equipment; the same system was also used on the Oliver Model 18 pull-type combine. A hydraulic lift on the 12-foot header permitted a cutting range of 1 1/2 to 30 inches.

THE NEW OLIVER MODEL 33 SELF-PROPELLED GRAIN MASTER

A NEW PROFIT-PRODUCER FOR GRAIN, BEAN AND SEED GROWERS AND CUSTOM OPERATORS

strength

life

here's the backbone of the Model 33

Six forward speeds were built into the Oliver Model 33 Grainmaster. Optionally, the Model 33 could be equipped with a Thomas Vari-Drive unit for an additional $510. The base price of this machine was about $4,500. Cylinder width was 35 inches, ahead of a full-width separating unit. Oil-filled gear cases were used throughout, and pressure-type grease fittings were used extensively. All essential bearings were of either the ball or the roller type. Operating weight of this machine was about 7,200 pounds.

OLIVER

Oliver Model 33 self-propelled combines were powered with a Continental F-226, six-cylinder engine. This curiously, even though Oliver was building its own tractor engines and stationary power units. A tubular steel member constituted the backbone of the Oliver Model 33. It provided the needed flexibility needed for field work, yet provided the strength and rigidity needed for constant alignment. Empty weight was of the Model 33 was about 7,100 pounds. Loading the 45 bushel grain tank added considerable weight; this, coupled with hill climbing and soft ground necessitated tremendous strength in the frame design.

Priced at about $4,500 the Model 33 was quite competitive with its peers. This field scene illustrates a typical harvest operation. Special shoe sieves were available for various seed crops, and a Hart Scour-Kleen recleaner was a $106 option. Electric lights, permitting night operation, were available for $35. The Oliver straw walker system was designed with a flat deck to prevent bunching and permit a smooth, even flow of straw to the rear of the machine. Fishbacks were welded to the sides of the walkers for additional pitching and tossing action.

Oliver Model 33 Grainmaster combines were available in special designs for special crops. Included was an Edible Bean Special, designed especially for navy beans. A 'sacker' version was available, using a sacking platform in lieu of the standard grain tank. The Ricefield Special was built in 12 and 14-foot sizes, with the smaller model listing at $5,885. A special feeder house for combining flax added $175 to the base price, and rubber bean bars added $37 to the retail tag. Production of the Model 33 began in 1950 and ended in 1956.

Combines

Straw walkers were a design feature of the Oliver Model 35 combine. A 10-foot header was standard equipment, along with a Continental F-226, six-cylinder engine. The standard machine listed at $5,200, but was also available as a Ricefield model at $6,885. Another option was a special Ricefield model with tracks in lieu of rubber tires. This machine sold for $8,775. To accommodate certain crops, the Model 35 was also available with a spike-tooth cylinder at an extra cost price of $169. The Thomas Vari-Draulic drive system added $575 to the base price. While the 10-foot machine was standard, the Model 35 was also available with 12 and 14-foot headers.

In 1958 Oliver introduced their Model 40 Self-Propelled machine. Production of this machine ended in 1963. Also of note during this period was the Model 25 SP combine. Built in the 1961-63 period, it is not illustrated for lack of a usable photograph. New features of the Model 40 included full-time power steering, a choice of gasoline or diesel engines, live-axle drive and double-disc brakes. An easily removable deck cover gave easy access to the cylinder, and the 57 bushel grain tank was equipped with a big 9-inch unloading auger. Empty weight was about 8,875 pounds.

In 1957 Oliver introduced the Model 9 corn head for the Model 25 and Model 40 combines. Concurrently introduced were the Model 12 head for either the Model 25, Model 40, or Model 430 combines. A Model 49 row-crop header was also built for the Model 35 and 40 combines, first beginning in 1957. Stripper plates were used instead of snapping rolls. Model 40 combines were priced with a 10-foot grain table, but 12, 14, and 16-foot sizes were also available. The 10-foot size sold at $6,925; a comparable Edible Bean Special retailed at $7,100. By comparison the Model 40 Rice Special listed at $8,900. The Model 49 row-crop header had a retail tag of $1,620.

Oliver combines took on an entirely new appearance with the 1964 introduction of the Model 525 combine. Produced until 1972 this popular machine was based over an 11-foot cutting width, although 12 and 13-foot headers were available at slight additional cost. Power steering was a standard feature, as were the electric lights. A combination gearset and variable speed drive permitted infinitely variable adjustment of ground travel. Optionally, the reel could be adjusted from the operator's platform.

Model 512, Model 522, and Model 531 corn heads were optionally available for the Oliver 525 combines. The 531 was a three-row design. Like the other two noted above, it was introduced in 1967. The Model 531 corn head sold at approximately $4,400, while the base machine was priced at $8.930. Standard equipment included a Chrysler Industrial 251 engine, with the numerics referring to the ci displacement of this six-cylinder engine.

For special crops the Model 525 was available with a spike-bar cylinder in place of the usual rasp-bar design. These machines were also built in a special Edible Bean version. Thus equipped, and carrying an 11-foot header the E.B. Special sold for $9,180. With an 83 horsepower engine, a 62 bushel grain tank, and a cylinder width of 28 inches, the Model 525 was intended as an all-purpose combine for the average-size farm. A quick-attach header design permitted easy interchange with the 2-row or 3-row corn heads. Oliver corn heads were adjustable to the exact row spacing.

Oliver Model 12 corn heads were built for the Model 25 and the Model 40 combines. The Model 512 corn head was built for the 430 and 525 combines. As previously noted, the Model 531, three-row corn head was built for the 525, 535, and 540 combines. During 1967 Oliver introduced the 541, four-row corn head for the 535 and 545 combines. At the same time came the 544 corn head for the Model 535 and 545, plus the Model 544 corn head for the Oliver Model 5555 combine. The latter model listed at $6,066 in 1967.

Production of the Oliver 430 and 431 combines began in 1963, or just a few months before the popular 525 model. The 430 was slightly smaller than the concurrent 431, but both used the same Chrysler 265 Industrial engine. This six-cylinder design carried a 265 ci displacement and developed 93 horsepower. Deep five-step straw walkers were a regular feature. Another interesting feature was a tailings diverter. By simply moving a lever the tailings could be sent back to the front of the cylinder for rethreshing or behind the cylinder to simply reclean. The cylinder width of 34 inches provided ample threshing capacity; this big cylinder was 22 inches in diameter.

An aftermarket parasol is installed on the Model 430 to shield the operator from the hot sun. Cylinder speeds ranging from 227 to 1,060 rpm were possible on the Model 430. The cylinder drive was a double-strand roller chain with bolted sprockets. Four different sprocket sizes could be installed on the beater shaft and five different sprockets could be mounted to the cylinder shaft. Using various combinations of these bolted sprockets, any of twenty different cylinder speeds could be obtained.

Apparently the 430 and 431 Oliver combines were the first from this company to offer a cab as an option. This option was so popular that within a few years the cab became standard equipment. In 1967 this option added $482 to the base price. Standard features of the Model 430 included power steering and infinitely variable ground speeds ranging from 7/10 to 15 mph. Over 3,000 square inches of cleaning area was built into the 430, and only five units on the entire machine were built with grease fittings.

By the time production of the Model 430 combine ended in 1967 it was carrying a base price of $7,787. A comparable machine as an Edible Bean Special sold for $8,107. In addition, Oliver built this model as the 430-R Rice Special in cutting widths of 12 or 14 feet. The latter size sold for $9,173. The Rice Special included a spike-tooth cylinder as regular equipment, along with extra-wide flotation tires and other features unique to the rice harvest.

Following the same general lines, the Model 431 was produced during the same 1963-67 period as the Model 430. The major difference was that the Model 431 used a big eight-bar, 42-inch rasp cylinder, and had a cleaning unit area of over 3,800 square inches. The grain tank capacity was increased from 60 bushels for the 430 up to 75 bushels for the 431, and the latter model included five straw walkers, compared to only four in the Model 430. However, both the Model 430 and the Model 431 used the same Chrysler 265, six-cylinder, 93 horsepower engine.

At an additional cost the Model 430 and 431 combines could be furnished with a spike-tooth cylinder, A hydraulic reel lift was another option, as was a pickup feeder. Instead of a grain tank these combines could be furnished with a bagger attachment. For those preferring manual steering, this was also available, although power steering came as standard equipment. The semi-revolving reel was yet another option which minimized grain shattering and was very useful in down and tangled grain.

Apparently the Oliver 431 straw chopper was offered late in the production run of this series. In addition to this special equipment item were numerous others, including header stone guards, slow-speed sprockets, and an optional $65 straw spreader. Model 431 combines with a 12-foot header listed at $8,920. Header widths of 14 and 16 feet were also available. In addition, the Model 431 was built as a $9,300 Edible Bean Special and as a Rice Special with a price tag of $10,118. Production of the 430 and 431 machines was phased out during 1967.

Combines

Bring Big-Profit Harvests

During the 1966-69 Oliver offered its Model 542 self-propelled combine. The 542 used the same 42-inch cylinder width as found on the big 545 model, but was apparently offered only with the Chrysler 265 Industrial engine. No reference to a diesel engine option occurs in available product or industrial listings. While the base price of $9,070 included a 12-foot header, there were five additional header widths available, ranging up to 18 feet. This machine weighed 9,085 pounds. This machine was also marketed as the Wheatland 542; it was intended only for small grain, sorghum, and grass seed crops.

Oliver 535 combines were ordinarily furnished with a Chrysler 265 Industrial engine of 93 horsepower. Optionally, the 535 could be equipped with a Perkins 97 horsepower diesel engine. This machine, built in the 1966-72 period, was ordinarily equipped with a 12-foot header, but additional widths of 13, 14, and 16 feet were also available. With the 12-foot header this machine listed at $10,112. The specially designed 535 Rice Special retailed at $12,300. Corn heads of two, three, or four rows could also be attached. The 535 was designed to be an intermediate machine, using a cylinder width of 34 inches.

Three different engine options were available for the big Model 545 combine. The Chrysler Industrial 265 engine of 93 horsepower was standard equipment. One substitution was a 97 horsepower Perkins diesel, and yet another was a Chrysler 318 Industrial engine of 115 horsepower in a V-8 design. Speeds were infinitely variable from 3/4 to 16 1/2 mph. Concave adjustment from the operator's seat, on-the-go, was another option, but the big 22-inch diameter cylinder was standard equipment.

Along with several grain headers and their options, Oliver 545 combines could also be equipped with corn heads. Nearly 4,100 square inches of cleaning area was offered in the Oliver 545; in this respect it was the same as the Model 542. Production of this machine ran from 1966 to 1972. It listed at $12,450 with a 13-foot grain table. Larger grain tables and corn heads were all sold at additional cost. In addition, the 545 was available as a Rice Special having a list price of $14,450. The center-mounted grain tank was an excellent feature; with optional extensions it had a capacity of 110 bushels.

Grain headers to 18 feet
Corn heads adjustable
to exact row width

Introduced in 1969 the Oliver 5542 was also listed as White-Oliver. The same year this machine was introduced, Oliver became a subsidiary of White Motor Corporation, and subsequently, White Farm Equipment. Normally, the 5542 was furnished with a 93 horsepower engine, but optionally a 107 horsepower gasoline engine was used. Some advertising of the period designates this model as the 5542 Wheatland, denoting its specific application to small grains and other seed crops. Built into 1981 the 5542 retailed at about $27,600.

Combines

Oliver introduced the big 5555 combine in 1968, with production ending in 1970. At the time, this was the biggest machine in the Oliver fleet, with grain headers up to 22 feet. A big 150 horsepower V-8 gasoline engine was used, and the low-mounted fuel tanks held 76 gallons. The 170 bushel grain tank used a 12-inch auger capable of unloading at two bushels per second! A huge 52-inch cylinder was used, and as an option, it could be equipped with a variable speed drive. Likewise, the ground travel was infinitely variable from 0 up to 16 mph.

When Oliver introduced the 7300 combine in 1972 the company was a subsidiary of White Motors. During the first two years of production the 7300 was also sold by the Minneapolis-Moline subsidiary. The machines were the same, even to the model number; the major difference being a different serial number prefix. This machine was also sold as the Cockshutt 7300, reflecting White's acquisition of this firm. Production of this model ended in 1981.

A Chrysler 318 Industrial engine was standard equipment for the 7300 combine. Optionally, it could be furnished with a Perkins 6.354 diesel. This option added $1,100 to the base price of $11,580. Forward speeds were infinitely variable from 0.7 to 17 mph, using a variable pitch drive system. The cab shown on this machine was a $650 option. Oliver also built this machine as a Corn & Soybean Special, priced at $11,770. Five different headers widths were available ranging from 13 to 22 feet.

By the end of production in 1981, the Oliver logo was disappearing and the White logo was taking its place. By the time production ended the 7300 had undergone numerous enhancements, including the use of a 100 bushel grain tank as standard equipment. The last published retail price for this machine was about $32,800, reflecting both the changes in design and inflationary pressures. However, this price included a cab, power steering, and 18.4-26 inch tires.

The 7600 combine was sold variously under the Oliver, Minneapolis-Moline, and Cockshutt logos. In addition, the White logo may have also appeared late in production. Farmers also had the option of the familiar Meadow Green of Oliver, or the new Sumac Red of White. This transitional phase lasted for only a short time, with Sumac Red being the standard color. The 7600 had a base price of about $18,000; a 7600 Corn & Soybean Special listed for about $100 additional. The 7600 and 7800 combines were built in the 1972-75 period.

A 45-inch cylinder was used in the 7600 combine. Other features included a straddle-mounted grain tank with a capacity of 150 bushels. The 12-inch dump auger made unloading very quick. These machines also featured the White-Oliver Kwik-Switch header exchange system. Corn heads were available in 4 and 6 narrow row styles or 3 and 4-row wide styles. Grain headers were available in 13, 15, 18, 20, and 22 feet. This machine had a separating area of 6,750 square inches, along with 4,422 inches of cleaning area. Power came from a 128 horsepower engine. The 7800 combine was of similar design, but used a 52-inch cylinder and a 155 horsepower engine.

White introduced their 8600 combine in 1974, continuing it in production until 1977. While the variable pitch drive system was standard equipment, the 8600 could be supplied with an infinitely variable hydrostatic drive for an additional cost of $2,139. The base price of about $36,000 included a 354 ci diesel engine, but for a $2,000 deduction from the base price the 8600 could be supplied with a V-8 gasoline engine. Various grain tables and corn heads were available. In addition, the 8600 was also offered as a Corn & Soybean Special. Beyond this, the 8600 was built in a special Ricefield version.

White 8800 combines were built in Grain, Corn & Soybean, and Ricefield versions. A hydrostatic drive was available as a $2,000 option. All three styles listed in the approximate area of $40,000. Ordinarily this machine was furnished with a Perkins T6-354.3 turbocharged diesel engine. In lieu of this, and for about $2,000 less cost the 8800 could be supplied with a Chrysler 400 Industrial gasoline engine. With its large unloading auger, the 170 bushel grain tank could be emptied in about 100 seconds.

Combines

Many different grain tables and corn heads could be supplied for use with the White 8800 combines. The grain header options included a hydrostatic reel drive, on-the-go reel adjustment, and a separate reel-drive clutch. The snapping roll stripper plates for the corn head were adjustable. Weighing about 16,900 pounds, the 8800 was ordinarily furnished with 23.1-26 tires. Ricefield versions could be equipped with a spike-tooth cylinder, but for other applications the standard rasp-bar design was supplied.

Between 1977 and 1981 the White Harvest Boss line included this 8650 pull-type combine. It could be furnished with grain tables of 8, 10, or 12 feet. No corn head could be supplied. This machine used a 44-inch rasp-bar cylinder and required 100-plus horsepower at the pto shaft. Weighing 9,500 pounds, this machine carried a retail tag of $25,500. Many different attachments were available for special seed crops. In fact, this model is shown with a pick-up attachment for windrowed grain. Remote electronic monitoring was a standard feature.

White 8900 combines were offered in a standard Grain version, and were also built as the 8900 Harvest Boss. The latter was a Corn & Soybean Special. With that exception, both machines were virtually the same. Both used a 145 horsepower, 354 ci turbocharged diesel engine. Options covered virtually any demand; corn heads and grain tables were built for virtually every crop or farming preference. Serial number records indicate that the 8900 Grain model was built in the 1978-81 period, followed in the 1982-84 period with the 8900 Harvest Boss.

White introduced their 9700 Axial Harvest Boss in 1984, building it into 1986. The huge machine was powered by a 243 horsepower engine and used a 265 bushel grain tank. However, in November 1985 Allied Products Corporation purchased certain assets of White Farm Equipment. The combine line was sold to Massey Combines. What a long journey from the crude Nichols & Shepard separators of the 1840s to this huge axial machine. On the other hand, the Nichols & Shepard Vibrator thresher cost a few hundred dollars, while this huge axial-flow machine was priced at well over $100,000.

Corn Pickers

Oliver corn pickers were developed from designs originated by Nichols & Shepard. To be sure, Oliver's own engineers perfected the early Grain Master, but obviously built on the pioneering work of Nichols & Shepard.

The early Grain Master corn pickers were probably no better, nor any worse, than comparable pickers of the 1930s. Regarding these early machines, one old-timer probably came close to being accurate by saying that, "They picked almost all the leaves, a few of the stalks, and some of the roots." Yet, mechanized corn harvesting finally brought corn to the foreground as a major cash crop. Hand harvesting precluded this, simply for lack of manpower.

By 1940 Oliver had developed a reasonably efficient corn picker by then-contemporary standards. In fact, some of the Oliver designs of this period remained on the Oliver picker line for decades. However, with better hybrids, commercial fertilizer, and improved crop methods, yields continued to increase. This overburdened the machine, and as a result, new machines were introduced on a regular basis. They reflected not only the improvements in design, but also contemplated the needs of farmers for an efficient, high-capacity machine.

During the early 1950s came a subtle change. The concept of the corn combine was about to be unfurled. The change took place slowly at first, but gained momentum during the 1950s. During the 1960s this idea gained speed, and by the end of the 1970s the transformation was essentially made from the time-honored corn picker to the corn combine.

Despite tremendous research dollars and countless, laborious efforts of designers, the corn picker as a distinct entity lasted for only about forty years. It was but another step in an evolutionary process which probably will see even more changes over the next four decades.

Oliver's corn picker line grew from the foundation laid by Nichols & Shepard Company. The latter had developed a corn picker in the late 1920s, and had marketed a limited number of these machines. Perfecting the corn picker was a slow process, and in fact, the corn harvest was one of the last major farm tasks to be mechanized. Shown here is an early one-row, semi-mounted corn picker developed by Nichols & Shepard specifically for the Fordson tractor. Appearances are that Nichols & Shepard introduced this machine about 1926.

Oliver introduced its two-row Corn Master in 1932. This machine was radically different than its ancestors. Long sweeping lines are evident from the points of the snouts to the back of the snapping rolls. The outer snouts were flared out gradually to enhance the entry of corn into the snapping rolls. Special pto equipment was available to permit use of this machine with almost any tractor having a pto drive. A wagon hitch, not shown here, was also available. Otherwise it was necessary to drive in synchronism with the picker.

Corn Master two-row corn pickers retailed at $625 in 1938. By this time the steel wheels of earlier machines had been replaced with rubber tires. Although this machine made heavy use of sheet steel design, it nevertheless weighed 3,000 pounds. Alemite grease fittings were used extensively, and this was a modern step forward in machine design. Despite its relative inefficiency by later standards, the Corn Master was indeed a major leap forward in mechanizing the corn harvest.

Corn Pickers

The No. 1 Corn Master first appeared about 1940. This machine had a unique design with gathering chains being used to carry the ears of corn upward. This design required the long extensions to make a trough or channel for the purpose. Oliver built the No. 1 Corn Master until about 1948 when it was apparently replaced with the new Model 15, also a one-row machine. In the late 1940s this model was retailing at about $800. It weighed about 1,800 pounds.

Oliver Model 2 Corn Master pickers were built until 1957. During the 1940s it was priced at about $1,100, but by the end of production the price had risen to about $1,550. The Model 2 underwent various modifications and improvements subsequent to its 1940 introduction. However, the basic design remained the same during its production run. Model 2 pickers used eight husking rolls having a length of 33 inches. The snapping units were designed on 41-inch centers, thus presuming that the crop was planted either in 40 or 42-inch rows.

Oliver's Model 5 one-row snapper was offered in the 1951-54 period. Priced at only $895 it was a low-priced alternative to hand picking, and was within the budget of even the smallest farmer. Farmers generally were more than ready to buy a corn picker as soon as they became generally available. While a few people enjoyed picking corn by hand, the majority found the task to be sheer drudgery. Curiously, a small minority preferred picking by hand, even into the early 1950s. For most, the annual 'battle of the bangboards' had ended a decade earlier.

In 1951 Oliver introduced their Model 5 picker. It was available either as a picker-husker, or as a snapper. The latter was identical to the husker, except that it had no husking bed. These machines remained in production until 1954. Oliver sold the Model 5 as a picker-husker at about $1,075, but the Model 5 snapper saw a substantial reduction in price to only $895. For small farms the one-row machine was often the preferred choice, but the great majority of farmers opted for the two-row machines.

Between 1955 and 1960 Oliver offered their Model 6 corn picker. It was available as a picker-husker at about $1,060 or as a snapper at $990. This one-row semi-mounted design was preferably used with certain Oliver tractors, and is shown here on an Oliver Super 55. However, it appears that adapter kits were available, making it possible to use the Model 6 on other selected tractor models. Demand for the one-row design diminished rapidly in the late 1950s. By that time farmers were looking toward the combine as the machine of choice.

Model 4 Oliver mounted pickers made their first appearance in 1951. With various changes and modifications this style remained in the product line until 1964. Initially the Model 4 was built for use with Oliver Row-Crop 70, "77" and "88" tractors. Mounted pickers had the advantage of unobstructed view for the operator and the distinct disadvantage of subjecting the operator to a constant bombardment of dust. A lever within reach of the operator permitted on-the-go adjustment of the snapping rolls whenever necessary. In 1957 this machine sold for about $1,950.

Mounted pickers were of particular advantage for opening fields or working in contoured rows. The Model 4 featured roller-type gathering chains for longer life and used snapping rolls with live points. In addition, the snapping roll speed was increased for greater capacity and picking efficiency. Oliver was the first to introduce the live pto shaft system, and this was a distinct advantage with a mounted picker. In reality, the live pto dated back to the days of Hart-Parr with their 'live' pto driven from the counterbalance pulley on the engine.

Serial number listings indicate that the first Oliver Model 74 mounted picker was built in 1963. This machine was available as a husker with an 8 or 12-roll husking bed, a snapper, or as a picker-sheller. The latter style was available as late as 1967. Model 74 mounted pickers embodied the latest in design, including an extra-large husking bed and a high-volume cleaning fan. The husker, snapper, and sheller units were easily interchangeable, and the big sheller unit had a capacity of 360 bushels per hour. It used a 64-inch shelling cage. Oliver priced the picker-husker at about $3,000.

Corn Pickers

Built in the 1964-67 period, Oliver's Model 74 picker-sheller reflected the change in farming practices from ear corn storage to direct field shelling. During this period however, many farmers were opting for the self-propelled combine with a corn head. However, the Model 74 was an alternative to this method that still permitted direct shelling. By 1966 the Model 74 picker-sheller was retailing at about $3,550, or about $200 more than a comparable picker-husker. By comparison, the Model 74 picker-snapper was priced at only $2,750.

Beginning in the late 1950s Oliver provided corn harvesting equipment for almost every requirement. For a time the company went so far as to offer a portable recirculating corn dryer. In the 1957-60 period this Oliver Model 73 picker-sheller was available. Ear corn dropped into the shelling unit and from there was conveyed into a trailing wagon or an accompanying truck. This was possible by use of a unique corn auger which could deliver either to the side or to the rear. For storage purposes the auger could be swung to the front to reduce machine dimensions.

Oliver announced the Model 83 corn picker in 1966, but it does not appear that full-fledged production began until 1967. Initially the Model 83 was built with an eight-roll husking bed, but in 1968 it was also offered with a twelve-roll bed. Production of the Model 83 series ended in 1976. The husking and shelling units were interchangeable and the Model 83 could also be furnished to accommodate narrow or wide rows. Improvements of this machine over previous versions also included blade-type snapping units, a feeding beater and an overhead raddle. By the time production ended in 1976 the Model 83 husker with an eight-roll husking bed retailed at $4,440, while the twelve-roll style listed at $4,900.

Model 83-S Oliver picker-shellers sold for about $4,250 in 1976, the last year of production. This machine had a huge 64-inch shelling cage to accommodate 150-bushel corn yields without difficulty. However, by the 1970s the majority of corn growers were opting for the corn combine. The latter could be equipped with a four-row, or even larger head, thus hastening the harvest. With the decline in sales for conventional corn pickers, production finally came to an end, closing out an interesting era in farm machinery development.

Corn & Cotton Planters

While perhaps not as significant to the Oliver line as their tractors or combines, the Oliver planter line was nevertheless of major importance. Historically, the Oliver Farm Equipment merger was an ideal one in many respects. Applied to the product line, it brought together an excellent machinery line with little overlapping of products. The planter line had been developed by American Seeding Machine Company and was sold under their Superior banner. Oliver continued to sell their planters as Oliver-Superior into the 1950s. This alone testifies to the high quality of the Superior planter line.

Unfortunately, research efforts for this book came up short regarding literature and information of the Oliver planter line, especially for the 1940s and 1950s. Given the usual requirements of completing a project as quickly as possible, and since two years were spent in research of the Oliver line, it was expedient to move forward with the project, even though a gap obviously exists in the Oliver planter line.

With the 1969 acquisition of Oliver by White Motors the planter line lost its distinctive identity. Thus, White planters are not included under this heading.

For some years before merging into Oliver, the American Seeding Machine people had been offering an array of planters and drills. Included were various styles of cotton drills. One well-known variety was the No. 4 Superior cotton drill. It was available with a plain runner or with a disc opener. This small one-row unit was also made with a plain seed box as shown, or could also be supplied with an additional fertilizer box. Due to certain farming practices, these small planters were offered by Oliver at least until the early 1940s.

In trashy or rocky ground the disc openers were preferable. This Superior No. 5 check-row planter was thus equipped, and also includes optional fertilizer boxes for banding in the row. Unquestionably, the Oliver planter line was based over that developed by Superior. Thus, with the Oliver Farm Equipment merger a fully developed planter line came into the picture. During the 1930s Oliver made further developments, and by 1940 the Oliver-Superior 9-D planter appeared.

Oliver's corn planter line traced its ancestry back to the American Seeding Machine Company, one of the merging partners that formed Oliver Farm Equipment Company. The Superior line of American Seeding Machine Company quickly became the Oliver-Superior line. In fact, Oliver used the 'Superior' logo on numerous farm implements for at least a decade. Initially the Oliver-Superior line differed little from that previously offered by American Seeding Machine Company. Included was this Superior No. 3 one-horse fertilizer corn drill of the 1930s.

Superior offered an extensive variety of fertilizer drills, including the No. 5 one-horse machine with five discs. Although these implements were not commonly used in the small grain areas of the west and midwest, they saw wide use in the southern states, particularly as applied to the cotton crop. Again, farmer preference prevailed. Superior was sensitive to the need, as was Oliver. Thus, these Superior and Oliver-Superior drills were available approximately up to the onset of World War Two.

Corn & Cotton Planters

During the 1950s Oliver made many improvements to its planters. The horsedrawn planter came to an end, and a series of modern four-four row designs followed. The 540 planter shown here was a popular model. It was available in a four-row design with width adjustment ranging from 28 to 40 inches in 2-inch steps. It could also be furnished as a six-row planter, using a 166-inch frame. The latter design permitted row widths of 28 or 30 inches. The time-honored check-row system came to an end during the 1950s.

Steel press wheels were often a problem in sticky soil. In fact, wheel cleaners were a necessity. This problem ended with the use of rubber press wheels. Oliver planters like this 340 were thus equipped. Large 16-inch press wheels were used and an adjustable mounting permitted calibrating them for a precise and uniform planting depth. By the 1960s the Oliver planters were using fiber glass fertilizer boxes which were impervious to the rusting effects of commercial fertilizers.

By the 1960s Oliver was also offering huge tool bar planters, with this huge twelve-row design being typical. The tool bar design permitted setting the planting units to any desired width. Some Oliver planter designs used a combination hill drop and drill boot. Converting from one planting method to the other was very simple, requiring only that each hopper bottom be turned 180 degrees. The combination boot contained both a feed wheel and a drill tube. These planters were also available with a cast iron boot for drilling only.

This No. 3600 Tool Bar Planter was of 1969 vintage. It represented the latest in planter design. Eight planting units are shown here, but the total number varied, depending on the row width selected. Some twenty years earlier, Oliver was offering their small Superior No. 44 and No. 44-T planters. These were two-row tractor planters, essentially built over the earlier horsedrawn designs. Another innovation of the 1950s was the No. 1009-D and the No. 1012-D planter. These were two and four-row units built for direct tractor mounting. Another important design was the No. 452 four-row pull-type planter of the mid-1950s. However, technology and farming practices were changing so rapidly during the 1950s and 1960s that it was difficult to stay abreast of industry changes and farmer demands.

So far as can be determined, Oliver began producing cotton harvesters in the late 1940s, with 1950 being a probable starting date. Little information has surfaced on these machines during the course of present research. The Model 10 cotton stripper was built until 1958. This pull-type machine had a nearly identical partner in the Model 20 stripper, except that the latter was built for mounting on tractors. Oliver also produced a two-row pull-type machine during the same general period.

In the late 1950s Oliver introduced their Model 23 cotton harvester. In a short time it was replaced with the Model 23-A, and this machine remained on the market until 1970. The Model 23-A was built in both the mounted and pull-type varieties, each having their own advantages. Cotton was the last major farm crop to be mechanized, although efforts continued for some years to mechanize harvesting of garden crops. In 1965 the Model 23-A pull-type machine listed at about $1,950.

Oliver Model 43 cotton harvesters made their debut in 1966, with production continuing until 1971. The Model 43 was built for basket or trailer delivery, with the trailer style being shown here. It simply involved the use of a towed trailer. This model was considerably less expensive than the basket style machine, having a list price of about $2,800. Cotton harvesters eliminated the time-consuming and back-breaking task of picking cotton by hand, as it had been done in all the centuries preceding the development of this unique machine.

Following the Model 43 Oliver cotton harvesters came the Model 23-B cotton harvester from White Farm Equipment. It was an improved, pull-type version of the earlier Model 23-A machine. As with the entire Oliver and White cotton harvester line, virtually no information has surfaced on these interesting machines. Despite their importance to the cotton grower, it does not however appear that Oliver's cotton harvester line ever became a major source of income compared to the overall factory output. In 1991 this Model 23-B sold for about $2,900. With the November 1992 announcement that the White factory at Charles City, Iowa would be closed, it is to be assumed that production of this machine might be acquired by another manufacturer, or be completely ended.

Model 43 cotton harvesters could be supplied in a basket design in lieu of the trailer delivery style. The basket style machine made this an entirely self-contained unit, but it was priced considerably higher than the trailer delivery machines. In 1971 the Model 43 shown here sold at $3,760. Once the basket was full it could be emptied into a waiting truck for a trip to the processing plant. No production figures have been located for the Oliver cotton harvester line.

Cultivators

Oliver's cultivator line of 1932 differed little from that previously offered by Oliver Chilled Plow Works. While a few farmers opted for tractor cultivators by 1930, the vast majority still used live, animate horsepower for the task. However, during the 1930s and 1940s the transformation was essentially completed. Shown here in the Oliver No. 35 cultivator. Besides the pioneering work of Oliver Chilled Plow Works in cultivator development, it appears that American Seeding Machine Company, another partner to the Oliver merger, was also involved to a lesser degree.

While one-row horse cultivators were far more popular, the two-row style was also sold to some degree. Most two-row designs used two poles and three horses. This Oliver design of 1932 is typical. Four levers are provided for individual depth control of each gang. In addition, a single hand lever is provided to raise and lower the entire cultivator. With the coming of tractor cultivators, many of these implements found their way to a convenient grove, awaiting the eventual coming of a salvage dealer.

Until the 1850s, the majority of field cultivation was done with a hoe. An entire family could keep only a small field under cultivation. Thus, row crops were far more labor intensive than small grain crops such as wheat, oats, and rye. From the historical perspective then, cultivators of any type are a relatively recent invention.

Initially, cultivators were built with wooden wheels and a wood frame. There was no seat; the concept of riding instead of walking was virtually anathema to most farmers of the time. This concept remained viable into the early 1900s. Many farmers were of the opinion that riding on the cultivator was an additional, and unnecessary burden on the horses.

Oliver Chilled Plow Works began developing and marketing cultivators in the latter part of the nineteenth century. From their pioneering efforts came a full-blown line of horsedrawn cultivators by about 1900. Within a couple decades the tide was changing. Various companies were offering motor cultivators by 1915, and it was increasingly obvious that the days of the horsedrawn cultivator were numbered.

Cleveland Tractor Company endeavored to adapt cultivators to their tractors, and Oliver Chilled Plow Works was instrumental in achieving that goal. Developmental work continued for some years, but Oliver Farm Equipment Company had no tractor cultivator of its own when the company was formed in 1929. By the next year, Oliver had introduced its 18-27 row-crop tractor, and with it, Oliver was able to furnish a two-row cultivator. Designed especially for this tractor, this was a rather heavy implement, but it was, like its horsedrawn predecessors, part of an evolutionary development.

As tractor designs improved, so did the cultivator line. For some years the front-mounted design was considered optimum, but with the development of the three-point hitch, rear-mounted cultivators gained in popularity. Changes in cropping practices and the use of specific herbicides came in the 1960s. Over the next twenty years herbicides have reduced the need for cultivators. Essentially, killing weeds by mechanical means has been largely replaced by chemical weed control. Thus, this most important secondary tillage tool has largely disappeared from the scene.

With the 1930 introduction of the Oliver 18-27 row-crop tractor, Oliver also provided a tractor-mounted cultivator. This two-row unit is mounted on an Oliver 70 tractor. It was adjustable for row widths varying from 28 to 42 inches. Oliver's advertising of the 1930s laid heavy stress on the importance of timely cultivation. Usually, corn was cultivated at least three times, often four times, and rarely, even more. The obvious point of the sales pitch was that with a tractor cultivator, this once-laborious task was made efficient and easy to accomplish.

Cultivators

The 1000 Series cultivators were introduced about 1949 and continued into the late 1950s. Oliver built a total of 27 different styles in two-row and four-row sizes within this series. Various changes followed, including the 300 Series cultivators of 1960 and subsequently. Larger tractors and larger farms demanded larger cultivators. This 1961 model is of the eight-row variety. Gauge wheels at each gang provided stability and kept each gang at its preset operating depth.

In the late 1950s Oliver introduced a series of cultivators designed for the three-point hitch. These rear-mounted cultivators became very popular. Despite quick-attach systems and other devices to simplify attaching the front-mount styles, it remained a laborious task. The three-point design permitted a farmer to back up to the cultivator, attach the lift arms and link, and begin cultivating. If another job came along the next day, it was just as easy to drop the cultivator and go to the next task.

No. 640 cultivators appeared in the late 1950s, and this one is shown attached to an Oliver 770 tractor. At an earlier time the gauge wheels were of steel. This modern design used semi-pneumatic gauge wheels which tended to shed themselves of accumulated soil. The gangs were adjustable over a wide range to suit varying row widths. Likewise, the gauge wheels were also adjustable over a wide range. As another major improvement, hydraulic systems of the 1940s and following, eliminated a tiring hand lift.

This No. 36 Surface and Subsurface Cultivator of 1932 was a carryover developed earlier by Oliver Chilled Plow Works. Certain soil types demanded a heavy implement like this to break up hardpan. Considerable power was required by this unit, but increasingly large tractors of the 1930s made the No. 36 a valuable tool. A large crank handle permits precise adjustment of the operating depth. Traction wheels are provided to actuate the power-lift device. It was controlled by a convenient rope from the operator's seat.

For certain applications the surface cultivator was the tool of choice. The flat, sharpened shovels operated just beneath the soil surface. Weeds were effectively controlled by having the roots cut off just below the surface. In dry weather the surface cultivator had the further advantage of permitting cultivation with a minimum exposure of moist soil to drying winds. The No. 44 beat and bean cultivator shown here was yet another tool carried over from Oliver Chilled Plow Works directly into the Oliver Farm Equipment Company line.

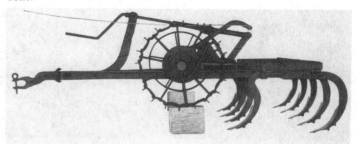

Cultivators

Disc cultivators were popular in certain areas and were ideal for specific crops. This No. 627 front-mounted design was, like others of the 1950s, capable of wide adjustment. As shown here, the discs are turned for hilling or turning dirt toward the row. The discs could also be adjusted to carry soil toward the center of the row if desired. Either way, the primary goal was to destroy weeds, as well as to loosen and aerate the soil. Front mounted cultivators were difficult to attach and detach, compared to the three-point, rear-mounted designs.

About 1969 Oliver introduced their No. 374 rear-mounted cultivator; this one is connected to an Oliver 1555 tractor. The latter was also sold as the White-MM G550 tractor in 1971. Rear-mounted cultivators used a stabilizing device to minimize the natural side shift inherent with the three-point system. In some instances, as with the Oliver cultivator, a large coulter blade was used to stabilize the machine. By the 1970s many farmers were opting for chemical weed control, thus eliminating the need for a cultivator.

This 1971 design illustrates the Oliver "Cutter Wheel" cultivator. It was fully introduced for the 1972 crop season. The rolling cultivator wheels were adjustable to achieve the desired degree of aggressiveness. They could be turned toward the row for hilling, or away from the row to maintain a level seedbed. Two large rolling-type stabilizers are evident, as are the large rear sweeps to further loosen and aerate the soil surface.

Field cultivators with mechanical lifts were eventually replaced with new designs operated with hydraulic power. This No. 247 chisel plow cultivator was a pull-type model, but Oliver also built a wide variety of mounted styles. Pull-type and mounted field cultivators each had specific advantages, and often, this resolved itself into simple farmer preference. The No. 247 was offered in several different styles and sizes. Various sweeps could be secured, depending on the desired application.

During the 1960s, and perhaps at other times, Oliver offered a heavy subsoiler mounted on a tool bar. Since the subsoiler operates at a substantial depth, only a few teeth will suffice to fully load even a very large tractor. Depending on the soil type and other field conditions, the number of teeth was easily varied to suit the available power. In some instances, as few as three teeth were all that could be handled, but for other soils, five or more teeth could be used.

Disc Harrows

The disc harrow did not come into general use until the 1880s. Spike tooth harrows appeared long before, but the first patent for a gang disk did not appear until 1854. Oliver Chilled Plow Works began marketing their version during the 1890s. Essentially the design saw little change for nearly forty years. With the arrival of tractor power the disc (also spelled 'disk') harrow underwent a complete change of design. These new implements were heavier and used larger blades than formerly. Again, the early tractor discs saw little change until the 1950s. About that time increased tractor horsepower and larger farms predicated the need for bigger, heavier, and more aggressive disc harrows.

A notable change in farming practices began during the 1950s, in that the disc harrow was becoming a favored primary tillage implement over the plow. In order to achieve the desired results, disc harrow designs were modified to provide an implement having greater penetration than earlier models. New blade designs, larger blades, heavier frames, and numerous other changes were the result. In today's agriculture the disc harrow has become a favorite tillage implement, and has largely rendered the moldboard plow obsolete.

When Oliver Farm Equipment Corporation was formed in 1929 the new company instantly acquired a complete line of tillage implements. Oliver Chilled Plow Works had developed this line over some seventy years, so these implements had already achieved rights of passage in the industry. This Style NTDH disc harrow of 1932 was but one of numerous styles and sizes offered by Oliver during the 1930s. In fact, the disc harrow line was so well established that few changes were evident until the late 1940s.

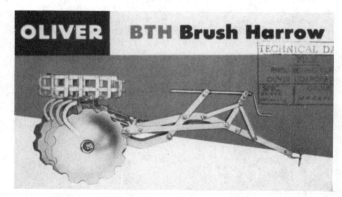

Oliver Chilled Plow Works introduced their BTH brush harrow already in the 1920s, and Oliver was building essentially the same unit into the early 1950s. This model was exceptionally heavy and rugged to withstand the loads to which it was subjected. The notched blades were 24 inches in diameter, and a substantial weight box was provided for better penetration. Oliver also suggested the BTH for deep tillage in orchards and for heavy stubble. A simple adjusting screw permitted changing the angle of the gangs at will.

A 1957 advertising brochure describes the Oliver Power-Angled double disc harrows. Double or tandem disc harrows achieved a degree of popularity during the 1930s but failed to overtake the single gang unit in popularity until the 1950s. Angling or straightening the gangs was achieved by the use of a latch combined with a telescoping tongue. Raising the latch and driving forward angled the gangs. Again raising the latch and backing up straightened the gangs into a transport position.

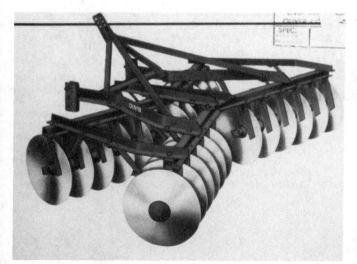

In the early 1950s Oliver introduced its No. 330 tandem disc harrow. This was a three-point hitch design and was offered in 7 1/2 and 9-foot sizes. Designed especially for small or irregular fields, the No. 330 could be used with any tractor having the three-point hitch system. At this point in farm implement development some manufacturers were using their own unique 'fast-hitch' system. In many instances, only specially designed implements could be used. For the No. 330, this was no problem, and this was an obvious sales advantage.

Disc Harrows

About 1955 Oliver introduced their No. 240 wheeled tandem disc harrow. This ushered in a new era for Oliver's disc harrow designs. The No. 240 was operated hydraulically. Rubber tires carried the disc when in the raised position, permitting a farmer to travel on the road from one field to another. Oliver offered the No. 240 in 9 1/4, 10 1/2, 11 3/4, and 13-foot sizes. Blades were available in 16, 18, and 20-inch diameters. About 1958 Oliver followed with their No. 241 disc harrow. It was a heavier machine that featured prelubricated, sealed-for-life ball bearings.

During the late 1950s Oliver introduced the 260 Series disc harrows. Variations remained available into the 1960s. This No. 261 illustrates the improvements in design over the earlier styles. A heavier frame was used, and angling or straightening the gangs was easily achieved. Ever increasing tractor horsepower and constantly larger farm units demanded larger sizes. Heavier and larger blades promoted better penetration. All of these factors helped to popularize the disc harrow as a primary tillage tool.

During the 1960s, as the disc harrow rose in favor over the moldboard plow, it also was required to do a better job of field tillage. This No. 262 disc harrow is thoroughly establishing a new seedbed. As is obvious, heavy trash is in its path, but behind the No. 262, little is present except for nicely tilled soil. Although it requires considerable power, this 16-foot model will cover a large acreage every day. This lowers the overall input cost while lessening the labor requirements.

After acquiring Oliver in 1969, White Motors continued with essentially the same line of disc harrows that had been pioneered by Oliver. This White No. 263 disk harrow is in the process of tilling and leveling a large field. Larger tractors have permitted greater ground speed. This in turn has permitted the disk harrow to achieve its potential as a ground leveler and as a clod buster. Certain soils tend to form clods, and they in turn, are not conducive to forming the optimum seedbed. A great many disk harrows are equipped with an attached harrow to assist in seedbed formation. Oliver began offering these devices already in the 1950s.

This big Oliver 2655 is coupled to a No. 271 Oliver disk harrow. Hydraulics are a boon; this hydraulic fold model can be closed or extended from the tractor cab. Obviously, a rigid frame design would be impractical, but hinging the outer gangs and actuating them with hydraulic power solved the problem. By the 1970s, the 20-inch blade had become the rule rather than the exception, and some disk harrows use even larger blades. By comparison, disk harrows of the 1930s commonly used 14 and 16-inch blades.

Drills

Unquestionably, the grain drill line from American Seeding Machine Company was the latter's most important contribution to the 1929 merger. Granted, American Seeding Machine had developed ancillary lines, but of these, none was as important as the grain drill. Of course, American Seeding Machine was itself the product of an earlier merger that brought together several product lines and several unique designs into a single focus.

Oliver Farm Equipment, and later, Oliver Corporation continued to use the 'Superior' tradename in connection with their grain drills. This tradename had been applied to grain drills for half a century prior to the Oliver merger, and continued under Oliver, and then, White Farm Equipment, for almost fifty more years.

A descriptive analysis of grain drills is an arduous and difficult task. Yet, the grain drill was one of the kingpins in farm mechanization. Its role in this regard cannot be overemphasized.

Early models used wooden wheels and a wooden frame. Most other parts were of cast iron. The design remained virtually unchanged into the 1940s. The wooden wheels were replaced with steel in the 1920s, and in the 1950s Oliver announced an entirely new line of grain drills. The latter were built almost entirely of formed sheet steel built over a steel superstructure. Rubber tires came into use, and from this new foundation came additional developments during the 1960s and following years.

Oliver's grain drill line was simply a continuation of the drills built by American Seeding Machine Company. The latter was formed by a 1903 merger of several grain drill manufacturers. Obviously, the merger lessened competition, but it also brought together several unique designs which were incorporated into a single unit. Shown here is an Oliver-Superior No. 26 grain drill of 1932. It is a double-run drill with disc openers. The machine shown here is actually a fertilizer drill, but it could also be furnished as a plain grain drill as the No. 26-A.

This No. 8 Oliver-Superior beet and bean drill is equipped with special irrigating shovels. Many other attachments could be supplied for Oliver-Superior drills. In addition, the Oliver-Superior line included disc drills and hoe drills in many different sizes and styles. Even before the 1929 Oliver merger, Superior had developed a hitch conversion that permitted the ordinary drill to be used as a tractor drill. Press drills were yet another option available in the Oliver-Superior line.

Oliver's drill line extended far past the ordinary grain drill to include beet and bean drills. This No. 8 unit of the 1930s had been previously developed by Superior. The four-row design contained features unique to the requirements of these important crops. Grain drills gained their first major impetus with Jethro Tull in England during the eighteenth century. While some thirty grain drill inventions were recorded in America prior to 1840, the actual manufacturing of these implements did not begin in the United States until about 1850. After that time this machine developed rapidly. Concurrently, specialized equipment such as this beet and bean drill made their appearance.

Drills

This Oliver-Superior furrow drill was first offered in 1930. It was intended for tractor power. Oliver took great pride in offering a drill which with extremely accurate feed regulation. The company referred to this furrow drill as being equipped with 'Plowfur' single disc openers. Pointing to the accuracy of these drills, Oliver noted that ninety different settings were available 'without putting anything on or taking anything off.' Fifteen different changes in feed rate were possible without so much as stopping the drill.

American Seeding Machine Company had previously developed this broadcast lime sower. It was intended for simple broadcasting of lime and commercial fertilizers. The No. 2 was a two-horse machine with a width of eight feet, and had a hopper capacity of ten bushels. A one-horse unit was also available in a width of 5 feet. Wide-based wheels were used to prevent them from sinking in the ground. This unit could be adjusted to broadcast anywhere from 75 to 3,000 quarts of lime or fertilizer per acre.

Oliver-Superior alfalfa and grass seed drills had been previously offered by American Seeding Machine Company. These drills were somewhat different than the ordinary, in that they used a four-inch disc spacing. Plain drill usually were built with a seven-inch spacing. Oliver stressed the advantages of this drill, noting that the ideal seed placement was in the ground, rather than on top. Economy was another factor. For instance, an early Oliver-Superior catalog notes that in broadcasting, an average of 66 clover seeds are deposited on each square foot of soil, this being many times that needed for a good crop. By using a drill, the amount of seed was substantially reduced.

About 1940 Oliver introduced a new line of superior plain drills with a steel hopper. They were built with 7, 8, and 10-inch spacing, and with anywhere from 12 to 28 runs. Ordinarily this drill was supplied as an open delivery, single disc style. It could also be supplied with the closed disc or 'Plowfur' style, and with a horse hitch. A tractor hitch was optionally available. This Oliver-Superior grain drill is being drawn by an Oliver 70 standard-tread tractor.

Into the 1950s Oliver offered their No. 26 Superior grain and fertilizer drills. They were available with power or hand-lift as desired. The power lift mechanism was mechanically operated from the drill wheels. Another 1950s option was the use of a hydraulic lift system. Oliver-Superior drills used the double-run force feed system that had been developed by American Seeding Machine Company many years before. In the double-run force feed the feed wheel separates the feed cup into two parts. One side has a larger opening for large seeds, and the other side is smaller for small seeds. Oliver used an exclusive spring-locked cover to close the side which was not in use.

About 1955 Oliver introduced a new Oliver-Superior model, the No. 64. It utilized an entirely new concept in design and construction, but retained the traditional features inherent with the Superior designs. The low-profile design was only 3 1/2 feet to the top of the seed hopper. Lifetime sealed disc bearings were a new feature, and the fully-enclosed and lubricated transmission provided 144 different seeding rates. A traditional design, the double-run feed distributor, was retained in this new drill. Numerous options and special equipment was available for the No. 64 Oliver-Superior.

A major new feature of the No. 64 grain drill was a redesigned disc furrow opener. It was intended for high drilling speeds to reduce planting time. The No. 64 used a staggered mounting pattern for the openers. This provided extra trash clearance. The single-disc openers were 14 inches in diameter, while the double-disc openers were 13 1/2 inches in diameter. Spring-break hoe openers were available for use in stony or root-infested fields. A new disc scraper design was included in this drill, along with the choice of 15- or 20-inch tire equipment.

Oliver's No. 76 grain drills were introduced in the early 1970s. Even at this date, the Superior trade-name is evident, once again paying homage to the grand heritage shared by the Oliver-Superior line. Production of the No. 76 grain drill was eventually centered at the Shelbyville factory, in keeping with White's gradual consolidation of the various implement lines. Unfortunately, the entire farm equipment industry was undergoing dramatic change and consolidation of the equipment lines would prove to be insufficient to retain profitability.

One of the last Oliver grain drill styles was the ultra-modern No. 96 shown here. Fully hydraulic control was a standard feature, along with the latest in openers, press wheels, and other components. Although the double-run force feed system common to the Superior line remained intact, it had been updated and revised to reflect higher field speeds and modern technology. Grass seed could be sown in bands or broadcast, depending on preference. The rear-mounted hopper assures shallow placement and the rubber-tube conductors were a major improvement over the steel spiral tubes of earlier models.

Oliver followed the earlier example of Cleveland Tractor Company in offering various equipment built over its tractors. Actually, this "3A-48" trencher does not appear to have been built by Oliver, but by another vendor. However, it is a most substantial machine, apparently capable of large trenches when required. Note that the seat is pivoted to permit adequate visibility of the trencher, as well as providing a forward view. A bulldozer blade is also provided for backfilling of the ditch.

Although Oliver built a limited amount of earthmoving equipment, the company's emphasis seems to have been far more oriented toward its agricultural lines. By purchasing Be-Ge Manufacturing Company of Gilroy, California in 1952, Oliver added substantially to its industrial line. Be-Ge specialized in scrapers, land levelers, and hydraulic cylinders.

Additional impetus toward earthmoving equipment came from the 1944 acquisition of the Cleveland Tractor Company. The latter aimed its crawler tractor line primarily toward the farm scene, but its larger tractors in particular, were destined primarily for construction work. During the 1950s in particular, Oliver made a serious attempt to enter the market of earthmoving equipment. However, crawler tractor production ended in 1960, forcing Oliver to base its earthmoving machinery over wheel tractor designs.

This Oliver-Cletrac OC-3 crawler is equipped with a Jet backhoe. Adding this machine greatly increased the usefulness of the OC-3. In addition, this small machine was able to work in areas impossible to access with larger equipment. The crawler design was inherently capable of negotiating wet areas impossible for wheel tractors, providing yet another advantage. Much of the development of these small and very useful machines was predicated on the previous development of economical and reliable hydraulic systems.

When Oliver bought out Be-Ge Manufacturing Company it acquired a line of trenching machines which had been developed by the latter company. This photograph illustrates a Be-Ge trencher mounted on a J. I. Case Model VAI industrial tractor. Oliver's advertising pointed to the great usefulness of this machine to contractors, plumbers, and other building trades. Likewise, it was aimed at farm drainage contractors and others having need for this specialized equipment.

Oliver's acquisition of the Cletrac line placed the company into the construction machinery business. Cleveland Tractor had developed their crawlers to a high degree. A sad, but very real legacy of World War Two was that it greatly hastened development of hydraulics. After hostilities ended this relatively new technology was widely applied to farm and industry alike, and with dramatic results. This Oliver-Cletrac is equipped with a fully hydraulic loader. Previous to the end loader, most truck loading was done by conveyors or a gargantuan steam shovel.

**The "Quick Change"
BULLDOZER and ANGLEDOZER — Combined**

Oliver's "77" Industrial of the 1948-54 period could be furnished with the 'Strait-Line' hydraulic loader, shown on the rear of the tractor. It could also be furnished with a "Quick-Change" combined bulldozer and angledozer. The dozer blade was 7 feet long and 29 inches high. It could be pivoted to the right or left simply by moving two pins. A third pin permitted a 6-inch offset of the blade. Removing only four pins would completely dismount the loader.

The Oliver backhoes were built primarily at the Shelbyville factory. However, much of the technology came from the acquisition of Be-Ge Manufacturing Company, especially since the latter had been engaged in manufacturing hydraulic cylinders. For some years Oliver offered backhoes adaptable to certain Oliver tractor models. For instance, the 508, 510, and 613 backhoes were built for mounting on the Oliver 550 tractor. The 615 backhoe was built for the 770 tractor. Oliver 1615 backhoes could be used with the 1550 or 1650 tractors, and the 1617 backhoe was for use with the Oliver 1650 model.

Oliver's No. 70 trencher was designed specifically for mounting to the 550 tractor. This 550 is also equipped with the Oliver No. 558 front-end loader. The backhoe used a 12 cubic foot bucket. Maximum lift was 8 1/2 feet, and the No. 70 had a breakaway force of 3,500 pounds. While these small machines were not intended to replace older and larger styles, they reduced labor costs in construction to a great degree. Much of the small work previously done by hand methods was now mechanized.

The Tampo roller shown here was not built by Oliver; however, the latter provided the engine for this machine. Designed and built by Tampo Manufacturing Company at San Antonio, Texas this roller was a major development with its use of pneumatic tires instead of a steel drum. Between 1938 and 1967 Oliver supplied many manufacturers with the Engine-over-Axle (EOA) equipment for use in their specific applications. Oliver also supplied a substantial number of engines for these and other industrial applications.

**No. 70 Trencher
for 550 Tractor**

Oliver's revolutionary double-end loader could dig either in the front or to the rear of the tractor, but always dumped in the front. Since rear loading necessitated moving the load over and above the operator, the steel canopy was an essential feature. Oliver pointed out that whenever extra traction was needed, it was easy to obtain by simply loading the bucket at the rear and gaining considerable ballast. This design also made steering easy. Despite the unique design of the Strait-Line loader, it does not appear to have gained great popularity.

The LIGHT way to do a HEAVY Job!

A very faded photograph remains as testimony to the early Hart-Parr engine developments. This small pumping engine was likely built prior to 1905. Hart and Parr wrote a significant thesis on gas engine design while students at the University of Wisconsin. Many of the principles they outlined in this thesis were then embodied in the Hart-Parr stationary engines, and later, in their tractor engines. The walking beam pump appears to have been built entirely from wood.

Until about 1920, Hart-Parr offered various of their tractor engines as stationary styles. These could be furnished on wood skids, cast iron base, or on portable trucks. With the introduction of the New Hart-Parr in 1918 the company phased out these large stationary units, and in 1921 began offering a series of stationary engines identical to those available in the tractor line. This "24" power unit was the identical engine as used in the 12-24 Hart-Parr tractor. After the 1929 Oliver merger, the latter continued to offer these stationary power units as late as 1936.

Each of the parties to the 1929 Oliver merger contributed mightily to the new corporation. Without a doubt, the Hart-Parr engines and tractors were a major part of the new company. Hart-Parr began in the 1890s by building engines. From its first tractors to the last, the engines were built within the Hart-Parr factories. Stamina and reliability were always hallmarks of the Hart-Parr design; this was proved in the field thousands upon thousands of times.

Hart-Parr began operations at Madison, Wisconsin by building stationary and portable engines. After tractor building began at Charles City, the company continued to offer stationary and portable engines, using the power plant from the tractors. This practice continued into and after the Oliver merger. At one point, Oliver offered the so-called Oliver-Hercules engine line, having used Hercules engines on some of its combines. At another point, Oliver also offered the famous line of Stover stationary engines, and even produced an Oliver-Stover catalog in the 1930s. These ventures were all of short duration; the company's primary emphasis was on building power units based on current tractor engine styles. Until 1967 Oliver also built Engine-Over-Axle (EOA) transmission assemblies for use with its own engines, or others having the same mounting design. Many different styles and sizes of EOA equipment were built at the Charles City plant.

Power units were manufactured at the South Bend plant until 1958 when production was moved to Charles City. All power unit production ended in 1960.

The Hart-Parr "36" stationary engine was identical to that used in the 18-36 Hart-Parr tractor. It remained on the market until about 1936, although sales of the power units were quite small. Hart-Parr pointed to the durability of these engines, noting that one of them had been operated for forty days and nights without being shut down. Hart-Parr also offered the "36" as an air compressor. One cylinder provided power and the other was fitted with a Buhl compressor head.

The "50"

A 1936 Oliver catalog illustrates the Hart-Parr "50" stationary engine. It remained available, despite the fact that production of the 28-50 Hart-Parr tractor had ended in 1930. This large stationary engine was easily capable of 50 horsepower. It was fitted with a heavy cast iron base for mounting to a concrete foundation or heavy wood sills. By 1936 the market for heavy two-cylinder stationary engines had declined markedly, with customers preferring smaller, multi-cylinder power units.

An advertising folder of the 1930s illustrates the Oliver-Hercules power unit. Two sizes were available, the Model B at 43 bhp, and the Model D with 51 bhp. In this instance, Hercules built the engine, with Oliver serving as a jobber of same. However, these small engines were ideally suited for feed grinders, sawmills, and other machinery. Many areas had no electrical power in the 1930s, so the small, lightweight Oliver-Hercules engines found a ready market.

Oliver sold the Model 50 power unit as early as 1930, continuing its production until about 1937. This engine was the same as that used in the 28-44 tractor built during the same period. The four-cylinder design carried a 4 3/4 x 6 1/4 inch bore and stroke for a displacement of 443 ci. The bare engine weighed over 1,200 pounds and featured nickel alloy iron cylinders with removable sleeves. Oliver could, and did, supply this engine with a transmission and special clutch assembly for use with road graders and other construction equipment.

The Model 35 power unit was essentially the same engine as used in the Oliver "80" tractors. Of four-cylinder, valve-in-head design, its 298 cid resulted from cylinders of 4 1/4 x 5 1/4 inch bore and stroke. Weighing 975 pounds as a bare engine, this style was apparently sold individually or as a companion to the Engine-Over-Axle (EOA) units built by Oliver. Production of the latter began in 1938 and continued until 1967. This engine had a rated speed of 1,200 rpm.

Production of the 166 power units began in 1950. These were the same engines as used in the Oliver 66 tractors. When Oliver changed over to the Super 66 tractors in 1954, the power units followed, maintaining the same specifications as the comparable tractor. Shown here is a Super 166 diesel, complete with clutch. This unit is entirely self-contained, although fan-to-flywheel engines were also available for OEM applications. Power unit production was centered at the South Bend factory until 1958 when production was moved to Charles City.

Engines & Power Units

Oliver built 166, 177, and 188 power units during the same time period as the Oliver 66, 77, and 88 tractors. With the 1954 changeover to the Super series, the engines likewise followed with identical specifications. This 188 power unit is typical of the period. While the 177 power unit carried a 3 1/2 x 3 3/4 inch bore and stroke in its six cylinders, the Super 188 used six cylinders with a 3 3/4 x 4 inch bore and stroke. This yielded over 55 belt horsepower.

Oliver's Super 99 tractor carried a six-cylinder Oliver-built diesel engine. Likewise, this 199 Oliver power unit utilized the same engine with its 4-inch bore and stroke. Capable of nearly 75 horsepower, this unit was built in the 1950-60 period. Production peaked in 1954 with the sale of 474 units; other years averaged less than 200 engines for a twelve month period. In addition to a substantial number of OEM and EOA applications, many of these engines were used for irrigation.

Although this Super 225 power unit was assembled at South Bend, it did not use an Oliver engine, but one built by Hercules. First offered in 1957, the Super 225 diesel remained available from Oliver until 1960. During 1957 and 1958 only nineteen units were sold. A total of 8,723 serial numbers were issued for the Super 225 in 1959. However, it is unknown whether Oliver actually sold all 8,000-plus of these engines or whether substantial blocks of the assigned serial numbers remained unused.

White Motors acquired Oliver as a wholly owned subsidiary in 1960. White Farm Equipment Company was not formed until 1969 when Oliver and several other companies were merged into WFE. However, with the 1960 acquisition, power unit production ended, as did numerous other facets of the Oliver operation. However, Oliver continued with their Power-Pak series of power units, based primarily on the 770 tractor engine. Production of this series also came to a gradual end, disappearing entirely by 1965.

Between 1953 and 1960 Oliver offered a series of small portable generators. Approximately ten different models were offered during this period. However, a check of the serial number listings shows that only 2,000 numbers were assigned to these units. No information has been located to positively show that all of these numbers were actually attached to electric plants. Presumably, the entire unit was purchased from another manufacturer, especially since there is no indication that Oliver was able to build electric generating equipment within a very competitive market.

Fallovators

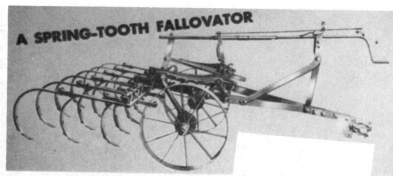

During the 1930s Oliver introduced a new implement, or perhaps, an implement with a new name. It was the Fallovator. Oliver advertising noted that [the Fallovator marks] a new day in summer fallowing---in weed eradication. Claimed to be two machines in one, the Fallovator depended on two different sets of shovels for two distinctly different jobs. One was with duck foot shovels for cultivating summer fallow. The other was with spring teeth to dig out deeply rooted plants such as quack grass, Johnson grass, and Canada thistle.

A 1944 Oliver advertising brochure shows the No. 1 Fallovator. This implement was also quite useful for summer fallow cultivation; that is, keeping the soil loose and free of weeds while not being cropped. Oliver built the Fallovator in a 7-foot model having either 13 or 15 spring teeth. It was also built in a 10-foot style which could use either 19 or 21 teeth. The big 13-foot Fallovator weighed nearly a ton and required considerable power if working at any substantial depth.

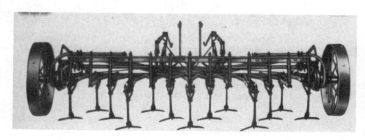

For those with fields infested with quack grass, Oliver recommended the following, "Take the Fallovator into your most heavily infested field of Quack. Use it persistently, correctly, and Quack Grass will cease to choke out paying crops." More detailed instructions follow, but essentially the process consisted of going over the field several times, each time in a different direction. For each trip over the field the Fallovator was set slightly deeper. With the root system thoroughly destroyed and brought up to the top, sun and wind finished the job.

Forage Equipment

In 1954 Oliver introduced their Model 200 forage harvester. Three different heads were available to accommodate windrowed hay, standing hay, or row crops. The Model 200 was a cylinder-type cutter and was available with either four or six knives, at the option of the original purchaser. Separate chopping and loading were possible with this design; Oliver pointed to this system as a major reason for the great capacity of these machines. All controls were within easy reach of the operator. The Model 200 left production in 1960.

Forage Equipment

White-Oliver Model 830 forage harvesters were introduced in 1969. This model remained on the market until 1976. The base unit included a six-knife cylinder cutter and was priced at $2,800. A pickup attachment was priced at $800, while the standing crop head sold for $1,550. Oliver also offered one-row and two-row heads; the latter size sold for $1,550, while the single-row version retailed at $735. This high-capacity machine was apparently a complete redesign of the earlier Model 200 which had gone out of production several years before.

As part of an overall forage equipment line, Oliver offered their Model 820 blower. It was available with the choice of a shaker-hopper or with a drag conveyor. This high-capacity blower was able to fill the tallest silos with ease, depending of course, on sufficient horsepower at the pto shaft. Oliver's late entry into the forage equipment business made it very difficult to reserve a substantial niche in the marketplace, and the company left this endeavor after only a few years.

The White-Oliver Model 840 forage harvester was a self-propelled design. It was built in the 1970-76 period. This high-capacity machine had a variable ground speed ranging from 1/2 mph all the way up to 18 mph when moving down the highway. Oliver built this machine with three different engines. The Chrysler 440 gasoline model was ordinarily supplied. With this engine the Model 840 sold at $11,200. When furnished with a GMC 478 gasoline engine the price came to $11,430, and with a Hercules 478 Diesel engine, Model 840 forage harvesters retailed at $12,920. Head equipment was not included in the base price.

Forage boxes were yet another part of the overall forage equipment line. Oliver truck-mounted this particular example, but by far the most of these forage boxes were mounted on heavy-duty wagon gears. As with the other components of the forage equipment line, Oliver's entry into the market was of relatively short duration. During the 1950s Oliver entered an expansionary phase, attempting to flesh out its product line to better serve the needs of the market. Consumer loyalty to a specific product line had long been a major factor. Following World War Two, so-called 'color loyalty' diminished to a considerable degree. A dark green line of all-Oliver equipment was indeed an unusual circumstance. Thus, Oliver's attempt to enter the forage equipment ended in only a few years.

Forage Equipment

Oliver's forage equipment line eventually included this mower-conditioner unit. The Model 437 mowed, conditioned, and windrowed the hay crop in a single operation. It utilized a full 9-foot cut, straight-flow feed, and featured a cam action reel to feed hay into the machine. With adequate tractor power, the Model 437 could operate at field speeds all the way up to 8 mph. Oliver offered this unit for only a short time. Like other components of the forage equipment line, Oliver entered this arena rather late.

In 1959 Oliver introduced their Model 95 hay conditioner as part of the overall forage equipment line. This model used 80-inch rolls to handle a full 7-foot swath. A unique feature was the triple v-belt drive to cushion the shocks associated with a hay conditioner. Individual compression springs were located at each end of the rolls to insure complete conditioning of the crop. Another feature was a design which located the wheels in alignment with the pickup roll. The Model 95 could be pulled by itself, or could be coupled to a special hitch and pulled directly behind the mower, as shown here. Several other models were offered during the 1960s.

The Model 642 flail chopper was built for a number of years, beginning about 1960. This machine could be used with the forage hood shown here for direct wagon loading. It was built with a six-foot cut, and the flail knives operated at 1,600 rpm. A simple diverter permitted the Model 642 to be used for shredding cornstalks, leaving the cut material evenly on the ground. Oliver also suggested pulling a disk harrow behind the 642 in order to accomplish two jobs, shredding and disking at the same time.

In addition to the Model 642, Oliver also built the 644 and 646 shredders. The 644 was 12 feet wide and could accommodate four corn rows with its 72 rotating knives. Both the 644 and the 646 could be supplied for use with 540 or 1,000 rpm pto shafts. Due to the size of the 646 with its 96 knives, an extra-heavy pto shaft was available as an option. As with many of the lesser-known Oliver products, information on this series of flail shredders is rather scarce.

Grinders & Hammer Mills

Until the 1950s Oliver made little effort to enter the market for feed grinders and related equipment. During the late 1930s Oliver contracted with Stover Mfg. Company at Freeport, Illinois to sell their engines, feed mills, and other equipment under the Oliver-Stover logo. This venture was short-lived however, and the company quickly retreated from the field. During the 1950s Oliver once again entered the arena, this time with a combination grinder and blower. The 408 machine shown here was essentially a grain and forage blower equipped with a regrinder.

Oliver's 408 Grinder/Blower was convertible to a hammermill if desired. Recutting or regrinding reduced the volume of forage and grain, permitting up to 30 percent more material to be stored in the same area. Oliver advertising noted that given a tractor of adequate horsepower, the 408 was capable of reducing a ton of haylage in about 3 1/2 minutes, and a ton of corn silage in even less time. This machine was available for use with 540 or 1,000 rpm pto speeds, as desired.

For a time Oliver built complete grinder-mixers. These were constructed over the basic 300 and 400 hammermills. The 305 grinder-mixer used a 55 bushel mixing tank, while the 306 and 406 grinders each carried a 95 bushel tank. A chain conveyor is obvious; it was easily moved to any desired position and could be quickly swung into a transport position. Several of the full-line manufacturers had been in this endeavor for many years, and several short-line manufacturers specialized in grinding equipment. Thus, Oliver's attempt to enter this very competitive market met with only fair success.

Harrows

The spike-tooth harrow is likely one of the oldest farm implements, probably even older than the plow. A precise dateline has been lost to antiquity. However, Oliver Farm Equipment was fortunate in having several different field tillage lines come into the 1929 merger. This early Evans triple harrow was from American Seeding Machine Company, and had been developed by A. C. Evans Company. The latter was a partner in the American Seeding Machine merger of 1903. This harrow consisted of wooden bars through which the harrow spikes were driven. Oliver offered numerous styles of spike tooth harrows subsequent to the merger.

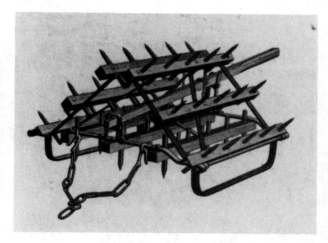

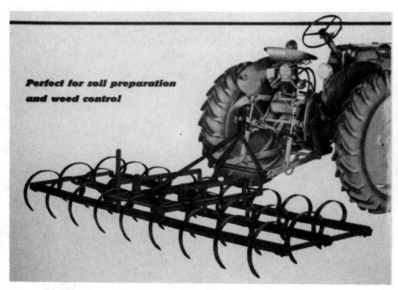

Perfect for soil preparation and weed control

This Series 3000 spring tooth harrow was designed specifically for the three-point hitch system. Spring tooth harrows have been a fairly recent development, dating back to the 1870s. While the spring tooth harrow immediately gained favor, horsedrawn styles were not nearly so effective as tractor harrows. Tractors were able to operate at consistently higher ground speeds. This greatly improved the soil-shattering action which greatly improved the effectiveness of the spring tooth harrow.

Oliver's harrow line included the 283 and 383 spring tooth harrows. The 283 was a wheeled, pull-type unit, while the 383 was for the three-point hitch. As spring tooth harrows evolved, various design changes took place. The size and form of the spring itself was modified to achieve better tillage, and various styles of points were available for specific requirements. As tractor horsepower increased, so did the size of the harrows. The addition of hydraulics did much to improve the ease of operation.

Lawn & Garden Equipment

Illustrated here is the Oliver 105 tractor. This 10 horsepower model was equipped with a Kohler four-cycle engine. It featured a four-speed transmission with available speeds ranging from 3/4 to 7 1/2 mph. Other features included electric starter, electric clutch, and large, flotation tires. This unit was priced at $1,185. Built in 1973 and 1974, the 105 had a smaller companion in the Oliver 75. The latter style was equipped with a 7 horsepower engine. It sold for $760.

In the late 1960s Oliver initiated a line of lawn and garden equipment. Small lawn and garden tractors were becoming increasingly popular, along with related equipment from snow blowers to rotary tillers and log splitters. Under the leadership of White Farm Equipment the line became quite extensive. Initially these products were sold under the Oliver logo, but eventually were built strictly as White products. Specific details are not available, but it is likely that at least some of the lawn and garden products were not actually manufactured by White Farm Equipment (WFE) but were contracted from other manufacturers.

White's lawn and garden equipment line came into full bloom during the 1970s. A plethora of attachments were developed for the Yard Boss tractors. Numerous styles of walking and riding mowers were available, along with an extensive line of snow throwers, rotary tillers, and other equipment. Examples of many different items in the lawn and garden equipment line are shown here.

Numerous attachments were available for the Oliver lawn and garden tractors. Included was this front-mounted snow thrower. The Oliver 125 was essentially built over the same chassis as the Oliver 105. The major difference was that a 12 hp engine was used. Thus equipped, it sold for $1,285. Oliver also offered a 125-H model; the major change being the use of a hydrostatic transmission instead of a four-speed gear box. Oliver 125-H tractors retailed at $1,480. These models were built during 1973 and 1974.

Although the Oliver 145 includes sleek body lines in its design, it nevertheless displays an aura of industrial construction as a tribute to its heavy duty components. This 14 horsepower model was built with a hydrostatic transmission. It is shown here with a rear-mounted rotary tiller. Electric starting, lights, and an electric clutch were all standard features. Its weight of 850 pounds is further proof of its heavy duty construction. Production began in 1973 and ended the following year.

White began offering the GT-Series tractors in 1976. They were built in 10 and 16 horsepower sizes. At the same time, the T-Series tractors were introduced in sizes of 8 and 10 horsepower. These models reflected the general cosmetic lines of the concurrent White farm tractor models, and this is particularly evident over the hood. Numerous attachments were available for all sizes, including the mower deck shown on this GT-1620 model. It was equipped with a 16 horsepower engine.

Another segment of the White lawn and garden tractor line was this LGT 1100 model. It was equipped with an 11 horsepower engine. Topping the line was the big LGT 1655 with a 16 horsepower engine. All were equipped with electric starting and hydrostatic drives. The mower deck is but one of many attachments available for this model. Beyond the usual snow throwers and other attachments, White also offered a small plow, disk harrow, and other garden implements for these tractors.

For a time White built the R-82 and R-50 Yard Boss tractors; the Yard Boss terminology is a registered trademark of White. These models were dedicated primarily for lawn mowing duties, while most of the other lawn tractors were multiple purpose machines. This economical style was without many of the cosmetic features found on the regular lawn tractor line. A one-piece steel frame is evident; it provided great strength and durability with a minimum of weight.

White's lawn equipment line also included a series of walk-behind lawn mowers. About ten different sizes and styles were available. Included was the Lawn Boss, a 5 horsepower, power-propelled unit intended primarily for the professional, but equally adapted to those with large lawns. Numerous safety features were built into these machines, and like other equipment in the White product line, these units were built with the utmost in utility and durability.

Yet another product of the White lawn and garden equipment line was the Shred Boss, a powered shredder with a built-in bagger. Shown here in actual operation, leaves and lawn clippings were raked into the hopper where they were shredded and delivered into an attached plastic bag. This machine was very useful to those who saved the material for garden composting. A precise production period has not been located within the current research.

Lawn & Garden Equipment

For a time White offered a heavy duty high pressure washer. Numerous styles and sizes were available, including this WM 1622. It had a working pressure adjustable from 500 to 1,000 psi for virtually any kind of duty. Depending on the model, a duplex or a triplex plunger pump was used. These units included a concentrate tank and pump in the unit for adding suitable cleaning agents whenever desired. Except for a small amount of advertising material, little else has been located regarding this particular product line.

For a time, White offered a chain saw as part of the overall lawn and garden line. Built by another manufacturer, it was built to White's specifications and carried the White logo. Marketing of the White chain saw seems to have been short in duration. Attempting to carve a market niche in this very competitive market was a tremendous challenge, especially given the financial rewards. Shown here are the 12 and 14-inch White chain saw models.

White's Snow Boss snow throwers entered the market in the 1970s. Shown here is the Snow Boss 800, one of many different sizes and styles. It is a two-stage unit having a front auger and a rear-mounted blower. It is also equipped with power-propelled drive wheels. The Snow Boss 800 used an eight horsepower engine; other models included the 3 hp Snow Boss 300 and the 5 hp Snow Boss 500. A small push-type blower was also built.

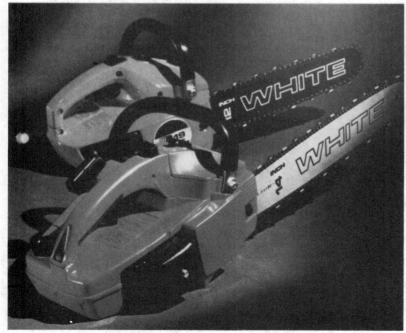

White's garden tiller line included the Roto Boss 300, a 3 horsepower size weighing only 55 pounds. The Roto Boss 500 was a 5 horsepower machine with a Briggs & Stratton four-cycle engine. This machine used 16 forged steel tines and was power-propelled. This model was also convertible to a snow thrower if desired. An optional adapter kit permitted the owner to use it with the White LGT tractor series. White's Roto Boss 802 garden tiller was the largest of the line; it was equipped with an 8 horsepower Briggs & Stratton engine.

Listers

Listers, occupied but a small part of the overall Oliver farm equipment line. Initially developed by Oliver Chilled Plow Works, this important is noted under that heading, as well as under the *Corn Planter* heading of this volume. To avoid redundancy wherever possible, listers are already included under these headings and are not illustrated here as a separate line.

Loaders

Industrial loaders and farm loaders were both part of the Oliver product line. With the development of live hydraulic systems the farm loader became a distinct reality, especially when compared to the heavy and cumbersome mechanical loaders of earlier years.

We have elected to include industrial and farm loaders within the *Tractors* section of this book. This provides a better forum for illustrating them, especially in showing the specific tractor models used with various Oliver loader models. Combining several product lines under a single heading is always a problem, but reproducing the same illustrations several times is likewise a problem. Thus, the better course seemed to be the avoidance of further redundancy.

Middlebusters

Under the *Oliver Chilled Plow Works* section earlier in this book, and the *Plows* section which follows, middlebusters are illustrated. Very important to some farming practices, the middlebuster is not widely known nor at all used in the majority of farming operations. Due however to its importance, this important implement is already shown in the two sections previously cited, and the reader is directed to these sections for further information.

Mowers

NEW EIGHT FOOT CUTTER BAR FOR

NEW IMPROVED NO. 82 MOWER

During the early 1930s Oliver continued to offer horsedrawn mowers. However, with the development of the "60" and "70" tractors came a newly developed tractor mower. A 1941 brochure illustrates the Model 21-B. This semi-mounted design was available with bar lengths of 5, 6, and 7 feet. By 1950 Oliver had developed the Model 22-A power-driven mower. This improved design used two swinging caster wheels. Only two drawbar bolts were needed to attach the mower. It could also be fitted to the Oliver-Cletrac HG-42, HG-60, and HG-68 tractors. About 1954 the Model 22-B mower appeared. The flexible mounting system of the 22-B permitted this machine to follow field contours independently of the tractor.

Oliver's No. 82 mower was but one of several new Oliver designs introduced in the late 1950s and the early 1960s. The No. 82 was available with an eight-foot cutter bar. This, together with other improvements permitted a fifteen percent increase in acreage cut per hour. Standard features of the Oliver mower line included a direct-drive power take off system, together with a positive roller chain drive and an enclosed safety clutch. The roller chain drive and slip clutch were all enclosed in a sealed gear case.

During the 1950s Oliver developed a series of mowers designed for the three-point hitch system. Included was this No. 356 mower, an immediate successor to the No. 355 model. This style was available with a six or seven-foot cutter bar, as desired. On raising the three-point hitch the entire cutter bar floated, and this was a distinct advantage on rough or uneven ground. Connecting this mower required only the connecting of the three-point pins and hooking up the pto shaft. The hazards of high speed mowing were minimized by the use of a positive safety release.

Hay conditioners were developed in the 1950s as a way of improving hay quality. Initially this machine was pulled by one tractor, while another tractor operated the mower. Within a short time a special hitch was developed for the mower so that one tractor could operate both machines simultaneously. The next logical step was to combine both components into a single machine. This Oliver No. 129 mower-conditioner of 1972 is one of the various combination units emerging from the drawing boards and the factories. By the time this machine emerged though, Oliver Corporation was a subsidiary of White Motors.

Outboard Motors

The Oliver outboards saw first light in 1955. Their Outboard 5 shown here was a small unit weighing but 50 pounds. It featured Oliver's Tend-A-Matic remote fuel tank, shown in this illustration. Oliver's expansion into the outboard motor business likely had roots with the sagging farm implement business of the mid-1950s. Presumably, it was thought that expanding into other areas would enhance the year-end balance sheet, thus the announcement of numerous small equipment lines.

Oliver introduced two outboard models in 1955; the Outboard 5 and the Outboard 15. Both models were offered into 1957. Serial number information is almost entirely lacking on the outboard motor line, making it very difficult to determine sales of these units, even on a very approximate basis. The only indication appears in a report to the stockholders which that 'sales of outboard motors, while still small in relation to total sales of the Company, approximately doubled in 1956.'

The Oliver Mohawk 6 hp outboard first appeared in 1958. This model was rated at 4,500 rpm. Weighing but 57 pounds, it was capable of a stern lift of 15 to 17 inches. A conventional 8-inch propeller was used. Other features included a Dura Drive lower unit, Tenda-Matic fuel tank, spiral gears, and underwater exhaust. A 1958 report to company stockholders indicates that the outboard line had lost money the two previous years, but a break-even, or even a modest profit was anticipated for the coming year.

In 1956 Oliver introduced the Outboard 35. This big unit was capable of tremendous thrust. Two of the Outboard 35 engines are shown in this photograph. The counter-rotating Oliver 35's could easily raise outboard runabouts and cruisers to planing position in seconds. Despite the quality of the Oliver outboards there is no indication that sales approached the hopes or expectations of Oliver management. However the company hoped to generate additional business by manufacturing an extensive line for a chain of automotive stores.

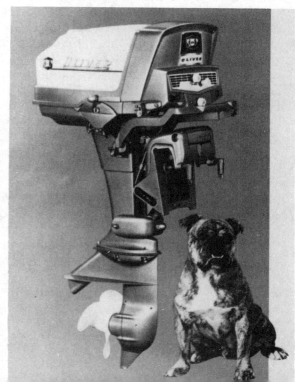

Outboard Motors

During 1958 Oliver announced its Ranger and Lancer 16 horsepower outboard motors. The Ranger weighed 79 pounds and used a 9-inch propeller with an 11-inch pitch. Both styles featured an engine having a 2 1/2 x 2 1/32 inch bore and stroke. Other features included reed valves, anti-friction bearings, and a 6 1/2 gallon Tenda-Matic fuel tank. Silencing included a rubber mounted shroud, rubber suspension, and intake baffles. Spiral gears were used, along with an underwater exhaust. These models could be furnished with the choice of dashboard mounted starter, remote controls, lower unit extension, and a power propeller selection. The Lancer weighed 92 pounds.

The Bulldog 35 horsepower outboard remained in production from 1956 to 1960. This 125 pound unit used an engine rated at 4,500 rpm, and was designed with a 3 1/16 x 2 7/8 inch bore and stroke. For 1960 Oliver announced that F. Perkins Ltd. of Peterborough, England would be manufacturing the Oliver outboard motors. These were the first and only American-designed and British-built motors to be sold in quantity in the United States. However, 1960 was also the last year of production for the Oliver outboard motors. After that year, they disappeared from the scene.

Plows

Obviously, the Oliver plow line was initially a continuation of the plows previously built by the Oliver Chilled Plow Works. As noted under the latter heading, it was James Oliver who gave the world the chilled plow. Going all the way back to the 1850s, James Oliver began perfecting the design. By the time of the 1929 Oliver Farm Equipment Company merger, the Plow Works had nearly 80 years of experience in plow building.

Walking plows, and later the sulky plow and various gang plow models were developed at the Oliver Works. In addition, Oliver was almost prematurely early in offering tractor plows. By 1911 Oliver was building several styles of large tractor plows, going so far as to build a gigantic fifty bottom plow for demonstration purposes. Unquestionably the Oliver approach to plow building was eminently successful. Granted, there were other plow builders, in fact, there

were a great many of them. Yet, Oliver continued to maintain a position of superiority throughout the years. Clever marketing might have achieved this goal in the short term. Yet, Oliver was in the plow business to stay. To accomplish that goal, there was no choice but to build first-class plows, and Oliver did that very well.

Using the vast experience gained by the Chilled Plow Works, Oliver Farm Equipment was able to move forward with the same essential line initially. In addition, the Oliver name was well recognized by the farmer, and this too, was a distinct advantage. Plows of many sizes and styles were a part of the Oliver line until the acquisition by White Motors. The latter continued offering plows for a few years. However, changing farming practices and the introduction of minimum tillage systems brought the plow market to a close. Yet, for over a century, the Oliver name was synonymous with quality plowing equipment.

When Oliver Farm Equipment Company was formed in 1929, the new company continued offering most of the line previously built by the Oliver Chilled Plow Works. Shown here is the James Oliver No. 11 sulky plow of 1932. This horsedrawn style had been introduced several years earlier for the company's founder and namesake, James Oliver. The latter began experimenting with various chilled plow designs in 1855. Although he went through many lean years in his quest, James Oliver was ultimately successful.

Oliver plows were available with a multitude of moldboard designs, each intended for specific soils and conditions. The slatted moldboard was used extensively in some areas, although it was completely useless in others. Even this walking plow of the 1930s is equipped with a slatted moldboard. Oliver Farm Equipment continued to offer walking plows through the 1930s. As with most other farm equipment companies of the time, it appears that much of their horsedrawn equipment was available until the early years of World War Two. Due to defense demands, production of non-essential equipment ceased, and most factories were converted to war production. After hostilities ended, production of horsedrawn machinery never resumed.

Numerous styles of Oliver walking plows were available in the 1930s. As otherwise noted, much of the earlier line developed by the Chilled Plow Works remained in production until about 1940. Styles such as this No. O-98 series included reversible points. This was a great advantage. If the point was damaged or broken in the field, it could be turned over in a few minutes so that work could continue. Likewise, when the point finally was worn out, it was relatively easy to present a new point to the furrow, for a cash savings as well.

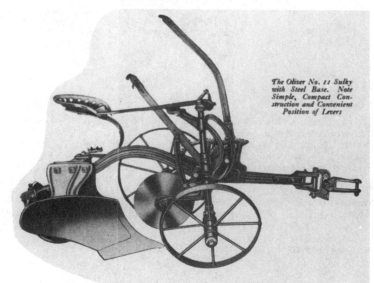

The Oliver No. 11 Sulky with Steel Base. Note Simple, Compact Construction and Convenient Position of Levers

Easy to Operate

Oliver sulky and gang plows of the 1930s were built in many styles and models. In addition there was an extensive variety of moldboards, coulters, jointers, and other attachments available for each model. In effect, this gave Oliver literally hundreds of possible configurations. This Oliver No. 11 sulky plow was built with a steel base. Its rolling landside reduced draft, giving this model the lightest draft of virtually anything built. Features included a renewable shin and a simple lift mechanism.

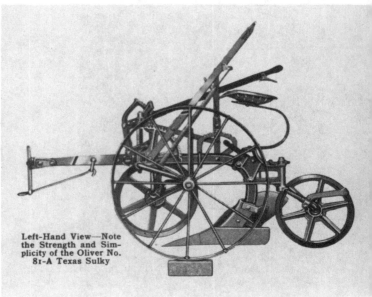

Left-Hand View—Note the Strength and Simplicity of the Oliver No. 81-A Texas Sulky

Oliver's Dixiana walking plow was intended primarily for light loam, mellow and sticky soils. A feature of this style was the high throat for ample clearance. The 'Oliver Plow Book' noted that 'When a walking plow is properly adjusted it can be operated without the operator holding to the handles. The test of a man's ability to adjust a walking plow and sharpen the share is to make that plow operate correctly without holding the handles.' Unfortunately, a great many blacksmiths were less than successful in properly sharpening plow shares, and more than a few farmers were unable to properly adjust the plow.

The Oliver 23DXX Two-Way Sulky Plow.

This left-hand view shows the Oliver No. 81-A Texas Sulky. As the name implies, it was intended for the soils unique to Texas and surrounding areas. A given moldboard design would not work properly in all soils, so proper modifications were needed. In fact, some soils were found to be so sticky as to defy almost every kind of plow moldboard. Yet, Oliver was able to design plows that would work successfully in almost any soil type. Since Oliver was a leader in plow design their huge factories had the resources for the necessary development work. Smaller companies were at a disadvantage in this regard.

For small and irregular fields the Oliver two-way sulky plow was the answer. This No. 23 two-way was offered at least into the 1930s. The unique design permitted plowing from one side of the field to the other, with no need of back furrows or dead furrows. A mechanical lift is provided for each plow base. Sulky plows were usually pulled with three horses. In heavy sod or heavy sticky soil, four horses were sometimes used. By contemporary standards, this method of tilling the soil was extremely slow. Yet, this is precisely how many fields were moved from useless ground to productive acreage.

Oliver Chilled Plow Works had developed a series of tractor plows some years prior to the 1929 Oliver Farm Equipment merger. Many of these models remained in the lineup during the 1930s. Salient features of others were redesigned and retained in new models introduced in that decade and into the 1940s. The 218 and 318 Oliver plows were among the many different models offered during this period. Oliver's own advertising of the 1930s notes that in all, there were over 3,000 types and models of Oliver plows available. The 218 and 318 were big base plows, unique even to the extensive Oliver line.

Included in the Oliver plow line of the 1930s and 1940s was the 512-A and 514-A tractor gang plow. The latter was five bottoms with a cutting width of 14 inches, compared to five bottoms which each cut 12 inches for the 512-A model. Tractor plows gained considerably in popularity during the 1930s. Row-Crop tractors were making their appearance, and with them came even more mechanization of field work. After all, tractors were a tireless machine that could outwork even the best horses, and when day was done the tractor would be parked in a shed, requiring no feed, no grooming, and no attention until ready to go to work the following day.

The 218—an All-Round Plow—Very Widely Used with 2-3 Plow Tractors

The Oliver 514-A, a Tractor Plow of Great Strength and Great Capacity

Plows

Oliver Farm Equipment Company, like the earlier Chilled Plow Works, sent its plow experts into the field on a regular basis. By showing farmers how to adjust and operate their tractor plow, they could work more efficiently, use less tractor fuel, and do a much better job of plowing. For those who seriously studied the adjustment of their plows, the rewards were immediately obvious. Those who were content to turn over the soil in a haphazard way paid a price. Poorly plowed fields were very rough, and almost impossible to level with other equipment. Failure to do a good job of turning under last year's weeds were bound to be plagued with a healthy growth the following year.

Many thousands of acres of brush land were converted to useful and productive fields. Oftentimes this disagreeable task was accomplished with the use of an Oliver 22-A brush plow. Oliver guaranteed this outfit to turn even the toughest brush land into productive soil. Due to the heavy draft required for shearing off substantial roots and laying the brush into a furrow, only a single bottom was used. Even then the job often required a substantial tractor. The brush plow was an implement that was often used throughout a neighborhood, and once the available brush land was turned over, this unit was of little further use.

The 22-A Oliver Brush Sulky, showing view from the mouldboard side.

The New Oliver No. 21 Two-Way Tractor Sulky—Rugged in Strength Sure in Operation.

Oliver's No. 21 two-way tractor plow was a powered version of the earlier horsedrawn designs. To withstand the strains imposed by the tractor, it was of heavier construction. The two-way plow was often used in irrigated fields, hillside plowing, and soil conservation work. The No. 21 could be used for deep as well as for shallow plowing. All the controls were within reach of the operator's seat, and a quick-acting power lift system was a standard feature. Various furrow width adjustments were provided. In 1931 this plow sold for about $125.

Disc plows, like moldboard plows, were offered in numerous styles and sizes. These ranged from a small horsedrawn Pony disc plow up to large tractor-drawn styles. During the 1930s a three-disc variety would be priced at about $150, with this four-disc model being somewhat more expensive. Extension rims on each wheel provided the needed flotation in sandy soil, but the design permitted leaving them in place when working in ordinary or hard ground. Oliver disc plows were designed to withstand the strains imposed by the largest farm tractors of the time.

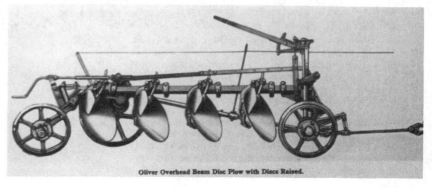

Oliver Overhead Beam Disc Plow with Discs Raised.

The 1950s saw the introduction of Oliver's famous heavy-duty plow line. Included were the 214-B, 316-A, 414-A, and the No. 516 plows. Oliver introduced their famous Raydex plow shares in 1940. These disposable plow shares were made of a special alloy that was rated to be 60 percent harder than anything on the market. Once these heavy duty points wore down, a new set was installed, bringing the plow back to as-new condition. Shown here is an Oliver 4340 pull-type plow of the late 1950s.

Oliver introduced their No. 3240 three-point, fully-mounted plow in the early 1950s. It was a convertible style and could be set up for two or three bottoms as desired. This model also had adjustable cutting width for 12, 14, or 16-inch bottoms. An option was the choice of rigid or spring-trip beams, and the No. 3240 could be equipped with 16 or 18-inch coulters, as desired. Shown here is a 1960s version known as the Model 3242. It is working behind an Oliver 1250 tractor. An intermediate model, the No. 3241 was introduced about 1958.

Late in 1960, Oliver introduced its Model 5540 plow. Essentially, it was a five-bottom version of the earlier 5440 plow; the latter being a four-bottom style. This model was designed for use with any tractor having a Category II 3-point hitch and a separate remote hydraulic cylinder. The four bottom style was capable of having one or two additional beams added, making it either a five- or a six-bottom plow. A special design feature was its capability to work properly behind tractors with an 80-inch wheel tread. This practically eliminated the need of changing wheels treads when going from plowing to row-crop work.

Oliver semi-mounted plows gained great popularity in the 1950s and subsequently. In fact, the mounted and semi-mounted designs all but eliminated the pull-type plows from the scene by about 1960. This No. 508 Oliver plow was especially popular. Its semi-mounted design also featured adjustable cutting widths. Due to the high horsepower on the front end of the plow, trip bottoms were encouraged. Snagging a buried stone or a large tree root with a single plow point could cause severe damage to the entire plow without this safety device.

Plows

The New Spring Automatic Reset 446 Drawn Plow

Oliver introduced their No. 446 pull-type plow about 1960. This large plow featured Oliver's spring-type automatic reset trip device on each plow beam. In all, Oliver offered five different beam trip assemblies to fit any soil condition. The pull-type 446 was available in sizes from 4 to 8 bottoms, with a basic main frame of 4, 5, or 6 bottoms. The cutting width was adjustable for 14 or 16 inches. Ample trash clearance of up to 27 inches was provided, and this model was designed with steerable tail and furrow wheels.

The No. 346 mounted plow was built in 3, 4, and 5-bottom sizes. This heavy-duty design included the automatic spring-trip safety device on each beam. Actually, the No. 346 was the smallest of this series. Other models were available, up to eight bottoms. All featured an adjustable cutting width of 14 or 16 inches. Another feature was a selective front or rear lift system. These plows could be furnished for use with Category II or Category III three-point hitches. Oliver also offered these plows with a hydraulic automatic-reset trip, cushion-action trip, or a shear-pin beam.

Oliver's semi-mounted No. 548 plow was convertible from 4 to 8 bottoms. The frame was adjustable for cutting widths of 16 or 18 inches. A selective hydraulic lift was standard equipment, along with the choice of Category II or Category III three-point hitch equipment. These plows were available with Oliver's clamp-on adjustable subsoilers. This unit clamped onto the plow beam and was designed to rip up the soil several inches below the furrow bottom to break up stubborn hardpan. Of course the Oliver Raydex plow bottoms continued as a major feature.

White Farm Equipment continued manufacturing plows after acquiring Oliver. However, farmers of the 1970s were rapidly moving toward minimum tillage or no-till systems that obviated the need for a plow. Thus, the market quickly changed, and established plow makers could find little market for this time-honored tillage implement. Additionally, plows were not quickly worn out, so the market was fairly saturated by this time, making sales of new plows even more difficult. Shown here is a White Model 348 plow of the early 1970s.

Rakes

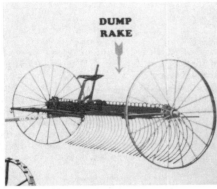

Oliver acquired hay equipment through the 1929 merger. During the 1930s this line remained essentially the same as it had been before, including various sizes and styles of dump rakes. Although the dump rake gathered hay into piles, it was no match for the side delivery rake, which laid the drying hay into a neat windrow. From the historical perspective the dump rake was really nothing more than a mechanized step above gathering hay into piles with a pitchfork. The side delivery rake mechanized the job somewhat further, and this brought an end to a venerable old implement.

Oliver side delivery rakes of the 1930s had been developed in the previous decade. Driving over the cut hay, the side rake lifted and carried the loose material to the side, leaving it in a neat, fluffy windrow. In this state, sun and wind were better able to hasten the curing process. When sufficiently dry, a hay loader carried the material onto a wagon for delivery to the barn. In every stage of farm mechanization, developmental mileposts are evident. With the hay harvest, it was the pitchfork, then the dump rake, then the side rake, and finally, wheel rakes of various styles.

In the 1950s Oliver developed their No. 2 side delivery rake. This model was intended solely for use with tractor power. New features included pneumatic tires, enclosed gears, and heavy-duty construction. Rake teeth could be attached individually to the pipe tooth bar. Some early designs placed the spring eye over the pipe, requiring removal of the pipe and all intervening teeth, just to replace a broken tooth.

By the late 1950s, presumably about 1959, Oliver introduced their No. 107 five-bar rake. It was designed to operate at higher speeds than earlier models, and the modern parallel raking-bar design shortened the route from swath to windrow. This made the machine more compact and lessened the loss of nutritious leaves. The five-bar design permitted a slower reel speed, even though it was capable of higher ground speeds. The No. 107 was ground-driven, automatically synchronizing bar speed to ground travel.

During the 1960s Oliver announced their No. 105 wheel rake. It used 40 or 48-inch spring balanced raking wheels. Oliver's Add-A-Wheel design made a sixth and seventh wheel optional, with the standard five-wheel design being shown here. Wheel rakes had the distinct advantage of requiring no ground-drive or pto mechanism, and offered the further advantage of delivering the hay gently, quickly, and efficiently into the windrow. Nothing more was needed than to drop in a drawbar pin and head for the field.

Rotary Hoes

Rotary hoes are a fairly recent development. The first appeared in the early part of the twentieth century as a horsedrawn implement. This implement is an effective weed destroyer if used shortly after weeds have germinated near the soil surface, and before they have begun sending out roots. Rotary hoes have also been used widely as a crust buster, caused by unusual climatic conditions. This three-point model of the early 1950s is attached to an Oliver "66" tractor.

An Oliver Super 55 is pulling this two-row rotary hoe of three-point design. Rotary hoes began to grow in popularity when it was discovered that high ground speeds greatly enhanced their effectiveness. At high ground speeds the rotary hoe is able to provide substantial soil-shattering action for destruction of germinating weeds, as well as to break up a surface crust caused by heavy rains and other conditions. The three-point design permitted complete control by the operator, as well as providing easy-on, easy-off use of this implement.

This four-row pull-type rotary hoe is typical of 1960s designs. In this case an Oliver 1600 tractor is on the tongue; it had sufficient power to move along at a fairly high ground speed. For weed destruction a fairly shallow penetration was all that was required. Since the growing crop was planted at a greater depth, very little damage occurred to the growing crop. Yet, the rotary hoe was able to surface till virtually every square inch of the field.

During the 1960s Oliver rotary hoes were offered in many sizes and styles. One basic model used 18-inch wheels having 12 teeth per wheel. It was available in five sizes from 2 through 8-row. The 2 and 4-row sizes were available with a three-point hitch mounting, and all sizes were available as pull-type units. For severe soil and weed conditions Oliver offered a rotary hoe having 21-inch wheels and 16 teeth per wheel. It was available in the same size configurations as the standard 18-inch size. Weight boxes were a standard feature, although no additional weight has been added to the unit shown here.

The Oliver-Iron Age line also included an extensive offering of dusters. Developed already in the 1920s, dusters were more popular than sprayers for certain applications, but with a greater sensitivity to environmental problems, dusters lost favor. This trailer-style unit required an operator to aim the duster chute, as well as to control the delivery. Much of the early developmental work in orchard dusters was carried out some years earlier by the Bateman Mfg. Company, Grenloch, New Jersey. Bateman had roots going back to 1836, but began the Iron Age line in the late 1800s.

Oliver-Iron Age Model 71 orchard sprayers featured a compact, fully-enclosed design. This pto model was less expensive, since no costly engine was required. Various capacities were available, ranging from 10 to 50 gpm, and all could be furnished with the standard pump having a rated capacity of 600 psi. In lieu of this, a 1,000 psi pump was also available. Additionally, metal or wooden tanks were available at the buyer's discretion.

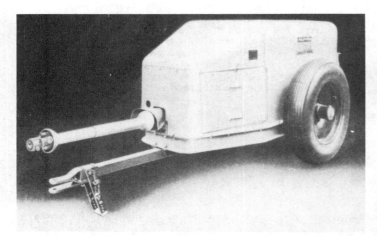

Farquhar had long made a specialty of building orchard sprayers. When Oliver took over in 1952 they continued in the same vein. However, the Farquhar line was not acquired in the White Motors takeover of 1960. Although Oliver as a subsidiary continued to build sprayers for a time, the Iron Age line came to an end. Shown here is an Oliver-Iron Age orchard sprayer of the 1950s. This basic Model 71 sprayer was available in literally dozens of configurations, including the choice of an independent engine drive or a pto drive.

Oliver bought out the A. B. Farquhar factory at York, Pennsylvania in 1952. The latter had previously acquired the Iron Age implement line of Bateman & Company. When Oliver took over, they continued to offer the Oliver-Iron Age line of sprayers and dusters. The Model 71 engine-driven model shown here was available as a pushcart, or could be furnished with the choice of automotive or tractor hitches. All used a Farquhar-designed pump capable of up to 400 psi.

1970 SPRAYER LINE

Oliver No. 301 sprayers utilized the tractor's three-point hitch for easy-on, easy-off use. This model of about 1953 is equipped with a side boom for spraying roadside ditches to kill noxious weeds. A simple control valve permitted the operator to open or close the spray valve as desired, and the pto-driven pump was of course, under the complete control of the operator. Oliver's No. 201 three-point sprayer had a capacity of about 100 gallons and could be furnished with extended spray booms for use in row crops.

Into the 1960s, Oliver was offering trailer-type sprayers in over a half dozen different styles and sizes. The smallest model used a pump having a capacity of 10 gpm, while the largest was capable of 50 gpm with a maximum pressure of 1,000 psi. In fact, the pump was essentially the same as that earlier developed by Farquhar. Oliver's 1970 sprayer line included this No. 622 tractor mounted design. The saddle-mounted tanks carried spray solutions for applications such as pre-plant incorporation of herbicides.

After buying out Farquhar in 1952, Oliver seriously got into the sprayer business, continuing to offer various models into the 1970s. This No. 683 is a large trailer-mounted style is of fairly recent vintage, and typifies the smooth lines and simple designs of the late model sprayers. A tank gauge is provided to accurately ascertain the amount of spray solution in the tank. Extensive offerings of boom equipment were made, including a host of different nozzles to suit specific applications.

Designed specifically as a chemical applicator, this No. 612 unit from Oliver was part of the 1970 line. It was highly accurate, and could be utilized to spray up to twelve rows at a time, assuming a 30-inch row spacing. It could also cover up to 30 feet or more at a single pass, using a center-mounted boom. Since the spray booms were carried forward on the tractor, there was no need to attach them to a planter, harrow, or other equipment. This No. 612 applicator was designed specifically for use with the Oliver 770, 880, 1550, 1600, 1650, 1750, 1800, 1850, and 1950-T row-crop tractors. It could also be used with similar models of other makes.

Spreaders

D. M. Sechler Implement & Carriage Company at Moline, Illinois developed the Black Hawk spreader. It was distributed by various companies, including the Oliver Chilled Plow Works, and later, the Oliver Farm Equipment Company. For several years it was sold by American Seeding Machine Company as the Superior-Black Hawk No. 26 spreader. Advertising of the day indicated that, "The Oliver-Superior spreader leads the way to increased fertility of the soil and bigger yields."

At some undetermined point, probably during the 1920's, American Seeding Machine Company assumed the manufacture of the New Black Hawk spreader. The stencilling on this one indicates that Brackett, Shaw, & Lunt Company functioned as the New England Distributor for the New Blackhawk. The latter was a very large eastern machinery distributor. Presumably, this arrangement ended when American Seeding Machine Company merged into the Oliver Farm Equipment Company in 1929, since the new company had its own distributors and branch houses.

A 1930s photograph epitomizes the 'good old days' of farming. This farmer has loaded the spreader by hand, using a four- or five-tine fork. Now he gets a chance to rest while driving his favorite team to the field and distributing the load. While probably very crude by today's standards, the manure spreader only came into being as a practical machine during the early 1900s. Prior to that time, livestock waste was loaded onto a wagon with a fork, taken to the field, and unloaded again, probably with the same fork!

Oliver-Superior spreaders of the 1930s had a capacity of 75 bushels. The wooden box was made of long-leaf yellow pine to better resist the corrosive effect of manure acids. The all-steel framework was of high carbon steel, and ran the full length of the bed. An adjustable feed mechanism for the apron could be set for anywhere from 4 to 28 loads per acre. A further advantage was the use of a standard wagon tread width; this permitted the Oliver-Superior to follow the same track as made by ordinary farm wagons.

About 1937 Oliver introduced their No. 75 spreader. It was an updated version of the earlier Oliver-Superior offering, but continued to use an all-steel frame lined with kiln-dried long leaf yellow pine. A major feature was the use of a spring mounting system whereby both the front and rear axles rode on heavy steel springs. Automotive steering had been used for some years, and continued as before. A color illustration of this model shows a bright red box and yellow wheels; the iron parts were painted either black or dark green.

Oliver's No. 7 Superior spreaders appeared in the late 1930s. This four-wheel No. 7-BW design was even equipped with rubber tires instead of the usual steel wheels. A comfortable seat and footboard are evident, and company advertising of the time notes that the tongue and singletrees were well varnished. Alas, a few loads of manure, and much of this brightly painted glamour disappeared. Frequently, the tongue was sawed off, suitable irons were installed, and the No. 7 was converted to a tractor spreader.

The Oliver-Superior No. 7 tractor spreader represented this company's earliest efforts to market a revolutionary new two-wheel tractor spreader. As is obvious, backing a conventional four-wheel spreader into a shed was far more difficult than backing this simple two-wheel, trailer-type design. The simple all-steel design was enhanced by the use of dark orange-yellow paint with large black lettering. Of course, since this was purely a tractor spreader, all controls were within convenient reach of the operator's seat.

Selected No. 1 long-leaf yellow pine lumber was used for the sides and floor of the No. 17 Oliver-Superior spreader. Introduced about 1952 this model had a capacity in excess of 75 bushels. Large roller bearings were used wherever possible, and the main cylinder was equipped with six bars. Full-length shields were used for extra safety, and a heavy angle iron frame was the foundation on which the No. 17 was built. The widespread attachment was designed to thoroughly pulverize and distribute the material over a seven-foot swath.

During the 1950s Oliver introduced newly designed and much larger spreaders than had been built in the past. The widespread use of hydraulic farm loaders and the use of larger farm tractors made it economically wise to carry a larger load to the field and reduce the number of trips. This No. 100 model of the 1950s utilized a capacity of about 100 bushels, somewhat larger than anything previously offered. In addition, the ground-drive system was eliminated in favor of a full pto drive line.

Spreaders

About 1959 Oliver introduced their No. 470 spreader. It featured a big 140 bushel capacity and utilized a pto drive. The 88 cubic foot capacity of the No. 470 made it ideal for fast cleanup of large feed lots and barns. Following it came the Oliver No. 471 spreader; it was essentially the same machine but contained numerous small improvements. It is shown here fully loaded, carrying approximately 140 bushels. Building these large spreaders was predicated on redesigning the apron and other components to handle the heavy strains imposed by these large loads.

About 1971 Oliver was building this big No. 590 spreader. Its design was virtually the same as the No. 490, except that this spreader had an even larger capacity. Various wheel rims were available, with an eye toward being able to use large truck tires to carry the load. Since these machines were carrying heavy loads at relatively low speeds, used truck tires were considerably less expensive than buying brand new tires. Due to an ample supply of used tires, replacements were also readily available.

Another Oliver offering was the No. 490 spreader of the 1960s. Curiously, earlier designs utilized a main beater, a top beater, and a widespread attachment. Later models like this No. 490 used only one main beater that also served as a widespread attachment. With the pto drive, this mechanism operated at a higher speed than the old ground-driven designs. The saw-tooth paddles bolted to the spreader shaft served to tear up and disintegrate the material, leaving it in an even swath for the entire load.

For the largest livestock operations, Oliver offered this huge 240 bushel, No. 570 spreader. Its tandem axle design permitted the necessary flotation for carrying such immense loads into relatively soft fields. Like others of the time, a pto drive system was used. Spreaders like the No. 570 might on occasion be carrying a load of six tons or more, exclusive of the weight of the spreader. Eventually though, White Farm Equipment specialized more highly in other endeavors than manure spreaders.

Stover-Oliver Equipment

During the 1930s Oliver Farm Equipment sold several auxiliary implement lines. Included was that of the Stover Mfg. Company at Freeport, Illinois. The latter was a well known and highly respected gas engine builder. In addition, Stover had developed an extensive line of small feed grinders, corn shellers, and other small farm equipment.

Proof of the Stover-Oliver connection lies in the fact that on November 1, 1933 Stover issued their Stover-Oliver Catalog No. 072. It contains virtually the entire Stover line, even including the recently introduced Stover diesel engines.

At least some of the Oliver retail price books of the 1930s contain a special section devoted to the auxiliary equipment lines. Included at one time or another are the lines of Stover Mfg. Company, Cockshutt Plow Company, and Peru Wheel Company. A 1937 Oliver price book also includes the Oliver-Cope line, the latter being products of the Western Land Roller Company at Hastings, Nebraska. While companies came and companies went during this period, Stover seems to have remained a constant entity, being shown in various Oliver price books throughout the decade of the 1930s.

The ever-changing farm scene was forever altered by the effects of the Great Depression. Many other factors were involved, including rural electrification, the introduction of row-crop tractors, and many and various social factors. This changing scene was bringing companies like Stover to their end. With rural electrification, Stover's gas engines were seldom needed, and sales continued to decline. Stover's corn shellers and corn grinders seldom wore out, the market was already saturated, and sales of these also dropped to virtually nothing. Thus the Stover line came to an end in the early 1940s.

During the early 1930s Stover introduced their Oil-Rite engines. They were of a totally enclosed design with automatic lubrication. No longer was it necessary to watch a sight feed lubricator, and no longer was it necessary to shut down the engine to lubricate the crank pin periodically. This engine was built in four sizes ranging from 1 1/2 to 5 horsepower, with prices ranging from $66 to $123. These engines were built in the hit-and-miss type for gasoline, or could be furnished in a throttling governor design for use with kerosene.

Harnessing the wind was the quintessential method of pumping water beginning in the 1880s, and continuing in some areas to this day. Stover began business by building windmills, but those of the 1880s were made almost entirely of wood. This late model Stover Oil-Rite windmill of the 1930s used roller bearings and ran in a constant oil bath. Stover's windmill line was as extensive as anyone in the industry, but their windmills seldom wore out, the market was saturated, and demand gradually declined during the 1930s. However, the Stover Oil-Rite windmills were available through Oliver dealers during the 1930s.

During the 1930s Stover modified their engine line to include smaller high-speed engines. Less weight meant less cost for iron, and obviously, less machine work to manufacture. In fact, these small engines could run at higher speeds with great efficiency, and could run for hours, and even days at a time with virtually no attention. Despite moderate popularity, the trend was becoming obvious; electric motors were about to eliminate the time-honored gas engine as a prime mover on the farm. With the onset of World War Two, the Stover-Oliver connection came to an end. The Stover factories were needed for war production, and besides, Stover was virtually out of business anyway!

Oliver's use of toolbars was not by any means limited to the Oliver wheel tractors. Oliver-Cletrac crawlers were well adapted to tool bar applications. This particular design of the 1930s shows an Oliver toolbar mounted on a Cat Twenty tractor from Caterpillar Tractor Company. Caterpillar had developed a rear double power take off and power lift, and the Oliver tool bar utilized these features when needed. This particular design controlled depth accurately by the use of heavy gauge wheels.

In the 1950s Oliver was offering an extensive line of toolbars and related equipment. Much of it had been developed in the 1940s, and even earlier. However, the advent of the three-point hitch created significant new toolbar designs, and greatly increased the possibilities for toolbar applications. This implement had the distinct advantage of having many different uses with a single bar. All that was required was to remove one set of tools from the bar, and replace these with an entirely different set. Row spacing was infinitely variable, and this too, was a distinct advantage in certain applications.

An Oliver toolbar design of the 1940s was this Universal Tool Bar mounted on the Row Crop 70 tractor. It is shown here with the 6-tooth spring tooth attachment in place. It made use of a rear mounting bracket, together with using the front-mounted pipes which ordinarily carried the cultivator. This particular attachment was recommended especially for wheel track eradication when cultivating corn and other row crops.

With ever-increasing tractor size, high-powered hydraulics, and other technological changes, Oliver tool bars gradually increased in size, as well as in their usefulness. The No. 3000 Oliver tool bar made its appearance in the late 1950s. It could be fitted with the No. 3003 middlebuster or the No. 3004 busterlister. The No. 3051 subsoiler was another possibility, as was the No. 3027 spring tooth attachment. Shown here is an Oliver mounted toolbar with a furrowing attachment. Disc hillers and numerous other attachments were also available.

C. W. Hart and C. H. Parr built the first factory devoted exclusively to the manufacturing of farm tractors, or as they were called in 1901, gasoline traction engines. The story is often told of how the term 'tractor' was coined by the Hart-Parr advertising people, but in fact, the term had been in use for centuries, although not in the context of a motor-powered machine. Earlier in this book the history of Hart-Parr Company is detailed, and there is no doubt that the company did indeed build some unique and innovative tractors. However, like many others of the time, the problem was not in building a tractor, but in building one that was suitable for row-crop work. Some folks attempted to build specialized motor cultivators, but these machines weren't of much use for anything else. Likewise, the heavy duty Hart-Parr tractors were no good for cultivating and other row-crop work.

During the 1920s Hart-Parr took the innovative step of offering a power take off shaft for their tractors. One of these units was driven directly from the crankshaft counterweight, and so it was in effect, a 'live' pto. Recognizing this, a separate clutch was used to engage and disengage the powered implement. The bottom line is that this was indeed an early example of a live pto, although it is likely that little thought was given to the idea at that time.

During the 1930s Oliver offered some sort of live pto as an option on a few models; in fact, it was billed more as an auxiliary system rather than being standard equipment. At various places, vague references indicate that Oliver engineers had been working on this idea in the 1940s but ran into patent problems. Nothing has surfaced to show whether these problems involved possible infringement of previous patents, or whether the problems were in building a patentable design. Eventually though, the Oliver 88 appeared, and with it came the full-blown live pto system. Within a few years virtually the entire farm tractor industry had adopted this concept in one form or another.

Another pioneering first was Oliver's use of a high-compression engine. There was no question that raising the compression ratio would also increase the power level, but many engineers of the 1930s scoffed at this idea as being too 'automotive' and as ultimately being unworkable. The concept of operating a tractor engine at say, 1,200 rpm, was not well received by many, and going even further, the notion of a six-cylinder tractor engine was even more remote. However, Oliver persevered in all of these directions. Ultimately, tractor builders generally, raised compression ratios, and increased the engine speed. Both of these changes raised the power level without adding substantially to the tractor weight. As one of the early tractor engineers put it, "For years we sold too much iron for too little money." With the emergence of the Oliver 70 came a whole new concept in tractor design, but on the negative side, Oliver continued to promote their Tip-Toe steel wheels for several more years, even though rubber tires were becoming increasingly popular.

Especially during the 1930s and 1940s, Oliver built numerous Industrial tractors. The company had obviously found a market for this specialized design, and had also coagulated its efforts so that relatively few changes were needed to convert an ordinary standard-tread tractor into an industrial model. The mechanization and expansion of commercial enterprises provided a new market for industrial tractors, and the company went so far as to provide fan-to-differential power units for use on industrial machinery. In addition, Oliver produced E.O.A. (Engine-Over-Axle) units from 1938 to 1967. This specialized design was especially popular for roadbuilding and other construction equipment.

During World War Two the company contributed mightily to the defense effort, although a few tractors were built during this time. Research on new models was very limited, but by 1948 Oliver was ready with an entirely new line of tractors. These were built over the successes of the past, including the Oliver 60, 70, and 80 tractors. The latter was even built with a diesel engine, although very few were sold. However, in the 1950s, Oliver was an industry leader through their promotion of diesel power over the conventional gasoline engine. Precise industry figures have not been located, but from all appearances, Oliver led the industry in the sale of diesel tractors for several years.

The Oliver 66, 77, and 88 tractors of the 1948-54 period marked an entirely new series of Fleetline models. Although the Oliver 66 was built only with a spark-ignition engine, the 77 and 88 tractors could be bought with either gasoline or diesel engines. During 1954 the company upgraded these tractors with the new 'Super' series models, and added the Oliver Super 55; it was the company's first compact utility tractor model. During these years Oliver also introduced their Hydra-Lectric hydraulic system, and built on their previous success with the live pto system. During the late 1950s Oliver actively entered the commercial market by offering numerous styles and sizes of forklifts, backhoes, and other industrial equipment. Oliver also bought out the Be-Ge scraper line and made a serious attempt to enter the heavy construction market.

In 1958 Oliver began marketing the new 660, 770, 880, and other new models. Typical of the period, these new models evidenced an increased power level and other new features. However, on November 1, 1960 Oliver Corporation was purchased by White Motor Corporation of Cleveland, Ohio. In February 1962 White Motors also bought the Cockshutt Plow Company at Brantford, Ontario, Canada. Thus, during the 1960s a substantial number of Oliver tractors were given a coat of red paint and a set of Cockshutt decals. These were sent to Canada and marketed as Cockshutt, although they were otherwise virtually the same as their American counterparts. During 1960 the Oliver 500 tractor was marketed; it was not built by Oliver but by David Brown of England. This marked the first instance of an Oliver tractor not being actually manufactured by Oliver.

In 1960 the new four-digit tractor models appeared. Among them were the 1600, 1700, 1800, and 1900 models. Numerous modifications and changes followed over the four year production run, and these models were available with new features that had previously been but a dream. Oliver had built a few of the 995GM tractors in the 1958-61 period, and this too, marked a departure from the conventional four-cycle designs.

Progress continued apace during the 1960s. Oliver Corporation no longer existed as a corporate entity, but was a subsidiary of White Motors. However, in 1969 White Motor Corporation formed White Farm Equipment Company. This internal merger combined the manufacturing efforts of Oliver, Cockshutt, and Minneapolis-Moline into a single venture. The latter had been acquired by White Motors in 1963, but had operated as a wholly-owned subsidiary. Consolidating the three product lines almost immediately led to a reduction in overlapping products and in manufacturing facilities.

Almost immediately after the formation of White Farm Equipment came a transitional period when virtually identical tractors were marketed under different tradenames. A few models were sold as Oliver, Minneapolis, or Cockshutt, the major difference being the paint color. As the transition continued, the White name was more and more applied to the tractor line, with the Oliver 2255, also known as the White 2255, being the last purely 'Oliver' tractor. With the introduction of the White 4-150 Field Boss in 1974 the White name would be used henceforth, to the exclusion of all others.

During all of these corporate and manufacturing activities some other, and more sinister, changes were taking place. The number of family farmers was decreasing rapidly, and the average farm acreage was increasing. Larger tractors and equipment meant fewer farmers. Within a few years the market for mid-sized tractors virtually disappeared. The standards established over many decades of tractor building had vanished! Added to all this were tough economic times that dramatically reduced sales of new tractors. These economic changes created difficult times for the industry, and much of the industry never survived; others, while not broke, were badly bent. Thus, the volatile tractor market became even more unpredictable and even more risky. As the farm economy improved, so did the balance sheet for tractor manufacturers, but gone were the halcyon days of yore...those grand times when a farmer might go to town and drive home a brand new Oliver 88 for the princely sum of $2,900.

White Farm Equipment Company was purchased by Texas Investment Corporation in December 1980. The latter operated WFE as a wholly owned subsidiary until Allied Products Corporation purchased selected assets on November 6, 1985. The Allied assets at the time included Bush Hog Implement Company, Kewanee Farm Equipment Company, New Idea Farm Equipment Corporation, Continental Gin Company, and the Lilliston Corporation. After the Allied acquisition of 1985, the WFE headquarters at Oak Brook, Illinois and the Central Parts Warehouse at Hopkins, Minnesota were both moved to South Bend, Indiana. During 1986 White Farm Equipment of the U.S. bought selected assets of the White Farm Mfg. Ltd. in Canada, but the Brantford (Ontario) combine plant was closed.

In May 1987 New Idea Farm Equipment Company and White Farm Equipment formed the White-New Idea Farm Equipment Company; its headquarters were established at the New Idea home base of Coldwater, Ohio.

Local newspapers announced on November 18, 1992 that the parent of White-New Idea (Allied Corporation) would be closing the Charles City, Iowa factory in mid-1993. With its closing, some nine decades of tractor manufacturing at the site of the Hart-Parr Tractor Company will come to an end.

After the 1929 formation of Oliver Farm Equipment Company, production of the Hart-Parr two-cylinder tractors continued apace. Almost immediately though, engineers and draftsmen were busy designing a new row crop tractor. A single copy had been built by March 1, 1930. Several more were built that month, and production of about 20 units a day began in April 1930. Over 2,000 units had been built by the end of June. Note the distinctive decals used on this early example. "Row Crop" is a single hood decal; the decal on the fuel tank includes the words, "Hart-Parr."

Originally, the Oliver-Hart-Parr Row-Crop tractor, as it was known, used a single front wheel. This configuration was used only in 1930 and 1931. The latter year, Oliver began a series using dual front, or a tricycle, front end. In 1937 this basic tractor model became the Oliver 80. The engine was essentially the same as used in the 18-28 standard-tread model. While it is commonly thought that the 18-28 and 28-44 tractors were built first, the Row-Crop style was in production some six months prior to either of the standard-tread models.

With the introduction of the Oliver-Hart-Parr Row-Crop, and the nearly concurrent introduction of the 18-28 and the 28-44 tractors, production of two-cylinder tractors ended. Granted, Oliver continued building the original Hart-Parr models for a couple of years, but this was essentially for the purpose of using up the parts inventory. Virtually from the beginning of production, this model could also be furnished with a wide-front, and even in a Western Special version. As a standard row-crop model, it sold for $985. The Western Special was the same, except that it used a Pomona air cleaner with a Donaldson auxiliary. This model was priced at $1,005.

Oliver Hart-Parr Row-Crop tractors of 1931 could also be furnished in a wide-tread design. This was the same as the standard model except that a special rear axle permitted a maximum tread width of 86 inches. It was priced at $1,005. The four-wheel, wide-front Row-Crop featured a special arched front axle with 16 3/4 inch center clearance, and a 59-inch center-to-center of the tread. This model sold for $1,035. Extension rims and various types of lug equipment were also available.

The Oliver Hart-Parr Row-Crop appeared at the Ne-braska Tractor Test Laboratory in April 1930. Appar-ently the 18-27 horsepower rating later ascribed to this model emerged from this test, No. 176. The rating was actually set by SAE and ASAE rating codes. The four-cylinder engine was rated at 1,190 rpm and used a 4 1/8 x 5 1/4 inch bore and stroke. It delivered a maximum of 30 belt horsepower. This model could be equipped with an option pto shaft for $8.50. Adding a K-W low tension lighting generator was a $71 option.

Production of the 18-27 dual-wheel model began in 1931 and ended in 1937. A precise date for this change has not been located. However, an Oliver price book, issued early in the year, lists only the single front wheel row-crop model, with the dual front, not even being shown as an option. This 1931 model is equipped with an Oliver No. 97 disc cultivator. It was adjustable for 38, 40, and 42-inch rows. Note also that the decal arrangement was changed for 1931; instead of a large hood decal, only the "Row-Crop" decal ap-pears on the fuel tank.

This illustration is taken from the cover of a 1935 Oliver catalog. It points out the many advantages of the Oliver design, including the "Power on Tiptoe" design which Oliver used for several years. Oliver pointed out that the success of this design, especially regarding a minimizing of soil compaction. This model was equipped with three forward speeds of 2.6, 3.2, and 4.15 mph. It was also pointed out that in Nebraska Test No. 176, the Oliver Hart-Parr delivered 82% of its belt horsepower at the drawbar.

Oliver pointed to a special advantage of their row-crop design, and this was their "Central Tool Mount-ing" system. The special equipment designed for use with the Row-Crop was jointly developed by the Oliver and American Seeding Machine Divisions. No doubt the engine design was engineered at the former Hart-Parr factory, since the latter had vast experi-ence in engine building. A big 2 3/8 inch crankshaft was used; it was supported by three main bearings. An entirely new cooling system design kept engine water temperature within about five degrees, while earlier designs commonly had a temperature differ-ential of 20 degrees or more. Note that this Row-Crop has been specially equipped with a road grading attachment.

Full pressure lubrication was a standard feature of the Oliver Row-Crop design. An oil filter was also standard equipment, and both of these features greatly prolonged engine life. The differential brakes could be operated either by foot pedals or automatically operated by the steering wheel. The latter was seen as an advantage when cultivating. Ball or roller bearings were used on all transmission shafts. Many different implements were tailored especially to the Oliver Hart-Parr Row-Crop.

This undated photograph illustrates a rear view of the Oliver Hart-Parr Row-Crop. In fact, the decals include the Oliver shield with 'Hart-Parr' and 'Row-Crop' as overlays. Unfortunately, the original photograph was not in color, nor have any color images appeared for the benefit of Oliver tractor enthusiasts. Note also that the skeleton wheel design is shown, although lugs have not yet been mounted. This unique design would be marketed for some years as "Power on Tiptoe."

No information accompanied this original Oliver photograph. However, it is significant that Oliver attempted to adapt their "Power on Tiptoe" concept even to their standard-tread tractors. Obviously though, this one does not yet have any lug equipment mounted. In fact, for moving about the factory yard on brick and concrete paths, the high steel lugs probably made it a rough ride indeed! Had this tractor been painted green, it would have shown up much darker in this black-and-white photograph. It is known that Oliver experimented with various colors initially, and this might well have been one of those experiments.

During the early 1930s Oliver proudly flew the Oliver Farm Equipment Company flag...its stripes bearing the names of Hart-Parr, Nichols & Shepard, Oliver, and American Seeding Machine Company. Much of this early advertising resolved itself into the famous Oliver Shield; it was used in various forms and with various color combinations at least into the 1960s. Recognizing that name recognition was an important ingredient in the farm equipment business, the Oliver flag with its combination of the four original partners was a clever method of maintaining product identity but still pointing to an entirely new organization.

The Oliver Hart-Parr 18-28 tractor made its debut in early 1930. This model used the same basic four-cylinder engine as was used in the concurrent Row-Crop. This 1930 photograph shows C. H. Parr, one of the Hart-Parr co-founders standing with the new 18-28 and old Hart-Parr No. 3. Although the 18-28 weighed much less than old No. 3, it was capable of almost the same horsepower output as its older, and much larger ancestor. Although C. W. Hart had left the company some years earlier, Mr. Parr remained with Hart-Parr, and later, Oliver for many years.

In 1931 the 18-28 tractor listed at $1,025. When sold as a Western Special the price was $1,045; the difference being that this model was equipped with a Pomona air cleaner. Ricefield 18-28 tractors were the same as the standard, except the 6-inch high lugs were used instead of 5-inch. Also a special 2-inch skid band was used on the front wheels. This extra equipment raised the price $10 over the price of the standard model. For $1,035 the 18-28 "Tiptoe" Ricefield was available; it used the skeleton wheels typical of the Row-Crop design. Another style was the 18-28 Orchard tractor. Essentially, this model used special hood and fender equipment, but this raised the price to $1,075. Another variation as an 18-28 high-speed tractor, with a maximum travel of 5.9 mph. The 18-28 could also be furnished as a low-speed model.

In July 1930 the 18-28 tractor appeared at Lincoln's Nebraska Tractor Test Laboratory and was tested under No. 180. This test revealed almost 24 drawbar horsepower. Although the 18-28 was initially offered only with steel wheels, rubber tires became optional equipment in the early 1930s. A 1935 catalog notes the "Air tires are available as extra equipment." An interesting, albeit a minor feature, was the use of a filter on the crankcase breather to deter the entry of dirt and grit into the lubricating oil.

Built in the 1931-37 period, the Oliver Hart-Parr "18" Industrial model was essentially an 18-28 tractor designed for industrial use. The most obvious difference was the use of heavy cast wheels with pressed-on hard rubber tires. This model had three forward speeds ranging up to 9.2 mph. There was no platform or fenders. This stock model is shown behind the Charles City factory, and displays no evidence of any decals or other insignia.

A catalog view of the Oliver Hart-Parr "18" Industrial tractor shows the designator on the fuel tank, along with "Hart-Parr" presumably cast into the side of the engine block. The "18" Industrial was built with this designation only in 1931. Serial number listings indicate that only five of these units were made in 1931. After that time this model was offered as the 18-28 Industrial, and was built with either pneumatic or with hard rubber tires.

When Oliver announced what would be the 28-44 tractor in 1930, it apparently began life as the Model A tractor, then as the "3-5 Plow" model, and later, as the 28-44. This illustration of the Model A on first glance looks identical to the 28-44, but a close inspection reveals a different front axle mounting, different oil filter, and more than likely, other differences. The Model A does not appear in the serial number listings under that designation, nor does the "3-5 Plow" title ever appear therein. Oliver rated this as a four-plow tractor, claiming it to be "The Most Powerful Tractor of its Size on Four Wheels."

When first announced in 1930 the 28-44 model was available only with steel wheels. Within a year or two, pneumatic tires became optional equipment. A rear view of an early 28-44 shows the pto shaft in place; it came only as an option. In October 1930, Oliver sent a copy of the 28-44 to the Nebraska Tractor Test Laboratory. Operating on kerosene fuel, it delivered a maximum of 49-plus horsepower on the belt tests. Not visible in this illustration is the spring-cushion drawbar design.

The 28-44 tractor was built in the 1930-37 period, essentially undergoing a metamorphosis into the Oliver 90 model. The four-cylinder engine used a 4 3/4 x 6 1/4 inch bore and stroke. When equipped with ordinary spade lugs, this model sold for approximately $1,325. In 1931 it was offered in Western Special and Ricefield versions; the latter style could also be equipped with "Tiptoe" rear wheel equipment. By 1935 the 28-44 was also available as a Thresherman's Special with cast disc front and rear wheels. High-speed and low-speed versions were available, as was a special high-altitude model.

During the early 1930s, pneumatic tire equipment became available as an option. A 1935 Oliver price list includes changeover equipment for tractors already in the field. If it was desired to convert the 28-44 to rubber tires, the cost was $353, plus of course, the cost of labor by the dealer. In addition to the Thresherman's Special model, it also appears that Oliver built an "Oliver Special" using the 28-44 tractor. However, this tractor has no horsepower rating stamped on the serial number tag. Little information has surfaced concerning this model, and it is not listed in the serial number compilations.

Various Oliver publications through the years point to the "28" Industrial as being the first model to be available with the choice of high- or low-pressure pneumatic rubber tires. The "28" Industrial was available in the 1931-37 period. After that time, it was also known as the "90" and the "99". Regular equipment with this industrial model included an upholstered seat, complete with backrest, emergency parking brake, dual air cleaner, and a pto shaft. Options included electric lights and a spring-mounted front axle.

Production of the Oliver 80 Industrial tractor began in 1932. Its immediate ancestor was the Oliver 18-28; essentially the tractor shown here was nothing more or less than an improved version of the 18-28. It used the same engine, and essentially the same chassis, but was suitably modified for industrial work in factories, storage yards, and on docks. Up to 1937 the 80 Industrial was available for use with gasoline or kerosene fuels, but in that year Oliver introduced the 80 Diesel Row-Crop. Apparently the diesel engine was also available as an option in the 80 Industrial model. Production ran until 1947.

Beginning in 1930, Oliver offered the "44" power unit shown here. It was essentially the engine and transmission assembly used in the 28-44 tractor, and included a special clutch arrangement. Likewise, the engine and transmission components of the 18-28 tractor were sold thus. Other manufacturers used these units to power road graders and various other equipment, especially in the roadbuilding industries. Production of the "28" and "44" power units ran from 1930 to 1937.

Shown here is an Oliver "44" power unit set up for use with a road grader. In this example, a company making a road grader would build their unit, taking the detached front axle shown here, and mounting it to the front of the grader chassis. Likewise, the engine, transmission, and rear wheels would be installed on the grader. Production of the "28" and the "44" power units is buried within the serial numbers for the comparable tractors, so no determination can be made regarding production of these unique and rather specialized units.

During the 1932-47 Oliver offered the 99 Industrial model. This was basically the 28-44 Industrial model, but with a different model designator. Meanwhile, the other 28-44 models ended production in 1937. This 99 Industrial was originally built as the Oliver Special High-Compression 28-44. Other modifications included the 99 in Ricefield and Thresherman's Special editions. This tractor offered four forward speeds up to 6 mph. It weighed over 6,900 pounds.

An Oliver advertisement of the 1940s illustrates the "99" in use as an airport tractor. A perusal of the Oliver serial number lists indicates that sales of this particular model were never very large from year to year. However, since it required only minimal change to set this tractor up as an industrial model, it probably was a paying proposition to do so. Essentially, the engine and chassis remained the same, except for high-speed gearing. Different tire equipment was used, along with a different seat, and other minor items.

In 1935 Oliver introduced the famous Oliver 70. This new row-crop model used a smooth-running six-cylinder engine. Four forward speeds were available ranging up to 5.88 mph. Standard equipment included the unique skeleton wheels which Oliver called "Power on Tiptoe." As a result, many farmers simply dubbed this model as the "Tiptoe Oliver." This 1935 model used side panel latches similar to those on a Ford Model A car. In 1936 the side panel latches were changed to the familiar turnbuckle style. Also shown is the "Oliver" and "Row Crop" imposed over the Oliver shield. This decal arrangement was used only during 1935-37.

Tractors (Wheel)

During the 1930s Oliver heavily promoted their "Power on Tiptoe" concept. The open, or skeleton wheel design was light in weight, yet extremely strong. Various lug combinations could be used, but the concept was that these wide spade lugs would penetrate the soil and provide the needed footing with a minimum of soil compaction. In fact, it was even held that the action of the Tiptoe design would help to loosen and aerate the soil. However, pneumatic tires were also making an appearance in the 1930s. Many Oliver 70 tractors ended up at the local blacksmith shop to have the Tiptoe rims cut off, to be replaced with a set of rims and pneumatic tires.

A 1936 photograph shows an Oliver Hart-Parr 70 pulling a plow. Oliver began phasing out the Hart-Parr name in 1935, and finished the phase-out in 1937. Even this 1935 model manifests a much larger Oliver title on the radiator tank, with the Hart-Parr name being much less visible. Although Mr. Parr remained with Hart-Parr, and later on, Oliver Farm Equipment, virtually until his death, Mr. Hart left the company many years before. He never went back.

From its inception the Oliver 70 was available with a variety of options. A 1935 catalog, issued during the first year of actual production, shows that not only was the 70 available in a standard configuration, it was also available as shown here. All Oliver 70 models were available as the 70 HC (High Compression) style for using gasoline, or as the 70 KD (Kerosene Distillate) style for using either of these fuels. Both styles retailed at slightly over $900.

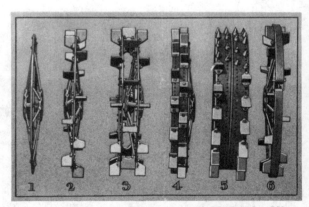

Various wheel equipment was available for the Oliver Row-Crop 70 tractor. In this illustration, No. 1 on the left shows a plain skeleton wheel with no lugs. No.2 shows the standard skeleton wheel with tiptoe lugs, as was used most commonly. For extra traction, No. 3 was a double-wide version of No. 2. A conventional rim with spade lugs is shown in No. 4, while a double-wide conventional rim is illustrated in No. 5. It is shown with spade lugs and with spud lugs, at the choice of the operator. No. 5 shows the overtire attachment for Oliver 70 lug equipment.

Although the Oliver 70 on steel retailed at about $900, the rubber-tired version was somewhat more expensive, selling at about $1,150. Yet, the advantages of rubber tires were obvious, and the transformation from steel wheels to rubber tires became a basic reality in the 1931-41 period. After that time, rubber tires were more of a dream than a reality for a few years, due to the demands of World War Two. Ordinarily the Oliver 70 was equipped with 5.25 x 16 dual front tires and 8.25 x 40 rear rubber.

When Oliver designed the Row-Crop 70, the 1935 model displayed a certain amount of streamlining, although this would be much more pronounced on the 1937 models. Even though this photograph of a 1935 Oliver 70 wide-front model is in black and white, it is obvious that the tractor was not painted green. Apparently the company was indecisive about the color to use on their new tractor, so they painted some green, some red, some orange, and perhaps even some other colors. They took this combination to various fairs in 1935 and left the farmers vote which color they like the best. Green won the balloting, and green it was from that point on.

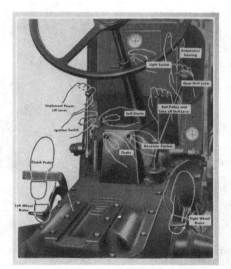

Oliver sent a copy of their new Model 70 tractor to the Nebraska Tractor Test Laboratory in April 1936. Since a great many tractors were tested during 1935, it is possible that due to the backlog, it was impossible to run the 70 through the tests in 1935. The results appear in Test No. 252. Similar tests, but using kerosene fuel appear in Test No. 267. The Oliver Row-Crop 70 appears again in 1940 under Test No. 351. Note the light-colored radiator grille on this copy. Apparently, it was of various colors during production. Most generally though, the opinion is that the grille was of galvanized metal, although some collectors claim that it was nickel plated.

A 1935 Oliver 70 catalog illustrates their so-called Finger-Tip Control, all the way from the self-starter to a convenient implement power lift lever. The smooth-running six-cylinder engine in the Oliver 70 was not built exclusively by Oliver. Waukesha built this and some other Oliver engines at least for a few years. The extent or the duration of this activity has not been ascertained with certainty; our research has revealed nothing in the serial number records, or even the rather incomplete production records of this period.

When the Oliver 70 was tested at Nebraska in 1936, it pulled over 89% of its own weight in the drawbar tests. This remarkable performance was probably due in part to the steel tiptoe wheels which Oliver used at the time. There appears to be no doubt that Waukesha built these engines, at least for a time. However, the application forms which Oliver submitted to the Tractor Test Laboratory list this engine as the company's own. After many decades, the conjecture is that Waukesha built these engines on a contract basis, and strictly to Oliver specifications.

Oliver 70 tractors were introduced in 1935. This model was built in two basic types and four regular models. Included was the standard 70 Row-Crop, the Standard-Tread 70, a four-wheel high-clearance model, and the Orchard & Grove 70. A six-speed transmission was provided. For tractors on rubber tires, the maximum speed was 13 1/4 mph, but this gear was locked out on tractors equipped with steel wheels. A separate clutch was provided for the pulley and the pto shaft. In effect, this was a 'live' pto system. This 1935 photograph shows George W. Bird standing by an Oliver 70 Standard. At the time Mr. Bird was the Shop Superintendent, and from 1944 to 1961 he was the plant manager of the Oliver plant at Charles City, Iowa.

Oliver apparently built some transitional models in the 1935-37 period. This Oliver 70 Standard demonstrates a different radiator grille than that shown above, yet it is not at all like the Oliver 70 of 1937 and following years. The side decal is placed on the fuel tank and simply has "70" in the background with "Standard" as an overlay. From a 1935 catalog it is ascertained that these models were all equipped with a flywheel ring gear, but electric starting was an extra-cost option. These models were ordinarily supplied with magneto ignition, even if using electric starting. In lieu of the magneto, a distributor system could be supplied at slight additional cost.

Oliver 70 Standard tractors were available with steel wheels if so desired, although rubber tires were usually preferable. A 1937 price list indicates that the Oliver 70 Standard retailed at $970 when equipped as shown here; substituting rubber tires raised the list price to $1,150. Both styles were of course available either with the HC (High Compression) engine for gasoline, or the KD (Kerosene-Distillate) engine for low grade fuels. The belt pulley was standard equipment, but the pto shaft was an extra cost option.

Another configuration of the Oliver 70 Standard was the Orchard 70. It could also be ordered as the Grove 70, although the only difference was in the stencils! A 1937 price book indicates that "If tractor with stencil reading "Oliver Grove 70" is desired, your order on plant must so state; otherwise tractors stencilled "Oliver Orchard 70" will be furnished." This model could be furnished with either the HC or the KD engine as desired, and the price with rubber tires was about $1,130.

The date of this photograph is unknown, but careful inspection manifests this as an Oliver 70 Standard. However, it uses an entirely different hood design and radiator grille than was found on the regular production models. Possibly it was a transitional or experimental design between the 1935-37 series and the streamlined models of 1937 and following. It also appears that the lower part of the main frame casting, directly beneath the radiator, was painted orange. In fact, the 1935 catalog for the Oliver 70 shows the Row-Crop to be painted thus, with the "70" cast into the front of the frame being highlighted in black, and the "Oliver Hart-Parr" at the top of the radiator tank is decorated in white.

Another experimental model was this air-tired model, probably of 1937, or perhaps slightly later. Again, the color scheme has changed. It is obvious that the orange highlight appears on the frame casting below the radiator, and extending back on each side toward the rear wheels. The Oliver shield trademark has undergone some change, and this experimental model manifests orange striping on the sidecurtain louvers. At one point in production an orange highlight was painted on the ridge of the hood, extending all the way from the radiator grille back to the instrument panel.

Oliver built numerous experimental models of the "70" series. Shown here is a photograph marked 'Experimental,' but bearing no date or other information. The rear wheels appear to be of a different design, and perhaps there were other changes as well. During the 1930s Oliver apparently spent a great deal of money in developing their row-crop tractor line. However, this work paid off, in that the series remained essentially unchanged for several years.

No information has been located on yet another Oliver experimental model. This Oliver 70 Standard has been mounted on a Rust high-clearance chassis. Possibly, the Rust chassis was developed by the Rust Cotton Picker Company of Memphis, Tennessee. However, beyond setting up this experimental model, it appears that Oliver took no further action in this regard. The extent of the Oliver experiments during this period proves that the company was highly motivated to develop, build, and sell almost any design that was needed for ordinary or for special uses.

Marked as an experimental model, nothing more accompanied the original photograph of this streamlined Oliver 70 Row-Crop model. Obviously it is distinctly different than the original 1935-37 design. The 'Hart-Parr' name is gone, and 'Oliver' is stamped on the vertical bar in the center of the grille. The main casting carries '70' in its center, and is apparently an orange highlight over the green finish of the tractor. However, more changes would take place during production, notably in the design of the stencils and in the overall color combinations.

Oliver 70 tractors were offered in two basic types, row-crop and standard-tread. Four regular models were built: Row-Crop, Standard, Orchard, and High-Clearance. The latter is shown here, and is somewhat unlike today's usual concept of a high-clearance tractor. In this instance, high-clearance meant a tractor equipped with an arched front axle, as with this 70 High-Clearance model. This design was intended for cultivating and other works in standing crops. Its chief advantage was the added stability gained from the wide-front axle, and this was particularly valuable when working in hilly terrain. In 1937 this model sold for $997.50.

Another interesting experimental model was this Oliver 70 built over a crawler attachment. More than likely, the track mechanism was built by someone other than Oliver, and possibly may even have been built by Cletrac. Since no information accompanied the original photograph, not even the date, any detailed discussion of this particular experimental model would likely be nothing more than pure conjecture.

Oliver's Row-Crop 70 of 1937 remained on the market until 1948. During this period it saw few major changes, except those very visible changes of a cosmetic nature. The engine remained virtually the same as with the 1935 model, and in fact, this streamlined model was the forerunner of the Oliver Fleetline series which would eventually include the 60, 70, and 80 models. Electric starting and lights were available as optional equipment. Although the "Tiptoe" wheels remained available virtually throughout production, few farmers of 1940 and following years were interested in anything but pneumatic tires.

Today's vintage tractor collectors, and even the dedicated Oliver collectors find considerable controversy regarding the various cosmetic changes on the Oliver 70 tractors. This 1948 model illustrates the orange striping which highlights the main frame casting from the radiator back to the transmission case. Yet, some of the earlier models do not display this highlight, while others used this attractive gambit. The Oliver 70 was tested at Nebraska again in 1940, this time under No. 351. The essential difference was that this test was run using rubber tires, while the previous test had been made on steel wheels.

This experimental Oliver 70 Standard of about 1937 illustrates a radiator grille design which apparently did not go into regular production. However, this front view illustrates a unique vertical bar over the grille; it extends back over the hood. At least in this experimental model, multiple pin stripes accentuate the design, along with the painted 'Oliver' placed vertically on the center bar. More than likely, the highlights were in orange, since this seemed to be Oliver's major choice for highlights on their tractors of the period. Note also that the main frame below the radiator is also highlighted, probably in orange, and probably extending back along the tractor frame all the way back to the differential case.

Another photograph of the Oliver 70 Standard of 1937 illustrates its sleek designs. In fact, this design is virtually the same as used on the production model, except for the grille design. As previously noted, the Oliver 70 series could be furnished with either the high-compression (HC) engine or the kerosene-distillate (KD) style for approximately the same price. The same basic engine was used; major changes included a different manifold, plus some minor changes. The side doors were intended to keep out dirt and dust, but a great many were permanently removed and consigned to a back wall of the tractor shed.

Tractors (Wheel)

During 1939 Oliver averaged about 26 Row-Crop 70 tractors per day, for a total of 7,860 units during the year. One trainload of Oliver 70 tractors is shown here, about to leave the Charles City factory for an unknown destination. During the same year, 1939, Oliver also built 1,896 of the Oliver 70 Standard tractors, plus another 15 copies of the Oliver 70 Industrial. The latter was built over the basic Oliver 70 Standard chassis, but suitably modified for this particular duty.

This Oliver 70 Standard has been converted to an Oliver 70 Industrial model. Pneumatic tires were available for the Industrial, but ordinarily this style was furnished with the solid rubber tires shown here. Hazards of working in a factory yard made pneumatic tires impractical, since the solid rubber tires could better withstand the snags and tears often encountered in these hazardous areas. A heavy front bumper has been added to this copy, probably to bump rail cars and other unspecified duties.

With the 1930 introduction of the Oliver Row-Crop, the company also designed and built a series of implements especially for this tractor. In the following years the mounted implement line was expanded and improved with great rapidity. Included were tractor-mounted planters, as shown here. These were built in two- and four-row versions. One of the most popular was the No. 1082-J two-row model, along with the 1083-J four-row style. These were runner planters, and were ordinarily fitted with the Oliver Power-Lift attachment.

The streamlined Oliver 70 Standard was built in the 1937-48 period. Although this one is on steel wheels, it evidences an electrical system complete with electric lights. This feature alone permitted many farmers to work late into the night when necessary. While give little thought today, adding an electric starter was indeed a major step forward in 1940; it eliminated the laborious, and sometimes dangerous task of cranking the tractor by hand.

The Oliver 70 Orchard in the streamlined series was built from 1937 to 1948. It was essentially an Oliver 70 Standard equipped with the special fenders and other modifications needed for orchard and grove work. Thus equipped, this model had a turning radius of 11 1/2 feet. The seat was of sponge rubber, upholstered with a comfortable back rest, and adjustable forward or back. Steel wheels were available, but preferable equipment were pneumatic tires. A special low auxiliary standing platform was mounted on the drawbar support. When equipped with rubber tires on cast disc wheels the Oliver 70 Orchard model weighed about 3,300 pounds.

Many Oliver advertisements of the period commented to the effect that "The Oliver 70 is fun to drive." To prove the point, this lady is doing a job once thought of only as being for men; she is putting in a day's work with an Oliver 70 and a two-bottom plow. While no one thought about it in the 1930s, World War Two was on the horizon. During those difficult years many women became more than the stereotyped housewife, they also became farmers in varying degrees.

Oliver 70 Industrial tractors paralleled the production of the 70 Standard model. As otherwise indicated, the 70 Industrial was nothing more than a suitably modified 70 Standard, as is evident from this illustration. In fact, this particular tractor differed little from the Oliver 25 Airport tractor, also built during the same 1937-48 period. Oliver 70 tractors in all versions used a six-cylinder engine having a 3 1/8 x 4 3/8 inch bore and stroke.

The 70 Standard was redesigned especially for airport utility work, and was then known as the Oliver 25 Airport model. This model featured six forward speeds up to 12 mph. Standard equipment included electric starter, lights, dual foot and hand brakes, front and rear drawbars, a side exhaust, and an upholstered seat. Actual production figures of this model are not available at the time of this research, and in fact, appear to be buried within the production of the Oliver 70 Standard model.

Oliver 50 Industrial models could be furnished with ordinary pneumatic tires or with the low-profile industrial design as shown here. This one is equipped with dual rear tires for improved traction, and is pulling a road grader. During the 1930s pull-type graders maintained a limited popularity. However, the advent of the motor grader all but ended demand for machines of this caliber, and the demand virtually disappeared by the early 1940s.

In the 1937-48 period the Oliver 50 Industrial model was part of the line. This four-cylinder model was a continuation of the 32-50 Special High Compression model built only in 1936 and 1937. The latter has serial numbers corresponding to the regular 28-44 model. As previously noted, the 28-44 Industrial became the Model 99. Electric lights and rubber tires were standard equipment for this heavy-duty model. Since its size and horsepower rating closely duplicated some of the existing product line, its value to the overall picture remains undetermined.

Little information has been located on the Oliver 35 Industrial tractor. It was built only during 1937 and 1938. Only about 2,700 were built, or to be technically correct, only this many serial numbers were assigned. The 35 Industrial was a four-cylinder model slightly smaller in output than the 70-Series tractors. Apparently this model was intended both for industrial duty and for agricultural purposes, as desired.

The Oliver 80 Row-Crop came onto the market in 1937. It was a continuation of the Oliver Row-Crop initially marketed in 1930. The tractor shown here is fitted with a cultivator. Studying the photograph creates some questions regarding the color of the tractor. Unfortunately, no color photos exist. Yet, the darkness of the cultivator would give the impression that it was painted the usual green color, but the tractor appears to be a light color, perhaps orange or some other color. Possibly this was a prototype, and possibly this tractor emerged at a time when the company was in flux regarding the final color selection. Precise answers will probably never be found.

The Oliver 80 Row-Crop could be purchased with various wheel combinations. This one uses pneumatic fronts and Tip-Toe rear wheels. Easier steering was the result, while still providing the advantages of the unique rear wheel lug design. The original purchaser had the choice of the HC or the KD engine. The High-Compression style used a 4 1/4 x 5 1/4 inch bore and stroke in its four cylinders. Kerosene-Distillate (KD) models were essentially the same but carried a 4 1/2 inch cylinder bore.

Many different mounted implements were available for the Oliver 70 and Oliver 80 tractors, including this mounted mower. The Oliver Row-Crop 80 KD model developed nearly 39 belt horsepower in Nebraska Test No. 300 of May 1938. Distillate fuel was used for this test. A separate clutch operated the belt pulley and the pto shaft. Although Oliver pioneered this concept, live pto systems did not come into general use for some years.

4-Wheel High Clearance

Oliver 80 Row-Crop tractors were built from 1937 to 1948. This model was the second of the Oliver Fleetline Series. The latter was begun with the Oliver 70 in 1935, the Oliver 80 followed in 1937, and the Oliver 60 made its entry in 1940. When equipped as shown here the Oliver 80 was priced at approximately $1,350. It weighed about 4,850 pounds. Rated at 1,200 rpm, the Oliver 80 HC model delivered over 41 belt horsepower in Nebraska Test No. 365 of November 1940.

Another variation of the Oliver 80 Row-Crop was this special high-clearance version. The modifications consisted basically of a special arched front axle which provided maximum clearance for standing crops. Outside of this change, there was little difference between this model and the ordinary Row-Crop 80. It was however, substantially more expensive, being priced at $1,427 in 1938. This model was of course, advantageous for working in standing crops. It also provided much greater stability when working on hilly land.

The Oliver 80 Standard was another variation of the basic Oliver 80 design. This tractor model used a heavy duty engine having a 298 ci displacement. The crankshaft was 2 3/8 inches in diameter and operated in three large main bearings. The crank was drilled for full pressure lubrication of all main and connecting rod bearings. Power was delivered through a big 12-inch clutch, and finally emerged through heavy 2 3/4 inch heat-treated rear axles. An adjustable radiator shutter was furnished as optional equipment. Oliver concurrently built the "35" Industrial tractor; it was similar in design and construction to the Oliver 80 HC model. However, the "35" was available in various combinations of travel speeds, wheel and tire equipment, all for industrial use.

In 1940 Oliver built their first diesel-powered farm tractor. Initially, this tractor carried a Buda-Lanova diesel engine, but eventually an Oliver-designed diesel was used. However, it appears that only about 75 of the diesel Row-Crop tractors were built, and of these, very few still exist. Oliver also built even fewer of the 80 Diesel Standard tractors. Diesel engines of 1940 were still in need of further development and most farmers had little interest in diesel designs.

Oliver 90 tractors were built in the 1937-53 period. This tractor was essentially the same as the Oliver Hart-Parr 3-5 Plow tractor introduced in 1930 and tested at Nebraska under No. 183. In fact the same test number was used for the 28-44 and the Oliver 90. Rated at 1,125 rpm the four-cylinder engine carried a 4 3/4 x 6 1/4 inch bore and stroke. By 1948 the Oliver 90 was retailing at $1,983 on steel, or $2,347 on rubber tires. Equipped with pneumatic tires, it weighed 6,141 pounds.

The Oliver 90 and Oliver 99 tractors were essentially built on the same chassis. In fact, when the 99 was introduced in 1937, the basic difference was that the 99 used a high-compression four-cylinder engine compared to that used in the Oliver 90. However, the 99 was designed to operate only on 70-octane gasoline. Shown here is a 1946 photograph of a Model 99 with a Continental six-cylinder gasoline engine. This Model 99 is shown during testing at Tulare, California in May 1946.

The Oliver 99 was not tested at Nebraska until 1950, and results of this test appear under No. 451. A photograph of the actual test shows the early hood and grille design, with the streamlined hood and grille coming later. The subject of the test used a 4 3/4 x 6 1/4 inch bore and stroke in its four cylinders. This yielded a 443 ci displacement. In Test No. 451 the Oliver 99 yielded slightly over 62 maximum belt horsepower. In 1948 the Oliver 99 on rubber tires listed at $2,544.

Oliver 60 tractors made their debut in 1940. This little four-cylinder model carried a 3 5/16 x 3 1/2 inch bore and stroke. It operated at 1,500 rpm and had a 120 ci displacement. Oliver 60 tractors were available on Tip-Toe wheels as shown here, or could be furnished with rubber tires. The 60 HC tractor, operating on gasoline, was tested at Nebraska under No. 375 of 1941. This test was run using rubber tires, and yielded nearly 17 drawbar horsepower. On the belt, it yielded almost 19 horsepower. On steel wheels, as shown here, it sold for about $957.

An advertised feature of the Oliver 60, 70, and 80 tractors was the Oliver Fuel Miser. Essentially, this was a variable speed governor which regulated power and speed for the most economical use of fuel. A four-speed transmission was standard equipment, and a two-speed belt pulley drive was built into the design. Hood sides were standard equipment, along with force-feed engine lubrication, oil pressure gauge, water temperature gauge, radiator curtain, and differential steering brakes.

This 1940 photograph shows the Oliver 60, 70, and 80 tractors. With the introduction of the Oliver 60, the company's Fleetline series was completed. Many different mounted tools were available for the Oliver 60, including cultivators of every description, and the choice of two-row or four-row corn planters. A power lift was available as an option. Other options for the original model included electric starter and lights, fenders, and wheel weights.

Oliver 60 tractors could be fitted with various special equipment. One example is this road grader. It is unknown whether this particular attachment was developed by Oliver, but more than likely, it was actually built by a company specializing in this equipment. Whether any number of these special road grader units were built is unknown; there is nothing in the serial number records to provide any information in this regard.

The Oliver mounted planter was but one of many different implements and attachments available for the Oliver 60, 70, and 80 tractors. Shown here is an Oliver check-row planter, complete with check wire. For the benefit of younger readers, farmers of the 1940s had two choices; drilling corn or planting it with check wire. Buttons were spaced equally on the wire, and as the planter moved across the field, the buttons tripped the planter mechanism. Thus, corn was planted at an equal distance, both lengthwise and crosswise of the field. This permitted cultivation in both directions.

By the late 1940s Oliver had developed hydraulic loaders to fit the Oliver 60 and Oliver 70 tractors. The advantages of the hydraulic loader are obvious, and in an era when an occasional mechanical loader was the only alternative to hand labor, this device was a welcome addition to the farm equipment inventory of almost every farm. Various attachments were available, in addition to the manure bucket shown here. These included a backfiller blade, snow plow, snow bucket, and lifting boom.

Oliver 60 tractors were ordinarily furnished with dual front wheels. However, they could also be furnished in the wide-front style shown here. The high-clearance front axle permitted work in standing crops. It also had the additional, and perhaps greater advantage of providing extra stability for working in hilly ground. Oliver used various tradenames for special features of its "60" tractor. PowerMaster was ascribed to the engine, and Row-Vue was a name given to the tapered hood and chassis. The latter provided better visibility, and this was especially important when using mounted implements.

Apparently the Oliver 60 Row-Crop model was built with only the HC gasoline engine. If it was indeed available with the KD engine, existing advertising material makes little or no mention of this possibility. On the other hand, the Oliver 60 Standard could be purchased with either the HC or the KD engine. When making this change, the only change involved the fuel burning equipment. When equipped with steel wheels and the HC engine, this model carried a 1948 list price of $1,150. By comparison, the KD model on steel sold for $1,265.

Oliver 60 Standard tractors used the same four-cylinder engine as the Row-Crop. It carried a 3 5/16 x 3 1/2 inch bore and stroke. Five forward speeds ranged from 2 5/8 to 11 2/3 mph. When furnished with steel wheels the Oliver 60 Standard weighed 2,117 pounds, but on rubber tires the weight was 2,343 pounds. In addition to a different manifold, the HC model used a 6:1 compression ratio; this was changed to a 5:1 compression ratio on the KD model.

Another variety of the basic Oliver 60 was the 60 Industrial model. It was built over the Oliver 60 Standard, but was specially equipped for industrial work. This model was sold in limited numbers, but was a logical continuation of the industrial styles shown for the Oliver 70, the Oliver 80, and earlier models. The Oliver 60 series offered some innovative features. Included was an air intake under the hood with the opening in front of the radiator. Another regular feature was worm and sector steering of a semi-reversible design that permitted easier steering and handling of the tractor.

Production of the Oliver 900 Industrial tractor began in 1945 and concluded in 1951. This model used the same basic four-cylinder engine with a 4 3/4 x 6 1/4 inch bore and stroke that had been used on the 28-44 model. However, in this instance the compression ratio was raised to 5.1:1, and the speed was raised from 1,125 rpm to 1,200 rpm. These changes yielded approximately 64 belt horsepower. The four-speed transmission had speeds ranging up to 16 mph.

This Oliver 900 Industrial is pulling a Be-Ge scraper. Oliver bought out Be-Ge in 1952, and obviously was working with this company for some time prior to actually acquiring the firm. This model could be used with any commercial grade fuel. Company records indicate that production of the 900 Industrial was moved from the Charles City plant to the South Bend, Indiana plant in 1950. Six-volt starting and lighting came as standard equipment. Two headlights and a rear tail light were included. A convenient foot starter switch was used.

Independent hydraulic brakes were used on the Oliver 900 Industrial tractor. A third pedal was included for an equalized service brake. Rear tires were of 14.00 x 32 inch size, but the 900 Industrial could also be furnished with dual 13.00 x 32 tires or with 18.00 x 24 tires. Rear wheel weights were available for a maximum total tractor weight of 15,800 pounds. As shown here, hub caps were provided to give a smooth one-piece appearance. Also featured was an upholstered two-passenger seat.

By the beginning of 1948, Oliver had developed an entirely new tractor, the Oliver 88. Apparently, Oliver had been working on various aspects of a new tractor line for several years. Unfortunately, World War Two intervened, and all but the most essential design work came to a halt in the interim. However, this new six-cylinder model incorporated many new features, including the live pto shaft and an entirely new hydraulic system. Note that this experimental model uses the old-style streamlined grille, along with ordinary front wheel rims. Both were modified shortly after.

The Row-Crop 88 went into production with the old-style grille and hood as shown on this 1947 experimental model. This style remained in effect during approximately the first 1,300 units. At that time an entirely new grille, hood, and fenders were installed. By the time the 88 went into full production, it also appears that the two-piece front wheel rims were standard equipment. Live pto equipment had apparently been in the works for some time, but had not gained any ground due to patent problems.

Initially, Oliver did not offer their 88 tractor with a butane fuel option. However, this experimental model is thus equipped. But, the company took great pride in offering the 88 with three distinct fuel options; gasoline (HC), distillate (KD), and diesel. Initially, the diesel was intended primarily for the export market and for certain areas wanting this engine style. Within a few years the diesel engine gained ground, and eventually brought a virtual end to the spark-fired engines of all types. Higher octane values for gasoline permitted still higher compression ratios. Thus, the pressures within the engine were beginning to approach those of the modern high-speed diesel. This permitted greater use of a single engine design for a consequent reduction in production costs.

The Oliver 88 HC engine was of six-cylinder design, using a 3 1/2 x 4 inch bore and stroke. The 88 KD engine was also of six-cylinder design, and also of 4-inch stroke, but carried a 3 13/16 inch bore. Apparently this style was discontinued in 1949 when the 88 Diesel replaced it. Both the gasoline and diesel engines had a 231 ci displacement. Considerable engineering work resulted in a great many parts being interchangeable through the 88, 77, and 66 tractors. For instance, the self-contained belt pulley and drive case were interchangeable between the 77 and 88 tractors.

A front view of this early Oliver 88 provides an excellent picture of the grille layout and the paint scheme. Only about 1,300 of these tractors were built with this design, but a surprising number still exist, to the great joy of vintage tractor enthusiasts. Adding the live pto system also permitted new advances in a constant-power hydraulic system. Prior to 1948, Oliver saw little advantage in offering a hydraulic system which did nothing more than raise and lower implements, and at a very high production cost, compared to the mechanical lift system already available.

Oliver 88 tractors went to the Nebraska Tractor Test Laboratory and the results for the Row-Crop appear in Test No. 388. Gasoline fuel was used, and in this test the 88 delivered nearly 42 belt horsepower, along with a maximum of nearly 37 drawbar horsepower. The six-cylinder motor operated at 1,600 rpm. Six forward speeds ranged from 2.62 to 12.32 mph. The Hydra-Lectric lift was standard equipment, along with the pto, complete electrical system, and other accessories. This Oliver 88 is shown pulling a land leveler.

Tractors (Wheel)

Many front-end options were available for the Oliver 88 including this single-front tire as shown here. Oliver's advertising pointed to the ease of changing front axle. Apparently, it was necessary only to block up the tractor, disconnect the steering shaft, and remove the mounting bolts. In some areas this was an advantage, since not all axle configurations were suited to all conditions and cropping practices. The Oliver 88 was also built as an Orchard tractor using a standard-tread design.

Production of the Oliver 88 tractor ran from 1948 to 1954. Apparently, the six-speed transmission could be optionally replaced at the factory with a different design having four forward and four reverse speeds, and apparently, this modification was available for all models and styles of the 88 tractor. In addition, the company was able to configure special transmissions for unique situations. Oliver was the first to adopt the recommendations of the SAE Tractor Technical Committee regarding standardization of tire sizes. This Oliver 88 is shown with a two-row cultivator, but four-row styles were also available. In addition to the standard axle configuration, the Oliver 88 was also available with a special 100-inch axle which permitted wheel spacings up to 122 inches.

Oliver finished development of the 88 tractor in 1947, and in fact, it was tested at Nebraska in October of that year. However, the Oliver 88 Diesel did not go into production immediately, probably not until 1949. This model was not tested at Nebraska until October 1950, and the results appear in Test No. 450. It is worthy of note that a photograph of the actual test tractor illustrates it to be using the old-style hood and grille, not the wide-bar grille shown in this high-clearance model. Production of the high-clearance model was probably rather limited, especially since little reference can be found regarding this model. Conversely, the Oliver 88 with an adjustable wide-front axle was optionally available in lieu of the tricycle front.

By the time production of the Oliver 88 ended in 1954 the regular row-crop style was listing at $2,810. The single-front design shown here added only $11 to the list price, but the adjustable wide-front added $78. An hour meter was a $14 option; it would later become standard equipment. A mechanical power lift was available for $95, and wheel weights were priced at $41 per pair. For those who did not want the Hydra-Lectric hydraulic system there was a $295 deduct from the list price. When the Oliver 88 Row-Crop was equipped with Ricefield tires and equipment, the total list price was $3,079.

Unlike some of their competitors, Oliver does not appear to have gone into butane or propane fuel equipment to any large extent. This option was indeed available as an extra-cost option, although industry guides of the period do not even include this derivation. Curiously, the steel Tip-Toe wheel of long standing remained available on the Oliver 88 as optional equipment. The special Tip-Toe wheels bolted directly onto the cast wheel rim in place of the pneumatic tires.

The Oliver 88 was the first of Oliver's new Fleetline Series which would also include the 66 and 77 models. With the introduction of these tractors the 60, 70, and 80 tractors went out of production. It is significant that the new 88 Series went into production in 1948, and this coincided with the beginning of the second century for the corporation. This early style of the Oliver 88 Industrial shows the first version of the hood and radiator grille, and as previously noted, only about 1,300 total units were thus equipped. After this time the tractor was modified to included the familiar horizontal bars in the front grille. Concurrent with this change, the engine was modified slightly and used larger frost plugs as the most visible change.

Oliver 88 Standard tractors were another option in place of the usual Row-Crop design. This fixed-tread model was tested at Nebraska under No. 391, where it delivered 44.96 maximum belt horsepower. The gasoline version was priced at $2,806, while the 88 Diesel Standard sold for $3,456. A Model 88 Orchard was built over the Standard, and it was priced at $2,603. Model 88 Orchard Diesel models retailed at $3,253. Meanwhile, the 88 Diesel Row-Crop tractor sold for $3,460.

Oliver Industrial 88 tractors were built essentially over the 88 Standard-tread chassis, and in fact, there appears to have been little difference when the 88 Industrial was equipped with regular rear rubber in lieu of industrial treads. Again, the early style grille is shown. Many modifications are obvious in this new design, but many more were not manifested by a casual look at the tractor. Included was the use of a new style front wheel bearing that did a better job of sealing out dirt and moisture. In addition, the steering mechanism was improved to provide a shorter turning radius on both the row-crop and the standard-tread versions.

THE "88"

In 1948 Oliver printed an internal memo, comparing the Oliver Standard 88 with old Hart-Parr No. 3 of 1903. The latter was capable of about 30 belt horsepower, and about 18 horses at the drawbar. It weighed about 19,000 pounds. By comparison, the 88 Standard weighed only 4,350 pounds and delivered almost 29 drawbar horsepower, plus nearly 38 horsepower on the belt. Old Number 3 had a displacement of 2,042 ci and operated at 350 rpm. The 88 Standard operated at 1,600 rpm and had a displacement of 231 ci. Power in No. 3 came from a pair of huge 10 x 13 inch cylinders; the 88 used six cylinders with a 3 1/2 x 4 inch bore and stroke.

Oliver 88 Industrial tractors were adapted to many new applications. Included was this heavy-duty front end loader. The 88 Industrial was designed with a very substantial front axle, larger spindles, and bigger tires to handle the loads to which it was subjected. Various other equipment was also adapted to the 88 Industrial, including backhoes, blades, industrial brooms, and equipment too numerous to mention. While the 88 Row-Crop and 88 Standard were finished in the usual Oliver Green, the 88 Industrial was finished in orange with black trim.

Another example of the Oliver 88 Industrial is this road grader; it even includes the words, "Oliver 88 Industrial" stencilled on the side of the main frame. Apparently this model made heavy use of hydraulics, since the various blade motions are obviously controlled by hydraulics. Even the steering was achieved by means of hydraulics, rather than a complicated system of shafts and universal joints. The latter was also much easier for the operator, since hydraulics took over the turning effort.

Oliver 77 Row-Crop tractors saw first light in 1948. Apparently some experimental models had been built during 1947. Cast iron or stamped steel wheels were an option, as was the use of the Tip-Toe steel wheel. However, the latter would fit only on the cast wheels. The same mounted tools could be used with this model or with the 66 and 88 models interchangeably. Likewise, it appears that virtually all of the previous mounted implements could be used on these tractors. The great success of the 66, 77, and 88 tractors was due in part to the standardization of parts and to the heavy use of interchangeable parts. This made it easier for the dealer to keep all parts on hand, it reduced the parts inventory at the factory, and of course, reduced manufacturing costs.

Oliver 77 tractors were tested at Nebraska in late 1948 under No. 404. This test used gasoline fuel and revealed a maximum output of 37.17 belt horsepower. It was tested again in 1949 under No. 425, and this test revealed a maximum of 38.82 belt horsepower. The Oliver 77 LP-gas version came to Nebraska in April 1952 under No. 470 and shows 38.10 maximum belt horsepower. The latter model is illustrated on page 168 of the Author's *Nebraska Tractor Tests Since 1920.* In 1952 the tractor shown here retailed at $2,477.

Many parts for the Oliver 77 interchanged with the concurrent Oliver 88. Like the Oliver 88, this model initially offered the HC and the KD engines, but in 1949 the kerosene-distillate (KD) style was taken from production and replaced with an Oliver-designed six-cylinder diesel engine. The Oliver Hydra-Lectric hydraulic system went into full production during 1949, although it may have been available on a limited basis in 1948. Presumably, it was possible to retrofit tractors already in the field with Hydra-Lectric hydraulics.

Oliver tractors like virtually all others, saw numerous homemade attachments. Included was this front-mounted buzz saw. Granted, the blade is shielded on the back side, but the open drive belt would probably make today's safety engineers shudder. This writer recalls one situation of the early 1980s where a farmer ran the belt off an outfit like this and tried to run it back on without stopping the tractor. The result was that he got his arm caught, dislocating a shoulder, plus other bumps, bruises, and lacerations. As a result he filed suit against the tractor manufacturer! Be warned, stay out of things like that. Besides, Oliver didn't make the saw and this photograph is placed here to illustrate the many uses of tractor power, not to provide grist for some unnamed litigant!

Little information can be located regarding this Oliver 77 High-Clearance model. Presumably a limited number were built, yet even the 1952 Oliver price book does not include this option. More than likely this option was available only on a direct factory shipment. During 1952 the Oliver 77 Row-Crop listed at $2,350. This included the Oliver Ridemaster seat. This specially designed unit used rubber torsion spring units and was introduced with the new Fleetline Series tractors.

Tractors (Wheel)

Oliver 77 tractors were available in numerous configurations. As previously noted, the dual-front style listed at about $2,350. Adding the optional adjustable wide-front axle raised the list price another $80. The single-front axle style sold for $2,379. Buying the 77 KD model added $111 and the LP-gas model was $180 higher than the regular. However, LP-gas equipment was also available as a field option for $185. The Oliver Hydra-Lectric hydraulic system was priced at $289. Oliver 77 Diesel Row-Crop models sold for $2,867. Not required, but highly recommended was the double-battery option for greater cranking power on this model. This option added $33 to the list price.

Oliver 77 Standard tractors were built during the same 1948-54 period as the 77 Row-Crop models. The 77 Standard with HC gasoline engine was tested at Nebraska in October 1948 under No. 405. A similar model with a diesel engine appears in Test No. 457 of May 1951. Fully equipped, the gasoline model was priced at $2,411, while the 77 Diesel Standard sold for $2,950. Many different devices could be attached using the threaded pads at the front of the tractor. The diesel model was virtually identical to the gasoline style, save for the different engine.

LP-gas models of the Oliver 77 Standard were an attractive option for a few years. For this model, the factory-installed cost was $180 over the normal list price, but these tractors could be converted in the field for the price of a $185 kit. Oliver also offered KD equipment as a factory option priced at $111. Numerous other options were available, including a magneto in lieu of battery ignition for the price of $36. Particularly for the Industrial styles, metallic clutch facings were a worthwhile option for only $20 additional.

Oliver 77 Orchard tractors were essentially built over the 77 Standard chassis. Every effort was made to remove obstructions from the hood and sides of the tractor that would snag tree branches, causing damage both to the trees and to the tractor. The Orchard 77 was available ordinarily with the HC gasoline engine, and was priced at $2,270 in 1952. By comparison, the Orchard 77 Diesel sold for $2,807. A belt pulley came as standard equipment, thus increasing the usefulness of the tractor. All other options available for the 77 Standard were also available for the 77 Orchard in both the gasoline and the diesel versions.

A heavier front axle and larger front tires were a major difference between the Oliver 77 Standard and the 77 Industrial model. As previously indicated, suitable mounting pads were strategically situated on the tractor for the mounting of various equipment, including this heavy duty backfill blade. The blade itself could be removed and replaced with a bucket, or even with a v-type snow plow when desired. Virtually all engine and accessory options offered with the 77 Standard were also available with the 77 Industrial, including a wide variety of tire equipment for almost any conceivable application.

The Oliver 66 was introduced in 1949, with production ending in 1954. This was the third model in the so-called New Fleetline series. Oliver made several changes in the design and colors of the decal work. Initially, it appears that the "Row-Crop 66" was in red, and that a yellow stripe was painted over the top of the hood. This lasted for a year or so. It also appears that the first two or three years of production, a darker color of green was used than after perhaps 1952. There seem to be no definite answers, and probably never will be. Shown here is an early Oliver 66 with the red lettering on the side decal. Beginning about 1953, yellow lettering was used.

A head-on view of the little Oliver 66 reveals its attractive grille styling. This little four-cylinder tractor was initially offered with the choice of the HC engine, having a 3 3/16 x 3 3/4 inch bore and stroke, or the KD engine using a 3 1/2 inch bore. Essentially, the 66 and the Oliver 77 used the same engine, except that six-cylinders were used in the latter model. Thus, a great many parts were interchangeable between these two models. In fact, parts interchangeability was carried through into the Oliver 88 as well, with many parts being common to all three models.

The Oliver 66 was tested at Nebraska in June 1949. Results appear in Test No. 412. This little tractor delivered 21 drawbar and nearly 25 belt horsepower. Rated speed for the 66 was 1,600 rpm, and its six forward speeds ranged from 2 1/2 to 11 1/2 mph. When furnished with dual front wheels as shown here, plus the pto shaft, belt pulley, and Hydra-Lectric lift system, this tractor was priced at about $1,810. Numerous options were of course, available at additional cost.

Initially at least, not all the New Fleetline series was available in an orchard version, but this situation soon changed. Shown here are all three New Fleetline models, the 66, the 77, and the 88 in an Orchard style. In addition to the spark-fired models, the Orchard tractors could also be purchased with a diesel engine. In 1954 the 66 Orchard sold for $1,840. The 77 Orchard was priced at $2,380, and the 88 Orchard was tagged at $2,600.

Oliver 66 tractors when equipped with the KD engine were $75 higher than the comparable HC model. Special long rear axles were available for an extra $10; this option permitted wheel settings up to 106 inches. A special low-speed transmission was an $18 option, and metallic clutch facings could be included for an extra $15. In addition, a magneto could be used instead of battery ignition for an additional $19. Apparently, not all of the early 66 tractors were equipped with the rubber torsion spring seat, but this could be converted in the field for $40. An endless variety of other options were available.

The Oliver 66 was also available with a diesel engine. Production of this model began in 1951. It was also tested at Nebraska in October of that year, with the results being tallied in Test No. 467. Both row-crop and standard-tread versions were built, as with the spark-fired models. The four-cylinder engine carried a 3 5/16 x 3 3/4 inch bore and stroke for a displacement of 129.3 ci. In 1954 this model sold for $2,300 as a row-crop, or for $1,863 in the standard-tread style shown here. Oliver 66 Orchard Diesel tractors were priced at $2,330. Operating weight of the tractor shown here was about 3,000 pounds.

Oliver 66 Industrial tractors were essentially built over the 66 Standard, whether in gasoline or diesel versions. During the early 1950s Oliver claimed to have been the undisputed leader in sales of diesel-powered farm tractors. In fact, Oliver was heavily promoting the diesel at a time when many other manufacturers were making a major push toward the use of LP-gas as a tractor fuel. The latter certainly offered certain advantages, but also had the great disadvantage of complicated fuel handling equipment. This Oliver 66 Industrial is towing an unidentified aircraft into its hangar.

Oliver 66 Industrial tractors could be fitted with numerous attachments. Some were built by Oliver, and others could be supplied through their dealer organization. In addition, many other attachments were available from various short-line companies specializing in such equipment. Finally, there were custom-built attachments built at local welding shops or in a farmer's machine shed. Shown here is an attractive v-type snow plow of substantial capacity.

With the advent of the 66 Standard and its brother, the 66 Industrial, Oliver was rapidly moving toward a small utility tractor; one that could be adapted to many other farm, commercial, and industrial duties. For example, this fully hydraulic loader is but one such application. Designed especially for the purpose, this unit included a special radiator guard, plus the additional rear counterweight needed to offset the weight of a loaded bucket. Thus, the Oliver 66 saw wide duties; units like this were used in applications from cattle lots to gravel pits.

Interchangeability was a cardinal feature of the New Fleetline Series built by Oliver. This applied also to many components of the Industrial line, particularly since it was basically a modified version of the 66 Standard. For instance, Oliver announced that the same basic high-clearance front axle would be used on all three models, the 66, the 77, and the 88. On the single-front row-crop model, the same front unit was used on all three. Oliver felt that the cost penalty of using a heavier-than-necessary unit on the 66 and 77 models would be more than offset by the reduction in tooling, manufacturing, and inventory costs.

During the 1950s Oliver helped make the diesel-powered farm tractor a viable option. The company also did extensive research on spark-fired engines, and this resulted in the purely experimental Oliver XO-121 model. Built on an Oliver 88 chassis, the XO-121 was a revolutionary new design in spark-fired engines, in that it used a 12:1 compression ratio. The fuel for this experimental tractor was processed by the Ethyl Corporation. In the historical perspective, it was Hart-Parr Company that came forth in 1901 as the first company solely dedicated to building the gasoline tractor. During the 1930s it was Oliver that developed the concept of a high-compression tractor engine; it first appeared on the Oliver 70 of 1935.

In this photograph, A. King McCord, who at the time was president of the Oliver Corporation took the wheel of the XO-121 tractor. This experimental model was developed to determine the feasibility of the design, and in fact, decals on the side of the tractor read, "Ahead of Tomorrow." In the 1950s and early 1960s the question remained as to what type of engine would be used in the future. The possibilities which Oliver explored included this high-compression design. Since raising the compression ratio also increased the power level, the problem was in finding a fuel which would not pre-ignite. Thus, the Ethyl Corporation assisted in formulating a fuel suitable for this design.

Oliver's XO-121 used a four-cylinder engine having a 3 3/4 x 4 1/2 inch bore and stroke, for a displacement of 199 ci. Rated speed was 1,600 rpm. The special fuel had an octane rating of over 100, and in various tests, the XO-121 delivered 44% more horsepower than the Oliver 77, with a gain in fuel economy of over 30%. This engine was the subject of an engineering paper prepared by T. H. Morrell and K. S. Minard for the September 1961 meeting of the Society of Automotive Engineers under No. 395B. Full details of this engine may be found in this narrative.

In 1954 Oliver introduced its first utility tractor, the Super 55. The agricultural version shown here featured an adjustable front axle. It had a width range of 48 to 76 inches. Super 55 tractors were built in gasoline and diesel models. New features included a hydraulic system integrated with the transmission. A three-point hitch was optionally available. The six-speed transmission had a range up to 14.25 mph. Engine speed was rated at 2,000 rpm.

An Oliver Super 55 gasoline (HC) tractor was tested at Nebraska in September 1954. This test, No. 524, shows a maximum of 30.75 drawbar and 35.88 belt horsepower. The four-cylinder engine, rated at 2,000 rpm, used a 3 1/2 x 3 3/4 inch bore and stroke and had a displacement of 144 cubic inches. The rated speed of 2,000 rpm was primarily for belt work. For drawbar work the recommended engine speed was 1,750 rpm. Ordinary equipment included 11-28 rear tires.

Oliver also built the Super 55 in a diesel-powered model. This tractor also carried a 144 cubic inch, four-cylinder engine, but with a compression ratio of 15.75:1. Weighing about 3,500 pounds, the Super 55 Diesel was tested at Nebraska in September 1954. It delivered nearly 29 maximum drawbar horsepower, along with slightly over 34 belt horsepower. While the Super 55 HC model was priced at about $2,075, the Super 55 Diesel listed at $2,560. These prices included lights, belt pulley, pto shaft, and hydraulic lift system.

With the introduction of the Oliver Super 66 a 12-volt electrical system became standard equipment. The Oliver 66 used a four-cylinder motor with a 3 5/16 x 3 3/4 inch bore and stroke. It was rated at 1,600 rpm. Oliver Super 66 tractors also carried a four-cylinder engine, but the cylinder bore was raised to 3 1/2 inches, and the speed was raised to 2,000 rpm for belt work, and to 1,750 rpm for drawbar duty. In this model the compression ratio was set at 7.0 to 1, compared to 6.75:1 for the earlier Oliver 66 model. These and other changes raised the power level to nearly 30 drawbar horsepower, compared to about 22 horses on the earlier Oliver 66 model.

The Oliver Super 55 Industrial was essentially the same as the Agricultural model, except that this industrial style had a fixed front axle. In addition, the Industrial was equipped with a special foot accelerator. The Super 55 Fork Lift shown here was built during the same 1954-58 period as the Super 55 Agricultural model. Power steering was an extra-cost option on all styles. The fork lift shown here was but one of many different options available for the Super 55. Shown here is a Sherman fork lift mast attached to the Super 55. It was available in numerous configurations and with special fork equipment if so desired.

Oliver Super 66 tractors were available in numerous configurations, including the single-front axle shown here. Also built was an adjustable wide-front axle. The Super 66 could also be secured in a diesel version. The latter was the subject of Nebraska Test No. 544, where it delivered a maximum of 29.09 drawbar horsepower. Oliver sold the diesel row-crop version for about $3,300, while the comparable gasoline style was priced at $2,700. Both used an engine having a displacement of 144 cubic inches.

Oliver Super 66 tractors could be purchased with an adjustable wide-front axle as shown here. These tractors were ordinarily furnished with a package that included lights, pto, and other accessories. However, other extra-cost options were also available. Included was power steering for $198; power-adjustable rear wheels for $205, and a belt pulley for $71. During the 1950s the transition from belt drives to pto drives became increasingly evident, and in fact, is shown here, with the pulley being an option, rather than standard equipment.

This ordinary Super 77 farm tractor has been adapted to commercial duty by the installation of a large mower. Safety chains are used to prevent injury or damage. The Super 77 appeared in 1954 and was continued until 1958. This model could be purchased with the adjustable width front axle as shown here, or the usual tricycle front. Many other options were available, including the single-front axle. As with other Oliver models, front mounting pads were provided for mounted implements, and the Super 77 boasted of Oliver's exclusive Hydra-Lectric hydraulic system, a live pto shaft, and independent disc brakes.

The wide-ranging Oliver tractor options included a special high-clearance design, as shown here. This was an extra-cost option over the $3,250 for a Super 77 with dual front wheels. Using a six-cylinder engine having a 3 1/2 x 3 3/4 inch bore and stroke, the Super 77 was rated at 1,600 rpm. The compression ratio was 7.0 to 1, and displacement was 216 ci. When equipped with a diesel engine as shown here, the Oliver Super 77 listed at $3,967. Power steering added about $200 to the list price, but this option soon became standard equipment on virtually all farm tractors, since it greatly relieved the tedium of a day in the field.

Oliver Super 77 tractors were built in a standard-tread with a fixed-width front axle during the same 1954-58 time frame as the Super 77 row-crop models. In Nebraska Test No. 542 the Super 77 delivered 40.16 belt horsepower using gasoline fuel. The comparable diesel model gave a performance within fractions of its spark-fired counterpart. This Super 77 is shown with the optional belt pulley attachment; it was a $71 option.

Oliver Super-Series tractors were also available with an LP-gas conversion at an extra cost of $258. Another style was the Super 77 Orchard tractor, and this one also includes the LP-gas equipment. Beyond this, the Super 77 Orchard was also available as a diesel model. An ordinary gasoline-fired version of the Super 77 Orchard listed at $4,160, while the diesel-powered counterpart sold for $4,875. Much of the extra cost for these Orchard models was in the special sheet metal work. Shielding was required around the engine, and of course, the fenders were designed to minimize damage to trees and vines.

An Oliver Super 77 Industrial tractor was also available in the 1954-58 period. This model was essentially the same as the Super 77 Standard, except that different wheel equipment was used, and many specialized options were available. When equipped with an Oliver Super 77 Loader, these attachments included a parallel lifting fork, boom attachments, backfiller blade, reversible snow plow, snow bucket, coal bucket, and digging bucket. Some of this equipment was built by Oliver, but other items may have been supplied by other companies through the Oliver dealer network.

It is a curious anomaly of tractor design that the wide-front axle existed long before the first row-crop models of the 1920s. Yet, the wide-front made its return, and in particular, the adjustable wide-front design. Many farmers preferred the latter due to its increased stability, especially on hilly ground. For others, the preference was based on their specific cropping practices. However, Oliver was quick to respond to the needs of the farmer by offering many different options. Included was this Oliver Super 88 which appears to use a fixed-width front axle design.

Whether in a gasoline or a diesel version, the Oliver Super 88 engine was of six-cylinder design and used a 3 3/4 x 4 inch bore and stroke for a displacement of 265 ci. Nebraska Test No. 525 was run on the gasoline model, and Test No. 527 shows the performance of the Super 88 diesel. The two subjects were remarkably close in their power level; both delivered a maximum of nearly 50 drawbar horsepower. The present research has no way to substantiate the claim, but Oliver advertising of the time noted that they had sold about 90% of the diesel-powered tractors of this period.

Tractors

Oliver Super 88 tractors included a special high-clearance version as shown here. The gasoline-powered high clearance model sold for $4,561, compared to only $3,850 for the ordinary dual-front row-crop version. A Super 88 Diesel High-Clearance tractor listed at over $5,300, but the Super 88 Row-Crop diesel was priced at $4,600. Yet another option was the Super 88 with an adjustable front axle; Oliver also referred to it as a Rice or Cane model. This one with a gasoline engine sold for $4,112. Like others in the 'Super' series, LP-gas equipment was available for an additional $260 in lieu of gasoline and a carburetor. Power steering was a $200 option.

The Super 88 tractor was also built as an Industrial model. It was of course, built over the basic Super 88 Standard chassis, but included the usual extra accessories needed for industrial and commercial applications. Another change for this model was the use of an entirely different hood and grille design. The heavy front bumper became standard equipment, and it was designed with a heavy front drawbar. Tire equipment was available for almost any application, and the Super 88 Industrial could be purchased with gasoline, LP-gas, or diesel engines.

Tractor duals were relatively uncommon in the early 1950s. Yet, as tractor power levels increased, so did tractor weight, and as a consequence, so did soil compaction. Thus, Oliver began experimenting with dual wheel equipment for their tractors in the early 1950s, and perhaps even earlier. Shown here is a factory photograph that illustrates the Oliver engineering approach at the time. The axle-mounted duals would eventually become widely used, and in the interim, so would clamp-on dual wheels. Regardless of the mounting method, dual wheels improved performance, lowered slippage, and minimized soil compaction.

Super 44 Utility tractors were initially built at the Battle Creek, Michigan plant, and production was then shifted to South Bend. Built only in 1957 and 1958, the Super 44 Utility carried a four-cylinder Continental engine. The high-clearance frame and the adjustable wheels made this an ideal tractor for commercial gardeners and nurserymen. Of course it was also a very useful hired hand for many other applications within its capabilities. After production of the Super 44 ended, came the Oliver 440 tractor. It was an improved version, and was built at the Charles City, Iowa factory.

Production of the Oliver 99 began already in 1937. In the twenty years up to 1957, various changes and modifications occurred. In fact, it appears that the Super 99 may have been introduced already in 1954; Oliver's own serial number lists suggest that it was 1957, yet the industry listings show that this happened in 1954. To support the latter contention, Oliver Super 99 tractors were tested at Nebraska in August of 1955. Only the diesel version was tested. The conventional Oliver diesel style is shown in Test No. 557, and the Super 99 with a GM Diesel engine is manifested in Test No. 556.

Oliver Super 99 tractors were available with gasoline or diesel engines. Of the latter, two styles were offered...the conventional six-cylinder Oliver diesel, or the three-cylinder, two-cycle GM diesel. The latter was offered with a torque converter unit which was another 'first' for an Oliver tractor. The GM diesel used a 4 1/4 x 5 inch bore and stroke for a 213 cid. Rated speed was 1,675 rpm. This delivered about 80 belt horsepower, making it one of the most powerful farm tractors in existence at that time.

An Oliver advertising brochure of March 1955 calls the Oliver Super 99 GM Diesel the 'most powerful general-purpose farm wheel tractor built!' This big tractor included a recirculating ball-type steering gear, with power steering available as an extra-cost option. Another feature was the front axle construction which moved the kingpin inward, almost to the centerline of the front tire. This relieved much of the shock and impact on the steering gear, and ultimately, on the operator. A large, roomy operator's platform was featured, along with a rubber spring seat for greater comfort. Another option was a padded backrest for additional comfort and safety.

Many different options were available for the Super 99, including this operator's cab. Although it had no heater or air conditioning unit, it nevertheless was another step forward in operator comfort and safety. Double-disc differential brakes were a standard feature. The could be easily adjusted from the outside of the tractor with only a wrench. Other standard features were big 15-34 rear tires, a complete array of gauges on the dash, plus a combination tachometer and hour meter.

General Motors first introduced its two-cycle diesel engines in 1938. Subsequently, the GM diesel proved itself throughout the world. This Model 3-71 used a 16.0 to 1 compression ratio; air was supplied by an externally situated rotary blower. The unit fuel injector system was designed so as to automatically purge entrapped air. No central metering or pressurizing pump was required, and thus, there were no high-pressure fuel lines. The unit injectors could be replaced in the field with a minimum of difficulty.

In Nebraska Test No. 556 of 1955, the Oliver Super 99 GM made a maximum drawbar pull of 10,075 pounds, or slightly over five tons! This tractor also delivered nearly 79 belt horsepower. The belt pulley was rear-mounted, and attached to the pto shaft housing. It was removable, and could be installed in the field at any time. Also featured was an independent pto shaft which was driven directly from the engine flywheel, and completely independent of the tractor clutch. Option included an over-center hand clutch that could be operated by hand or with a foot pedal. Dual air pre-cleaners were yet another option.

In addition to the GM diesel engine option, Oliver Super 99 tractors were also available with an Oliver diesel engine, or the company's gasoline-powered version. However, the latter was never tested at Nebraska. Both models used an Oliver six-cylinder engine having a 4-inch bore and stroke for a 302 ci displacement. Rated speed was 1,675 rpm. The gasoline style used a 6.2 to 1 compression ratio, and the Oliver diesel engine was built with a 15.5 to 1 compression ratio. The diesel model continued to use the Lanova-type combustion system.

Production of the Oliver Super 99 series closed out in 1958. Initially, the Super 99 was built at the South Bend plant, and production was later transferred to Charles City. The Super 99 with a gasoline engine listed at $4,675, while a comparable diesel model sold at $5,500. Buying a Super 99 with a GM diesel engine raised the price to $7,146. If however, if the Super 99 GM diesel with a torque converter was wanted, then the price jumped to $8,126. The torque converter style was available only with the GM diesel engine. Numerous attachments were available, both from Oliver and in the extensive aftermarket.

Oliver's own six-cylinder diesel was available in the Super 99. Thus equipped, it delivered about 65 maximum belt horsepower, and a maximum of about 61 horsepower on the drawbar. These results appear in Nebraska Test No. 557. Another feature of the Super 99 was the use of a pressurized cooling system that included a bypass thermostat. The diesel model featured an ether injector for cold weather starting, and a four-stage fuel filter system was standard equipment. To operate a loader or other auxiliary equipment, a second hydraulic pump could be added to the front of the tractor.

In 1955 Oliver began building its 990 Speedhaul scraper. It remained in production until 1957. This unit was powered by an Oliver Super 99 GM tractor unit sans the front axle. The scraper pivot was situated ahead of the rear axle for greater traction and better stability. At the time, Oliver was directing much of its advertising toward soil conservation work, such as grass waterways. One advertising brochure noted that 'twenty years of conservation [work lies ahead] for farmers and land improvement contractors.'

Oliver's 55 tractor first appeared in 1958; it was a streamlined update of the earlier Super 55 tractor. Production of the 550 continued, albeit with various changes, until 1975. This 1958 model uses an altogether different grille than the 1961 models. Also, the decal arrangement is entirely different. Oliver 550 tractors could be furnished with gasoline or diesel engines; both were a four-cylinder design with a 3 5/8 x 3 3/4 inch bore and stroke. Rate speed was 2,000 rpm.

Although the lower part of the original photograph is damaged, it nevertheless illustrates the original grille and decal design as used on the Oliver 550. In fact, this is the actual test tractor used in Nebraska Test No. 698 for the 550 Diesel version. This model used a 16 to 1 compression ratio, while the gasoline model of Test No. 697 was designed with a 7.75 to 1 compression ratio. Beginning in 1935 Oliver pioneered the concept of high compression ratios for gasoline tractors, and eventually applied the same concept to their diesel tractors.

Oliver 550 tractors of 1961 retained the original grille styling of the original offering. However, by this time the decals and highlights have been changed substantially from the original design. Oliver 550 tractors could be purchased with a fixed-width front axle, or with an adjustable-front style. This little tractor had a wheelbase of under 73 inches, and an overall length of 10 feet. With a 52-inch wheel tread, it had a turning radius of nine feet, making it a very handy utility tractor, as well as providing up to 45-plus brake horsepower when needed.

By 1963 the Oliver 550 had taken on a different appearance. Major components were essentially the same, but the new open grille styling gave the 550 and entirely different look than before. Again, the highlights, including the decal design and placement changed. Standard equipment on the agricultural models included a three-point hitch and Oliver's integral hydraulic system. These were extra-cost options on the Oliver 550 Industrial model.

A coat of red paint replaced the usual Oliver green on this Cockshutt 550 tractor. With that change and somewhat different decals, the Cockshutt 550 and the Oliver 550 were essentially the same identical tractor. Standard equipment for this model included a live pto drive; it could operate at 540 or 1,000 rpm. In 1962 the 550 gasoline version sold for $3,270, while the comparable diesel version was priced at $3,770. This price included three-point hitch, power-adjustable rear wheels, and power steering. A belt pulley was available for $81.

Oliver 550 Industrial tractors were basically the same as the Agricultural style. This Oliver 550 fork lift was offered in the 1958-60 period, and was simply an improved model of the Super 55 fork lift previously offered. Power steering was standard equipment at this juncture, and the tractor has been suitably modified for fork lift service. This included heavy counterweights to the rear, plus the adaptation of the seat, steering wheel, and operating controls for this specialized duty.

With a pent-up demand for small backhoes and excavators, Oliver attempted to tap into this market with their 550 Industrial and their 613 backhoe, together with the 615 loader. Again, the tractor was essentially the 550 Industrial model, but was equipped with a much larger hydraulic pump to accommodate the needs of backhoe work. The backhoe was detachable from the tractor, although this required a bit of effort. Small backhoe units like this were easily maneuvered into small, tight areas that formerly required hand work, since the huge equipment of earlier days was simply impractical in these situations.

In the 1960-64 period, Oliver offered this No. 551 fork lift as an improvement over the earlier 550 fork lift. This model used a 12-foot mast having a lifting capacity of 2 1/2 tons. The large tires made this unit quite suitable on construction jobs and other areas with rough ground, mud, snow, and other problems with which to contend. Numerous attachments were also available. In 1965 the No. 552 appeared as another upgrade, and with the latter model, mast sizes were available with lifts up to 21 feet. Numerous other features were also found on the Oliver 552 fork lift tractor. A bit of confusion exists over the production of the 550 tractor, since the serial number listings also list this model as the 2-44 beginning in 1966 and continuing to 1975.

LP-gas fuel could be used in the Oliver 770. This option added $280 to the base price of $4,200, and an example is shown in this photograph. Oliver promoted LP-gas as a tractor fuel to some extent during the 1950s and into the early 1960s. However, the company's major emphasis was on diesel tractors. In this assessment of the future, Oliver's engineers would vindicate themselves, since by 1970 the gasoline engine was rapidly fading from the tractor scene; diesel engines were rapidly taking the lead in the choice of tractor power.

Oliver 770 tractors saw first light in 1958. This model was a major revision of the earlier Super 77, and the ancestry can be traced back even further to the Oliver 77 model. This model carried a six-cylinder engine with a 3 1/2 x 3 3/4 inch bore and stroke. Gasoline, LP-gas, and diesel versions were available. The gasoline model used a 7.3 to 1 compression ratio, and all styles carried the valve-in-head design customary virtually all the Oliver models. Oliver 770 diesel tractors carried a 16.0 to 1 compression ratio.

Numerous frame configurations were available in the 770 series, including this rather unusual high-crop design. It was essentially the 770 agricultural row-crop model, except that offset and extended rear axles were used, along with an extended front pedestal. Special bracing was extended from the front of the tractor frame to the final drive housings. These tractors were built for various purposes, probably including mounted cotton pickers. These special high-clearance models were likely built only on factory order, and appear to have been available during the 1958-67 production run of the 770 tractors.

After White Motors acquired Oliver and Cockshutt, some Oliver models were sold in Canada under the Cockshutt logo, but were nothing more or less than the same tractor with red paint instead of green. Shown here is a Cockshutt 770 Wheatland model; it was the same as the Oliver 770 Wheatland, and both were essentially a 770 standard-tread tractor. However, the Wheatland could be furnished with larger tires, along with some other modifications for this specific duty.

Oliver 770 tractors were tested at Nebraska in the gasoline and diesel versions. The gasoline model appears in Test No. 648, where it delivered over 51 belt horsepower. Test No. 649 was run on the 770 diesel, and shows and output of nearly 51 horsepower. With the tricycle front end, the 770 gasoline sold for $4,200, while the comparable diesel was priced at $4,900. A 770 gasoline standard-tread was priced at $4,400, and when using a diesel engine it retailed at $5,100. Wheatland tractors were available with gasoline or diesel engines. The latter model was priced at $5,015 and the gasoline model sold for $4,300.

Another high-clearance design is shown with this Oliver 770 model. Instead of the extended axles and the dual-front wheels, this model used an adjustable width front axle of a high-clearance design. While the 770 extended axle version shown in an adjacent photograph uses the original grille design, this model is furnished with the redesigned grille. From all appearances, this change occurred about 1962 or perhaps in 1963. During the transitional period of this change, it appears that tractors came off the production line using both grille styles, apparently until the supply of the earlier style was exhausted.

The Oliver 770 Orchard tractor was equipped with special fenders and other accessories for this specialized work. This platform view illustrates the clean lines of a 770 Orchard model. It was built over the 770 standard-tread model, but the additional sheet metal work and accessories raised the price considerably. With Oliver's new Power Booster transmission the 770 Orchard with gasoline power sold for $4,200, and the diesel-powered version raised this price by another $700.

This early version of the 770 Orchard tractor is obvious by the grille design, as well as the Oliver decal (within an ellipse) on the side of the fuel tank. A unique feature was the specially formed exhaust pipe. It emerges from the side of the hood and is bent downward, enters the fore part of the fender, and finally emerges at the rear of the tractor. With the introduction of the 770 tractors, Oliver again changed the paint color slightly, this time adopting meadow green and clover white as the official color combination.

Oliver attempted to find many commercial and industrial uses for the 770 engine. In this instance, the company experimented with an Oliver 770 engine as power for a truck. Little is known of these experiments, but legend has it that after some experimental work with heavy loads the truck frame folded up and that essentially ended the project. More than likely, this unit was used in and around the Oliver plant, but there is no indication that Oliver 'trucks' were seriously contemplated as a production line venture.

During the same production period as the 770 agricultural models, Oliver Corporation offered the 770 Industrial Power-Pak units to OEM manufacturers. This Tampo road roller was one such unit, and it carried a pair of the Oliver 770 Power-Paks. Essentially, this was an engine/transmission unit, complete with final drives. The manufacturer then adapted their own equipment to the Power-Pak. In addition to the road roller shown here, Oliver furnished the Power-Pak for many other applications.

Oliver 770 Industrial tractors were built during the same 1958-67 period as the agricultural models. This early copy, probably of 1958 vintage, displays the grille design and decal arrangement as originally used on the agricultural models. 'Oliver' appears within an ellipse, both on the radiator grille, and on the side of the hood. The 770 Industrial was of course built over the standard 770 Standard chassis. However, it carries an exceptionally heavy front axle, and is equipped with rear tire equipment suited especially to industrial duty.

Two transmission styles were offered with the 770 tractors. The regular six-speed style included two reverse speeds, and a maximum forward speed of 11 mph. The high-speed transmission raised the speed level in all gears, culminating in a top speed of 13 mph. A 10-inch dry-type single plate clutch was used, and these tractors featured full-time power steering as a standard feature. Diesel models could be equipped with a Chevron starting aid for cold weather, along with a 1000 watt coolant heater.

Oliver 770 Industrial models could be furnished with numerous attachments, including this heavy-duty end loader bucket. Ostensibly designed for the heaviest work, it likely underwent tests which strained its durability at times. The heavy radiator guard was a standard feature with this loader, and full hydraulics were of course, standard equipment. During World War Two, hydraulic systems were highly developed for defense purposes. After hostilities ended, much of the new technology redounded to the great benefit of civilian applications.

Oliver 880 tractors were offered with the choice of gasoline, LP-gas, or diesel engines. All styles used a six-cylinder engine having a 3 3/4 x 4 inch bore and stroke for a displacement of 265 ci. Rated speed was 1,750 rpm. Oliver sent a copy of the 880 Diesel to Nebraska in April 1958. Results appear in No. 650, and indicate a maximum output of over 56 drawbar horsepower. This diesel-powered model with dual front wheels listed at about $5,700. Features included Oliver's new Power-Booster drive, full-time power steering, and new Powerjuster rear wheels.

A wide-front axle was an option for the Oliver 880; it added $105 to the regular list price of $4,925 for the gasoline model with dual front tires. The 880 gasoline model was tested at Nebraska in early 1958; results appear in Test No. 647. In this test the 880 on gasoline developed a maximum of 64 belt horsepower. Oliver's advertising of the period pointed with pride to this new model, commenting on its "Bold new styling...clean refreshing lines in sparkling Meadow Green and Clover White."

LP-gas models of the 880 Oliver were priced as a $290 addition over the base price using a regular gasoline engine. Thus, this 880 LP-gas model with a dual front axle was priced at slightly over $5,200. Oliver's standard six-speed transmission was combined with the optional Power-Booster drive to give a total of twelve forward speeds. These overlapped sufficiently to provide virtually any required ground speed within the range of the transmission. In addition, the Power-Booster included a special creeper drive which gave speeds as low as 1 mph.

Yet another available option for the 880 agricultural series was this extra-high clearance model. It was available both in the gasoline and diesel versions, with the latter being priced at $6,425. This special design gave a front axle clearance of nearly three feet, and only slightly less at the rear axle. Another design feature was the adjustable drawbar setting. In the lowest position it provided 15 inches of clearance. The middle setting was 18 inches, and in the top mounting the drawbar was 21 inches above the ground. For cultivating and other applications not needing a drawbar, it could be completely removed for maximum clearance under the rear axle.

Oliver 880 Wheatland models offered either 15-30 or 18-26 rear tires, while the regular row-crop models used either 34 or 38 inch tires. This model weighed about 5,300 pounds, compared to 5,000 pounds for a gasoline row-crop model. An 880 Wheatland Diesel was priced at about $5,775, or about $800 higher than a comparable gasoline model. Sales literature of the period indicates that the power-adjusted rear wheels, pto shaft, power lift system, and other features were over and above the base price for the tractor, but were incorporated into various package options.

Sometime during the 1958-63 production run of the Oliver 880, the company built this special twin-engine industrial model. It used single front and rear axles, but used dual transmissions. No information has been located regarding specific features of the design, including the method of tying the two power plants into an integral and synchronized affair. Given the power level of about 55 drawbar horsepower for each engine, it would appear that there was more than enough horsepower for the amount of rubber in contact with the ground.

Oliver 880 Industrial tractors featured a shuttle-drive which Oliver called their 'Reverse-O-Torc" design. A simple flick of a lever mounted on the steering post provided forward and reverse movement of the tractor. Power was delivered through a single-stage torque converter. The 880 Industrial was also available with a conventional transmission. When equipped with a front-end loader, the Reverse-O-Torc transmission made the 880 Industrial an ideal tractor for loading purposes, since clutching was eliminated and slack time was reduced.

During the late 1950s and early 1960s Oliver engineers spent at least a limited amount of time trying to adapt the 880 engine into a truck. This experimental unit apparently was used within the Oliver plant at Charles City for several years but was eventually scrapped. It was however, fitted with air brake equipment and a fifth wheel for moving semi trailers and other equipment in and around the factory.

Oliver 660 tractors were introduced in 1959 and remained in production until 1964. This model was an evolutionary progression from the earlier Super 66 model, and was built with the choice of gasoline or diesel engines. The four-cylinder motor carried a 3 5/8 x 3 3/4 inch bore and stroke with a governed speed of 2,000 rpm. Shown here is the 660 with dual front wheels, as regularly supplied. This model in a gasoline version sold for $3,185; a comparable diesel model was priced at $3,685.

As with other Oliver tractor models, the 660 was available with several front axle configurations, including the adjustable wide-front axle shown here. This option added about $100 to the regular list price. A single front wheel design added $170 to the base price, but this included power steering. In buying the 660 gasoline model at nearly $3,200, the Hydra-Hitch system was included, along with power-adjustable rear wheels, and live pto system. Oliver continued to build their gasoline engines with fairly high compression ratios; the 660 had a compression ratio of 7.75 to 1.

Oliver sent a copy of its new 950 tractor to Nebraska in July 1958. This model featured Oliver's six-cylinder, four-cycle diesel engine. Rated at 1,800 rpm, it had a 302 ci displacement. Bare weight of this tractor was over 10,000 pounds. It featured six forward speeds ranging up to nearly 13 mph. During Test No. 660 the Oliver 950 delivered nearly 50 drawbar horsepower. The tractor is shown here during this test. Production of the 950 began at the South Bend factory but was eventually transferred to Charles City. The 950 was built in the 1958-61 period.

990 GM Industrial Wheel Tractor

Oliver 950, 990, and 995 tractors all used the same essential chassis. The major difference was that the 950 was equipped with a six-cylinder Oliver diesel, while the 990 and the 995 models were built with a GM three-cylinder, two-cycle diesel engine. Additionally, the 995 Lugmatic tractor used a torque converter instead of a conventional transmission. The 950 used a 12-inch clutch, but the 990 was furnished with a 14-inch clutch. A recirculating ball-type steering gear was standard equipment on all three models. Shown here is an Oliver 950 model.

Oliver 950, and 990 tractors were available in agricultural and industrial versions, with the latter being shown here. Possibly the 995 was also available as an industrial model, although available data makes no indication one way or the other. The 990 was tested at Nebraska in July 1958 under No. 661. This model delivered a maximum pull of 12,629 pounds at the drawbar. The three-cylinder GM engine was of two-cycle design and used a 4 1/4 x 5 inch bore and stroke. In the 990 tractor the engine was governed at 1,800 rpm, but in the 995 Lugmatic the governed speed was raised to 2,000 rpm.

Tractors

Oliver bought out the Be-Ge Manufacturing Company, thus acquiring the latter's Roto-Haul scraper, as shown here. It could be matched to the 950, 990, or 995 tractors with good success, although it appears that the 995 was the tractor of choice, due to its torque converter transmission. At the time, Oliver was promoting this pair for waterway conservation work and similar duties. It is an interesting sidelight that the Oliver Chilled Plow Works had been promoting the concept of soil conservation practices already in the 1920s, and perhaps, even earlier.

The Oliver 995 Lugmatic tractor was not confined to purely industrial work, but was also a logical addition to various farm operations. Oliver claimed that their torque converter design offered up to 11,400 pounds of drawbar pull and utilized up to 95% of the horsepower. The 995 also offered live pto by using a unique hollow shaft design in the torque converter. This permitted live pto operation while having no effect whatever on ground travel. For those desirous of a gasoline engine, the 950 was offered with this version, but of course it was not available in the 990 and 995 models.

Oliver sold the 950 gasoline version at about $5,475, but the comparable 950 diesel retailed for $6,325. An Oliver 990 tractor was essentially the same except for the GM engine. However, it retailed at nearly $8,100, and the 995 Lugmatic with the torque converter drive sold for almost $9,400. These prices included power steering, hydraulic lift, and the pto system, although the three models of this series could be purchased without these options. The 950 gasoline version was not tested at Nebraska.

In 1958 Oliver coupled one of their 995 Lugmatic tractors to a Be-Ge Speed-Haul scrapers for an integrated unit. In the 1955-57 period, Oliver offered their 990 scraper using an Oliver Super 99 GM tractor as the power source, and integrated it with a Be-Ge scraper. This unit was an upgraded version of the design, but apparently never sold in quantity, despite its attractive appearance. At this point in time, Oliver, like many other farm equipment manufacturers saw new and potentially rewarding markets in construction equipment. For Oliver, success in the scraper business was less than might have been desired.

During 1960 Oliver produced their little 440 tractor. It was an upgraded version of the earlier Super 44 series. This model used a small four-cylinder Continental engine with an L-head design. Rated at 1,800 rpm, it carried a 3 3/16 x 4 3/8 inch bore and stroke. The offset design made it an ideal cultivating tractor, and the adjustable wide-front axle was standard equipment. Oliver Corporation might have continued this tractor in production for a few years. However, on November 1, 1960 the Oliver Corporation became a wholly owned subsidiary of White Motors. With a change in corporate management, the vision for the future obviously changed.

In the 1960-63 period Oliver offered the Model 500 tractor. This tractor was built expressly for Oliver by David Brown of England. This was the first foreign-built tractor offered by Oliver. Gasoline or diesel engines were offered, both of which used a four-cylinder design, and developed about 30 drawbar horsepower. Initially, the Oliver 500 was distributed from the Cleveland, Ohio plant but with its closing, dealer sales were moved to Charles City, Iowa. A three-point hitch, hydraulics, differential lock, and pto shaft were among the standard equipment package. Options included power steering, the Oliver Powerjuster rear wheels, and remote hydraulics.

Oliver 1800 tractors were first introduced in 1960. The Series A was built from 1960 to 1962, the Series B was built in the 1962-63 period, and the Series C was produced during 1963 and 1964. The Series A was tested at Nebraska under No. 766 of October 1960. This gasoline model used an Oliver six-cylinder engine with a 3 3/4 x 4 inch bore and stroke for a displacement of 265 ci. Rated speed was 2,000 rpm. In Nebraska Test No. 766 the 1800 (A) developed nearly 74 pto horsepower. An LP-gas conversion was also available.

Oliver 1800 (A) tractors were available in many configurations. The gasoline tricycle style listed at $5,500. Another option was the 1800 Wheatland, priced at about $5,750, or the 1800 Riceland at $5,850. Yet another option was a front-wheel-drive version, and it sold for about $7,900. The gasoline model used an 8.5 to 1 compression ratio; the engine used aluminum pistons, removable wet-type sleeves, and a pressurized cooling system.

An Oliver advertising brochure of 1961 points to the company's celebration of 25 years of six-cylinder power. In retrospect, when Oliver introduced the six-cylinder tractor engine in 1935, much of the industry was of the opinion that the idea would never work. However, the same company which had produced the Oliver 70 in 1935 went on to build the ultra-modern XO-121 tractor in 1954, and ultimately, went on to build the 1800 with its high-compression six-cylinder engine. Shown here is an Oliver 1800 with a fully enclosed cab. It is unknown whether this cab was fabricated in the Oliver shops or purchased from an outside vendor.

Various changes occurred during the production of the 1800-Series tractors. This photograph illustrates an 1800 with an entirely different color scheme than was ordinarily used, yet no information can be located regarding this unique copy. Possibly it received a special paint job for a trade show, or perhaps the company was considering a new color scheme. After all, Oliver was now owned by White Motors (1960) and perhaps the new management had some new ideas about color schemes.

Oliver 1800 (A) diesel tractors used an engine with a 3 7/8 x 4 inch bore and stroke. The 1800 (B) increased the stroke to 4 3/8 inches for a 310 ci displacement. The latter design was tested at Nebraska in November 1962 and the results are shown in Test No. 831. The Row-Crop models were available with a dual-front or an adjustable wide-front axle, along with various standard-tread styles, including the Riceland and Wheatland styles. All models featured Oliver's Hydra-Power Drive system.

In Nebraska Test No. 839 Oliver submitted their 1800 (B) gasoline model; it was essentially the same as the (A) model but the engine size was raised to 3 7/8 x 4 inches. Test No. 846 was run on the same basic tractor, but with the four-wheel-drive option. Likewise, the Oliver 1800 (B) diesel was tested under No. 832 with the four-wheel-drive option. The actual test model is shown here during the drawbar testing. This model delivered almost 77 pto horsepower. Test No. 832 was run in November 1962.

In addition to the many options available with the 1800 Agricultural models, Oliver also built the 1800 Industrial model. It was essentially a standard-tread model, but included the necessary modifications for specialized work. The four-wheel-drive option was expensive...the tractor shown here was listing at about $8,900 in 1964. Many exciting new features were included in the 1800 tractors, including a dual-speed pto, power steering, and a draft-sensitive three-point hitch system. During the production run Oliver used several different decal configurations, but detailed information regarding these changes is now unavailable.

Oliver 1900 tractors were built in the same 1960-64 period as the smaller 1800 model. Three versions were offered, all using a General Motors diesel engine. The 1900 (A) used a four-cylinder, two-cycle design with a 3 7/8 x 4 1/2 inch bore and stroke, operating at 2,000 rpm. The 1900 (B) was first built in 1962. It used the same Series 453 GM engine, but in this instance, it was a Model 5221, while the 1900 (A) carried the Model 5121 engine. Essentially, the difference was that the 1900 (B) and 1900 (C) tractors operated at 2,200 rpm.

The 1900 (A) tractors used a GM diesel engine with a 17 to 1 compression ratio. This tractor was tested at Nebraska under No. 768, yielding over 89 pto horsepower. This test was run in October 1960. In September 1962 the 1900 (B) tractor was tested under No. 824. This test used the same GM four-cylinder engine, but the compression ratio was raised to 21 to 1. This boosted pto output to slightly over 98 horsepower. Again in 1963 the 1900 tractor went to Nebraska, but while the subject of No. 824 was a conventional two-wheel-drive design, the latter model featured a front-wheel-assist. It is also noteworthy that the 1900 (B) and 1900 (C) tractors operated at 2,200 rpm.

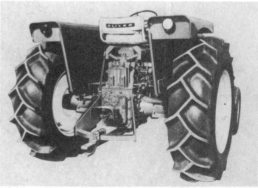

A four-wheel-drive version of the Oliver 1900 tractor was priced at about $11,600, substantially more expensive than the conventional design. With its capability of a 12,000 pound drawbar pull, the 1900 was rated as an 8-plow tractor. Many new features were built into the design, including an arched front axle, dual-speed pto shaft, a fully enclosed operator's platform, and a newly designed seat, complete with backrest. This Oliver 1900 is fitted with a front-mounted snow blower and an operator's cab. The snow blower was built by another manufacturer, but the cab may have been fabricated in the Oliver factories.

Oliver 1900 Ricefield tractors were available in addition to the 1900 Wheatland model customarily furnished. Except for special rice tire equipment, this model was virtually the same as the Wheatland model. Fully equipped, the 1900 two-wheel Wheatland version sold for about $8,800, while the 1900 Riceland was priced at $8,925. Power steering was included as a part of the standard package, but conventional steering was available for a cost savings of $200.

Tractors

In addition to the Oliver 1900 Wheatland and Rice-field tractors, this model was also available in an Industrial version. The front axle and wheel equipment varied, as did the rear tires. Oliver claimed that the GM engine used in the 1900 tractor was extremely economical to operate, and in fact, it ranked among the better of the lot for fuel economy. This two-cycle engine also could run for long periods with minimal attention, and some were known to have operated for 8,000 or more hours before an overhaul was needed. The Hydra-Power drive system included a creeper gear for special jobs, and Oliver continued to use their unique Hydra-Lectric hydraulics.

In June 1963 Oliver sent one each of their 1600 gasoline and diesel tractors to Nebraska for testing. The results appear in Test No. 840 for the diesel and 841 for the gasoline model. Production of the 1600 began in 1962 and continued into 1964. Initially the 1600 gasoline model used a six-cylinder engine with a 3 1/2 x 4 inch bore and stroke, but the second series raised the bore to 3 5/8 inches. The diesel engine used a 3 3/4 x 4 inch bore and stroke throughout its production run. The first series was built into 1963.

Oliver's 1600 Diesel tractor delivered nearly 58 pto horsepower in Nebraska Test No. 840. This model was rated at 1,900 rpm; it also was designed with a compression ratio of 16.25 to 1. Displacement was 265 ci. While the regular row-crop style with a dual front sold for about $5,100 with a diesel engine, the comparable tractor with a gasoline motor listed at $4,500. By comparison, the 1600 Wheatland Diesel was priced at $5,700, about $600 more than a comparable gasoline tractor.

Apparently, the 1600 four-wheel-drive model was not available until 1963. This model was built in gasoline and diesel versions, with the latter being priced at $7,800, and about $700 less for the gasoline style. The latter was also available with LP-gas equipment at $330 over the base price for a comparable gasoline tractor. From all appearances, Oliver built a minimal number of LP-gas tractors, and it also appears that the special modifications required to the hood and sheet metal work were done on a custom basis in the Oliver shops.

The 1600 tractor was also built in an Industrial version, complete with a heavy front axle. Special tire equipment was available for both the front and the rear axles. Many of these tractors were used for highway maintenance and similar applications, including airport work. Others were fitted with special hydraulic loaders which converted the 1600 into an effective front-end loader. Six forward speeds were built into the 1600 tractors, and the Hydra-Power drive came as standard equipment.

In 1960 Oliver introduced the 500 tractor, built by David Brown Tractors of England. The Oliver 600 shown here was introduced in 1962 and offered into 1963. It too was built by David Brown, apparently to Oliver's specifications. This model used a four-cylinder diesel engine with a 3 5/8 x 4 1/2 inch bore and stroke. Operating at 2,000 rpm, it was capable of about 48 pto horsepower. A three-point hitch and two-speed pto were standard equipment, but power steering, remote hydraulics, and the Oliver Power-juster rear wheels were extra-cost options.

Oliver 1650 tractors were built in the 1964-69 period. As previously noted, many options were available, and this 1650 includes the single-front axle and the LP-gas conversion equipment. The latter was priced as a $400 extra-cost option, and apparently was fabricated only on customer orders; it does not appear that any number of LP-gas tractors were built as standard factory production. The single-front axle was also an option, as was the Hydra-Power drive; it added $383 to the base price.

With the 1964 introduction of the 1650 Oliver came the company's new Certified Horsepower rating. Every 1650 coming off the assembly line was hooked to a dynamometer and was required to deliver no less than 66 pto horsepower before it could be shipped. A sticker was attached to each tractor certifying the observed horsepower and the name of the inspector. As with other Oliver models, the 1650 was available in many different styles and configurations. Shown here is a gasoline model with dual front wheels. This tractor listed at about $7,000.

In addition to the dual-front axle, Oliver 1650 tractors could be furnished with the adjustable-width wide-front design. It was available in two different styles, with width adjustment ranging all the way up to 89 inches. The adjustable wide-front axle was preferred by many farmers for its added stability, particularly when working on hilly ground. This style also was distinctly preferable in muddy conditions, since the dual-front design tends to plug with mud and field debris. However, the adjustable-front axle was an extra cost option.

Oliver built the 1650 in a high-clearance design; it provided over three feet of clearance under both the front and rear axles. The front axle had a width adjustment ranging from 65 to 89 inches. Both the gasoline and diesel models of the 1650 were sent to Nebraska's Tractor Test Laboratory in November 1964. The results appear in Test No. 873 for the diesel model, and No. 874 for the gasoline style. Both tests saw a pto output of slightly over 66 horsepower, and as previously noted, under the Certified Horsepower plan, no 1650 was shipped until it had developed at least 66 pto horsepower coming off the assembly line.

Shown here is an Oliver 1650 Ricefield tractor. Except for the special tire equipment, this model was basically the same as the 1650 Wheatland. With a diesel engine, the 1650 Ricefield was priced at about $7,500, while the comparable Wheatland tractor sold for $7,400. The extra $100 essentially paid for the special tire equipment used on this model. Ricefield models could be furnished with a three-point hitch or with a special wide-swing drawbar. The gasoline and LP-gas engines were of course, of six-cylinder design, using a 3 3/4 x 4 inch bore and stroke. The gasoline model was designed with an 8.5 to 1 compression ratio, and a ratio of 9 to 1 was used for the LP-gas model.

Little is known of this special high-clearance four-wheel-drive version of the 1650 tractor. The front-mounted hydraulic pump for the front-wheel-drive is hidden beneath a shield. Evidently the company did build a few of these tractors as production units, but there are no specific figures, since all of the 1650 production is included in the same series of serial numbers, regardless of the tractor style or configuration. It is an interesting observation that engineers had tried for many years to build four-wheel-drive tractors, but with varying degrees of success. With the advent of hydraulic power many of the former problems disappeared.

Oliver offered the gasoline model with the extra-cost option of LP-gas equipment for $400 over the base price. When the 1650 was introduced in 1964, a limited amount of farm equipment was being designed around the 1,000 rpm pto shaft in lieu of the ordinary 540 rpm. To make the tractor usable for either circumstance, Oliver designed the 1650 with interchangeable pto shafts. Other options included the Hydra-Power drive which added $385 to the base price, and the Over/Under Hydraul-Shift which raised the price by $550.

The 1650 Diesel used a six-cylinder Oliver engine with a 3 7/8 x 4 inch bore and stroke. Designed with a 16.5 to 1 compression ratio, it was rated at 2,200 rpm. Other standard features included metered low pressure lubrication, a 12-volt electrical system, dry-type air cleaner, and a wide array of instrumentation that included a tachometer and odometer. Another option was the external radiator screen. It was easily removable for cleaning at any time. With the Hydra-Power drive the 1650 was also equipped with a creeper gear for special jobs.

While the conventional 1650 Diesel with dual-front wheels was priced at $7,700, the 1650 Diesel with four-wheel-drive sold for $9,900. Although production of the 1650 began in 1964, it does not appear from industry reports that the four-wheel-drive option was sold prior to 1965. Under adverse conditions the four-wheel-drive system could provide up to 40% more pull. Under these circumstances the extra $2,200 cost was more than justified. With the introduction of the 1650 Oliver appears to have gone from the customary generator to an alternator. An unnoticed feature of the Hydra-Power drive was that its design included water cooling to provide for uninterrupted use with no fear of damaging the system.

During 1964 and 1965 Oliver offered the 1750 model as an update of the 1800 (C) tractor. Both the gasoline and diesel versions used the same basic engine as was used in comparable 1800 (C) tractors, but while the latter used a rated speed of 2,200 rpm, this was raised to 2,400 rpm for the 1750 models. This change raised the rated pto output from 77 to 80-plus pto horsepower. From 1966 to 1969 the 1750 was built in its own right, rather than being an upgraded version of the earlier 1800 (C) tractor. The high air stack with a visible precleaner is obvious on this 1965 model; it was replaced with a low air stack on the Oliver 1750 introduced in 1966.

with 80 Certified pto Horsepower

New for '65

Nebraska Test No. 961 covers the 1750 gasoline model and the 1750 diesel is tabulated in No. 962. Both models delivered slightly over 80 pto horsepower. The 1750 Row-Crop listed at about $7,200 with a gasoline engine, while the diesel model sold for about $7,900. Whether in gasoline or diesel versions, the 1750 was also available as a Wheatland, or as a Ricefield tractor at additional cost; Oliver's Wheatland tractors were essentially a standard-tread design. In addition, the 1750 could be purchased with a four-wheel-drive option, along with a factory cab, fender tanks, and many other convenience features.

In 1964 Oliver sent a total of four 1850 tractors to Nebraska for testing. Diesel and gasoline versions of the standard two-wheel drive were included, along with one each of the diesel and gasoline-powered four-wheel-drive tractors. While actually introduced in 1964, the 1850 tractor was fully launched for the 1965 season. The gasoline style delivered over 77 drawbar horsepower with the two-wheel drive; these tabulations are included in Test No. 875. No. 876 illustrates the 1850 gasoline model with a four-wheel-drive option, and it delivered over 86 drawbar horsepower.

The Oliver 1850 was available with many new options, including a fully-enclosed cab. Another important option were the large fender tanks. Gasoline models were ordinarily priced at about $8,000, but optional LP-gas equipment was available for an additional $400. Fully hydraulic power steering came as standard equipment, along with the choice of Hydra-Power Drive or the Over/Under Hydraul-Shift system. Standard tire equipment included 18.4-34 rear tires.

With the acquisition of Oliver by White Motors, Cockshutt of Canada also came into the fold. For some years, Oliver tractors were painted red instead of green and given a set of Cockshutt decals. Essentially, this was the only difference between many of the models, including this 1850 Cockshutt Wheatland tractor. It was available with virtually all the options and features of the comparable Oliver 1850. The 1850 Diesel used a Perkins six-cylinder engine rated at 2,400 rpm, and carrying a 352 ci displacement. Bore and stroke dimensions were 3 7/8 x 5 inches.

Oliver 1850 tractors could be equipped with a front-wheel-drive system. In 1969 an 1850 Diesel, thus equipped, sold for about $11,650. Ordinarily, this was a mechanical drive, but Oliver could also supply the 1850 four-wheel-drive as a hydraulically operated unit, with one example being shown here. A special front-mounted hydraulic pump was used. This option permitted simple on-the-go shifting of the front-wheel-assist into gear or out of gear as desired.

A General Motors four-cylinder, two-cycle, Series 4-53 diesel engine was used in the Oliver 1950. This design included a 3 7/8 x 4 1/2 inch bore and stroke, with a rated speed of 2,400 rpm. It was certified to deliver 105 pto horsepower. Other engine features included a 21.0 to 1 compression ratio and four exhaust valves per cylinder for a superior power level in comparison to engine weight. The 1950 Row-Crop in a two-wheel drive design was tested at Nebraska under No. 871.

When equipped with the dual-front axle the 1950 Oliver sold for about $10,500. It was also available in a Wheatland version with a price of $11,250, or as a Ricefield model at $11,400. The adjustable wide-front axle shown here added slightly to the base price; even the standard agricultural model was available with several different tire options. A pto-mounted belt pulley was optionally available, along with front-end weights and rear wheel weights. Like others in this series, the 1950 could also be furnished with a two-speed pto shaft.

The Cockshutt 1950 diffe... ...er 1950 only in the paint color and th... ...rwise, it was the same tractor. A hea... ...lar drawbar ordinarily furnished... ...lar drawbar could be replaced... ...rawbar that mounted on the th... ...was built for Category II equip... ...Power system permitted shiftin... ...lown provided about 36% more... ...uced speed by about 26%. Th... ...advantage of permitting l... ...rning without touching the...

Model 1950 Power-Pak

In addition to a full series of 1950 tractor models, Oliver also offered the 1950 Power-Pak. This was essentially a complete tractor minus the front and rear wheels, fenders, and drawbar. Manufacturers of commercial equipment such as road rollers could simply drop the Power-Pak into place, attach their own final drives, and have a complete machine. Few details have been located regarding this venture. Presumably, a limited number of units were sold, but the extent of this specialized diversion is now unknown.

The Oliver 1950 was available with a mechanical four-wheel-drive system, or an optional hydraulically operated front-wheel-assist. Oliver advertising brochures of the period indicate that the four-wheel-drive option was available for field installation, as well as on direct factory order. The 1950 Diesel Wheatland tractor sold at $11,250 with two-wheel drive, but this price jumped to $14,700 with the four-wheel-drive option. Presumably, the hydraulically operated version was somewhat more expensive.

Many options were available for the 1950 ... desi... were optional Terra-Tires, with ...tation. This 1950 is equipped mea... drawbar Oliver called this 'El Toro' deliv... a bull it was, with nearly 100 '50 Se...d almost 106 horses being Scope... A feature common to the of the...he use of Oliver's Tilt-O- and c...ermitted easy adjustment ...reater operator comfort

Oliver 1950 tractors, especially those with the four-wheel-drive option, were used to some extent for construction work. Up to this time the crawler tractor was virtually sacrosanct as the ultimate dirt mover. Yet, the development of large wheel tractors was a distinct advantage, since rubber tires could shorten the haul time considerably. For the contractor, saving time also saved money. Large tractors like the 1950 also required a substantial braking system, and this was secured through the use of triple-disc brakes.

In the 1967-69 period, Oliver built the 1950-T. This model carried a six-cylinder turbocharged Oliver engine, unlike the GM engine used in the 1950. This model was capable of over 105 pto horsepower; it was also available in row-crop, Wheatland, or Ricefield versions. Like the 1950, it could be furnished as a conventional two-wheel-drive tractor, or with a four-wheel-drive option. The latter design sold at slightly over $12,850. This big tractor weighed nearly 12,000 pounds. The dual-wheel equipment shown on this 1950-T came as a factory option.

Built between 1965 and 1969, the Oliver 1550 delivered 53 Certified PTO Horsepower using gasoline or diesel engines, and 51 horsepower on LP-gas. All three models carried a six-cylinder, 232 ci engine with a 3 5/8 x 3 3/4 inch bore and stroke. Rated speed was 2,200 rpm. The gasoline model used an 8 to 1 compression ratio, and this was raised to 8.75 for the LP-gas model. Diesel engines were designed with a 16.5 to 1 compression ratio. Shown here is a conventional 1550 gasoline model with a dual-front axle. It listed at about $5,850.

Oliver 1550 diesel tractors were priced at $6,525, compared to $5,850 for the gasoline model. However, an LP-gas conversion added $425 to the price of the gasoline style. The 1550 gasoline tractor was tested at Nebraska under No. 943, and the diesel model appears in Test No. 944. With an optional transmission and the Hydra-Power drive, up to twelve forward speeds were available, ranging all the way from 1.8 to 13.6 mph. A considerable overlap provided just the right speed for virtually any kind of drawbar work.

The 1550 could be purchased for LP-gas fuel as an extra-cost option. An noted previously, Oliver continued to offer LP-gas units into the 1960s, although the company does not appear to have promoted this tractor fuel to the extent of many competitors. Instead, Oliver opted for the diesel engine, and indeed, promoted it very heavily. In addition to the regular row-crop design, the 1550 was also available as a Utility tractor, and the entire 1550 series was also available under the Cockshutt logo.

Tractors

Yet another option for the Oliver 1550 was their Industrial version. It featured an extra heavy front axle and special front wheel equipment to accommodate a heavy front-end loader and other equipment. During this time Oliver was also promoting various industrial equipment, including backhoes, so the 1550 was an ideal choice. Unfortunately, the production figures of the various 1550 models are all blended into a single listing, so production figures for individual styles is now impossible.

Offered from 1965 to 1969, the Oliver 1250 was available with a 35 horsepower gasoline engine or a 38 horsepower diesel. The 1250 was essentially built in Italy by Fiat, but was built to Oliver's specifications. Gasoline models used a four-cylinder, 3 1/4 x 3 1/2 inch engine, while the diesel design used a 3 5/16 x 4 inch bore and stroke. The latter was designed with a 21.5 to 1 compression ratio. Both had a governed speed of 2,500 rpm. This tractor was also marketed as the Cockshutt 1250.

The Fiat-built Oliver 1450 was offered between 1967 and 1969. It was built to White-Oliver standards, and was furnished only as a diesel model. The four-cylinder, 268 ci design featured a 4 1/4 x 4 3/4 inch bore and stroke. Rated speed was 1,900 rpm. Designed for 55 pto horsepower, the 1450 was a mid-sized utility tractor weighing about 6,000 pounds. Options included power steering and a belt pulley, but a live pto came as standard equipment. This model could be fitted with the Oliver 1410 loader, making it an ideal 'chore' tractor.

A big 478 ci naturally aspirated engine was used in the Oliver 2050 tractor. Rated at 2,400 rpm, Oliver certified this engine at 118 pto horsepower. Row-Crop, Wheatland, and Ricefield versions were available, and within these, all were available with two-wheel or four-wheel-drive systems. Dual rear wheels were available as a factory option, while the planetary final drives came as part of the 2050 design. Built during 1968 and 1969, the 2050 Row-Crop sold for about $12,500, while the 2050 Wheatland model listed at $12,300. However, the 2050 Row-Crop with four-wheel-drive carried a price tag of $14,000. This tractor was tested at Nebraska under No. 987.

Oliver 2150 tractors were built during the same 1968-69 period as the 2050 model. Both used a White-designed Hercules diesel engine. However, the 2150 was turbocharged, while the 2050 was naturally aspirated. This raised the power level to 131 Certified PTO Horsepower. Due to the higher power level, the 2150 used a 14-inch clutch, compared to a 13-inch clutch on the 2050. Curiously, Oliver offered this model with the choice of a standard bull-gear final drive, or planetaries on the ends of the rear axles. The Over/Under Hydraul-Shift system was optional, but it provided three forward speeds for each gear. This tractor was tested at Nebraska under No. 986. As a Row-Crop it listed at about $13,250. The four-wheel-drive version sold for $14,700, and the 2150 was also available with an 'extra heavy duty' four-wheel-drive configuration at $16,250.

In 1969 the Oliver 1250-A tractor superseded the earlier 1250 model. This Fiat-built design from Italy was manufactured to White-Oliver specifications, and was furnished only as a diesel tractor. Rated at 38 1/2 Certified Horsepower, the 1250-A used a three-cylinder, direct-injection engine having a displacement of 142.8 ci. This model could be furnished as a Utility tractor with an adjustable front axle, a special Vineyard tractor, and with a four-wheel-drive option. Oliver 1250-A tractors were offered only in 1969.

Between 1969 and 1971 Oliver offered the 1255 tractor, thus coinciding with the introduction of the '55' series tractors in the fall of that year. It was essentially the same as the earlier 1250 model from Fiat, and completion was done at the Decatur, Georgia assembly plant of White Motors. Like the 1250-A, the 1255 was available in Utility, Vineyard, and four-wheel-drive configurations. It was also built as a high-clearance model, the latter being priced at $4,500, while the 1255 Utility model sold for $4,350.

The White-Oliver 1355, and in fact, all of the '55' series tractors were the beginning end for the Oliver logo as applied to farm tractors. Within a few short years the Oliver name would be dropped, as would the Meadow Green and Clover White colors used for decades. The 1355 shown here was built in the 1969-71 period, and was an extension of the Fiat-built tractors being offered by Oliver. Utility, High-Clearance, Orchard, and Four-Wheel-Drive models were available. Prices ranged from $5,100 for the Utility up to $6,500 for the FWD style.

Industry listings show the Oliver 1555 under the White Farm Equipment heading, and indeed, the company sometimes listed this model as the White-Oliver 1555. First built in 1969, the 1555 remained in the lineup until 1975. During 1971 it was also sold as the Minneapolis-Moline G550; the latter company having come under the WFE umbrella. The 1555 was available in Row-Crop, Utility, and High-Clearance models. Within the Row-Crop category it could be equipped with dual front, narrow-tread adjustable front axle, regular adjustable front axle, and single front wheel designs. It was also available in a short wheel base version.

Oliver 1555 tractors were also sold as the Cockshutt 1555. This was the same tractor except for a different paint color. Beyond all the many versions noted with the Oliver 1555, this model could also be purchased in Wheatland and Ricefield versions. As a regular row-crop tractor it sold for $6,135. The 1555 Utility row-crop design sold for $8,273, but this package included a full array of accessories. LP-gas equipment was also available as a $425 option.

Gasoline or diesel engines were available in the Oliver 1555 models. Both styles had a six-cylinder, 232 ci engine rated at 2,200 rpm and delivering 53 Certified Horsepower. A 540 rpm pto shaft was standard, but the 1555 could be purchased with a 1,000 rpm shaft, or with a dual 540/1,000 system. Double remote hydraulics were available, and double-disc brakes were standard equipment. Power steering came as standard equipment on this model.

In the 1969-75 period White Farm Equipment offered the White-Oliver 1655 tractor. In gasoline and diesel versions it delivered 70 pto horsepower, but this was reduced to 66 horsepower on LP-gas. All of the chassis and axle combinations available with the 1555 were also available for the 1655 model. In addition, the 1655 was available in a four-wheel-drive version. It had the further choice of differential or planetary gear reduction on the rear axles. Regular or high-speed versions of the six-speed transmission were available, and Oliver offered three auxiliary transmission styles. These included the Hydra-Power drive, Over/Under Hydraul-Shift, or the Creeper Drive. With the high speed transmission the 1655 had road speeds up to 22 mph.

Oliver used their own six-cylinder diesel engine in the 1655. This six-cylinder design included a 3 7/8 x 4 inch bore and stroke for a 283 cid. Rated speed was 2,200 rpm, and the compression ratio was 16 to 1. A diesel row-crop version listed at $10,800, and with the four-wheel-drive option, the price jumped to $14,612. The 1655 was tested at Nebraska in May 1970; the results appear in Test No. 1041. In this test the 1655 Diesel delivered slightly over 70 pto horsepower, and nearly 62 horses at the drawbar.

The Oliver 1655 gasoline model was priced at about $10,000 with a full equipment package. Adding the LP-gas conversion raised the cost by $425. Regardless of engine choice, the 1655 was also built in Wheatland and Ricefield versions. Options included the Hydra-Lectric hydraulic system, Depth-Stop hydraulics; the latter could be supplied with external valves or internal valves, as desired. Although the dual-front axle was still available, the adjustable front axle as shown here seems to have been far more popular. The 1655 Oliver tractor was also sold as the Minneapolis G-750 during 1971. During 1969 and 1970 the "55" Series tractors were also available in a 'Heritage' version. There were no changes, except that the tractor was finished in red, white, and blue.

White-Oliver 1755 tractors were produced in the 1970-75 period. This model was also sold during 1971 as the Minneapolis G-850 tractor. Nebraska Test No. 1056 was run on the gasoline version, and it evidenced a pto output of nearly 87 horsepower; the diesel model of Test No. 1057 was virtually identical. Both models used a six-cylinder engine rated at 2,400 rpm. The gasoline style carried a 3 3/4 x 4 inch bore and stroke for a displacement of 283 ci, while the diesel used a 3 7/8 x 4 3/8 inch bore and stroke for a 310 cid. The 1755 was available in many different axle configurations, including an optional four-wheel-drive system. With a diesel engine, the latter style carried a list price of over $16,000.

First appearing in 1969, the Oliver 1855 was produced until 1975. This tractor was also sold by WFE as the White M-M G-940 tractor in 1971. It was also available with the Heritage color scheme during 1969 and 1970. The 1855 used the same basic engine as the 1755 diesel, except that the 1855 was lightly supercharged. This yielded a pto output of 98 pto horsepower, compared to approximately 87 horsepower for the 1755. Seven main bearings were used. It appears that some 1855 diesel engines were replaced with the 1955 Oliver engine due to a persistent problem.

Oliver 1855 tractors were available in Row-Crop, Wheatland, or Ricefield models. In addition, the 1855 was available with a front-wheel-assist system as an option. The 1855 diesel was tested at Nebraska under No. 1040. Although the 1855 was also available with a gasoline engine, this model was not tested at Nebraska. Many options were available for the 1855; these included Powerjuster rear wheels, dual-speed pto drive, Category III three-point hitch, wheel guard fuel tanks, and a factory-installed cab.

A divided exhaust manifold terminated at the turbocharger on the 1855 tractors. This design split the firing sequence to drive the turbine more smoothly, regardless of engine speed. Oliver advertising brochures of the period note that the gasoline engine was optional for the 1755 and 1855 tractors, leaving the obvious connotation that the diesel was emerging as standard equipment. The "55" series diesels used a so-called 'slim-line' injector which was only 3/8 inch in diameter. This design, combined with extremely high injection pressure, helped to increase fuel atomization, and consequently, provided cleaner burning of the fuel. The six-cylinder engine had a displacement of 310 ci.

Oliver 1955 tractors, like most other Oliver models, used a six-cylinder diesel engine. Four styles of Row-Crop tractors were built, plus Wheatland, Ricefield, and four-wheel-drive models. Closed center hydraulics were another feature, along with the choice of Category II or Category III three-point hitch systems. Hydraulic triple disc brakes were featured, as was a hydraulically operated pto shaft. With the Over/Under Hydraul-Shift, the 1955 offered eighteen forward speeds, and with the Oliver Hydra-Power drive, twelve different speeds were available. Standard equipment included power steering.

Nebraska Test No. 1055 was run on the Oliver 1955 tractor in October 1970. This test revealed a maximum output of 108 pto horsepower. The 310 cubic inch, six-cylinder engine used a 3 7/8 x 4 3/8 inch bore and stroke. Rated speed was 2,400 rpm. Although the four-wheel-drive option was built with a fixed tread, the wheels could be switched for a tread width of 66 or 70 3/4 inches; with the use of spacers this could be extended to 80 inches. A factory option was the no-spin differential which operated automatically to reduce front wheel spin-out.

White Farm Equipment built the 1955 with several dual-wheel variations. Included were dual-flange hubs and 5 1/2 or 11-inch spacers. Double-bevel rims provided even more flexibility. Powerjuster or demountable rims were available at the purchaser's option. A roll bar was optional, as was a steel canopy. In addition, the 1955 could be furnished with a factory-installed, fully-enclosed cab. The 1755, 1855, and 1955 tractors used a hydraulically operated clutch which eliminated the need for occasional clutch adjustment.

The 2055 Oliver tractor was offered only in 1971. This model was virtually the same as the Minneapolis-Moline G-1050 tractor. In fact, it was built at Minneapolis, rather than at Charles City. This model was sold as a Minneapolis-Moline model in the 1969-71 period. A big 504 cubic inch, six-cylinder engine was used; it carried a 4 5/8 x 5 inch bore and stroke. Row-Crop and standard-tread versions were available, and the 2055 could be furnished with a diesel or a spark-ignition engine. Apparently the latter was offered primarily as an LP-gas model. The 2055 was capable of about 110 pto horsepower.

Only during 1971 was this tractor sold as the Oliver 2155. However, it was sold as the Minneapolis-Moline G-1350 tractor between 1969 and 1971. A big 135 horsepower engine was used; it was available in LP-gas or diesel models. The latter was tested at Nebraska in May 1971 under No. 1069. Although the diesel engine is listed as being manufactured by Minneapolis-Moline, it appears that it was actually built by M.A.N. in Germany. Many options were available including differential drive or planetary rear axles.

White Farm Equipment built this Oliver 1865 at its Minneapolis-Moline plant. The 1865 was built only in 1971. As the Minneapolis-Moline G-950 tractor, it was built in the 1969-71 period. The 1865 was available with an LP-gas engine, or it could be furnished with a naturally aspirated six-cylinder diesel. The latter used a 4 1/4 x 5 inch bore and stroke with a rated speed of 1,800 rpm. Roosa-Master fuel equipment was standard on the 1865. Row-Crop and standard-tread versions were available, along with the choice of two different transmissions, and numerous other options.

Tractors

A big 585 cubic inch engine was used in the Oliver 2655, also known as the White Plainsman, and the Minneapolis-Moline A4T-1600. Built by the WFE plant formerly operated by Minneapolis-Moline, it could be furnished either with LP-gas or diesel engines. The LP-gas version carried a 4 5/8 x 5 inch bore and stroke. Operating at 2,200 rpm, it delivered about 169 pto horsepower. The White Plainsman was offered only in 1970, and this model was also available that year with the special Heritage color scheme. Except for the red, white, and blue paint, the Heritage tractors were identical to their equivalent models painted in their ordinary colors.

Oliver 2655 tractors were identical to the Minneapolis-Moline A4T. The latter was offered in the 1969-71 period, while the 2655 was built only in 1971. This model was built in a naturally aspirated diesel with a 4 5/8 x 5 inch bore and stroke; at 2,200 rpm it delivered 139 horsepower, but the turbocharged model put out 151 horsepower. Priced at about $15,000 the Oliver 2655 weighed in at over 17,000 pounds. During Nebraska Test No. 1070 this tractor manifested over 123 drawbar horsepower, and made a maximum drawbar pull of 18,236 pounds.

In 1971 White Farm Equipment introduced the Oliver 1265 tractor. It was built until 1975. During the 1973-75 period this same model was built as the White 1270, but from 1971 to 1973 it was sold in Canada as the White 1265. White Farm Equipment also marketed this same tractor as the Minneapolis-Moline G-350 tractor in 1971. The 1265 was a diesel-powered utility tractor, but it could also be purchased with the four-wheel-drive option shown here.

White 1270 and Oliver 1265 differed primarily in the use of a different radiator grille. Otherwise, these two tractors were virtually the same. This tractor was built by Fiat, and used a three-cylinder, direct-injected engine with a 3.94 x 4.33 inch bore and stroke. This gave a displacement of 158.1 ci. In a standard two-wheel-drive configuration the 1265 diesel listed at about $6,650. However, the four-wheel-drive version sold for almost $9,800. Numerous features were built into the Oliver 1265, including a differential lock, power-adjusted rear wheels, three-point hitch, and a transmission with six forward and two reverse speeds.

The Fiat-built Oliver 1365 was marketed in the 1971-75 period. Two-wheel or four-wheel-drive was available, along with eight forward speeds, and two in reverse. The three-point hitch came as standard equipment and could be configured for Category I or Category II implements. This model also featured a combination live pto and ground-speed pto system. During 1971 the Oliver 1365 was also sold as the White 1365 for sale to Canada, and carried the additional logo of the Minneapolis-Moline G-450. Except for the grille design and the paint color, these three models were otherwise, virtually identical.

Beginning in 1973 the Oliver 1365 was marketed in Canada as the White 1370, even though the tractors were virtually the same. This Fiat-built model used a four-cylinder diesel engine having a 3.93 x 4.33 inch bore and stroke for a displacement of 210.9 cubic inches. The engine design utilized a 17.0 to 1 compression ratio. This resulted in an output of 59 pto horsepower. This direct-injection engine also featured a vibration damper for smooth operation. Oliver 1365 and White 1370 tractors were built in Row-Crop, Utility, or four-wheel-drive configurations. The latter style listed at about $11,800. Power steering was standard equipment.

Oliver 1465 tractors were available in the 1973-75 period. This model, like the 1265 and 1365 tractors, were built by Fiat. However, the 1465 was the largest of this specific series, having an output of about 70 pto horsepower. The four-cylinder, direct-injected diesel engine carried a 4.33 x 4.71 inch bore and stroke for a displacement of 278 cubic inches. The compression ratio was 17.0 to 1. Apparently, this model was available only as a Row-Crop tractor...there is no indication that it was built in a Utility model, nor can any information be located to determine whether it was available in a four-wheel-drive design.

White Motors purchased the Cockshutt Plow Company of Canada in February 1962. For several years thereafter, what were essentially Oliver tractors got a coat of red paint and Cockshutt decals for the Canadian market. In 1969 White Farm Equipment was formed to consolidate Oliver Corporation, Cockshutt, and Minneapolis-Moline into a single unit. However, the transition took place over several seasons, and until about 1971, Oliver tractors continued to be sold in Canada under the Cockshutt logo. However, in 1972 the transition continued, with White tractors being sent to Canada, but bearing a different model designator than the 'Oliver' equivalent. shown here is a Cockshutt 1465. It carries essentially the same radiator grille as the White 1470 which followed.

Following through in the transitional pattern established about 1971, White Farm Equipment sold their 1470 tractor to the Canadian market in the 1972-75 period. As otherwise indicated, this was essentially the same tractor as the Oliver 1465, albeit with a different radiator grille than was used on the Oliver. The simple fact was that White Farm Equipment was moving into the tractor business in its own right, and the Cockshutt, Oliver, and Minneapolis-Moline tractors were moving into the history books. Paradoxically, the same thing had happened nearly forty years before when Oliver Farm Equipment was formed from the toils of Hart-Parr, Nichols & Shepard, and others of an earlier merger.

The Oliver 2255 was the last tractor from White Farm Equipment to carry the Oliver name. Introduced in 1973, it was built until 1976. This big tractor was capable of over 126 drawbar horsepower, and could be configured for Row-Crop and four-wheel-drive equipment. The basic transmission design offered six forward and two reverse speeds. Options included the Over/Under Hydraul-Shift auxiliary transmission. Dual-wheel equipment as shown on this 2255 was available in several styles to accommodate various requirements.

Oliver 2255 and White 2255 tractors featured a Caterpillar V-8 diesel engine. Its 573 cubic inch displacement resulted from a 4.5 inch bore and stroke. This gave the 2255 about 145 pto horsepower. At some point in the 1973-76 production run a larger Caterpillar V-8 diesel was used; it carried a 4.5 x 5.0 inch bore and stroke for a displacement of 636 cubic inches. This change raised the power level slightly. The 2255 was tested at Nebraska in September 1973; the results appear in Test No. 1140.

White 2255 tractors were marketed in Canada. While many other of the tractors sent to Canada used a different grille than the 'Oliver' design, this one is obviously identical to the Oliver. Large fender tanks greatly increased the fuel capacity; a real necessity with a tractor of about 150 horsepower. Planetary rear axles are obvious, and this one is equipped with a factory-installed operator's cab. As otherwise indicated, the Oliver 2255 was virtually the end of the Oliver tractor line, since in 1973, White Farm Equipment began introducing a new series of tractors to the public.

In 1973 White Farm Equipment (WFE) introduced the 1870 and the 2270 tractors. These were equivalent to the Minneapolis G-955 and G-1355 tractors, respectively. Both used a Minneapolis-Moline engine and an Oliver power train. WFE apparently sold the White model in Canada, and the Minneapolis-Moline model in the United States. Both carried six-cylinder engines, with the 1870 also being available as an LP-gas model, in addition to the standard diesel design common to both. A 451 cubic inch engine was used in the 1870, while the 2270 carried a big 585 ci engine. Apparently the 2270 was available in Minneapolis Yellow or Oliver green for a time, but by the time production ended in 1974, the White designator had been adopted. These models virtually ended the transitional models, for in 1974 White introduced the first of their Field Boss tractors in new colors and with entirely new designs.

Production of the White 4-180 Field Boss began in 1975, and production of both the 4-150 and 4-180 tractors ended in 1978. Like the 4-150, the 4-180 Field Boss was designed with a Caterpillar 3208 V-8 diesel engine. Standard features included a luxurious cab with air conditioning, AM-FM radio, and other accessories. Two remote hydraulic outlets came as standard equipment, and additional units could be added if necessary. A feature common to the 4-150 and 4-180 tractors was a low profile drive system. No transfer cases were used, and power was transmitted in a straight line from the engine to both drive axles. When tested at Nebraska (Test No. 1184) the 4-180 Field Boss delivered over 155 drawbar horsepower.

WFE introduced their 4-150 Field Boss tractor in 1974. This was the first WFE tractor with the Field Boss styling and was the first WFE tractor to be marketed solely as a White. In other words, its introduction ended the days of Oliver, Minneapolis-Moline, and Cockshutt as distinct tractor entities. The 4-150 Field Boss was equipped with a 636 ci Caterpillar V-8 engine having a 4.5 x 5.0 inch bore and stroke. This direct injection design had a governed speed of 2,800 rpm. It was naturally aspirated. In Nebraska Test No. 1159 the 4-150 Field Boss delivered nearly 130 drawbar, and over 150 pto horsepower. It weighed about 15,000 pounds without added ballast, and sold in the vicinity of $37,000.

Between 1975 and 1982 White built the 2-105 Field Boss. This tractor was powered by a turbocharged six-cylinder Perkins diesel engine. Rated at 2,200 rpm, it used a 3.875 x 5.000 inch bore and stroke for a displacement of 354 ci. In Nebraska Test No. 1181 it delivered slightly over 105 pto horsepower. Numerous options were available, including the sound-protected cab shown here. Another option was a heavy duty fixed-tread front axle for a Wheatland conversion. The basic tractor was priced at slightly over $20,000. Options such as the front-wheel-drive added considerably to the cost.

White 2-85 Field Boss tractors and the 2-105 Field Boss models were virtually the same, except for the engine. In fact, the basic difference was that the 2-85 was naturally aspirated, while the 2-105 was turbocharged. Thus, turbocharging alone raised the power level from slightly over 85 pto horsepower for the 2-85 up to 105-plus pto horsepower in the 2-105 model. These engines featured complete pressure lubrication, even to the piston pins. The injection pump drive train was hydraulically loaded for optimum performance, and the high-capacity cooling system circulated nearly 40 gallons of coolant per minute.

The 2-85 and 2-105 Field Boss tractors continued with the Over/Under Hydraul-Shift transmission which had been developed previously by Oliver in 1967. This provided a total of eighteen forward speeds with a basic six-gear transmission. Only four gears were used in the Hydraul-Shift mechanism, and with the flip of a lever, the operator could operate in Under-, Direct-, or Over-Drive. A substantial overlap provided optimum ground speeds for virtually any field operation. Hydraulically powered brakes and hydrostatic power steering came as standard equipment.

Built in the 1975-76 period, the White 2-150 Field Boss featured a 585 cubic inch engine, the Over/Under Hydraul-Shift transmission, and triple-disc brakes. Closed center hydraulics, and planetary final drives were also part of the standard package. Silver and charcoal were the original colors of the Field Boss line, replacing the Oliver Green and Minneapolis Yellow of earlier years. A Category III three-point hitch was standard equipment, and up to three hydraulic outlets were available. This model was ordinarily furnished with a 1,000 rpm pto shaft, but a dual 540/1000 rpm style was optionally available.

White 2-150 Field Boss tractors utilized a White six-cylinder, 585 ci engine. This naturally aspirated design was rated at 2,200 rpm and carried a 4 3/4 x 5 1/2 inch bore and stroke. In Nebraska Test No. 1182 it delivered over 147 pto horsepower. The basic tractor listed at about $22,300 but many optional accessories were available, including this combined rollover frame and canopy. A fully enclosed cab was another option, and the cab tractors could be equipped with a 20 gallon auxiliary fuel tank for a total of 60 gallons onboard. In addition, fender tanks with a 78 gallon capacity were also available. However, the fender tanks could be used only on those models without the cab.

White 2-50 Field Boss tractors were available in the 1976-1980 period. This Fiat-built tractor carried a three-cylinder diesel engine having a 3.94 x 4.33 inch bore and stroke for a displacement of 158.1 ci. In Nebraska Test No. 1231 it delivered over 47 pto horsepower. Designed for row-crop and utility duties, the 2-50 was equipped with a High-Low transmission offering a total of eight forward and two reverse speeds. Options included a creeper gear, front and rear weights, belt pulley, power-adjusted rear wheels, and an underslung muffler. It was also available as a four-wheel-drive tractor.

The White 2-60 Field Boss was also available as a 4-60 Field Boss with the optional front-wheel-drive. Like the 2-50, this Fiat-built tractor utilized an engine having a 3.94 x 4.33 inch bore and stroke. However, the 2-60 was a four-cylinder design, while the 2-50 carried a three-cylinder engine. The tractor shown here had a displacement of 210.8 ci and in Nebraska Test No. 1232 it delivered over 63 pto horsepower. A differential lock was standard equipment on the 2-50 and 2-60 tractors, along with hydrostatic power steering.

Introduced in 1976, the White 2-70 Field Boss remained in production until 1982. This model was available with the choice of gasoline or diesel engines; the latter style having an output of about 70 pto horsepower. However, the gasoline version was not tested at Nebraska. The 2-70 gasoline tractor carried a six-cylinder motor with a 3.75 x 4.00 inch bore and stroke, for a 265 ci displacement. It was rated at 2,200 rpm. Thus equipped, the basic tractor sold at about $12,500. The Hydraul-Shift transmission was listed as optional equipment for this model, as was the roll-over protective frame and canopy.

A White 2-70 diesel tractor was tested at Nebraska under No. 1212. This test revealed a maximum pto output of 70.71 horsepower. The 2-70 six-cylinder diesel used a 3.875 x 4.000 inch bore and stroke for a 283 cubic inch displacement. Other standard features included a six-speed constant-mesh transmission, with the Over/Under Hydraul-Shift being optional. Open center hydraulics were used, along with a three-point hitch and double-disc brakes. A four-wheel-drive option was also available. White 2-70 diesel tractors listed as a basic package at about $15,000, although several of the options were widely used, and of course, increased the list price somewhat.

White 2-135 Field Boss tractors were built in three different versions during a 1976-87 production run. A 1976 offering is shown here; it used a gray stripe on the side, and was built until 1981. During the latter year the gray stripe was replaced with red, and the decals included the WFE designator. In 1982 the 2-135 was again changed, this time with a new modular design which integrated the steering unit and controls within the cab separately from the rest of the tractor. These changes helped to reduce the sound level within the cab.

The White diesel engine of the 2-135 tractor featured a combustion system designed by M.A.N. of Germany. A six-cylinder design with a 4.56 x 4.87 inch bore and stroke yielded a 478 cid. Also included in the design was a 17.0 to 1 compression ratio. In Nebraska Test No. 1275 the 2-135 delivered over 137 pto horsepower from its turbocharged engine. A new 3 x 6 Over/Under transmission was featured, and a new style Roosa Master injection pump came as regular equipment. Inboard planetary drives were a new design feature, and the Accra-Tach electronic monitor was also included.

Three different styles of the 2-155 Field Boss were built between 1976 and 1987. Initially a gray strip was used on the sides, as shown on this 1976 model. In 1981 the gray stripe was replaced with red and the WFE decals were added. The following year the 2-155 was fitted with the modular cab, as otherwise noted for the 2-135 model. This turbocharged diesel was of the same general design as the 2-135 but operated at a higher power level, although both styles had a 487 ci displacement. In Nebraska Test No. 1276 the 2-155 Field Boss delivered over 157 horsepower at the pto shaft.

Between 1977 and 1986 WFE built the 2-180 Field Boss tractor. It followed the same general design as the 2-135 and 2-155 models; like these tractors, the 2-180 underwent the same cosmetic changes. A naturally aspirated Caterpillar 3208 V-8 diesel engine was used in the 2-180. It was designed with a 16.5 to 1 compression ratio, used a 4.5 x 5.0 inch bore and stroke, and had a displacement of 636 ci. This engine was rated at 2,800 rpm. Standard equipment included the Accra-Tach digital tachometer. It read engine rpm, gave the ground speed in mph, the pto speed, and included an hour meter.

A Field Boss 2-180 tractor was tested at Nebraska under No. 1287. This test reveals a maximum pto output of over 181 horsepower. A huge 25-inch diameter fan was used to cool this mighty tractor, but standard equipment included only the ROPS framework and canopy; the fully enclosed cab was an extra-cost option, at least when the 2-180 was introduced in 1977. Long rear axles, dual wheel equipment, and power-adjustable rear wheels all came as options. The basic tractor package sold in the area of $55,000.

Iseki & Company, Tokyo, Japan built the White 2-30 Field Boss tractor. Built in the 1979-84 period, it featured a four-speed transmission with a High-Low range selector for a total of eight forward and two reverse speeds. The three-cylinder diesel engine incorporated a special swirl chamber, and was designed with a bore and stroke of 3.39 inches; this gave a displacement of 91ci. It also used a 20 to 1 compression ratio. Priced at about $9,100 as a two-wheel drive model, the 2-30 was also available with a power front axle; this four-wheel-drive package listed added about $1,700 to the basic package price.

Field Boss 4-210 tractors were first built in 1978, with production continuing until 1982. Inboard planetary final drives were a standard design feature, along with a 13-inch dual-plate ceramic clutch. Huge 19 3/4 inch self-adjusting hydraulic wet brakes were also used. This model used a Caterpillar 3208 V-8 diesel engine with a 636 ci displacement; it was rated at 2,800 rpm and carried a 4.5 x 5.0 inch bore and stroke. Retailing at over $70,000 this huge tractor was equipped with a special cab that included heating, air conditioning, and numerous accessories.

In the 1979-84 White Farm Equipment (WFE) offered the 2-35 Field Boss tractor. This Iseki-built model was sometimes given the White-Iseki title within the industry, although it was actually sold under the WFE logo. The Isuzu three-cylinder engine used a 3.386 x 4.02 inch bore and stroke for a displacement of 108.4 ci and an output of over 32 pto horsepower. This model was tested at Nebraska under No. 1374 of October 1980. The 2-30 and 2-35 tractors both carried the same basic equipment package, although the four-wheel-drive option was not available on the 2-35 tractors.

Between 1982 and 1986 WFE sold the White 2-62 Field Boss "Mudder" tractor. This was a specially designed four-wheel-drive model with high clearance. In fact, the ground clearance under the front axle was 30 inches! The drive train was completely enclosed and the drive shaft to the front axle was set as close as possible to the bottom of the tractor. Bevel gears in the steering pins to the final drive planetaries eliminated universal joints, and this feature permitted a shorter turning radius. The engine, transmission, and hydraulic equipment was the same as used in the 2-62 Field Boss tractor.

Nebraska Test No. 1395 was conducted on the White 2-45 tractor. Like the 2-30 and 2-35 tractors, this model was also built by Iseki & Company of Japan. The four-cylinder diesel engine carried a 3.858 x 3.62 inch bore and stroke for a displacement of 169.3 cubic inches. In Test No. 1395 the 2-45 tractor delivered over 43 pto horsepower. An independent 540 rpm pto shaft, differential lock, and power steering all came as standard equipment. In addition, the 2-45 could also be furnished with a powered front axle, as shown here; it then carried a 4-45 model designation.

Production of the White 2-62 Field Boss ran from 1980 to 1982. This Iseki-built model featured an Isuzu four-cylinder diesel engine. Rated at 2,200 rpm, it used a 4.016 x 4.330 inch bore and stroke for a displacement of 211 cubic inches. A total of twenty forward and four reverse speeds were featured in the 2-62, along with planetary final drives. A 2-62 Field Boss tractor was sent to Nebraska in June 1981, with the results appearing in No. 1396. Over 61 pto horsepower was developed, and the 2-62 Field Boss produced in excess of 51 horsepower at the drawbar.

During the 1982-88 period WFE offered the 2-55 and 2-65 Field Boss tractors. These two models had a lot in common, except for the engine. In fact, similarities also exist in this regard. The 2-55 carried a four-cylinder design with a 4.016 x 3.937 inch bore and stroke, for a 199.4 ci displacement. In Nebraska Test No. 1466 the 2-55 Field Boss delivered over 53 pto horsepower. By comparison the 2-65 Field Boss also used a four-cylinder engine; it carried the same 4.016 inch bore as the 2-55, but used a stroke of 4.646 inches. The additional stroke dimensions provided a total displacement of 235.3 ci. Thus, in Nebraska Test No. 1467 it yielded over 62 pto horsepower.

The date of this photograph is unknown. The appearance of the engine would lead to the conclusion that this little one-man cultivator was built in the late 1920s or early 1930s. The tracklayer design was ideal for cultivating in mucky ground, and in fact some of the track components have 'Cletrac' look. The front-mounted cultivator is a small-scale version of the concept established some years before in the Cletrac tractors and their mounted cultivators.

Cletrac AG-6 tractors were introduced either just prior to or shortly after the 1944 acquisition by Oliver. This small crawler design was offered by Oliver as late as 1957. It was designed with a Continental six-cylinder engine with a 3 5/16 x 4 3/8 inch bore and stroke for approximately 39 pto horsepower. AG-6 crawlers were also built as the AGH-6, the latter being a wide-gauge, hillside crawler. The AG-6 was an upgraded version of the Cletrac AG first introduced in 1936. This 1948 Oliver-Cletrac AG-6 tractor is equipped with a Ware hydraulic loader.

Cleveland Tractor Company introduced their Model AD diesel crawler in 1937; Oliver continued this basic model in production until 1959. The AD used a Hercules four-cylinder diesel engine having a 4 x 4 1/2 inch bore and stroke. Rated at 1,500 rpm, it had a displacement of 226 cubic inches. Toward the end of the production run this model was selling at about $5,800. Early examples of the Oliver-Cletrac appear to have been finished with the same orange enamel that had been used by Cleveland Tractor Company. Later production appears to have used an industrial yellow finish.

Oliver-Cletrac Model A tractors used a built-up main frame that was riveted together and supported on two heavy longitudinal springs. The track frames were built of riveted steel sections for the ultimate in strength and rigidity. The lower track wheels were designed with a double oil seal; this was an exclusive Cletrac feature. Many different grousers were available for the Model A tractors; in all, ten different varieties were available.

Tractors (Crawler)

This 1954 mockup photo of an ADH crawler illustrates the OC-12 type track frames used in the design. This series was available in several configurations. In addition to the regular AD style with 42-inch track centers, the ADH used a width of 50 inches. The ADL carried 42-inch track centers but was designed as a Logger's Special. Oliver-Cletrac ADHL crawlers were a Logger's Special, but in a 50-inch track gauge. The tractor of this 1954 photograph weighed 8,760 pounds.

Accessories for the Model A tractors, both diesel and gasoline-powered, were of every description. This 1952 photograph shows an ADH tractor equipped with an Anderson twin-cylinder hydraulic bulldozer. It was designed so as to not upset the balance point of the tractor to any degree. Electric lights could be furnished at nominal cost, as could a rear power take off shaft. Although a heavy steel radiator guard was furnished as standard equipment, a front bumper was also available. Winter and summer cabs were available, as was a rear power reduction and a rear-mounted belt pulley.

Cletrac BG tractors were introduced in 1935, and Oliver continued building the BG crawler until 1951. Initially, Cletrac equipped the BG with a Hercules six-cylinder engine having a 3 3/4 x 4 1/4 inch bore and stroke. At some point in production, the engine size was increased to a 4-inch bore. The latter style was capable of about 38 drawbar horsepower. Cast iron pistons were used on the AG and BG gasoline models, but the diesel-powered models used aluminum pistons. The Model A and Model B tractors all used electric starting as standard equipment.

The BD tractors were identical to the BG models except for the engine and its auxiliaries. When Cleveland Tractor introduced the BD in 1935 it was equipped with a Hercules six-cylinder diesel having a 3 1/2 x 4 1/2 inch bore and stroke. This tractor is shown in Nebraska Test No. 288 of September 1937. In August of 1939 the BD was again tested at Nebraska, this time under No. 325. The latter test shows a Hercules six-cylinder engine with the bore increased to 3 3/4 inches. Apparently this engine size was retained through the remainder of the production run which ended in 1956.

This 1953 Oliver factory photograph shows the 'Drawbar Test Tractor' which Oliver apparently used for its own testing of the BDH tractor illustrated here. Numerous changes were made to the BD during its long production run, but the essential tractor remained the same. Cletrac, and later, Oliver-Cletrac pointed with great pride to their Controlled Differential steering system. Despite some changes to the system over the years, it remained in principle, identical to the original design which was built into the very first Cletrac of 1916. Every Cletrac that was built used this same Controlled Differential system.

Cleveland Tractor Company introduced their D-Series tractors in 1936 with the gasoline model; the DD diesel style appeared the following year. A 12-volt electrical system was standard equipment. However, the DG tractor was not tested at Nebraska until November 1949. The DG delivered over 61 drawbar horsepower from the big six-cylinder Hercules engine. Rated at 1,300 rpm, it used a 4 5/8 x 5 1/4 inch bore and stroke. Although Cletrac, and later, Oliver-Cletrac heavily promoted these tractors for agricultural purposes, they also found extensive applications in construction work.

Cleveland Tractor Company introduced their little HG crawler in 1939, and Oliver kept in production until 1951. Cleveland Tractor sent the HG to Nebraska in August 1939, with the results appearing in Test No. 324. This model used a Hercules four-cylinder engine having a 3 x 4 inch bore and stroke. In fact, this was the same engine that Cleveland Tractor used in the GG rubber-tired tractor. However, the latter had disappeared from the scene by the time of the Oliver takeover in 1944. The original HG tractor with the 3 x 4 Hercules engine was capable of about 11 drawbar horsepower.

The Hercules engine built into the Oliver-Cletrac DD crawler was capable of over 61 drawbar horsepower. This mid-sized crawler weighed 13,700 pounds. Its six-cylinder Hercules engine carried a 4 3/8 x 5 1/4 inch bore and stroke. Oliver promoted the Cletrac models with a slogan, '365 Days of Usable Power.' The rear-mounted pto shaft was an extra-cost option, as was the belt pulley attachment. However, these were but a few of the many jobs for the Cletrac, and in fact, Oliver compiled a 24-page catalog in 1949 which did nothing but detail the many farm jobs within the capabilities of Cletrac Tru-Traction Tractors.

From all appearances the Cletrac HG continued using the same Hercules 3 x 4 inch, four-cylinder engine into the mid-1940s. However, a new style HG crawler was sent to Nebraska in November 1949. This model carried a somewhat larger Hercules engine with a 3 1/4 x 4 inch bore and stroke. It was rated at 1,700 rpm. Results of this test appear in No. 434; in this test the HG delivered about 16 1/2 drawbar horsepower. Two basic styles were offered; the HG-42 used a 42-inch center-to-center track width, and the HG-68 was widened out to a width of 68 inches. It was built especially for row-crop work.

Numerous attachments were available for the HG tractors. Included was this special fire line plow. The latter was also available in some of the 'OC' models. A comfortable seat with a backrest was standard equipment, and the drawbar could be easily removed for extra clearance in row crop work. In a 1949 catalog of the HG, many testimonials from farmers are included. One farmer said, "I pulled a manure spreader through 12 inches of snow, and spread manure with it when it was almost impossible to get horses to haul an empty wagon."

The Oliver-Cletrac HG tractor was not limited to drawbar work. This Oliver factory photograph shows a Ware hydraulic loader attached. This little machine was able to negotiate small buildings and other areas where big machines were unusable. Thus, tractor power found new applications and reduced manual labor. A belt pulley and pto shaft were extra-cost options for the HG, as were a variety of track pads to suit special applications. In addition track plates up to ten inches wide were available on special order.

Oliver could furnish numerous implements tailored to the HG tractor. Included was the Oliver-Cletrac front-mounted two-row cultivator. The Oliver-Cletrac two-row planter was another option, and the HG could be equipped with the Iron Age vegetable or tree sprayer. A front-mounted mower built by Detroit Harvester was also available for this tractor, along with weeders, dusters, and other equipment. For cold weather operation, the HG could be equipped with special cab equipment, and for operating under severe conditions, special air cleaner equipment was available.

Oliver OC-3 tractors were built in the 1951-57 period. This interesting little tractor was capable of about 22 drawbar horsepower. The four-cylinder engine carried a 3 1/4 x 4 inch bore and stroke for a displacement of 132.7 ci. Full pressure lubrication was a standard feature, and the lubrication system was designed to work positively on side grades of up to 35%, plus fore and aft grades of up to 45%. The crankcase and cylinders were cast en bloc, and the carburetor was gravity-fed.

Far ahead of its time was this rubber-tracked model of the HG crawler. The rubber tracks could operate on surfaced roads with no damage either to the machine or to the roadbed. This design also permitted higher ground speeds than were possible with conventional tracks. Unfortunately however, the tracks had a relatively short life, especially since they tended to stretch continuously. It is said that Oliver recalled these machines or retrofitted them with conventional tracks. Thus, very few of these original machines still remain. This factory photograph was taken in 1951.

Many variations of the OC-3 tractor were available. This 1952 Oliver photograph shows an OC-3 tractor equipped as a Cane Field model. It used the same Hercules IXB-3 engine as was standard for the OC-3 tractors. The OC-3 could also be equipped with a variety of loaders, dozer blades, and v-type snow plows. A standard design feature of the OC-3 was its unusually high clearance; this was a definite advantage for cultivating and other row-crop work.

This 1955 Oliver photograph shows the OC-3 equipped with Oliver '55' sheet metal. Other changes obvious in this photograph are the used of an upholstered seat and the use of four lower track wheel frames. The OC-3 was built in 31, 42, 60, and 68-inch track gauges. Each particular track width had its own place in the field, with the 68-inch width being popular for row-crop work. Special track equipment included the choice of 6, 8, 10, and 12-inch grousers, pressed steel pavement plates or special rubber block treads. Also available were special 6, 8, or 10-inch ice tracks.

Electric starting was furnished as standard equipment on the OC-3 Industrial with a 42-inch track width. It was extra equipment on all other OC-3 models. Engine side shields were standard equipment on the OC-3 with a 31-inch track width, but extra equipment on all others of this series. A pto shaft and belt pulley were optional, as were electric lights. A completely enclosed cab was available at extra cost, and a heavy duty radiator guard could be purchased. The latter was especially intended for the lumber and logging trades.

This undated Oliver photograph shows an OC-3 tractor that has been reworked to provide a clearance of 72 inches. The changeover was not done by Oliver, but by M. F. D. Incorporated of San Jose, California. Various other attachments and modifications were made for the OC-3, including a front-mounted forklift. This tractor could also be equipped with a dozer blade and a small hydraulic end loader. The Imp dozer was available, as was a substantially built rear-mounted winch.

Oliver OC-4 crawlers made their debut in 1956. This photograph was taken in August of that year; it shows the early OC-4 with a radiator grille and hood styling similar to that used on the Oliver farm tractors of the period. The engine was a three-cylinder style from Hercules; its 3 1/2 x 4 1/2 inch bore and stroke gave a displacement of 130 cubic inches. Rated speed was 1,700 rpm. Weighing 5,255 pounds, the OC-4 delivered nearly 18 drawbar horsepower in Nebraska Test No. 656. This test was run in June 1958, shortly after the OC-4 had been unveiled.

This photograph of an Oliver OC-46 Diesel was taken in 1958, yet the serial number listings do not show the OC-46 except in the 1962-65 period. Apparently, the latter listing refers to the new style hood and grille design incorporated into the OC-4 about 1959. However, it also appears that the OC-46 designator refers to the OC-4 with a bulldozer or a front-end loader. Two different transmission options were available; the 'Travel-Reverser' or the 'Slo-Low' design. The Travel-Reverser was essentially a shuttle clutch system.

Oliver OC-4 Diesel tractors carried a three-cylinder Hercules motor. This tractor was tested at Nebraska in June 1958 and the results appear in No. 655. It used the same 3 1/2 x 4 1/2 inch bore and stroke as the gasoline model, plus the same rated speed of 1,700 rpm. In the above test the OC-4 Diesel had a rated drawbar load of over 18 horsepower. Originally designed as an industrial model, the OC-4 achieved excellent balance with its four lower track wheel frames. Of course the Controlled Differential Steering system was retained, and Oliver noted that 'because the OC-4 has power on both tracks, an upper track wheel is not necessary.'

This 1959 company photograph shows an OC-4 Orchard tractor. This was but one of many different special styles available with the OC-4 tractors, whether in gasoline or diesel versions. Another choice was the Oliver two-point backhoe hitch. With the Oliver fast-lock hitch it only required a couple of minutes to attach or detach the backhoe. All that was required to remove this attachment was the removal of two pins and the hydraulic lines. Another option was the OC-46 hydraulic tool platform.

Another special version of the OC-4 was this Ski Slope Special. It was sized and equipped specifically for ski-lodge operators. This model used a 68-inch track gauge with special 30-inch grousers for only 1 1/2 psi of ground pressure. The Ski Slope Special could be equipped with a special blade for smoothing and filling on ski slopes, and could also be employed to clean up snow in the parking lots. During the summer months the special tracks could be replaced with regular grousers for even more usefulness.

For a time the Oliver OC-4 could be purchased on special order with a Air-Track system offering bogie-action. This special design was invaluable in logging operations ski-slope maintenance, and in orchards, mountain construction, and beach construction and maintenance. Research conducted for this book found little other information on this specialized version of the OC-4. However, there is no doubt that Oliver was determined to provide their crawler tractors with virtually any option that would enable them to do a specific job.

The OC-46 loader shown here was built in the 1962-65 period; in fact, 1965 virtually marked the end of the Oliver crawler tractors. In this instance, the loader was factory-engineered as a matched design for the tractor. The integrated construction of this machine included a bucket having a capacity of 5/8 cubic yard. A special rigid subframe helped to carry the load, as well as to carry the shocks and strains associated with this kind of work. The bucket was removable, and could be replaced with a loader boom, snow bucket, lift forks, and other attachments.

Little information has been found regarding the OC-4 Diesel with a special overhung design. This model of 1957 vintage is equipped with a backhoe, and also evidences exceptionally wide track pads. Another application was the mounting of an Oliver Model 125 skid-mounted mist sprayer on this special overhung chassis. No literature has been located in this regard, nor was any further data located among the Oliver Archives at the Floyd County Historical Society in Charles City. However, the OC-4-3D tractor is listed as having been available from 1957 to 1965.

Oliver OC-6 gasoline crawlers apparently carried the same six-cylinder engine as was used in the Oliver 66 Row-Crop tractor. This six-cylinder design included a 3 5/16 x 3 3/4 inch bore and stroke for a piston displacement of 194 ci. The diesel version of the OC-6 was equipped with an engine of similar design. In Nebraska Test No. 516 the OC-6 with a gasoline engine delivered nearly 33 drawbar horsepower. Test No. 517, run on an OC-6 Diesel, shows a maximum of over 34 drawbar horsepower. Both versions were available with either a 42-inch or a 68-inch track gauge.

The OC-6 crawlers were built in the 1953-60 period. Ostensibly designed as a farm crawler, the OC-6 also was available as the OC-66 end loader, at least during the latter years of production. The gasoline model, using the 42-inch track gauge, sold for about $5,200, while a comparable diesel listed at nearly $5,900. A three-point hitch was optionally available at $325, and the pto shaft was priced at $165. If electric lights were not wanted, this was a $25 deduct from the factory package price. Numerous other options were available, including full hydraulics, and a tool bar designed for the three-point hitch.

Numerous experiments were conducted, especially during the 1950s. No information accompanies this Oliver photograph; it shows a Ford tractor adapted to the Oliver crawler chassis. Lacking any definite information, the conjecture could be endless regarding this unusual combination. Could it be that Ford was interested in entering the crawler tractor business and was looking at a combination of their engine and chassis with the Oliver transmission and crawler components?

The Oliver OC-9 Diesel was built in the 1959-64 period, with the tractor shown here apparently being among the earliest production. A caption accompanying this photograph notes the 'This is the former OC-9 with a [Hercules] DJXC engine in place of the [Hercules] DOOC; all other material being OC-9.' Thus, it appears that various engine changes occurred early in production of this model, especially since a 1960 advertising brochure indicates that the OC-9 was equipped with a Hercules DD198 engine.

Early models of the OC-9 were also available with a gasoline engine, in fact, this photograph is noted as 'OC-9-Gas.' In addition, this model shows the radiator grille and hood styling that had been in use for some years. However, the old style louvered engine side panels have been discarded in favor of a streamlined design. Also of significance is a very attractive side decal which follows the basic pattern of the familiar Oliver Shield, but includes the OC-9 model designator.

Oliver OC-9 tractors from about 1960-64 were available with the TransOmatic Drive. This was a torque converter system especially designed for tractor duty. The four-cylinder Hercules engine used a 3 3/4 x 4 1/2 inch bore and stroke for a 198 ci displacement. It delivered about 57 flywheel horsepower. Rated speed was 2,200 rpm. Weighing some 9,675 pounds, the OC-9 was designed as an industrial machine, rather than being built for agricultural purposes. Due to the loads imposed, the transmission case was made of cast alloy steel, and all transmission gears were shaved for the highest possible finish and precision. This model was priced at approximately $9,200.

The Oliver OC-12 crawlers appeared in 1954, replacing the Oliver-Cletrac BG and BD models. The diesel model continued to use the Hercules DJXC engine as in the Model B, but the diesel model was improved substantially by the use of a Roosa-Master pump, plus a new head and manifold design. In addition, the rated speed was raised to 1,750 rpm. A brochure prepared for Oliver dealers compares the OC-12 in size to the Caterpillar D-4 or the International TD-9 tractors.

Five lower and two upper track wheels were used on the OC-12 This model was designed with a 60-inch track gauge, but was also available in a 44-inch track gauge. The latter style was designated as the OC12-44. Also available was the OC-126; it was a loader tractor assembled as a unit on the assembly line. The entire clutch mechanism could be removed through the top inspection cover, without removing any other guards, panels, or other components. A rubber-bushed coupling was placed between the clutch and the transmission; it could be replaced with the removal of only six bolts.

A 1958 Oliver factory photograph shows an OC-12 overhung chassis combined with a scraper. However, it does not appear that this device was marketed to any degree, if in fact, it was marketed at all. Oliver OC-12 tractors featured the Spot-Turn system. It used only two operating levers, and they controlled both the clutches and the brake bands. No foot brakes were needed. This was standard equipment on the OC-12. Since the entire Spot-Turn unit operated in oil, little maintenance was required, especially since the steering clutches were spring loaded. The entire mechanism could be removed through the final drive covers if required.

Many different options were available for the OC-12 tractors, and as previously noted, this chassis could also be set up for a bulldozer or an end loader. Several styles of grousers were available, including rubber treads and ice grousers. another option was the special Hi-Life track wheel units. This design required lubrication only once every 1,000 hours. Tapered roller bearings and face-type seals were features of this design. Standard features included an over-center hand clutch. The OC-12G (gasoline) model left the market in 1960, followed the next year by the OC-12D (diesel) model. The OC-12D with the Spot-Turn feature listed at about $9,000.

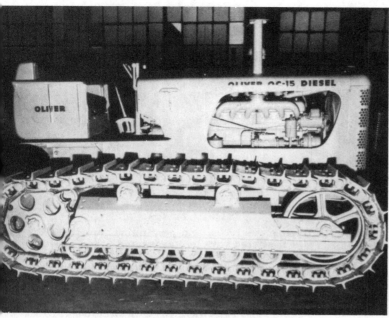

Oliver OC-15 crawlers are listed as being built between 1956 and 1961. This photograph of November 1955 shows the OC-15 Diesel, and an attached note indicates that it was built with the Hercules DRXB engine. The Spot-Turn system, instead of being hydraulically operated was instead, actuated by air power. In fact, Oliver's advertising brochures of the period indicate that air controls were standard equipment, both on the Spot-Turn and the Controlled Differential tractors. The transmission case was cast from Meehanite, a high-tensile iron alloy, and the OC-15 used sintered iron clutch facings as standard equipment.

In November 1957 Oliver sent a copy of their OC-15 tractor to Nebraska's Tractor Test Laboratory. The results, shown in No. 633, indicate an output of over 94 drawbar horsepower and a maximum pull well over 17,000 pounds. The six-cylinder engine used a 4 5/8 x 5 1/4 inch bore and stroke for a displacement of 529 ci. It was rated at 1,500 rpm. The test tractor used an Oliver engine. Weighing about 17,000 pounds, the OC-15 took on considerably more weight when equipped with a bulldozer, end loader, or the numerous other options available.

A Hercules DFXE diesel engine was used in the Oliver OC-18 tractor. This was the largest model in the Oliver line, weighing 16 1/2 tons, and capable of 133 drawbar horsepower. In low gear it had a maximum pull of over 31,000 pounds. An air-actuated differential was standard equipment on the OC-18, with foot operated brakes being standard, or air-actuated brakes being optional. Four forward speeds were provided, ranging from 1.5 to 5.5 mph. Six lower and one upper track wheels were used, and a 14-inch double plate clutch was standard equipment.

Oliver OC-18 crawlers used a big Hercules six-cylinder engine. This diesel design carried a 5 5/8 x 6 inch bore and stroke for a displacement of 895 cubic inches. Rated speed was 1,500 rpm. The crankshaft was 4 1/2 inches in diameter and operated in seven main bearings. The crankcase carried 8 1/2 gallons of oil, while the cooling system took 15 1/2 gallons. A 66 gallon fuel tank was used. Heat-treated track wheels were standard equipment, and as with other Oliver crawler models, a one-piece shaped and riveted frame was used for the maximum in rigidity. Production of Oliver crawler tractors ended in 1965.

Wagons

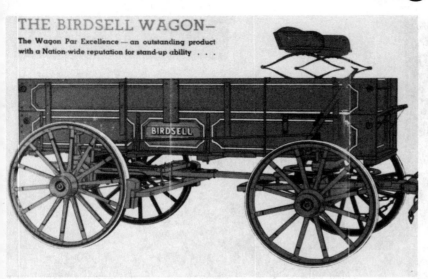

THE BIRDSELL WAGON—

The Wagon Par Excellence — an outstanding product with a Nation-wide reputation for stand-up ability . . .

During the early 1930s Oliver Farm Equipment Company sold the famous Birdsell wagons. Birdsell Manufacturing Company was established at South Bend, Indiana by the late John C. Birdsell in 1855. Birdsell was bought out by Allis-Chalmers in 1931, and continued making wagons and clover hullers for a short time thereafter. Of course, this was the same company which built the famous Birdsell hullers; these were developed and attained world renown through the genius of John C. Birdsell. The Birdsell line included everything from miniature to heavy mountain wagons.

During the 1930s, and continuing into the 1950s, Oliver offered various wagons and boxes. However, many of these were not built by Oliver, but by the Electric Wheel Company. In fact, some Oliver advertising brochures make reference to the Oliver-Electric wagons and boxes. From a 1950 brochure comes this illustration of the Oliver standard all-steel farm wagon. This model was made with an auto-steer front axle, but used plain bearings on tapered cast skeins.

Spring Bolster All Steel, Auto-Steer, Timken-Bearing Combination Wagon and Trailer

Roller Bearing Dairy Cart

Roller Bearing Dairy Cart with Box

In addition to the all-steel farm wagon, the Oliver-Electric was available on rubber tires. This one is shown with spring bolsters, but this was an option. In addition, the rubber-tire version shown here was equipped with Timken roller bearings. Generally, these wagons were capable of loads up to 5,000 pounds. The rubber tires and the Timken bearings permitted higher road speeds than were possible with earlier styles, and show the transition from small, lightweight wagons to heavier models that were designed for higher road speeds.

The Oliver wagon line also included various kinds of dairy carts during the 1930s and 1940s. Various platforms were devised; the upper style was a simple platform designed especially for hauling milk cans. The dairy cart with a box, shown in the center was a combination style that could be used for hauling milk cans or delivering hay and grain to hungry milk cows. In the bottom illustration is shown a dairy cart designed especially for cattle feed. Its height permitted the rationing of grain, oftentimes ground corn, to each cow while in the milking stall.

Wagons

An Oliver advertising brochure of the 1950s illustrates this Oliver-Electric wagon, complete with steel flare box and a hydraulic hoist. These wagons were built in two models; the 650 and the 760. The 650 had a capacity of 8,000 pounds gross load, while the Model 760 had a capacity of 10,000 pounds. Both used Timken tapered roller bearings running on high-carbon steel spindles. All styles could be equipped with either a plain bolster or a spring bolster. In addition, four different tongues or poles could be purchased; anything from a ball-and-socket hitch to a long pole for using the wagon with horses.

During the 1950s Oliver-Electric wagons included the Model 800 and the Model 640 styles. Both were of the fifth-wheel design. The Model 800 could be furnished with dual wheels at extra cost, and this provided considerably better flotation when working in soft ground. Model 640 wagons were built in a high clearance design which was advantageous for hauling in wet fields or unimproved roads. Oliver also marketed their Model 795 heavy-duty harvest wagon. Flare-type and barge-type boxes were also available from local Oliver dealers.

During the 1950s, Oliver advanced its forage equipment line. In addition to forage harvesters, blowers, and other equipment, Oliver also offered heavy duty forage boxes, complete with a suitable running gear. This Model 740 forage box is one of several different styles. A variation was the Model 740 equipped for handling baled hay. With a suitable bale thrower attached to the baler, this task became a one-man job, with the bale thrower delivering baled hay directly to the wagon.

Oliver's 470 gravity box was yet another part of the overall Oliver wagon line. With the development of the corn combine came the need for larger and consequently, more efficient methods of bringing the crop to the bin. However, there were numerous companies already in the wagon business, and in fact, some of them specialized in this endeavor. Thus, it does not appear that the Oliver wagons attained the popularity which they probably deserved. This 470 gravity box is shown behind an Oliver pull-type corn picker.

Windrowers

Oliver offered windrowers or swathers as a continuation of a line previously developed by Nichols & Shepard Company. Attendant to their development of a combine, N & S also built windrowers to meet the needs of those farmers preferring this harvesting method. In essence, the windrower passed through the standing grain, leaving it in a neat windrow for curing. After a suitable time, usually only a few days, the combine came through and harvested the windrowed grain. This model of the 1930s is ground-driven.

By the 1950s Oliver had developed this windrower, complete with pto drive, and equipped to accommodate the Oliver Hydra-Lectric hydraulic lift system. It was built in 8-foot and 12-foot sizes. Forged steel sickle guards were used on the 8-foot size, while the 12-foot model used malleable iron guards. A 40-inch canvas draper was standard equipment on both models; it delivered the cut grain to one side of the machine. Extras included transport trucks for moving from one location to another.

About 1955 Oliver introduced their self-propelled swather. It featured a wide range of cutting heights, ranging from 2 to 30 inches. Swathing and road speeds ranged from 2 to 8 mph. Built in 14 and 16-foot sizes, this model was equipped with a Wisconsin VF-4 air-cooled engine of some 23 horsepower. Electric starting was standard equipment. Canvas drapers were used, and the center delivery design is obvious. In addition, this unit could be easily converted to a self-propelled weed sprayer, complete with a 100 gallon tank, and a 46-foot boom.

During the 1950s and 1960s Oliver offered numerous styles and sizes of windrowers. At various times the company called these machines swathers, and at other times they were called windrowers. Semantics aside, they were the same machine. The Oliver No. 85 self-propelled model was built in 10-, 12-, and 14-foot sizes. It was built for grain swathing, hay mowing, and could be adapted as a sprayer. A generator, lights, and starter came as standard equipment, with dual drive wheels being optional. A semi-revolving, cam-type reel helped reduce grain shattering.

Serial Numbers

The following serial number listings are believed to be fairly inclusive and reasonably accurate. They are, for the most part, compiled from transcripts of various company listings. However, errors were found in these listings during compilation. In many instances the original records no longer exist, therefore, these listings are presented solely for the convenience of the reader, and are not to be construed in any way as being totally correct, despite our best efforts for accuracy.

HART-PARR COMPANY

STATIONARY ENGINES
1 - 1305	1898-1906

TRACTORS

No. 1 (17-30)
1205	1901

No. 2 (17-30)
1206	1902

No. 3 (18-30)
1207	1903

17-30
1208-1219	1903
1346-1347	1905
1435-1454	1906

22-45
1220-1245	1903
1306-1345	1904
1364-1393	1905
1414-1434	1905
1445	1906
1455-1604	1906

30-60
1605-1810	1907
1811-2014	1908
2432-3310	1910
3311-3999	1911
4212-4711	1912
4814-5261	1913
5262-5440	1914
5441-5521	1915
5522-5551	1916
5486-5640	1917
5641-5715	1918
4 built (spec order)	1924

40-80
2015-2018	1908
2019-2024	1909
2025-2100	1910
2101-2200	1911
2201-2275	1912
2276-2300	1913
2301-2324	1914

15-30
2332-2352	1910
2353-2382	1911
2383-2431	1912

60-100
4000-4100	1911
4101-4111	1912

20-40
4112-4211	1912
4714-4763	1913
4764-4813	1914

12-27
5816-5992	1914
5993-6039	1915

Red Devil
6219-6244	1914
6245-6743	1915
6744-6943	1916

18-35
6040-6153	1915
6154-6199	1916
6200-6215	1917
8201-8358	1917
8359-8400	1918

15-30 "A"
New Hart-Parr 12-25 first made 1918.
Subsequently sold as the 15-30 "A" tractor.
8401-9383	1918
9384-13025	1919
13026-17915	1920
18470-18850	1921
18851-19125	1922

Road King "35"
20001-20050	1919

10-20 "B"
35001-35216	1921
35217-35319	1922

10-20 "C"
35501-35527	1922
35528-35760	1923
35761-35922	1924

15-30 "C"
21001-21392	1922
21393-21898	1923
21899-22500	1924

Hart-Parr

22-40

70001-70020	1923
70021-70113	1924
70114-70250	1925
70251-70493	1926
70494-70500	1927

12-24 "E"

36001-36074	1924
36075-36600	1925
36601-37194	1926
37195-38118	1927
38119-39601	1928

12-24 "H"

39602-39686	1928
39687-42277	1929
42278-43253	1930

16-30 "E"

22501-22601	1924
22602-24000	1925
24001-25650	1926

18-36 "G"

26001-26359	1926
26360-28850	1927

18-36 "H"

28851-29635	1927
29636-34566	1928
34567-35000	1929
85001-89158	1929
89159-90698	1930

28-50

70501-70718	1927
70719-70967	1928
70968-71400	1929
71401-71707	1930

WASHING MACHINE
"A" Model

1001-2000	1924
2001-2700	1925
2701-3300	1926

"B" Model

3301-4571	1926
4572-5571	1927

Oliver Tractors & Power Units

Row Crop (Single Front)

100001-102648	1930
102649-103300	1931

18-28 (Includes "28" P.U.)

800001-800459	1930
800460-800963	1931
800964-800984	1932
800985-801050	1933
801051-801240	1934
801241-801989	1935
801990-801937	1937

"18" Industrial

900001-900006	1931

28-44 (Includes "44" P.U.)

500001-503599	1930
503600-506184	1931
506185-506211	1932
506212-506254	1933
506255-506400	1934
506401-507175	1935
507176-508015	1936
508016-508917	1937

Row Crop (Dual Front)

103301-103318	1931
103319-103617	1932
103618-104038	1933
104039-104850	1934
104851-107311	1935
107312-108573	1936
108574-109151	1937

80 Industrial

900007-900018	1932
900019-900021	1933
900022-900036	1934
900037-900072	1935
900073-900078	1936
900079-900086	1937
900087-900102	1938
900103-900127	1939
900128-900229	1940
900230-900315	1941
900316-900327	1942
900328-900339	1943
900340-900395	1944
900396-900633	1945
900634-900816	1946
900817-901124	1947

"99" Industrial

700001-700004	1932
700005-700033	1933
700034-700141	1934
700142-700239	1935
700240-700295	1936
700296-700326	1937
700327-700359	1938
700360-700421	1939
700422-700604	1940
700605-700777	1941
700778-701001	1942
701002-701147	1943
701148-701163	1944
701164-701225	1945
701226-701265	1946
701266-701287	1947

Oliver

Row Crop "70"

200001-200685	1935
200686-208728	1936
208729-219644	1937
219645-220425	1938
223255-231115	1939
231116-236355	1940
236356-241390	1941
241391-243639	1942
243640-244710	1943
244711-250179	1944
250180-252779	1945
252780-258139	1946
258140-262839	1947
262840-267866	1948

Standard "70"

300001-300633	1936
300634-302083	1937
302084-303464	1938
303465-305361	1939
305362-306593	1940
306594-307579	1941
307580-308187	1942
308188-308483	1943
308484-310217	1944
310218-311115	1945
311116-312689	1946
312690-314220	1947
314221-315420	1948

Oliver 25 Airport (1937-48)

See Oliver 70 Std above.

Industrial "70"

400001-400002	1936
None	1937
400003-400008	1938
400009-400016	1939
400017-400027	1940
400028-400047	1941
400048-400067	1942
400068-400096	1943
400097-400181	1944
400182-400800	1945
400801-401178	1946
401179-401690	1947
401691-402230	1948

"35" Industrial

220426-220694	1937
220695-223254	1938

"50" Industrial (1937-47)

See Oliver 99 numbers

Oliver "90"
Oliver "99"

Both were built under the same series of numbers.

508918-508934	1937
508935-509611	1938
509612-510067	1939
510068-510563	1940
510564-510976	1941
510977-511295	1942
511296-511473	1943
511474-512043	1944
512044-512820	1945
512821-513105	1946
513106-513855	1947
513856-514855	1948
514856-516275	1949
516276-516887	1950
516888-517873	1951
517874-518212	1952

"90" ended in 1952

518300-519244	1953
519245-519515	1954
519515-520353	1955
520354-520867	1956
520868-521255	1957

"80" Row Crop

109152-109166	1937
109167-109782	1938
109783-110220	1939
110221-110614	1940
110615-110944	1941
110945-111218	1942
111219-111390	1943
111391-111928	1944
111929-112878	1945
112879-114143	1946
114144-114943	1947
114944-115373	1948

"80" Standard

803929-803990	1937
803991-805376	1938
805377-806879	1939
806880-808124	1940
808125-809050	1941
809051-809990	1942
809991-810469	1943
810470-811990	1944
811991-813066	1945
813067-814563	1946
814564-815215	1947
815216-816241	1948

"60" Row Crop

600071-606303	1941
606304-607394	1942
607395-608525	1943
608526-612046	1944
612047-615627	1945
615628-616706	1946
616707-620256	1947
620257-625131	1948

"60" Standard

410001-410500	1942
410501-410510	1943
410511-410616	1944
410617-410910	1945
410911-411310	1946
411311-411960	1947
411961-413605	1948

Oliver

"60" Industrial

460001-460300	1946
460301-460500	1947
460501-460815	1948

"900" Industrial

710001-710077	1946
710078-710134	1947
710135-710227	1948
710228-710256	1949
None	1950
710257-710281	1951

"88" Row Crop

120001-120352	1947
120353-123300	1948
123301-128652	1949
128653-132862	1950
132863-138183	1951
138184-143232	1952
3500977-3511566	1953
4500076-4505123	1954

"88" Standard

820001-820135	1947
820136-821085	1948
821086-824240	1949
824241-825810	1950
825811-826916	1951
826917-827966	1952

"88" Industrial

920001-920015	1947
920016-920365	1948
920366-920505	1949
920506-920720	1950
920721-920955	1951
920956-921030	1952

"77" Row Crop

320001-320240	1948
320241-327900	1949
327901-337242	1950
337243-347903	1951
347904-354447	1952
3500001-3510830	1953
4501667-4504470	1954

"77" Standard

269001-269696	1948
269697-271266	1949
271267-272465	1950
272466-273375	1951
273376-274051	1952

"77" Industrial

403001-403010	1948
403011-403185	1949
None	1950
403186-403290	1951
403291-403515	1952

"66" Row Crop

420001-421588	1949
421589-426010	1950
426011-429770	1951
429771-431472	1952
3503990-3511337	1953
4500309-4504960	1954

"66" Standard

470001-470405	1949
470406-472390	1950
472391-474232	1951
474233-476408	1952

"66" Industrial

462001-462050	1949
462051-462110	1950
462111-462255	1951
462256-462405	1952

Industrial and Standard versions of the "66", "77", and 88 are included in the Row Crop listings for 1953-54.

Super "44"

1002-1550	1957
1551-1775	1958

Super "55"

6001-8290	1954
11887-31370	1955
35001-43647	1956
43916-56036	1957
56501-59033	1958

Super "66"

7085-7284	1954
14099-27842	1955
39371-42430	1956
45846-55800	1957
57858-72824	1958

Super "77"

8303-8988	1954
10001-29842	1955
38500-43637	1956
44167-55955	1957
56917-59008	1958

Super "88"

6503-8302	1954
10075-29347	1955
36774-43715	1956
43901-55607	1957
56580-59001	1958

990 Scraper

520226-	1955
520523-520755	1956
521084-521316	1957

Super "99"

521300-521495	1957
521496-521635	1958

950, 990, 995 Tractors

530001-530387	1958
71245-84376	1959
84487-95350	1960
110064-115469	1961

Oliver

995 Scraper
521580-521583	1958

550, 551, 552 Tractors
60501-70745	1958
72632-84415	1959
84416-110966	1960
111868-117540	1961
117541-123699	1962
127365-140619	1963
140620-149764	1964
162265-163114	1965
171923-176454	1966
186165-193085	1967
206095-207856	1968
213340-217921	1969
222833-223056	1970

Oliver 660
73132-84553	1959
86166-110955	1960
111213-117266	1961
117873-126294	1962
127356-136486	1963
141160-144039	1964

Oliver 770
60504-70891	1958
71011-84384	1959
84554-110967	1960
111472-117516	1961
117600-126208	1962
127319-138612	1963
141901-149064	1964
153255-165092	1965
171515-178936	1966
183649-195365	1967

Oliver 880
60505-71317	1958
71640-84335	1959
84555-110954	1960
111262-117504	1961
117640-126354	1962
128911-135054	1963

Oliver 440
85725-87817	1960

Oliver 500
100001-100500	1960
100501-101200	1961
101201-101700	1962
101701-102000	1963

Oliver 600
449800-452300	1962
452301-453700	1963

1600 - First Series
124420-127043	1962
127044-137709	1963

1600 - Second Series
137710-140262	1963
140723-147568	1964

1800 - Series A
90525-111024	1960
111025-117375	1961
118344-124395	1962

1800 - Series B
124397-126352	1962
129286-134683	1963

1800 - Series C
136501-140085	1963
140893-149818	1964

1900 - Series A
90532-111022	1960
111028-117374	1961
118356-124372	1962

1900 - Series B
124396-126355	1962
128422-135430	1963

1900 - Series C
138440-140066	1963
141168-148651	1964

1250 Tractor
705376-712832	1965
712833-725780	1966
728661-739518	1967
739527-742520	1968
742526-743152	1969

1250-A Tractor
305985-309380	1969

1450 Tractor
132382-147473	1967
147482-155196	1968
155479-159945	1969

1550 Tractor
157841-166406	1965
168919-181061	1966
184488-196205	1967
196301-208959	1968
213243-218186	1969

1650 Tractor
149836-152569	1964
153855-167667	1965
167668-183194	1966
183923-195765	1967
201091-209251	1968
212733-218193	1969

1750 Tractor
See 1800-C	1964
149835-149937	1965
181062-182126	1966
185301-200216	1967
200217-211777	1968
214936-218850	1969

Oliver

1850 Tractor
150421-153013 1964
153014-1167285 1965
168127-183381 1966
183382-199964 1967
200360-212448 1968
212673-218852 1969

1950 Tractor
150492-153011 1964
153016-167298 1965
168190-177661 1966
189008-199186 1967
200541-211167 1968
213355-218253 1969
223073-223109 1970
225820-226402 1971
233007-236363 1972

1950-T Tractor
188974-199339 1967
201931-211117 1968
213376-218449 1969

2050 Tractor
204444-212527 1968
212560-213932 1969

2150 Tractor
204480-212553 1968
212554-216595 1969

1255 Tractor
309381-360743 1969
312957-318393 1970
317338-318385 1971

1355 Tractor
503287-512149 1969
512698-525078 1970
523254-526640 1971

1555 Tractor
218128-220639 1969
221295-223072 1970
225914-230893 1971
232089-235984 1972
236883-242906 1973
244937-250430 1974
256165-262877 1975

1655 Tractor
218025-220399 1969
222600-222761 1970
225997-230735 1971
231772-235188 1972
236586-244447 1973
244735-255515 1974
257700-263340 1975

1755 Tractor
221603-223322 1970
226445-229636 1971
231415-236163 1972
238136-244369 1973
245667-253668 1974
257515-260346 1975

1855 Tractor
220640-221098 1969
221099-223507 1970
225508-231365 1971
231366-236584 1972
236585-244489 1973
247436-254772 1974
255727-255785 1975

1955 Tractor
222304-223439 1970
226858-230456 1971
232958-236326 1972
239032-244558 1973
247871-253050 1974

2055 Tractor
43100416-43100544 1971

2155 Tractor
43300043-43300253 1971

2255 Tractor
235598-235999 1972
237210-244214 1973
244825-252714 1974
258472-258571 1975
266683-266782 1976

2655 Tractor
45600188-45600700 1971
45600701-45601190 1972

1265 Tractor
302458-303466 1971
304497-307220 1972
307221-314368 1973
314369-319893 1974
317900-321497 1975

1365 Tractor
706251-706277 1971
710276-716975 1972
714614-730076 1973
725451-764138 1974
729125-766614 1975

1465 Tractor
827183-831562 1973
827580-839423 1974
827287-839487 1975

1865 Tractor
43600416-43600829 1971

Minneapolis-Moline Tractors

Includes late Twin City models. During the 1970-75 period, some WFE tractors were variously sold as Oliver, as Minneapolis-Moline, or as White. Some also may have been sold as Cockshutt. Refer to the text under (Wheel) Tractors in this regard.

This listing is fairly complete. However, some of the various M-M listings do not agree with each other, although this list is compiled from the company's own data.

16-30 Twin City

5501-6203 1936

17-28 Twin City

30104-30281	1930
30282-30298	1931
30299-30309	1932
30310-30333	1933
30334-30762	1934
30763-30808	1935

20-35 & 27-44 Twin City

250000-250730	1928-29
250731-250796	1930
250797-250799	1931
None built 1932-33	
250800-250805	1934
250806-250839	1935

21-32 Twin City

151797-154073	1930
154074-154123	1931
154124-154129	1932
None built	1933
154130-154275	1934

FT Tractor

46001-46004	1932
None Built	1933
46005-46029	1934
46030-only	1935
46031-46046	1936
46047-46074	1937

FTA Tractor

154300-155381	1935
155382-156247	1936
156248-156908	1937
156909-157229	1938

GT Tractor

160001-160076	1938
160077-160545	1939
160546-160878	1940
160879-161253	1941

GTA Tractor

162001-162300	1942
162301-162302	1943
162303-162659	1944
196660-162869	1945
162870-163219	1946
163220-163610	1947

GTB Tractor

164001-164178	1947
164179-164214	1948

016480000-016480600	1948
0164900001-0164901205	1949
0165000001-016501863	1950
01601864-01603396	1951
01603397-01604889	1952
01604890-01605972	1953
01605973-01606289	1954

GTB-Diesel

06800001-only	1953
06800002-06800850	1954

GTC Tractor

04700001-04700018	1951
04700019-04700676	1952
04700677-04701101	1953

GB Tractor

08900001-08901500	1955
08901501-08902601	1956
08902602-08903401	1957
08903402-08904251	1958
08904252-08904492	1959

GB-Diesel

09000001-09000850	1955
09000851-09001525	1956
09001526-09002145	1957
09002146-09002655	1958
09002656-09002790	1959

JT Tractor

550001-550025	1934
550026-551762	1935
551763-554554	1936
554555-556244	1937

JT Standard

600001-600469	1936

JT Orchard

625001-625103	1937
625104-625156	1938

KT Tractor

300001-300079	1929
300080-301583	1930
301584-301956	1931
301957-301981	1932
301982-301987	1933
301988-302078	1934

KT Industrial

40001-only	1932
40002-40004	1933
40005-40008	1934
40009-only	1935

Minneapolis-Moline

KTA Tractor
302200-302371 1934
302372-303825 1935
303826-304701 1936
304702-306281 1937
306282-306751 1938

LT Tractor
500001-500010 1930

MT Tractor
525001-525020 1930
525021-525095 1931
525096-525334 1932
525335-525345 1933
525346-525420 1934

MTA Tractor
525421-525490 1934
525491-526118 1935
526119-526960 1936
526961-528049 1937
528050-528645 1938

RT Tractor
400001-402200 1939
402201-405575 1940
405576-407950 1941
407951-408825 1942
408826-409357 1943
409358-410747 1944
410748-413754 1945
413755-416544 1946
416545-422057 1947

RTE Tractor
0044800001-0044800501 1948
0044900001-0044900315 1949
0045000001-0045000204 1950
00400205-00400281 1951
00400282-only 1952
00400283-00400287 1953

RTN Tractor
0034800001-0034800100 1948
0034900001-0034900200 1949
0035000001-0035000093 1950
00300094-00300173 1951

RTS Tractor
0024900001-0024900375 1949
0025000001-0025000300 1950
00200301-00200401 1951
00200402-00200551 1952
00300552-00200701 1953

RTU Tractor
0014800001-0014802402 1948
0014900001-0014903039 1949
0015000001-0015002155 1950
00102056-00103972 1951
00103973-00104823 1952
None Built 1953
00104824-00104831 1954

RTI-M Tractor
05500001-05500249 1953

"U" Tractor
310026-310500 1938
310626-312450 1939
312451-314892 1940
314893-316500 1941
316501-317701 1942
317702-318162 1943
318163-321101 1944
321102-325231 1945
325232-329751 1946
329752-337417 1947
337418-339682 1948

UDLX Tractor
310001-310025 1938
310501-310625 1938

UTC w/6 volt ignition
0154800001-0154800300 1948
0154900001-0154900100 1949
None Made 1950
01500101-01500180 1951
01500181-01500265 1952
None Made 1953
01500266-01500271 1954

UTC w/12 volt ignition
08800001-08800060 1954
08800061-08800110 1955

UTE Tractor
04300001-04300111 1951
04300112-04300261 1952
04300262-04300264 1953
04300625-only 1954

UTN Tractor
0385000001-0385000101 1950
03800102-03800204 1951
03800205-03800354 1952

UTS Tractor
0124800001-0124802276 1948
0124900001-0124903901 1949
0125000001-01203850 1950
01203851-01207138 1951
01207239-01210570 1952
01210571-01213219 1953
01213220-01213325 1954
01213326-01214125 1955
01214126-01215100 1956
01215101-01215150 1957

UTU Tractor
0114800001-0114802053 1948
0114900001-0114905000 1949
0115000001-01105383 1950
01105384-01110117 1951
01110118-01113449 1952
None Built 1954
01113450-01113453 1954
01113454-01113456 1955

UDJ Tractor
04900001-only 1952
04900002-04900030 1953

UDS Tractor
05000001-05000018 1952
None Made 1953
05000019-05000755 1954
05000955-05001154 1955
05002105-05002404 1956

UDS-M Tractor
05000756-05000954 1954
05001155-05002104 1955

UBU Tractor
05800001-05802912 1953
05802913-05804002 1954
05804003-05805077 1955

UBE Tractor
05900001-05900896 1953
05900897-05901068 1954
05901069-05901421 1955

UBN Tractor
06000001-06000202 1953
06000203-06000207 1954
0600208-only 1955

UBU Diesel
07800001-07800746 1954
07800747-07801041 1955

UBN Diesel
06900001-06900048 1954

UB Special
09700001-09701475 1955

UB Special Diesel
09800001-09800300 1955
09800301-09800464 1956
09800465-09800520 1957

YT Tractor
630001-630016 1937
630017-630025 1938

ZAU Tractor
0064900001-0064903013 1949
0065000001-? 1950
00605436-00609939 1951
00609940-00614658 1952

ZAS Tractor
0074900001-0074900150 1949
0075000001-00700480 1950
00700481-00701285 1951
00701286-00701910 1952
00701911-00702610 1953

ZAN Tractor
0084900001-0084900150 1949
0085000001-00800238 1950
00800239-00800442 1951

00800443-00800618 1952
00800619-00800620 1953

ZAE Tractor
0094900001-0094900301 1949
0095000001-00900373 1950
00900374-00900576 1951
00900577-00900997 1952
00900998-00901122 1953

ZBE Tractor
06300001-06300075 1953
06300076-06300306 1954
06300307-06300501 1955

ZBN Tractor
06400001-06400072 1954
06400073-06400106 1955

ZBU Tractor
06200001-06200957 1953
06200958-06202479 1954
06202480-06203059 1955

ZTN & ZTU Tractors
560001-560037 1936
560038-562974 1937
562975-565406 1938
565407-567154 1939
567155-568754 1940
568755-570821 1941
570822-571421 1942
571422-572967 1943
572968-575712 1944
575713-576813 1945
576814-578013 1946
578014-581814 1947
581815-585817 1948

ZTS Tractor
610001-610035 1937
610036-610388 1938
610389-610684 1939
610685-611087 1940
611088-611342 1941
611343-611446 1942
611447-611965 1943
611966-612485 1944
612486-612885 1945
612886-613085 1946
613086-613490 1947

ZTI Tractor
599001-599003 1936
599004-599016 1937
599017-599018 1938
599019-599022 1939

335 Utility
10400001-10400101 1956
10400102-10402087 1957
10402088-10402336 1958
10402337-10402439 1959
10402440-10402489 1960
10402490-10402539 1961

Minneapolis-Moline

335 Universal

11600001-11600301	1957
11600302-11600305	1958
11600306-11600334	1959

335 Industrial

11300001-11300440	1957
11300441-11300521	1958
11300522-11300596	1959
11300597-11300476	1960

445 Universal

10100001-10102854	1956
10102855-10104125	1957
10104126-10104804	1958
10104805-10104847	1959

445 Utility

10200001-10201445	1956
10201446-10202101	1957
10202102-10202242	1958
10202243-10202249	1959

445 Utility Diesel

15400001-15400018	1959

445 Industrial

11100001-11100075	1956
11100076-11100388	1957
11100389-11100645	1958

445 Industrial Diesel

15300001-15300025	1958

445 Military

15700001-15700074	1958

445 Universal Diesel

15200001-15200190	1958

Big Mo "400" (Gas)

16700001-16700100	1961
16700101-16700210	1962
16700211-16700360	1963
16700361-16700410	1964

Big Mo "400" (Diesel)

17000001-17000356	1959
17000357-17000632	1960
17000633-17000648	1961
17000649-17000652	1962
17000653-17000757	1963

Big Mo "500" (Gas)

16800001-16800160	1960
16800161-16800391	1961
16800392-16800606	1962
16800607-16800681	1963
16800682-16800746	1964
16800747-16800866	1965
16800867-16800881	1966

Big Mo "500" Diesel

17800001-17800065	1960
None Built	1961
None Built	1962
17800066-17800090	1963
17800091-17800115	1964
17800116-17800145	1965

Big Mo "600"

18400001-18400060	1960

4-Star Series (Gas)

16600001-16600890	1959
16600891-16601685	1960
16601686-16601860	1961
16601861-16602407	1962
16602408-16602537	1963

4-Star Series (Diesel)

18200001-18200050	1960
18200051-18200072	1961
18200073-18200097	1962

5-Star Universal (Diesel)

14400001-14400203	1957
14400204-14400785	1958
1440786-14401295	1959

5-Star Universal (Gas)

11000001-11001057	1957
11001058-11002067	1958
11002068-11002914	1959

5-Star Standard (Gas)

11200001-11200380	1958

5-Star Standard (Diesel)

14500001-14500165	1958
14500166-14500188	1959

5-Star Industrial (Gas)

11700002-11700006	1957
11700007-11700025	1958
11700026-11700084	1959

5-Star Industrial (Diesel)

14600001-14600010	1958
14600011-14600028	1959
14600029-14600060	1960

2-Star Crawler

12000001-12000051	1958

Motrac Crawler (Gas)

18500001-18500030	1960
18500031-18500038	1961

Motrac Crawler (Diesel)

18600001-18600160	1960
18600161-only	1961

Jet Star (Gas)

16500001-16500284	1959
16500285-16500834	1960
16500835-16501701	1961
16500702-16502439	1962

Jet Star (Diesel)

17500001-17500060	1960
17500061-17500135	1961
17500136-17500196	1962

Minneapolis-Moline

Jet Star 2 (Gas)
25800001-25801100 1963

Jet Star 2 (Diesel)
25700001-25700113 1963

Jet Star 3 (Gas)
28300001-28301000 1964
28301001-18301984 1965

Jet Star 3 Super (Gas)
28301985-28302055 1965
28302056-28302843 1966
28302844-28303565 1967
28303566-28304800 1968
28304801-28305085 1969
28305086-28305335 1970

Jet Star 3 (Diesel)
28400001-28400050 1964
28400051-28400200 1965
28400201-28400385 1966
28400386-28400466 1967
28400467-28400526 1968
28400527-28400601 1969
28400602-28400711 1970

Jet Star Orchard (Diesel)
34400001-34400020 1967

Jet Star Orchard (Gas)
30700001-30700050 1965
30700051-only 1966
30700052-30700070 1967

Jet Star 3 (LP-Gas)
36000001-36000010 1970

Jet Star 3 Industrial (Gas)
30800001-30800156 1966
30800157-30800191 1967

Jet Star 3 Industrial (Diesel)
30900001-30900050 1966

U-302 (Gas)
27600001-27601000 1964
27601001-27601300 1965

U-302 Super (Gas)
27601301-27602300 1966
27602301-27602425 1967
27602426-27602759 1968
27602760-27602859 1969
27602860-27602969 1970

U-302 Super (Diesel)
27700001-27700100 1967
27700101-27700150 1968
27700151-27700164 1969
27700165-27700190 1970

U-302 Super (LP-Gas)
36100001-36100025 1969
36100026-36100050 1970

M-5 (Gas)
17100001-17101535 1960
17101536-17103495 1961
17103496-17104707 1962
17104708-17105157 1963

M-5 (Diesel)
17200001-17201040 1960
17201041-17201999 1961
17202000-17202506 1962
17202507-17202656 1963

M-504 4-WD (Gas)
24300001-24300010 1962

M-504 4-WD (Diesel)
24200001-24200021 1962

M-602 (Gas)
26600001-26601275 1963
26601276-26602957 1964

M-602 (Diesel)
26700001-26700742 1963
26700743-26701772 1964

M-604 4-WD (Gas)
26800001-26800050 1963
26800051-26800053 1964

M-604 4-WD (Diesel)
26900001-26900050 1963
26900051-26900099 1964

M-670 (Gas)
29900001-29900006 1964
29900007-29901891 1965

M-670 (Diesel)
30000001-30000004 1964
30000005-30000819 1965

M-670 Super (Gas)
29901892-29903579 1966
29903580-29904454 1967
29904455-29904594 1968
29904595-29905004 1969
29905005-29905104 1970

M-670 Super (Diesel)
30000820-30001634 1966
30001635-30002309 1967
30002310-30002569 1968
30002570-30002860 1969
30002861-30003085 1970

M-670 Super (LP-Gas)
36200001-36200075 1970

G-vi Tractor (Gas)
16000001-16000876 1959
16000877-16001675 1960
16001676-16002032 1961
16002033-16002352 1962

G-vi Tractor (Diesel)

16200001-16200805	1959
19200806-16201890	1960
16201891-16202960	1961
16202961-16203235	1962

G-704 (LP-Gas)

23400001-23400081	1962

G-704 (Diesel)

23500001-23500123	1962

G-705 (LP-Gas)

23800001-23800078	1962
23800079-23800590	1963
23800591-23801092	1964
23801093-23801223	1965

G-705 (Diesel)

23900001-23900050	1962
23900051-23900898	1963
23900899-23901868	1964
23901869-23902094	1965

G-706 (LP-Gas)

24000001-24000072	1962
24000073-24000305	1963
24000306-24000350	1964
24000351-24000370	1965

G-706 (Diesel)

24100001-24100106	1962
24100107-24100549	1963
24100550-24100795	1964
24100796-24100821	1965

G-707 (LP-Gas)

31200001-31200283	1965

G-707 (Diesel)

31300001-31300415	1965

G-708 (LP-Gas)

31400001-31400031	1965

G-708 (Diesel)

31500001-31500075	1965

G-900 (Gas & LP-Gas)

33000001-33000110	1967
33000111-33000550	1968
33000551-33000670	1969

G-900 (LP-Gas)

36300001-36300160	1969

G-900 (Diesel)

33100001-33100316	1967
33100317-33101376	1968
33101377-33101946	1969

G-950 (LP-Gas)

43500001-43500060	1969
43500061-43500085	1970
43500086-43500186	1971

G-950 (Diesel)

43600001-43600210	1969
43600211-43600415	1970
43600416-43600829	1971
43600830-43600834	1972

G-955 Tractor

239825-243262	1973
244559-251357	1974

G-1000 Row-Crop, Gas & LP-Gas

30500001-30500450	1965
30500451-30500926	1966
30500927-30501041	1967
30501042-30501051	1968

G-1000 Row-Crop Diesel

30600001-30600500	1965
30600501-30601125	1966
30601126-30601285	1967
30601286-30601300	1968

G-1000 Wheatland, Gas & LP-Gas

32700001-32700796	1966
32700797-32701450	1967
32701451-32701774	1968
32701775-32702050	1969

G-1000 Vista (LP-Gas)

34500001-34500290	1967
34500291-34500390	1968
34500391-34500564	1969

G-1000 Vista (Diesel)

34600001-34600735	1967
34600736-34601185	1968
34601186-34601610	1969

G-1050 (LP-Gas)

43000001-43000040	1969
43000041-43000060	1970
43000061-43000105	1971
43000106-43000111	1972

G-1050 (Diesel)

43100001-43100285	1969
43100286-43100415	1970
43100416-43100544	1971

G-1350 Row-Crop (LP-Gas)

43200001-43200022	1969
43200023-43200044	1970
43200045-43200097	1971
43200098-43200108	1972

G-1350 Row-Crop (Diesel)

43300001-43300042	1970
43300043-43300253	1971
43300254-43300322	1972

G-1350 Wheatland (LP-Gas)

45300001-45300005	1969

G-1355 Tractor

236440-244184	1973
245258-252710	1974

A4T - 1400 (Diesel)

43900001-43900102	1969
43900103-43900247	1970

A4T - 1600 (Diesel)
45600001-45600187 1970
45600188-45600700 1971
45600701-45601190 1972

A4T - 1600 (LP-Gas)
45700001-45700126 1970
45700127-45700197 1971
45700198-45700257 1972

Uni-Tractor
75700001-75700254 1951

75700255-75701070 1952
75501071-75703118 1953
75703119-75704118 1954
08704119-08705418 1955
08705419-08706418 1956
08706419-08707687 1957
08707688-08708062 1958
08708063-08708488 1959
42200001-42200637 1960
42200638-42201134 1961
42201135-42201637 1962

Cletrac & Oliver-Cletrac Tractors

No yearly serial number listings for Cletrac have been located prior to about 1930. All that has been located is a listing show-ing the extent of the assigned serial numbers for the production period of each model.

R	1-1000	1916-17
H	1001-13755	1917-19
W (12)	13756-30971	1919-32
F	1-3000	1920-22
20K	101-10207	1925-32
30A	6-1421	1926-28
30B (B30)	1601-3057	1929-30
40	101-1833	1928-31
55-40	1835-1889	1931-32
55	1890-3852	1932-36
100	50-158	1927-30
15	76-11999	1931-33
20C	12000-14547	1933-36

Model GG (Wheel Tractor)
1FA000-5FA38 1939
5FA388-1FA0084 1940
1FA0086-1FA0164 1941
1FA1000-1FA6530 1941
1FA6532-1FA6886 1942

Model HG
1GA000-2GA882 1939
2GA884-5GA022 1940
5GA024-7GA482 1941
7GA484-8GA700 1942
8GA702-9GA628 1943
9GA630-13GA488 1944
13GA490-19GA992 1945
19GA994-25GA238 1946
25GA240-33GA144 1947
33GA146-41GA894 1948
41GA896-48GA426 1949
48GA428-48GA730 1950
52GA000-55GA856 1950
55GA856-59GA856 1951

Model ED-38 (ED-42)
1AA00-1AA76 1938
1AA78-1AA98 1939

Model ED-42
5AA00-5AA88 1938
5AA90-7AA22 1939

7AA24-8AA90 1940
8AA92-9AA00 1941

Model ED-2
1T00-1T12 1937
1T14-1T24 1938
1T26-1T42 1939
1T44-1T84 1940

Model ED2-38 (ED2-42)
1S00-1S08 1937
1S10-1S52 1938

Model ED2-42
5S00-5S90 1938
5292-6S58 1939
6S60-6S70 1940
6S72-6S80 1941

Model EHD-2
1V00-2V26 1938
2V28-3V50 1939
3V52-4V03 1940
4V05-4V13 1941

Model 20-C (AG)
12000-12552 1933
12554-13662 1934
13664-14550 1935

Model EN (E-31)
1B00-1B18 1934
1B20-6B48 1935
6B50-1B358 1936
1B360-1B630 1937
1B632-1B814 1938
1B816-1B946 1939

Model E-38 (EG-42)
2H000-2H226 1936
2H228-2H974 1937
2H976-3H168 1938

Model E-42
5H000-5H128 1938
5H130-5H410 1939
5H412-5H572 1940
5H574-5H584 1941
5H586-5H604 1942

Tractors (Crawler)

Model E

1A00-1A06	1934
1A08-6A78	1935
7A80-1A408	1936
3A000-3A246	1936
3A248-4A840	1937
4A842-5A070	1938
5A072-5A240	1939
5A242-5A314	1940
5A316-5A330	1941

Model EHG

1R00-1R06	1937
1R08-5R40	1938
5R42-7R70	1939
7R72-8R30	1940
8R32-8R52	1941

Model AG

14552-15662	1936
18000-18420	1936
18422-20200	1937
2X0202-2X0884	1938
2X0886-2X1700	1939
2X1702-2X2472	1940
2X2474-2X3100	1941
2X3102-2X3396	1942
Last One - 2X3548	

Model AD

1Z00-1Z50	1937
1Z52-5Z34	1938
5Z36-9Z30	1939
9Z32-1Z104	1940
1Z106-1Z688	1941
1Z690-1Z834	1942
None Built	1943
1Z836-2Z170	1944
2Z172-2Z670	1945
2Z672-3Z698	1946
3Z700-4Z910	1947
4Z912-6Z212	1948
6Z214-7Z388	1949
7Z390-7Z420	1950
7Z422-8Z134	1951
8Z135-8Z991	1952
3500000-UP	1953
4500000-UP	1954
8Z992-9X127	1955
9Z128-9Z177	1956
9Z178-9Z211	1957
9Z212-9Z225	1958
9Z226-	1959

Model AD-2

1N00-2N84	1937
2N86-4N64	1938
4N66-5N74	1939
5N76-5N80	1940

Model 25

76-200	1931
202-350	1932
352-632	1933
634-1174	1934
1176-1372	1935

Model 30 Gas
(Later BG)

1C00-2C78	1935
2C80-6C18	1936

Model BG

2C000-2C450	1937
2C452-2C576	1938
2C578-2C778	1939
2C780-3C336	1940
3C338-3C652	1941
3C654-3C736	1942
3C738-3C794	1943
3C796-4C858	1945

Model B-30

2556-3057	1930

Model 30 Diesel
(Later BD)

1D00-1D20	1935
1D22-6D98	1936

Model BD

2D000-2D092	1936
2D094-2D892	1937
2D894-3D706	1938
3D708-4D204	1939
4D206-4D236	1940
5D000-5D420	1940
5D422-6D030	1941
6D032-6D284	1942
6D286-6D780	1943
6D782-7D712	1944
7D714-8D472	1945
8D474-9D678	1946
9D680-11D222	1947
11D224-13D816	1948
13E818-15D656	1949
15E658-16D512	1950
16D514-17D683	1951
17D684-19D699	1952
3500000-UP	1953
4500000-UP	1954
19D700-20D219	1955
20D220-	1956

Model BD-2

1P00-1P06	1937
1P08-1P16	1938

Model 40/30
(Model 35) (CG)

76-381	1931

Model 35

400-452	1931
454-658	1932
660-1314	1933
1316-1924	1934
1926-2834	1935
2836-3246	1936

Model CG

5M000-5M188	1937
5M190-5M258	1938
5M260-5M308	1939
5M310-5M542	1940
5M544-5M602	1941
5M604-5M608	1942

Model 40

1600-1735	1930
1736-1888	1931

Model 55

1890-1930	1932
1931-2344	1933
2346-2578	1934
2580-3852	1935

Model 40 Diesel

10138-10190	1934
10192-10800	1935
10802-11520	1936
11522-11580	1937

Model DG

1E00-1E54	1936
3E00-3E66	1937
3E68-4E64	1938
4E66-7E66	1939
7E68-1E198	1940
1E200-1E362	1941
1E364-1E390	1942
1E392-1E462	1943
1E464-1E746	1944
1E748-2E354	1945
2E356-2E618	1946
2E620-2E850	1947
2E852-3E184	1948
3E186-3E296	1949
3E298-3E360	1950
3E362-3E401	1951
3E402-3E501	1952
3500000-UP	1953
4500000-UP	1954
3E502-3E515	1955
3E516-	1956

Model 35 Diesel (40-D) & (DD)

10000-10138	1934

Model DD

1L3000-1L3734	1937
1L3736-1L4218	1938
1L4220-1L5220	1939
1L5222-1L5642	1940
1L5644-1L6330	1941
1L6332-1L6558	1942
1L6560-1L6818	1943
1L6820-1L7420	1944
1L7422-1L8010	1945
1L8012-1L8790	1946
2L0194-2L2140	1947
None Made	1948
2L2142-2L3526	1949
2L3528-2L4128	1950
2L4130-2L5045	1951
2L5046-3L225	1952
3500000-UP	1953
4500000-UP	1954
3L226-3L403	1955
3L404-3L497	1956
3L498-3L595	1957
3L596-	1958

Model 80/60 (80 Gas) (FG)

101-252	1930
253-409	1931
420-562	1932
564-672	1933
674-732	1934
734-848	1935
850-986	1936
988-1044	1937

Model FG

1CA046-1CA054	1938
1CA200-1CA206	1938
1CA500-1CA530	1938
1CA532-1CA604	1939
1CA606-1CA794	1940
1CA796-1CA844	1941
1CA846-1CA878	1942
1CA880-Only	1943

Model 80 Diesel (Later FD)

6000-6068	1933
6070-6152	1934
6154-6314	1935
6316-6510	1936
6512-6688	1937
6690-6698	1938

Model FD

8Y000-8Y092	1938
8Y094-8Y364	1939
8Y366-8Y472	1940
8Y474-8Y682	1941
8Y684-8Y770	1942
8Y772-8Y908	1943
8Y910-9Y228	1944
Last One - 9Y228	

Model FDLC

1HA000-1HA074	1941
1HA076-1HA094	1942
1HA096-1HA102	1943
1HA104-1HA196	1944
Last One - 1HA272	

Model MG-1 (Built by Deere)

1DA000-1DA064	1942
1DA066-4DA948	1943

Model MG-1

1JA000-1JA234	1941
1JA236-7JA540	1942
7JA542-11JA412	1943
Last One - 15JA488	

Tractors (Crawler)

Model FDE

10Y000-10Y198	1945
10Y200-10Y478	1946
10Y480-10Y792	1947
10Y794-11Y120	1948
11Y122-11Y580	1949
11Y582-11Y788	1950
11Y790-12Y024	1951
12Y024-	1952

Model AG-6

3X0000-3X1510	1944
3X1512-3X3258	1945
3X3260-3X4584	1946
3X4586-3X6060	1947
3X6062-3X7642	1948
3X7644-3X8450	1949
3X8452-3X8454	1950
3X8456-3X8588	1951
3X8589-UP	1952
3500000-UP	1953
4500000-UP	1954
4X020-4X099	1955
4X100-4X215	1956
4X216-	1957

Model BGS

6C000-8C368	1945
8C370-9C060	1946
9C062-10C236	1947
10C238-11C456	1948
11C458-11C948	1949
11C950-12C228	1950
12C230-12C468	1951
12C469-12C699	1952
3500000-UP	1953
4500000-UP	1954
12C956-UP	1955

Model HG (Beginning s/n for year)

1GA000-	1939
2GA844-	1940
5GA022-	1941
7GA484-	1942
8GA702-	1943
9GA632-	1944
13GA422-	1945
19GA994-	1946
25GA240-	1947
33GA146-	1948
41GA896-	1949
48GA428-	1950
55GA858-	1951

Model HGR

1NA000-	1945
None Made	1946
1NA050-	1947
1NA706	1948

Model HGF

26GA108-	1947
35GA340-	1948
46GA508-	1949

Oliver Crawler Tractors

For the following tractors, the beginning number for each year is given.

OC-3

1WH000	1951
3WH712	1952
3500001	1953
4500005	1954
11WH760	1955
15WH306	1956
19WH090	1957

OC-4

1TG002	1956
1TG004	1957
4TG076	1958

OC-4-3G

1WR002	1958
2WR542	1959
4WR958	1960
6WR746	1961
800001	1962
800432	1963
801280	1964
801795	1965

OC-4-3D

1WD002	1957

1WD120	1958
1WD950	1959
2WD824	1960
3WD594	1961
800001	1962
800436	1963
801280	1964
801795	1965

OC-6G

3502785	1953
4500002	1954
1RM182	1955
1RM314	1956
1RM504	1957
1RM808	1958
2RM004	1959
2RM126	1960

OC-6D

3502776	1953
4500007	1954
1RC468	1955
1RC632	1956
1RC876	1957
2RC262	1958
2RC366	1959
2RC458	1960

Tractors (Crawler)

OC-9
1MA000	1959
1MA158	1960
1MA427	1961
800395	1962
800435	1963
801428	1964

OC-12G
1JR000	1955
1JR062	1956
1JR178	1957
1JR202	1958
1JR216	1959
1JR228	1960

OC-12D
1JX000	1954
1JX042	1955
2JX350	1956
2JX636	1957
4JX652	1958
5JX140	1959
5JX506	1960
5JX828	1961

OC-15
1VL000	1956
1VL060	1957
1VL164	1958
1VL378	1959
1VL526	1960
1VL640	1961

OC-18
1KS002	1952
3500127	1953
4500213	1954
1KS178	1955
1KS382	1956
1KS638	1957
1KS710	1958
1KS750	1959
1KS758	1960

OC-46
800010	1962
800443	1963
801286	1964
801793	1965

OC-96
1MB000	1959
1MB208	1960
1MB896	1961
800270	1962
800431	1963
801277	1964
801856	1965

Nichols & Shepard Company
Threshing Machine Serial Numbers

This listing begins in 1916, and no earlier listings have been located. Also, no serial number listings have been located for the N & S tractors. This listing arranged chronologically.

In order to reduce the bulk of the listing, it has been compiled to approximate year beginning and year ending numbers.

1916 25518-26039	**1923** 33366-34089	**1930** 46344-47961	**1937** None	**1944** 52424-52658
1917 26040-26911	**1924** 34090-34945	**1931** 47962-48396	**1938** 50713-51387	**1945** 52659-52842
1918 26912-28226	**1925** 34946-36978	**1932** 48397-48615	**1939** 51388-51773	**1946** 52843-53312
1919 28227-29793	**1926** 36979-39449	**1933** 48616-48708	**1940** 51774-51973	**1947** 53332-53581
1920 29794-31553	**1927** 39450-42148	**1934** 48709-48782	**1941** 51974-52123	**1948** 53582-53831
1921 31554-33063	**1928** 42149-43848	**1935** 48783-49612	**1942** 52124-52423	
1922 33064-33365	**1929** 43849-46343	**1936** 49613-50712	**1943** None Built	

About The Author

With this title, C. H. Wendel has completed eighteen books on various aspects of agricultural and mechanical history. What began as a labor of love in 1970 has become a full-time profession. For the past several years, Mr. Wendel has also been a columnist with *Gas Engine Magazine*, and also accepts occasional speaking engagements.

Over the past thirty years Mr. Wendel has amassed a sizable research library, and in addition to writing projects, he is also involved in historical research for various publishers, manufacturers, and other groups. Of particular value is a complete set of U. S. Patents ranging from 1872 to 1975, plus extensive runs of many technical journals ranging back to the 1850s.

Mr. Wendel has many hobbies, including a number of vintage engines and tractors. Many are restored, while others await their turn. Favorites include an 8 horsepower Mogul engine built by International Harvester Company in 1914. Another is a 5 horsepower diesel engine made by Witte Engine Works in 1938.

A confirmed bibliophile, Mr. Wendel has actively collected books over a lifetime. While the oldest book in the collection was printed in 1487, the book collection includes many technical titles, even including a few written in German or French. Beyond the history of technology, Mr. Wendel's book collecting interests also include an extensive gathering of titles on railroads and the Old West. A few choice biographies are included, such as the two-volume biography of Cyrus Hall McCormick. His favorite biographical subject is Thomas Edison; Mr. Wendel believes that Edison was to the world of invention what Johann Sebastian Bach was to music; Bach and Mozart are his favorite composers.

An avid interests in books and fine printing led to the 1989 acquisition of the Prairie Press, formerly of Iowa City, Iowa. This firm was established in 1935 and printed some of the finest private press books in the United States over a forty year period. The acquisition of the Prairie Press, plus numerous other purchases has brought the total inventory to half a dozen various letter presses, nearly 1,500 fonts of foundry type, a working Linotype, and numerous other accessories related to the printing art. Mr. Wendel has retained the Prairie Press name, inasmuch as it symbolizes the thrust of his historical work over the past quarter century.

Mr. Wendel is also involved in numerous church and civic affairs, and is a charter board member of the Old Threshers Foundation, Mount Pleasant, Iowa. He is also a member of the Amana Heritage Society, the Typocrafters, the American Typecasting Fellowship, and the Amalgamated Printers Association.

Many Thanks

This book would not have been possible had it not been for the kindness and the assistance of many different people. Standing at the very top of the list is the Floyd County Museum at Charles City, Iowa. All of the folks at the museum were very helpful while working there, and in particular, we thank Mary Ann Townsend for her nearly constant assistance while we spent days on end shooting pictures and making photocopies. These folks had the foresight to acquire much of the early material on Oliver, Hart-Parr and the related companies before it was destroyed. In so doing, they have preserved a valuable research base for the benefit of everyone interested in the products of these companies.

Many individuals also were very helpful. Mr. Robert Lefever provided the Author with a huge file of A. B. Farquhar material, and Mr. Ted Worrall loaned us a large amount of Oliver and Cletrac literature. Thanks also to Lee Pedersen, Walter Kasal, Ed Schmidgall, and Gary Spitznogle for their help.

Mr. Howard Ray loaned us a large packet of Cletrac literature, as did Paul Kesselring. During the research of Oliver tractors we frequently talked with Lyle Dumont who holds one of the largest collections of Oliver tractors to be found anywhere. Lyle has expert knowledge of the Oliver tractor line, and his assistance was greatly needed, and much appreciated.

Despite our attempts to keep a file of everyone who was of help, loaned literature, or rendered other counsel and aid, we almost certainly have neglected to mention some of those who have assisted in completion of this project. Whether named or not, our sincere thanks to each and all of you for your help. Had we not had your help, this book would be much smaller than the final result. If this book is ultimately successful, the credit goes to all of you; if it fails, then the blame is mine.

C. H. Wendel
January 4, 1993